犬夜叉
INUYASHA™

ANI-MANGA™

Vol. 9

CREATED BY
RUMIKO TAKAHASHI

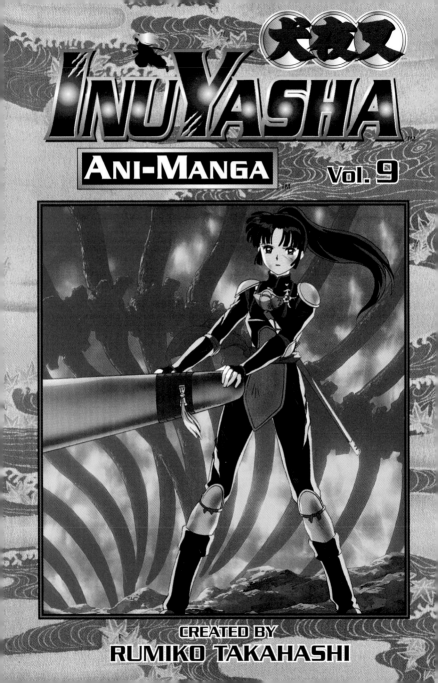

Inuyasha Ani-Manga™
Vol. #9

Created by
Rumiko Takahashi

Translation based on the VIZ anime TV series
Translation Assistance/Katy Bridges
Lettering/John Clark
Cover Design & Graphics/Hidemi Sahara
Editor/Frances E. Wall

Managing Editor/Annette Roman
Director of Production/Noboru Watanabe
Vice President of Publishing/Alvin Lu
Sr. Director of Acquisitions/Rika Inouye
Vice President of Sales & Marketing/Liza Coppola
Executive Vice President/Hyoe Narita
Publisher/Seiji Horibuchi

Published by VIZ, LLC
P.O. Box 77010
San Francisco, CA 94107

10 9 8 7 6 5 4 3 2 1
First printing, May 2005

www.viz.com

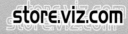

store.viz.com

Story thus far

Kagome, a typical high school girl, has been transported into a mythical version of Japan's medieval past, a place filled with incredible magic and terrifying demons. Who would have guessed that the stories and legends Kagome's superstitious grandfather told her could really be true!?

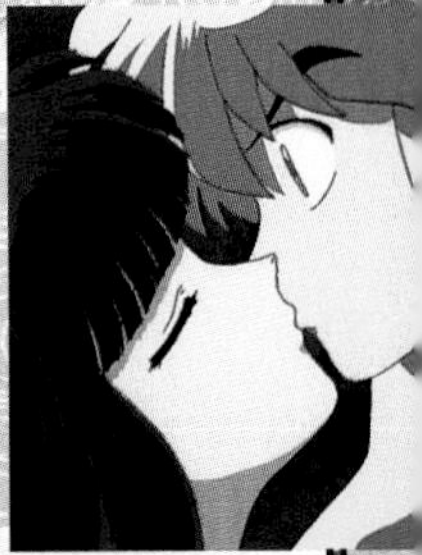

It turns out that Kagome is the reincarnation of Lady Kikyo, a great warrior and the defender of the Shikon Jewel, or the Jewel of the Four Souls. In fact, the sacred jewel mysteriously emerges from Kagome's body during a battle with a horrible centipede-like monster. In her desperation to defeat the monster, Kagome frees Inuyasha, a dog-like half-demon who lusts for the power imparted by the jewel, and unwittingly releases him from the binding spell that was placed 50 years earlier by Lady Kikyo. To prevent Inuyasha from stealing the jewel, Kikyo's sister, Lady Kaede, puts a magical necklace around Inuyasha's neck that allows Kagome to make him "sit" on command.

In another skirmish for possession of the jewel, it accidentally shatters and is strewn across the land. Only Kagome has the power to find the jewel shards, and only Inuyasha has the strength to defeat the demons who now hold them, so the two unlikely partners are bound together in the quest to reclaim all the pieces of the Shikon Jewel.

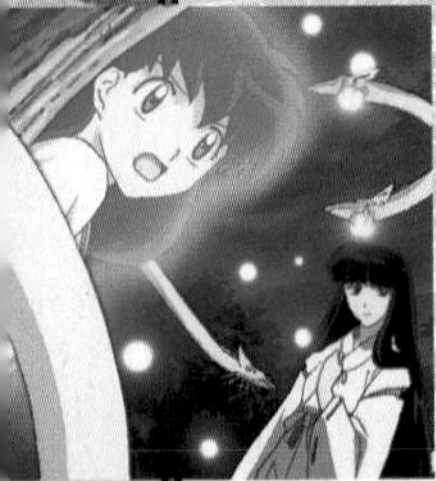

Inuyasha learns that Kikyo is alive and chases after her, hoping to reconcile with his former love. Kikyo, who was resurrected through the sorcery of an evil witch and whose life is sustained only through preying upon the souls of the dead, still believes that Inuyasha betrayed and murdered her 50 years ago. Kagome catches up to Kikyo first, but, rendered paralyzed and invisible by a spell, she can only watch as Inuyasha and Kikyo confront one another and share a passionate kiss! Kagome is heartbroken to see the enduring strength of Inuyasha's love for Kikyo, but Kikyo becomes jealous when it is Kagome's voice that draws Inuyasha out of his amorous reverie. Meanwhile, Naraku, the villain who orchestrated the plot that led to Kikyo's death, engages in more deception. He tricks a demon slayer named Sango into believing that Inuyasha attacked her town and annihilated the villagers, and Sango vows to avenge their deaths by killing Inuyasha!

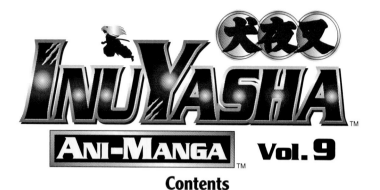

INUYASHA™
ANI-MANGA™ Vol. 9

Contents

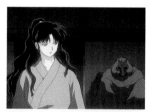

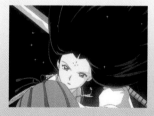

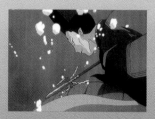

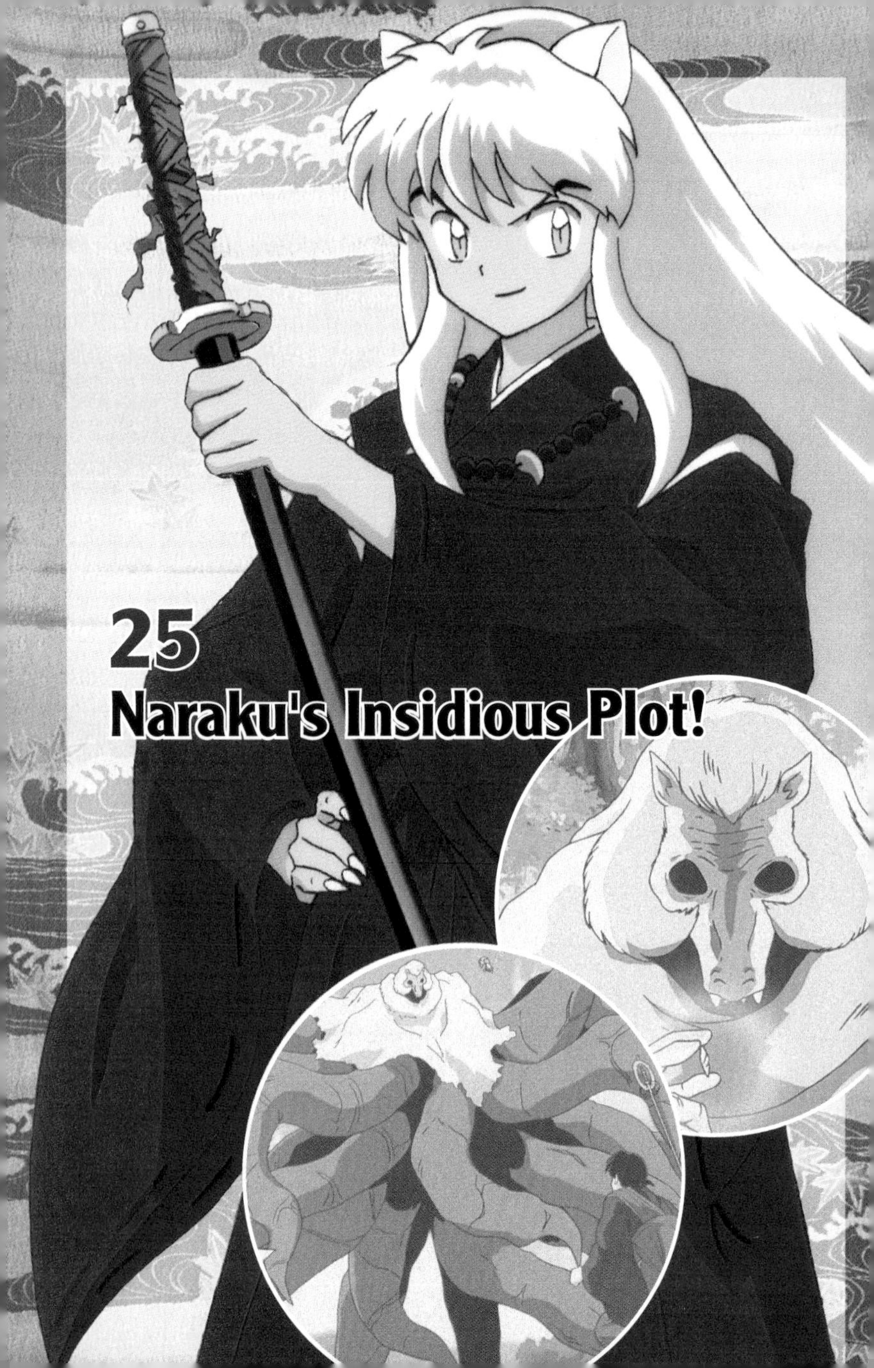

25
Naraku's Insidious Plot!

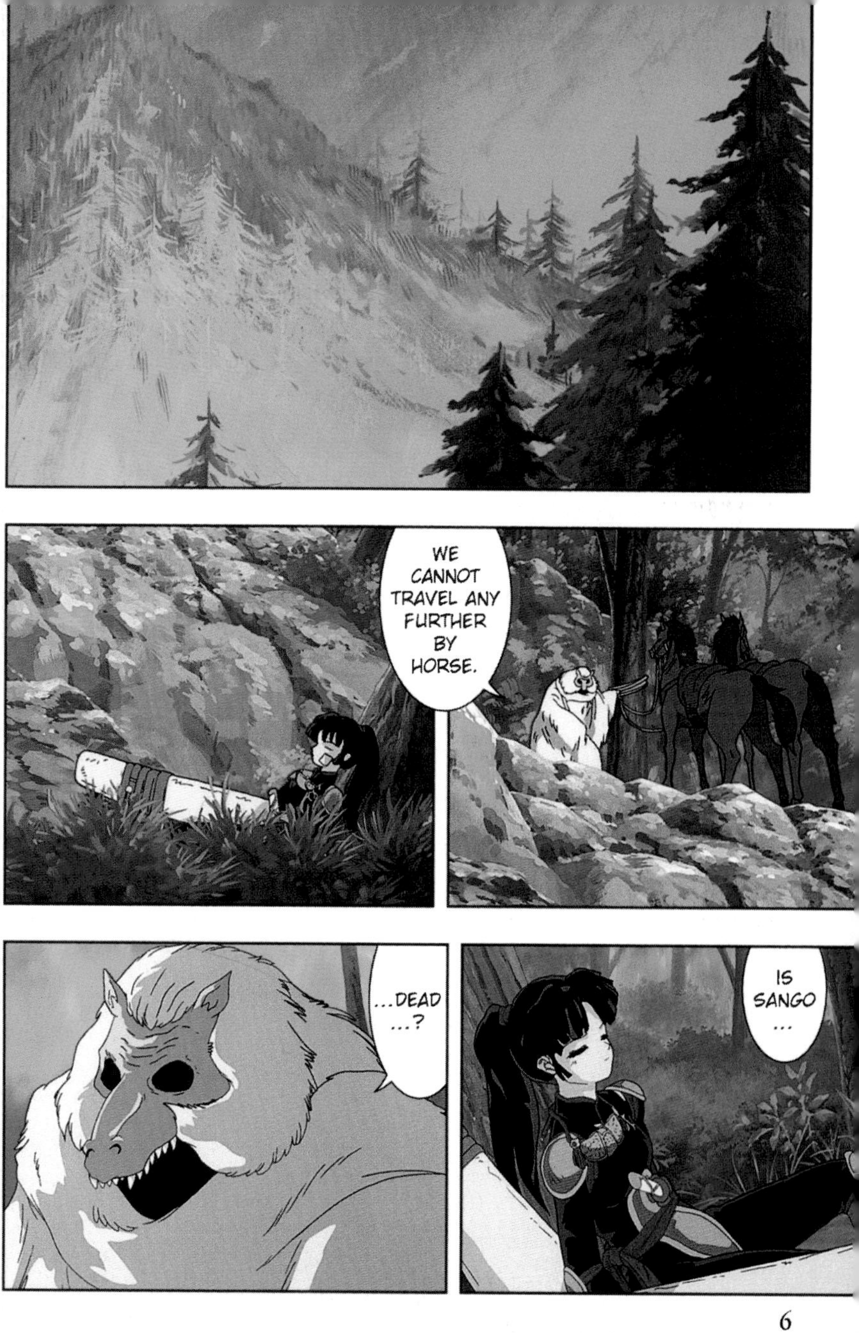
WE CANNOT TRAVEL ANY FURTHER BY HORSE.
IS SANGO ...
...DEAD ...?

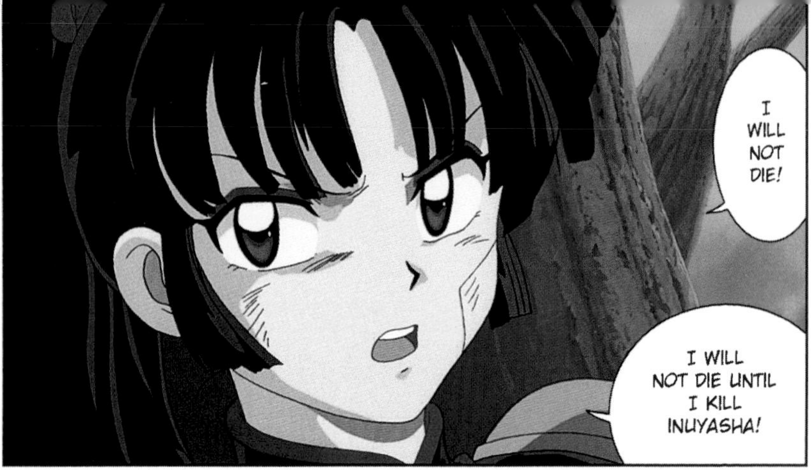
I WILL NOT DIE!
I WILL NOT DIE UNTIL I KILL INUYASHA!
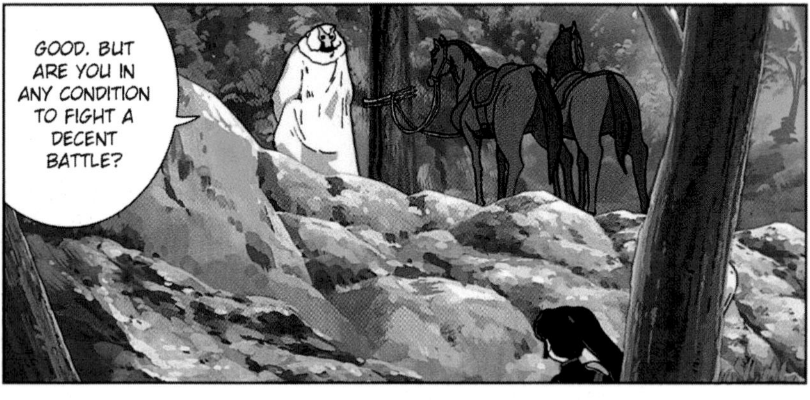
GOOD. BUT ARE YOU IN ANY CONDITION TO FIGHT A DECENT BATTLE?
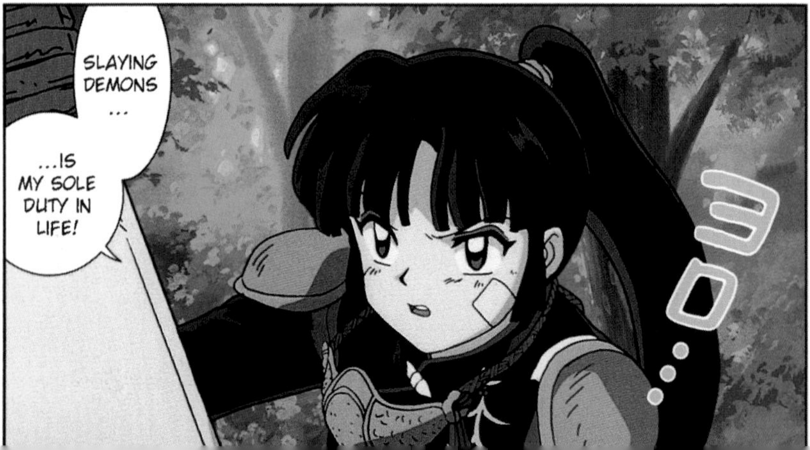
ヨロ...
SLAYING DEMONS ...
...IS MY SOLE DUTY IN LIFE!

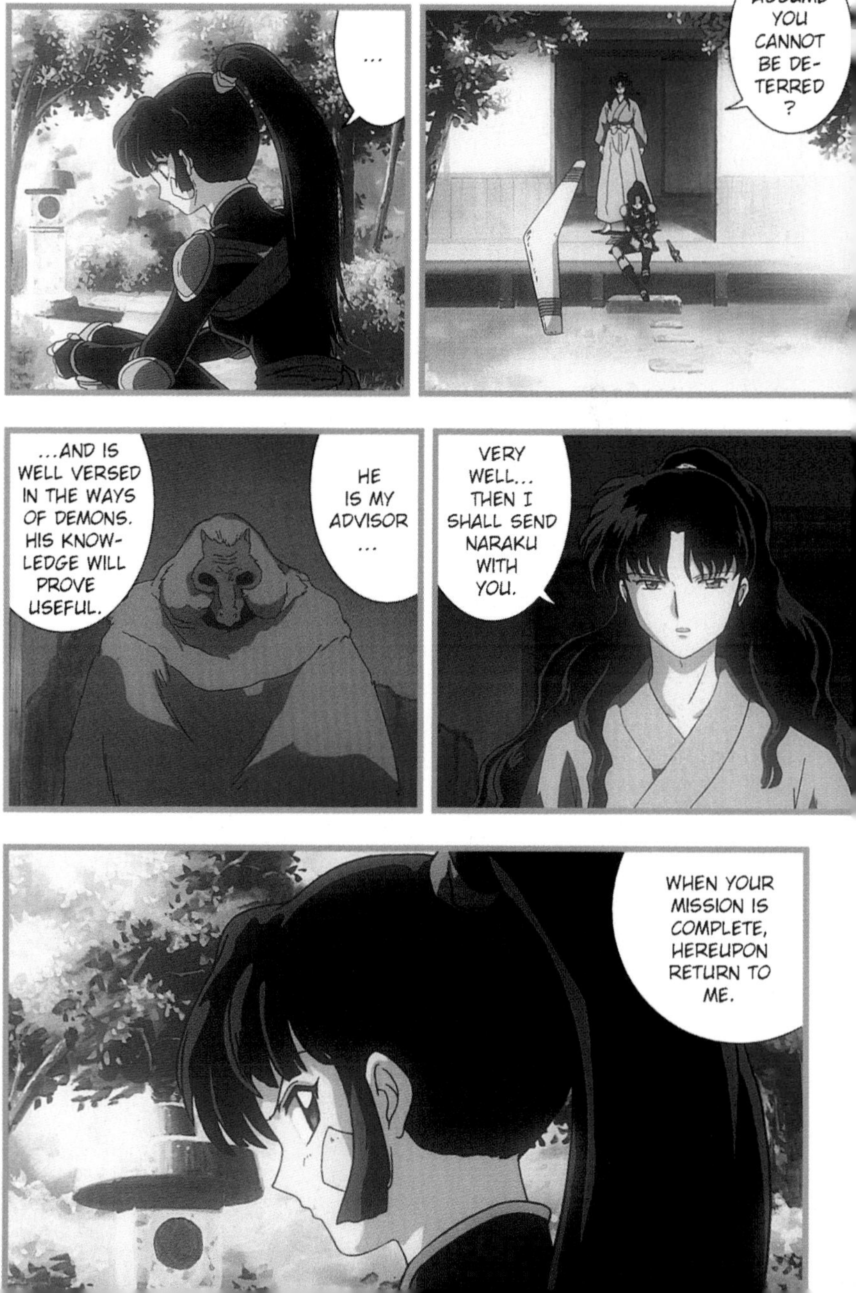
I ASSUME YOU CANNOT BE DETERRED?
...
VERY WELL... THEN I SHALL SEND NARAKU WITH YOU.
HE IS MY ADVISOR...
...AND IS WELL VERSED IN THE WAYS OF DEMONS. HIS KNOWLEDGE WILL PROVE USEFUL.
WHEN YOUR MISSION IS COMPLETE, HEREUPON RETURN TO ME.

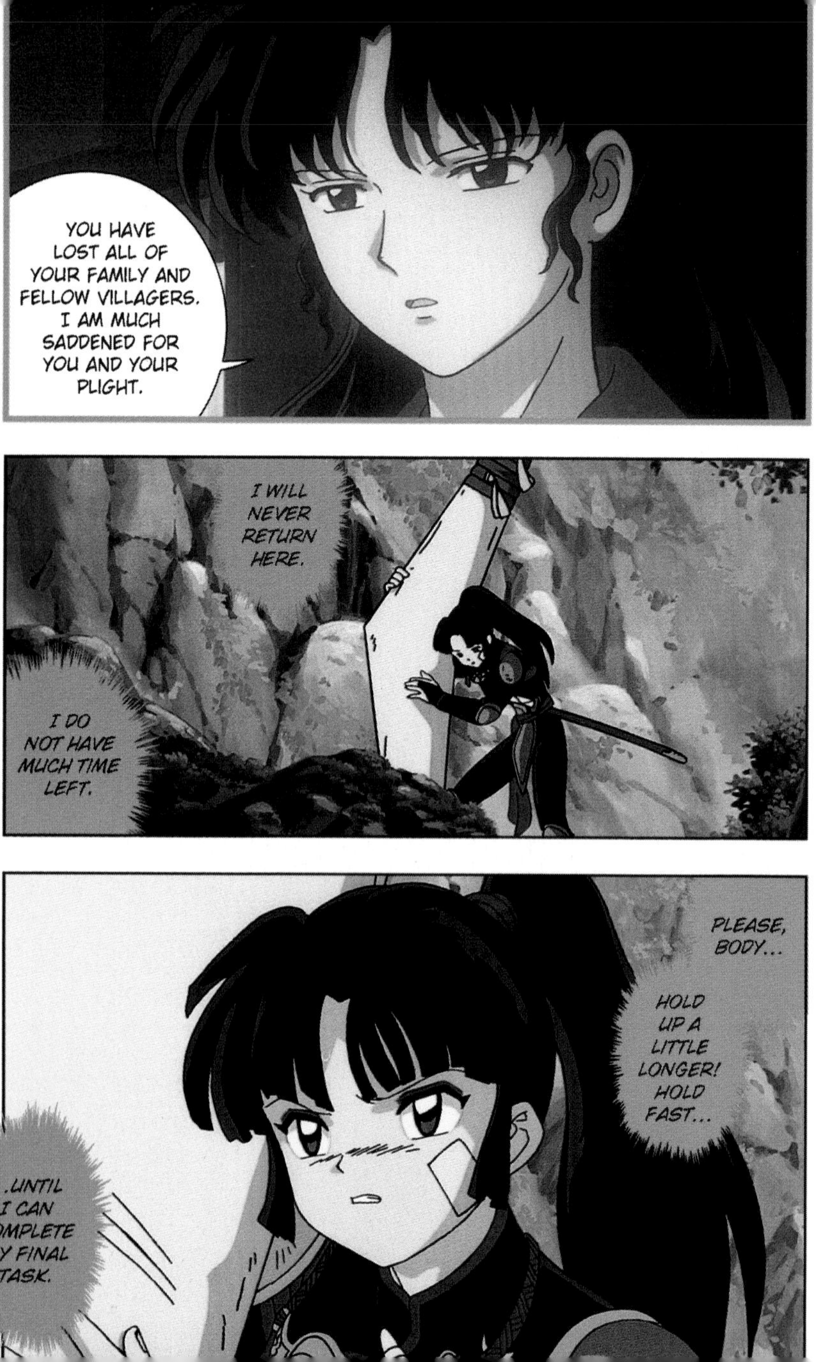
YOU HAVE LOST ALL OF YOUR FAMILY AND FELLOW VILLAGERS. I AM MUCH SADDENED FOR YOU AND YOUR PLIGHT.
I WILL NEVER RETURN HERE.
I DO NOT HAVE MUCH TIME LEFT.
PLEASE, BODY...
HOLD UP A LITTLE LONGER! HOLD FAST...
...UNTIL I CAN COMPLETE MY FINAL TASK.

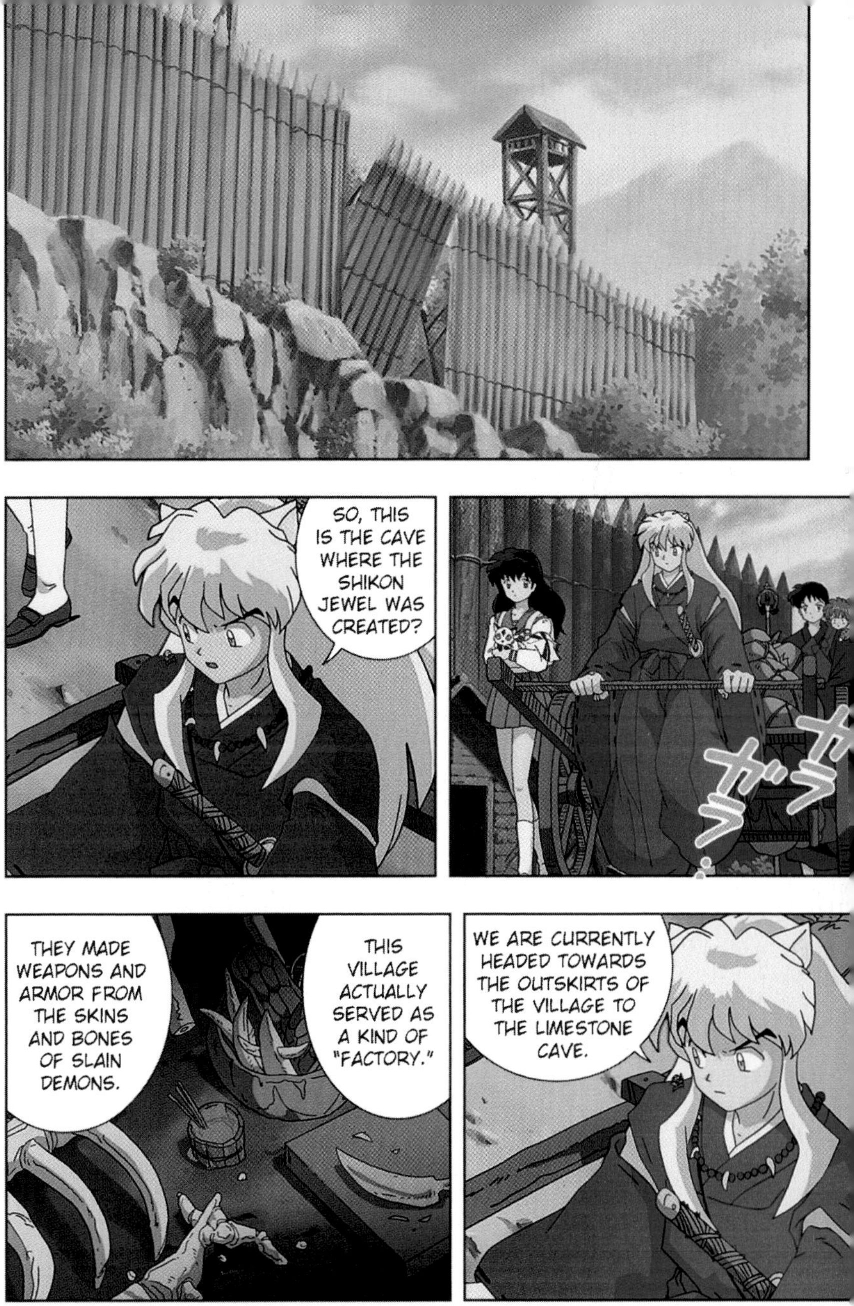
ガラ
SO, THIS IS THE CAVE WHERE THE SHIKON JEWEL WAS CREATED?
WE ARE CURRENTLY HEADED TOWARDS THE OUTSKIRTS OF THE VILLAGE TO THE LIMESTONE CAVE.
THIS VILLAGE ACTUALLY SERVED AS A KIND OF "FACTORY."
THEY MADE WEAPONS AND ARMOR FROM THE SKINS AND BONES OF SLAIN DEMONS.

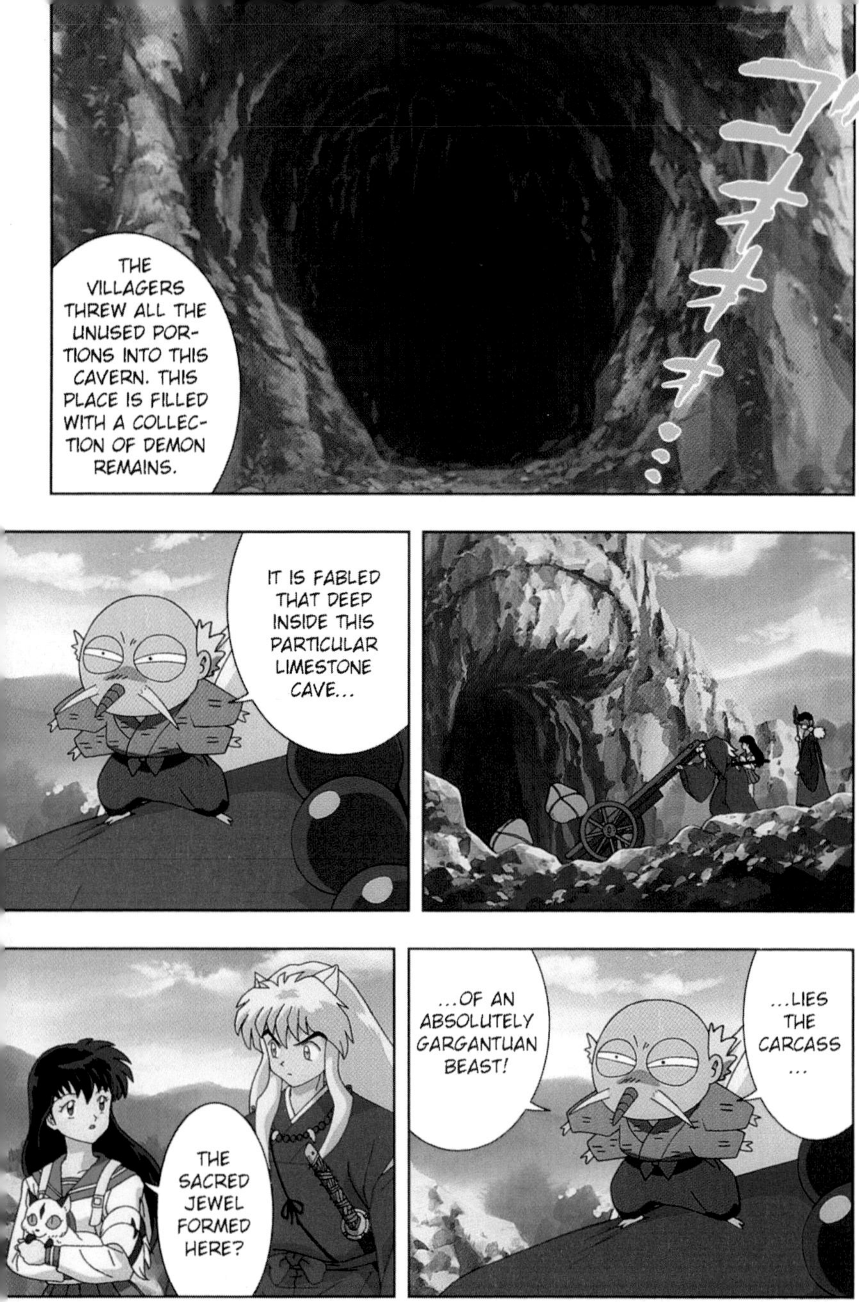
THE VILLAGERS THREW ALL THE UNUSED PORTIONS INTO THIS CAVERN. THIS PLACE IS FILLED WITH A COLLECTION OF DEMON REMAINS.
IT IS FABLED THAT DEEP INSIDE THIS PARTICULAR LIMESTONE CAVE...
...LIES THE CARCASS...
...OF AN ABSOLUTELY GARGANTUAN BEAST!
THE SACRED JEWEL FORMED HERE?

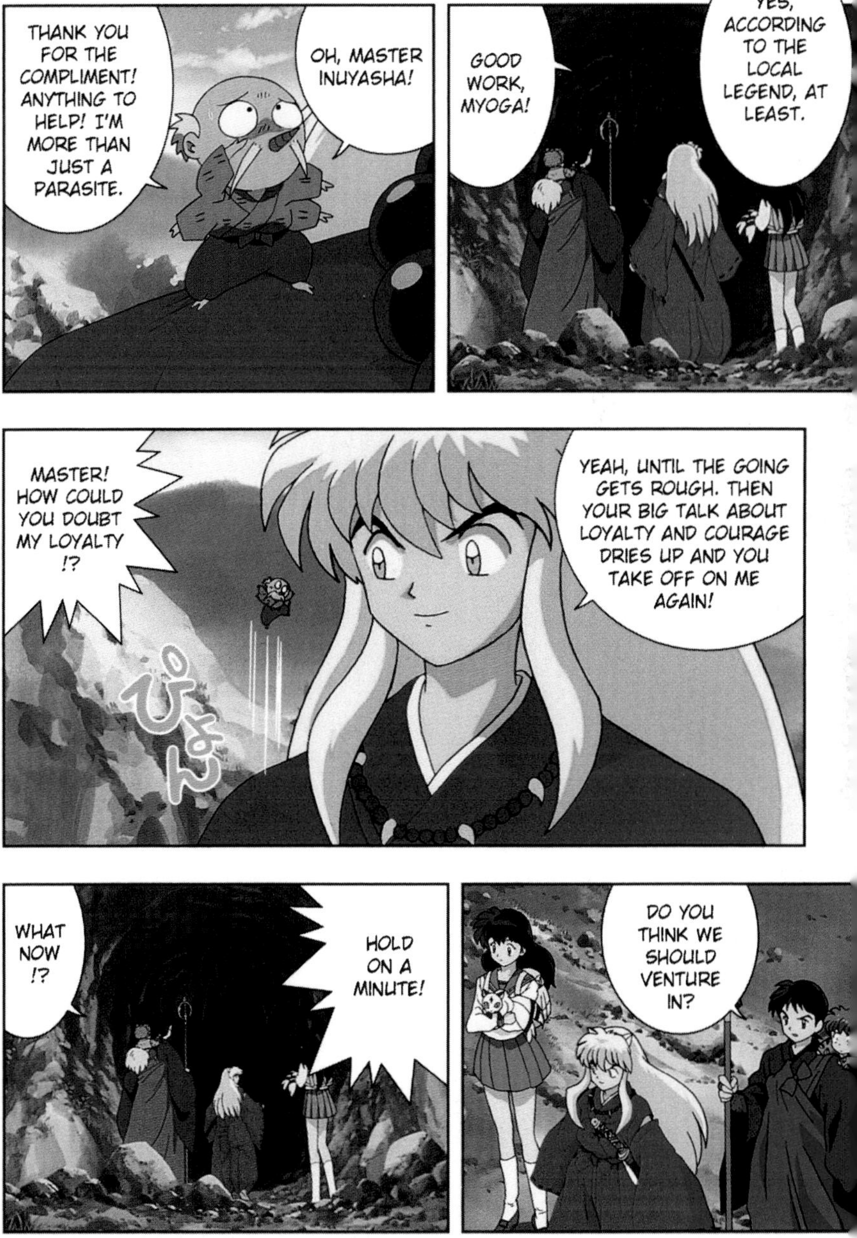
YES, ACCORDING TO THE LOCAL LEGEND, AT LEAST.
GOOD WORK, MYOGA!
OH, MASTER INUYASHA!
THANK YOU FOR THE COMPLIMENT! ANYTHING TO HELP! I'M MORE THAN JUST A PARASITE.
YEAH, UNTIL THE GOING GETS ROUGH. THEN YOUR BIG TALK ABOUT LOYALTY AND COURAGE DRIES UP AND YOU TAKE OFF ON ME AGAIN!
MASTER! HOW COULD YOU DOUBT MY LOYALTY !?
ぴょん
DO YOU THINK WE SHOULD VENTURE IN?
HOLD ON A MINUTE!
WHAT NOW !?

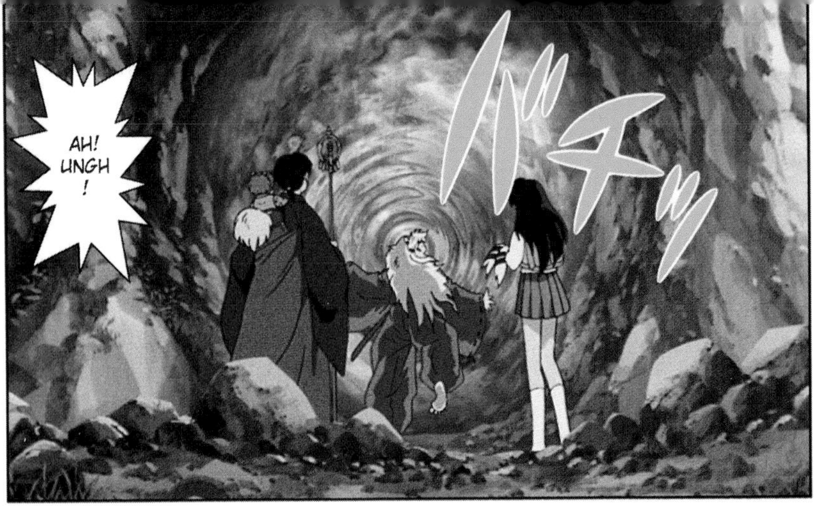
AH! UNGH !
バチッ
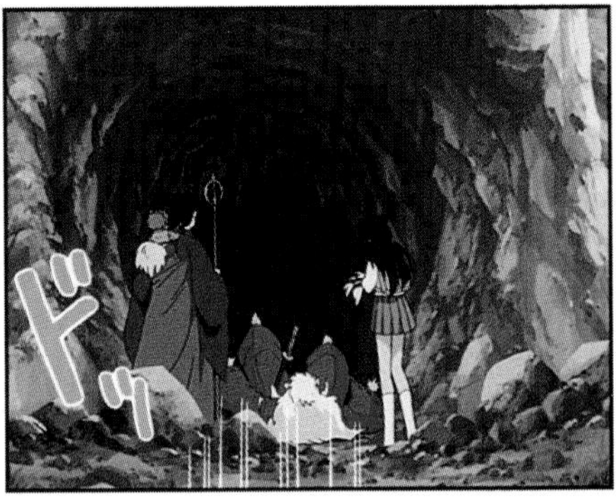
ドッ
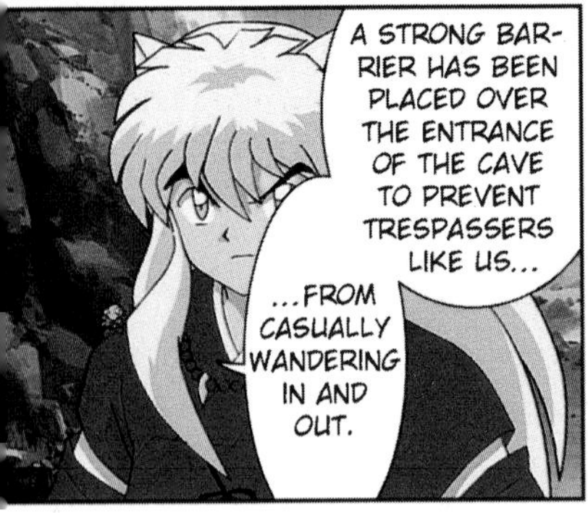
A STRONG BARRIER HAS BEEN PLACED OVER THE ENTRANCE OF THE CAVE TO PREVENT TRESPASSERS LIKE US...
...FROM CASUALLY WANDERING IN AND OUT.
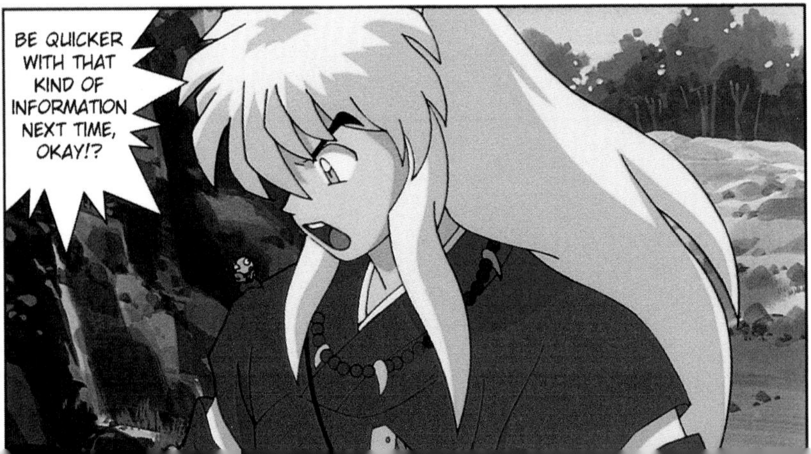
BE QUICKER WITH THAT KIND OF INFORMATION NEXT TIME, OKAY!?

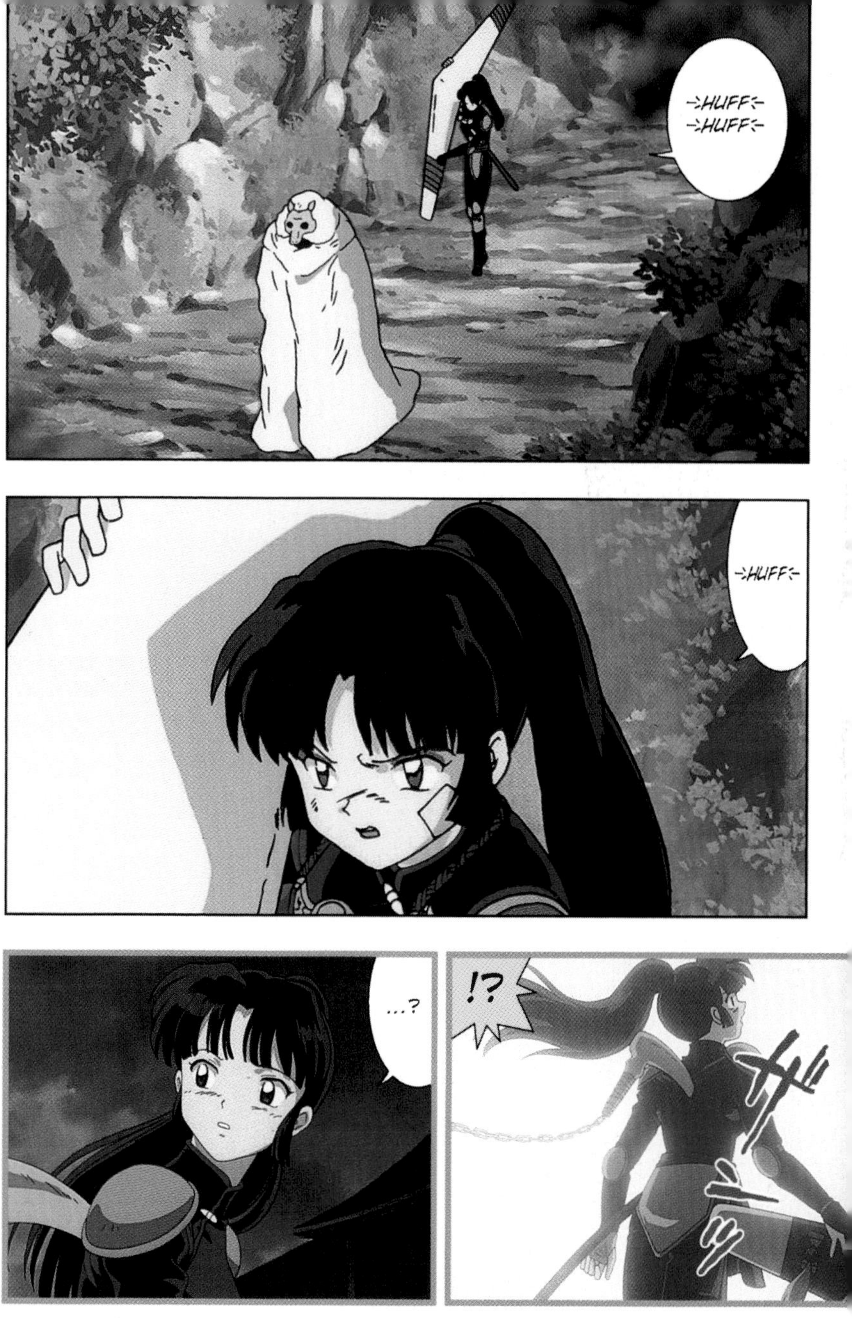
HUFF
HUFF
HUFF
!?
...?

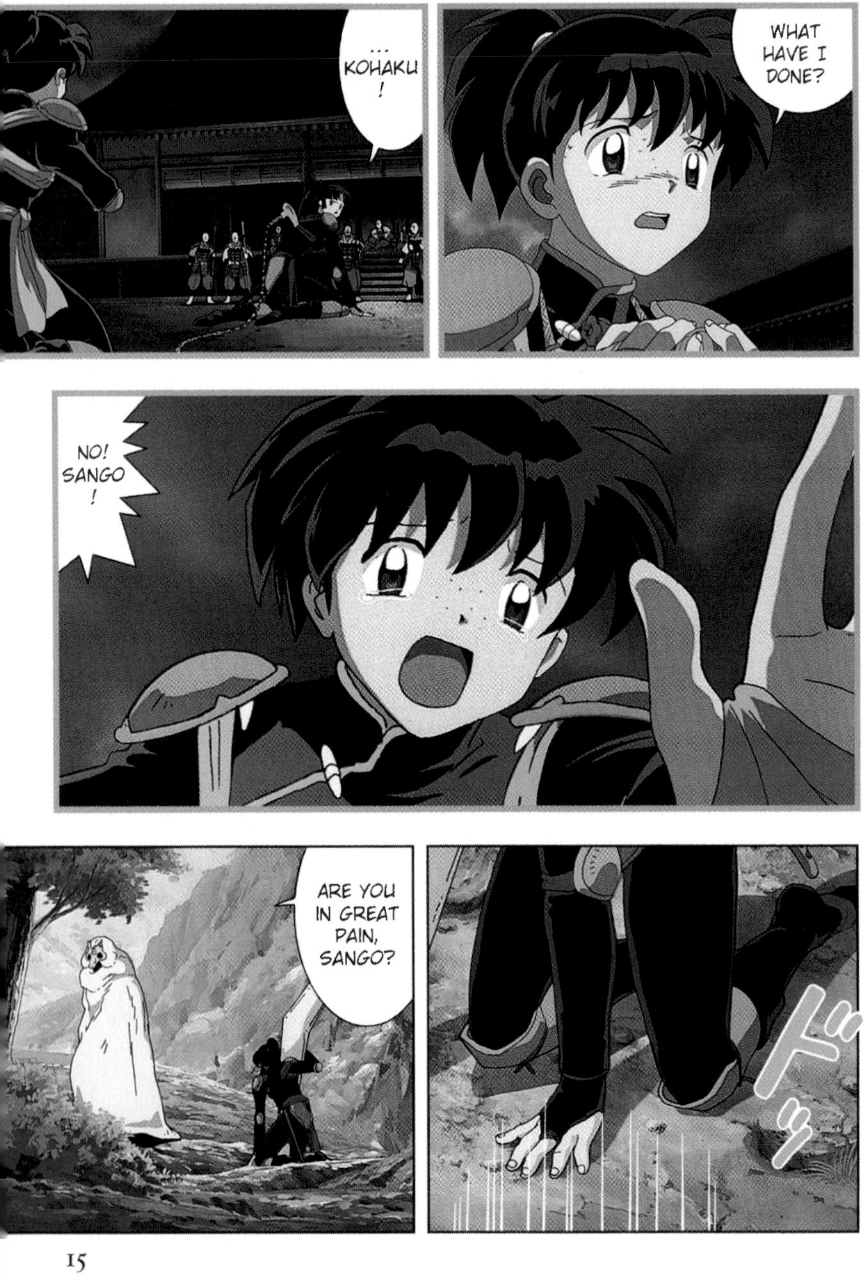
WHAT HAVE I DONE?
... KOHAKU !
NO! SANGO !
ドッ
ARE YOU IN GREAT PAIN, SANGO?

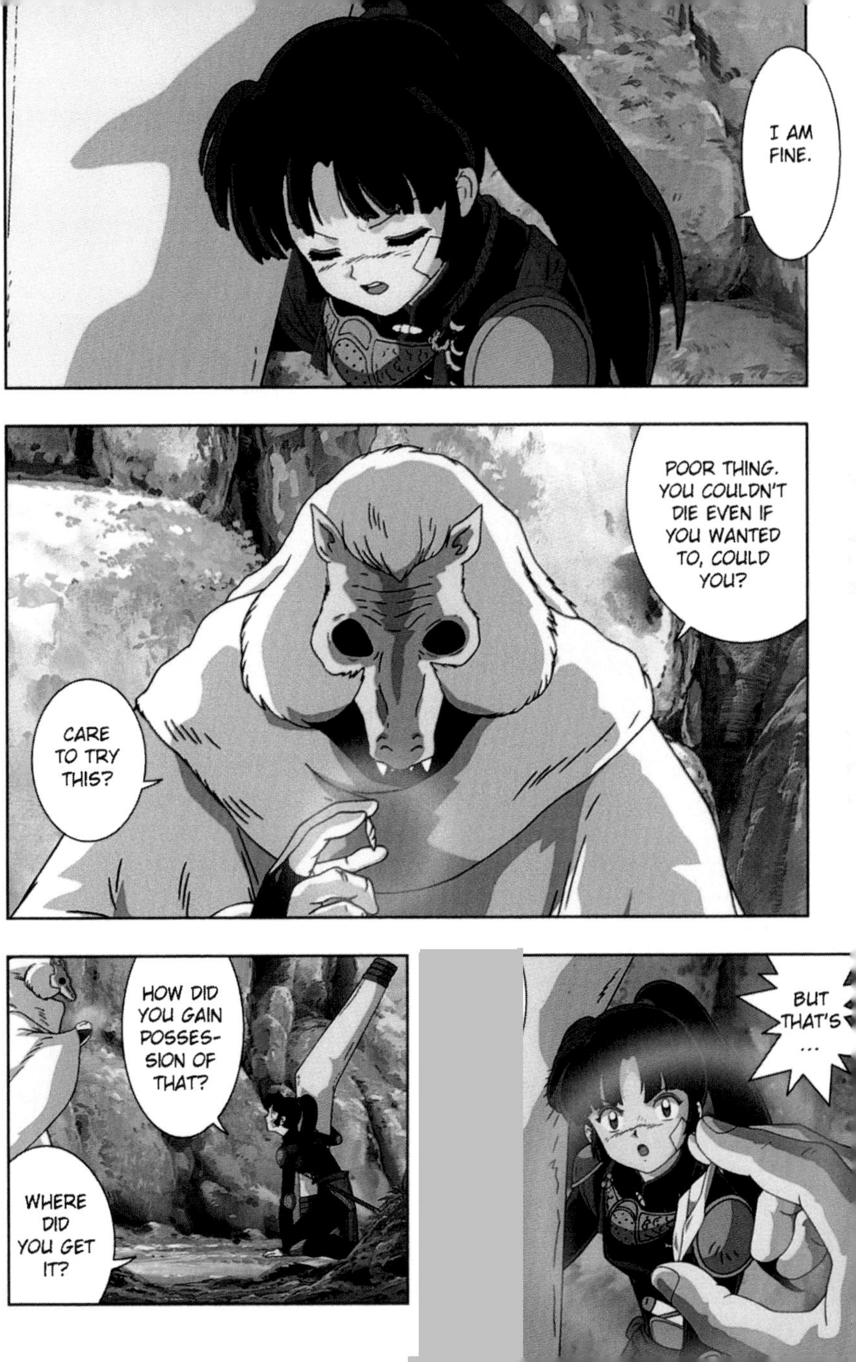
I AM FINE.
POOR THING. YOU COULDN'T DIE EVEN IF YOU WANTED TO, COULD YOU?
CARE TO TRY THIS?
BUT THAT'S ...
HOW DID YOU GAIN POSSES-SION OF THAT?
WHERE DID YOU GET IT?

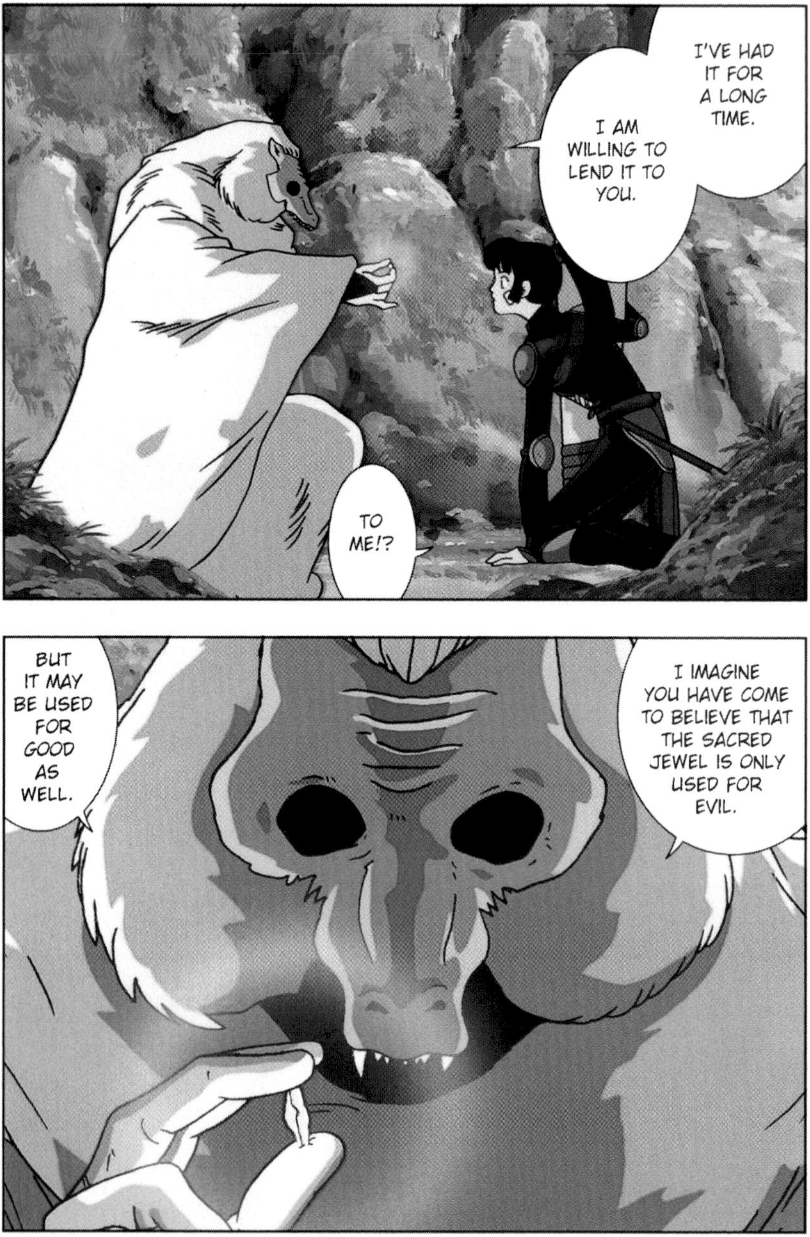
I'VE HAD IT FOR A LONG TIME.
I AM WILLING TO LEND IT TO YOU.
TO ME!?
I IMAGINE YOU HAVE COME TO BELIEVE THAT THE SACRED JEWEL IS ONLY USED FOR EVIL.
BUT IT MAY BE USED FOR GOOD AS WELL.

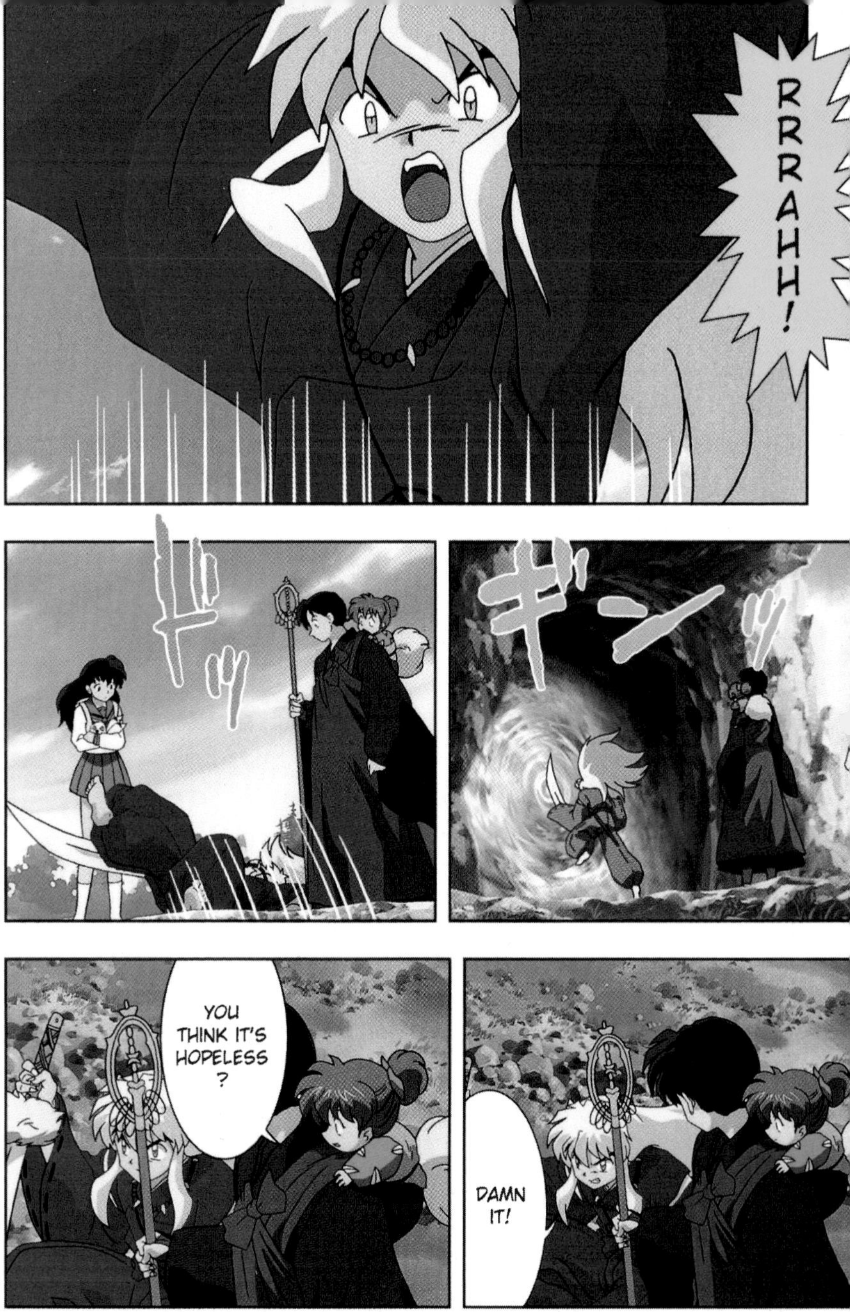
RRRAHH!
ギンッ
ドッ
DAMN IT!
YOU THINK IT'S HOPELESS?

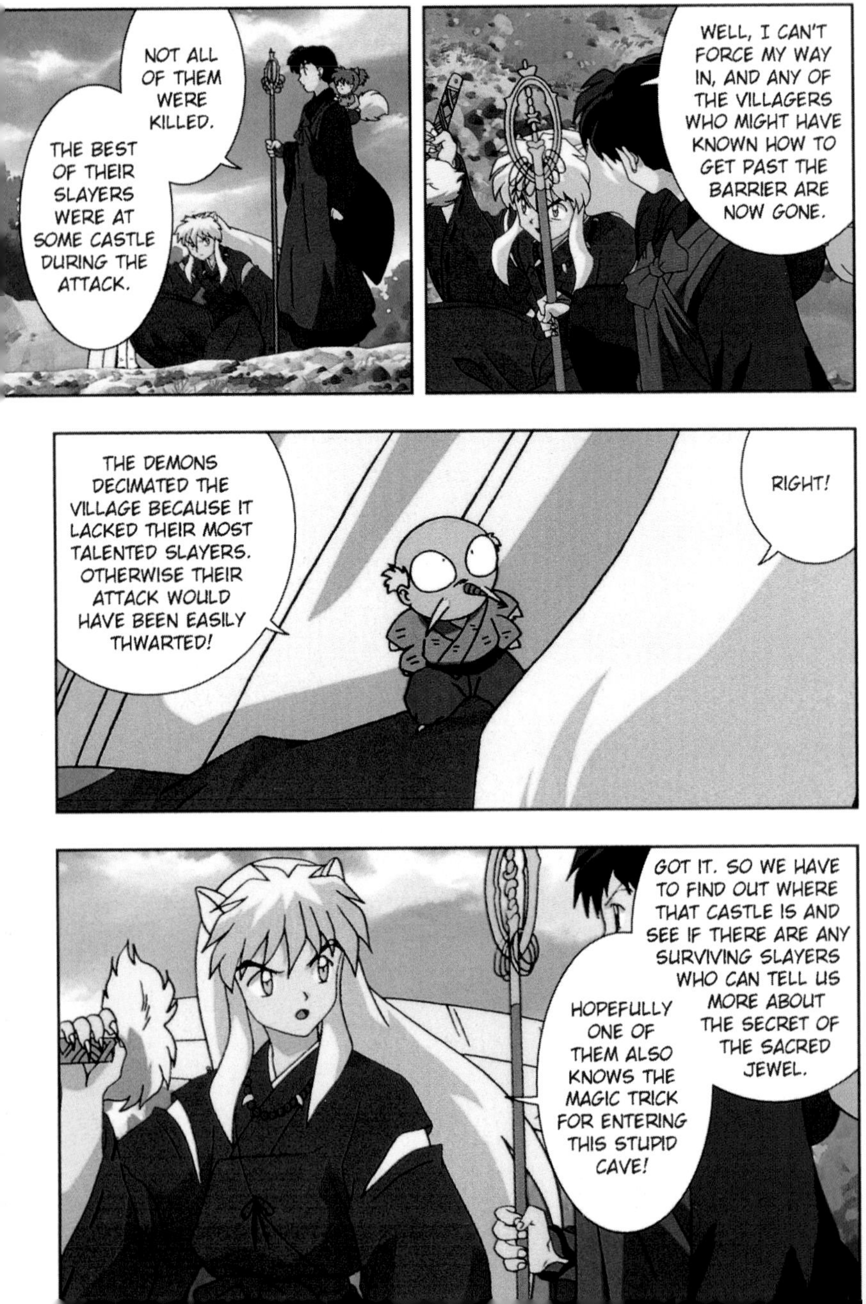
WELL, I CAN'T FORCE MY WAY IN, AND ANY OF THE VILLAGERS WHO MIGHT HAVE KNOWN HOW TO GET PAST THE BARRIER ARE NOW GONE.
NOT ALL OF THEM WERE KILLED.
THE BEST OF THEIR SLAYERS WERE AT SOME CASTLE DURING THE ATTACK.
RIGHT!
THE DEMONS DECIMATED THE VILLAGE BECAUSE IT LACKED THEIR MOST TALENTED SLAYERS. OTHERWISE THEIR ATTACK WOULD HAVE BEEN EASILY THWARTED!
GOT IT. SO WE HAVE TO FIND OUT WHERE THAT CASTLE IS AND SEE IF THERE ARE ANY SURVIVING SLAYERS WHO CAN TELL US MORE ABOUT THE SECRET OF THE SACRED JEWEL.
HOPEFULLY ONE OF THEM ALSO KNOWS THE MAGIC TRICK FOR ENTERING THIS STUPID CAVE!

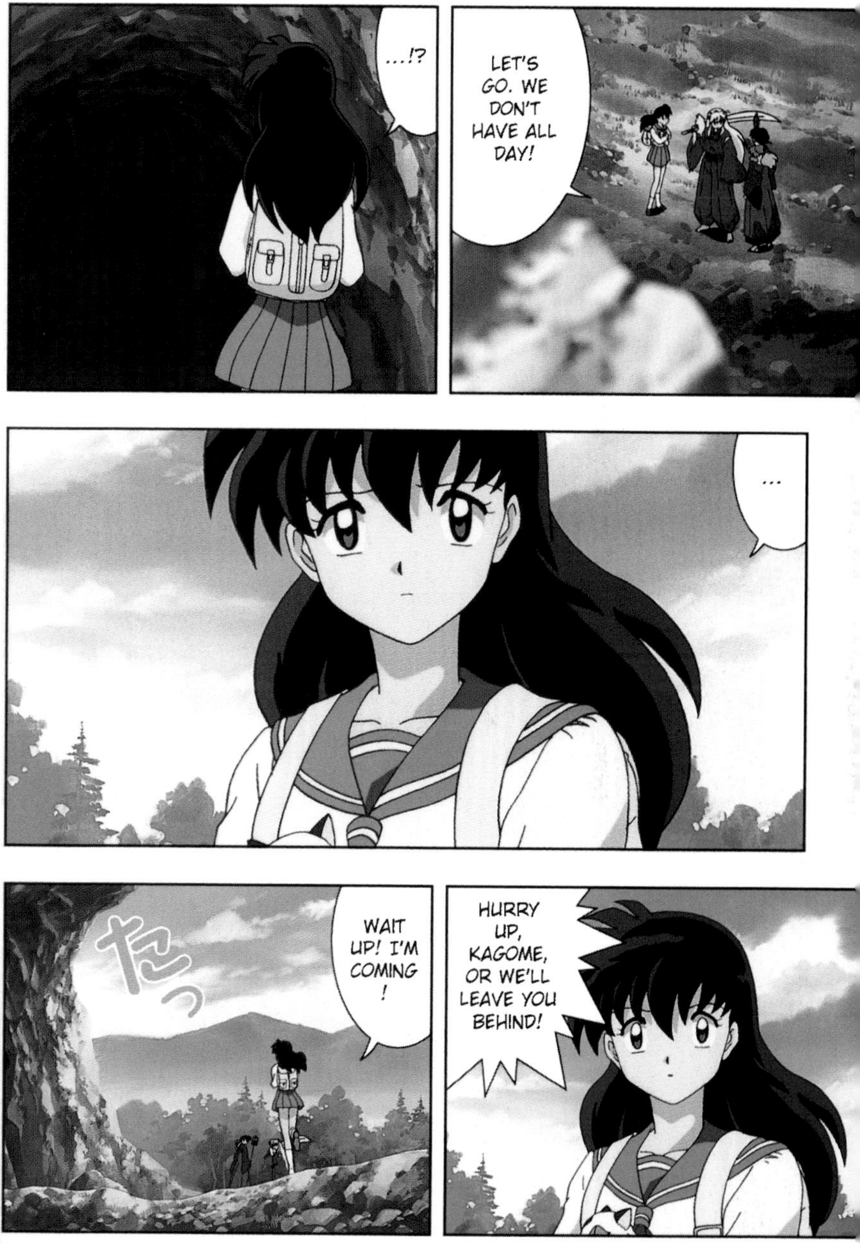
LET'S GO. WE DON'T HAVE ALL DAY!
...!?
...
HURRY UP, KAGOME, OR WE'LL LEAVE YOU BEHIND!
WAIT UP! I'M COMING!
たっ

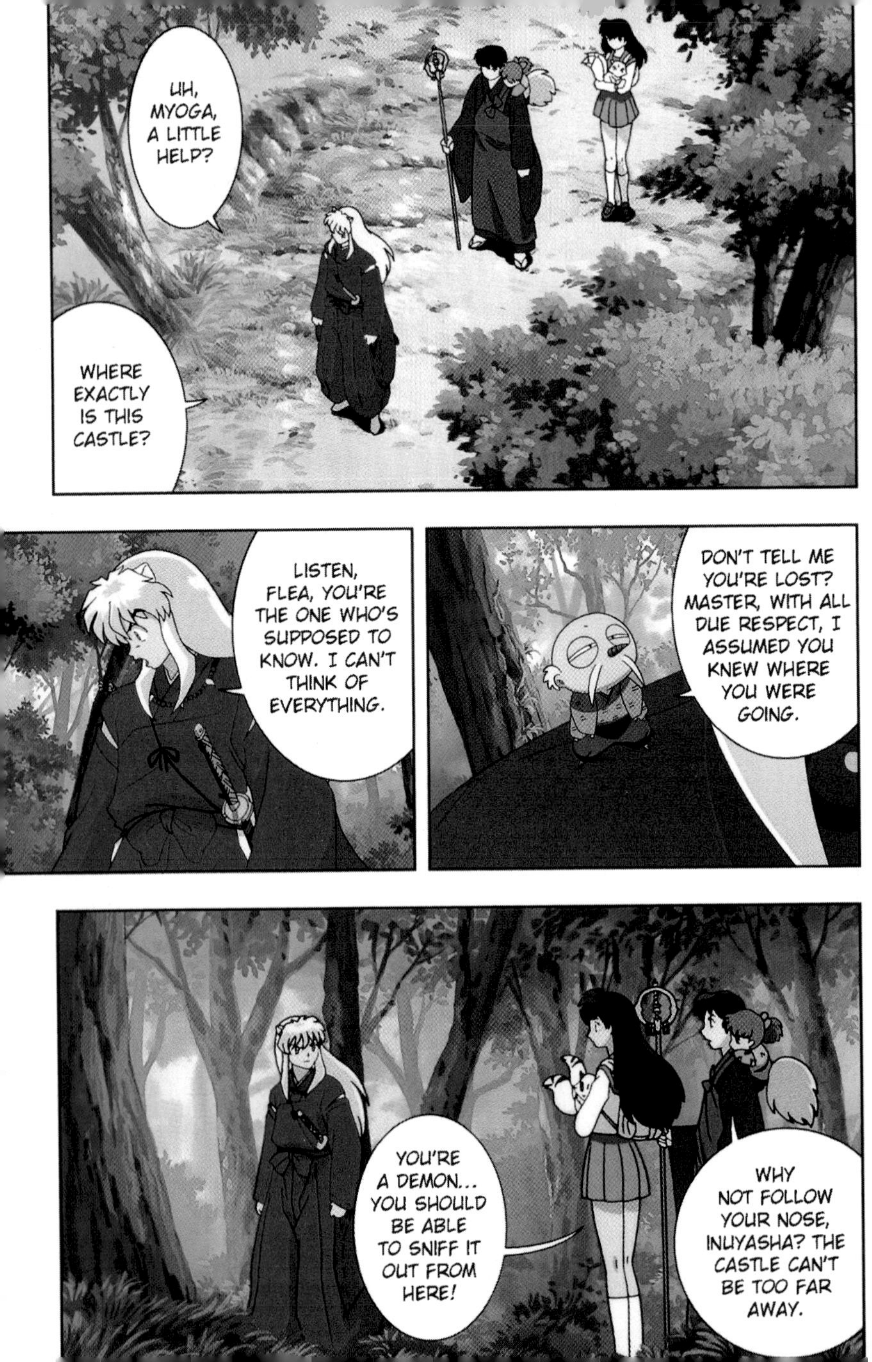
UH, MYOGA, A LITTLE HELP?
WHERE EXACTLY IS THIS CASTLE?
DON'T TELL ME YOU'RE LOST? MASTER, WITH ALL DUE RESPECT, I ASSUMED YOU KNEW WHERE YOU WERE GOING.
LISTEN, FLEA, YOU'RE THE ONE WHO'S SUPPOSED TO KNOW. I CAN'T THINK OF EVERYTHING.
WHY NOT FOLLOW YOUR NOSE, INUYASHA? THE CASTLE CAN'T BE TOO FAR AWAY.
YOU'RE A DEMON... YOU SHOULD BE ABLE TO SNIFF IT OUT FROM HERE!

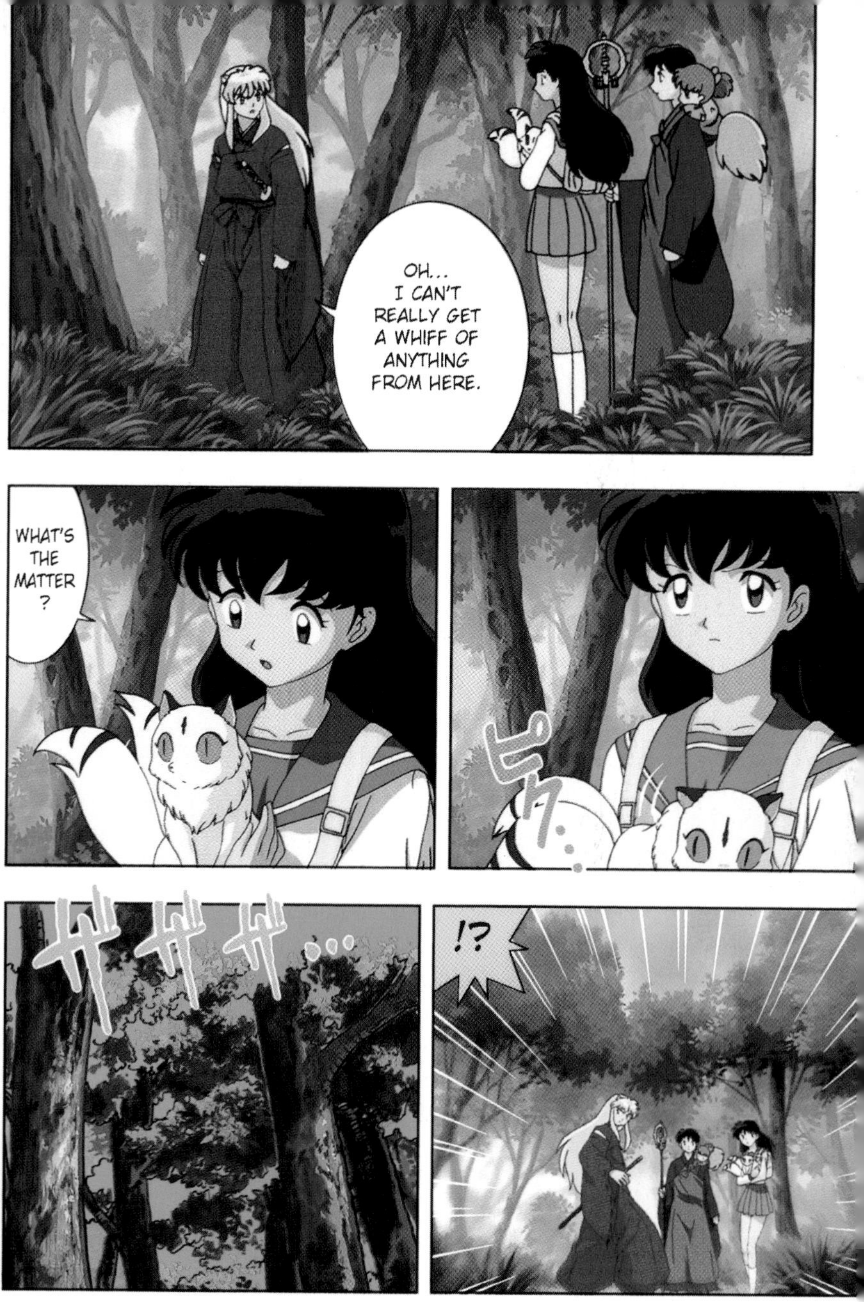
OH... I CAN'T REALLY GET A WHIFF OF ANYTHING FROM HERE.
ピク...
WHAT'S THE MATTER?
!?
ザザザ...

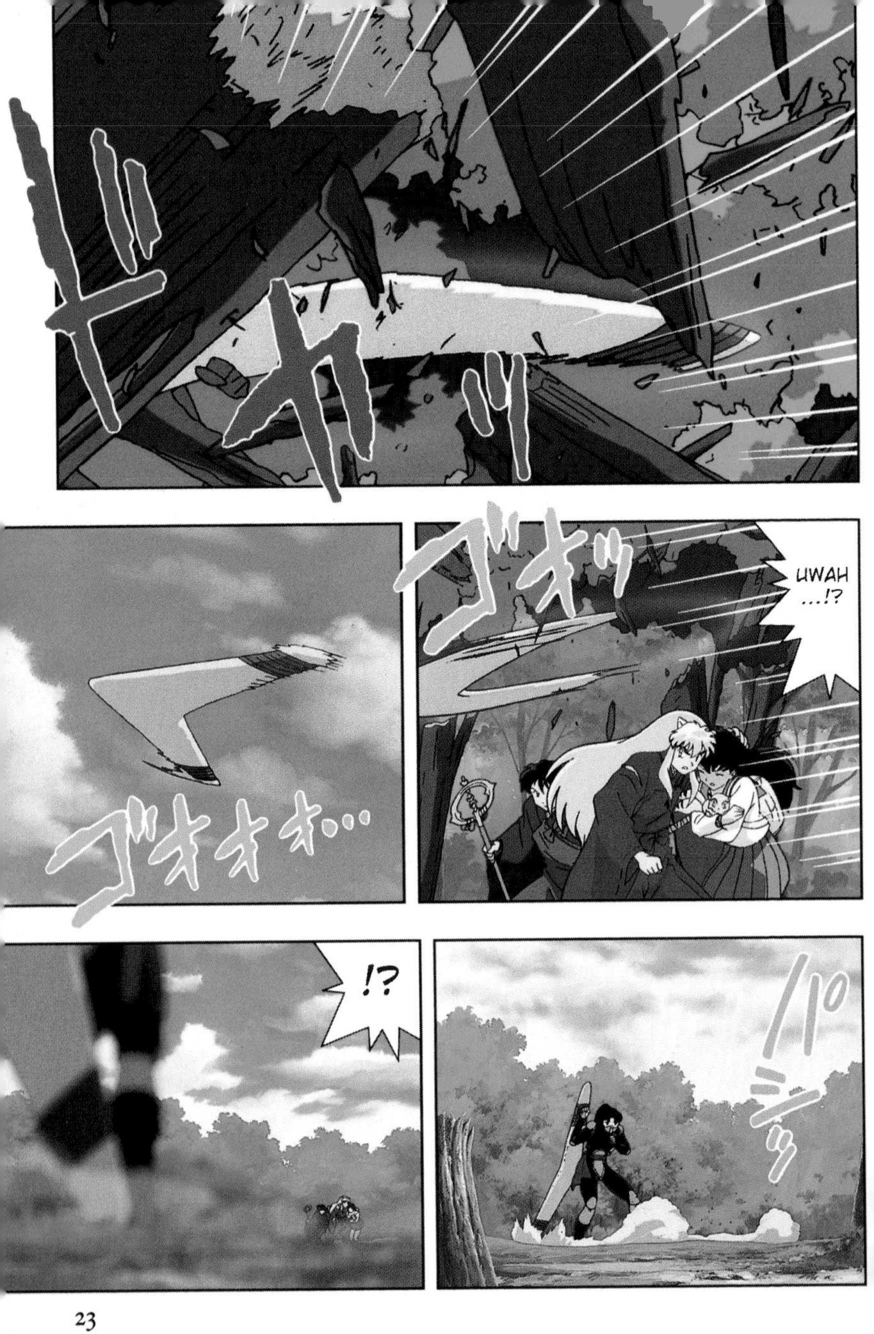
ドガッ
ゴオッ
UWAH ...!?
ゴオオオ…
パシッ
!?

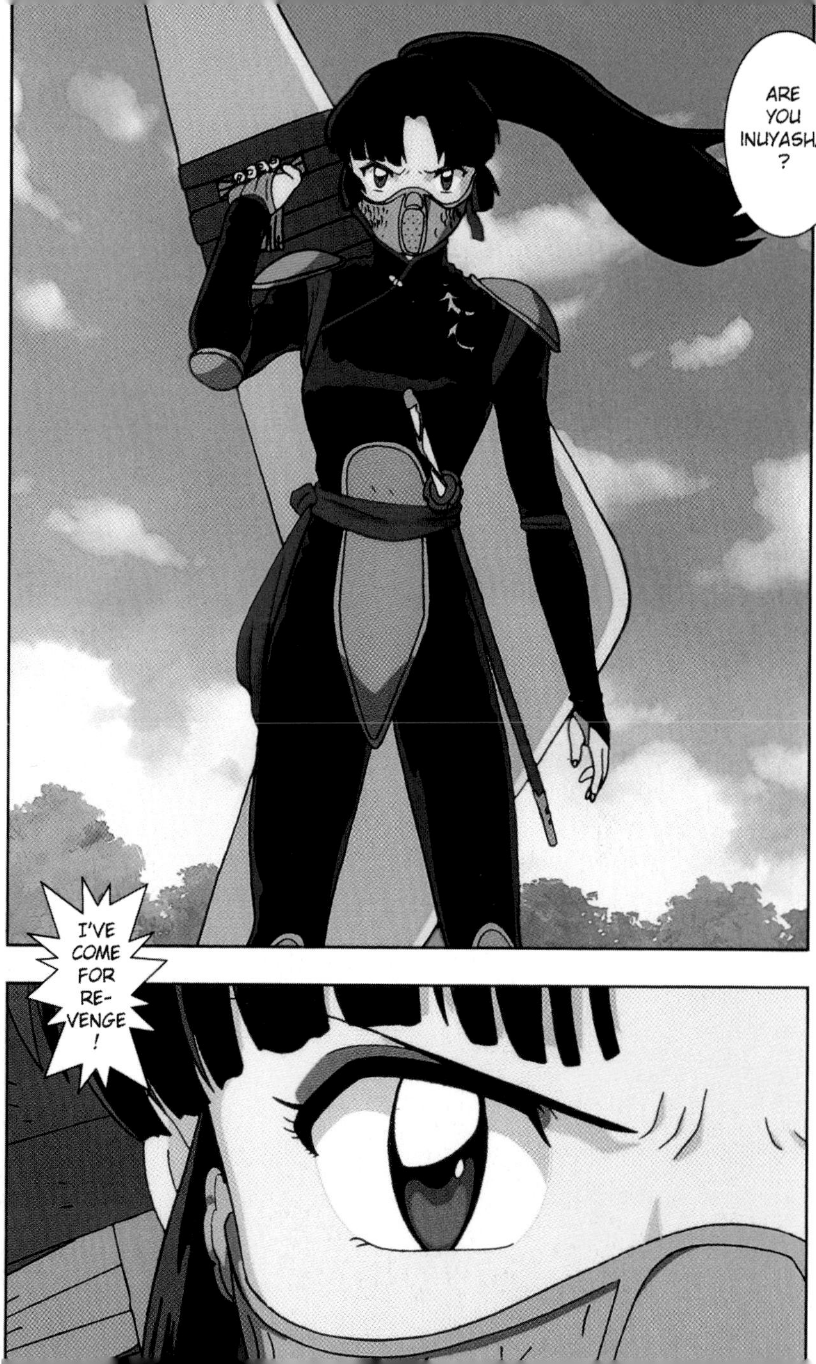
ARE YOU INUYASHA?
I'VE COME FOR RE-VENGE!

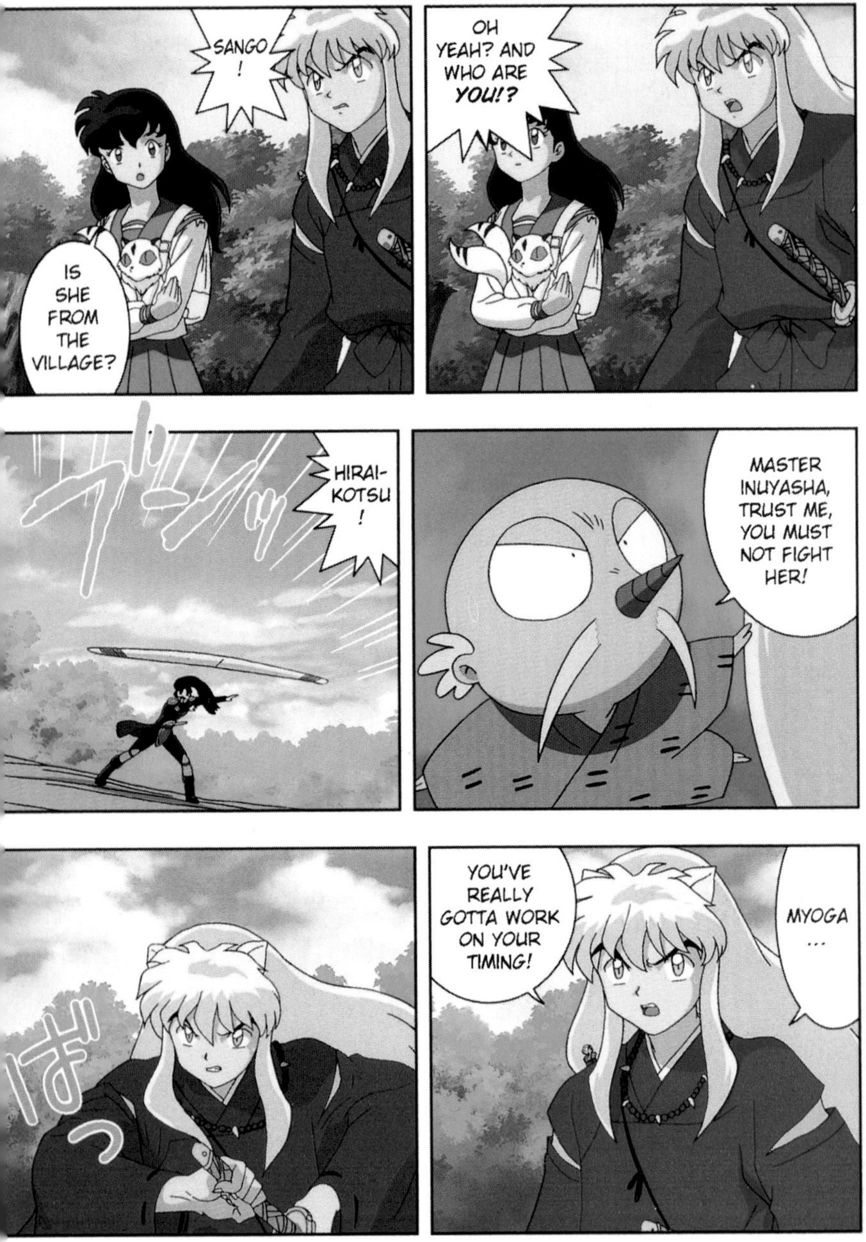

OH YEAH? AND WHO ARE *YOU!?*
SANGO!
IS SHE FROM THE VILLAGE?
MASTER INUYASHA, TRUST ME, YOU MUST NOT FIGHT HER!
HIRAI-KOTSU!
MYOGA...
YOU'VE REALLY GOTTA WORK ON YOUR TIMING!
ばっ

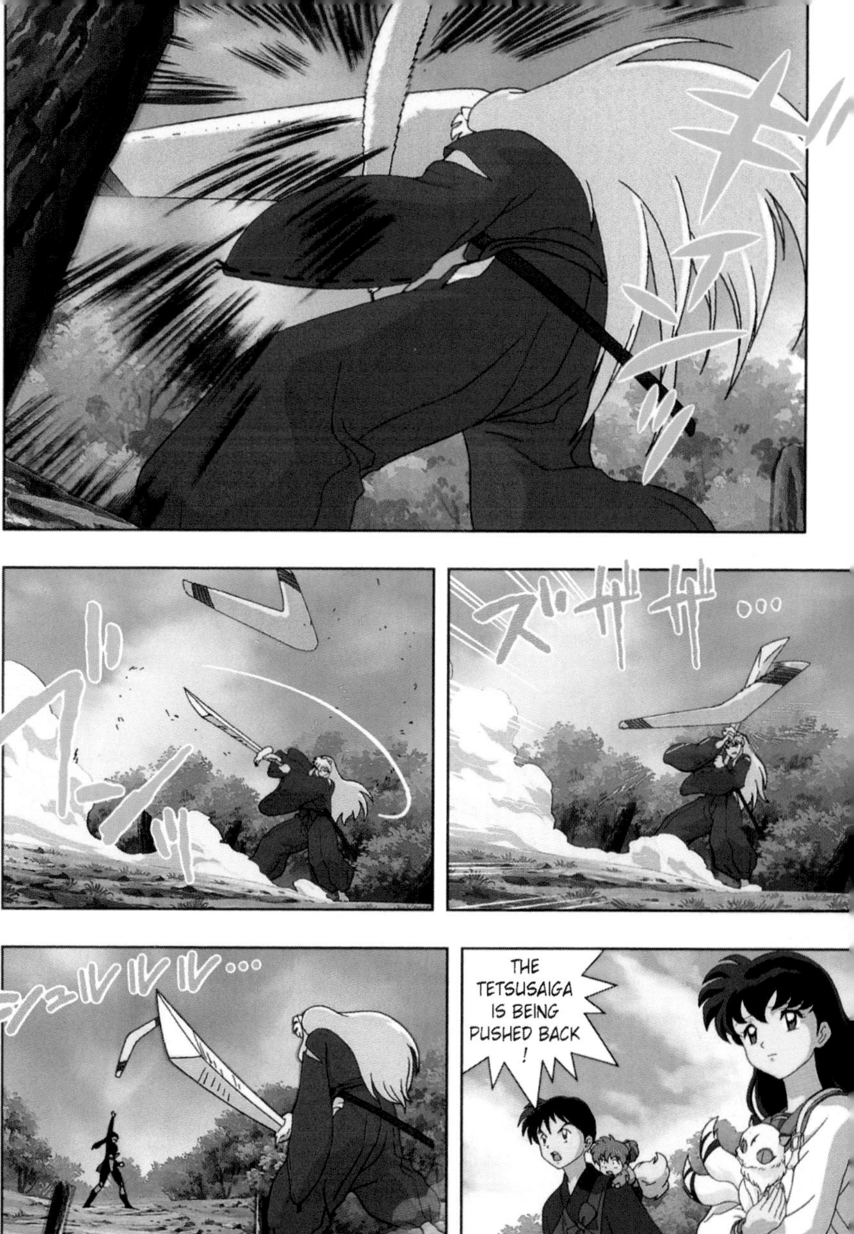
ズザザ…
THE TETSUSAIGA IS BEING PUSHED BACK!
シュルルル…

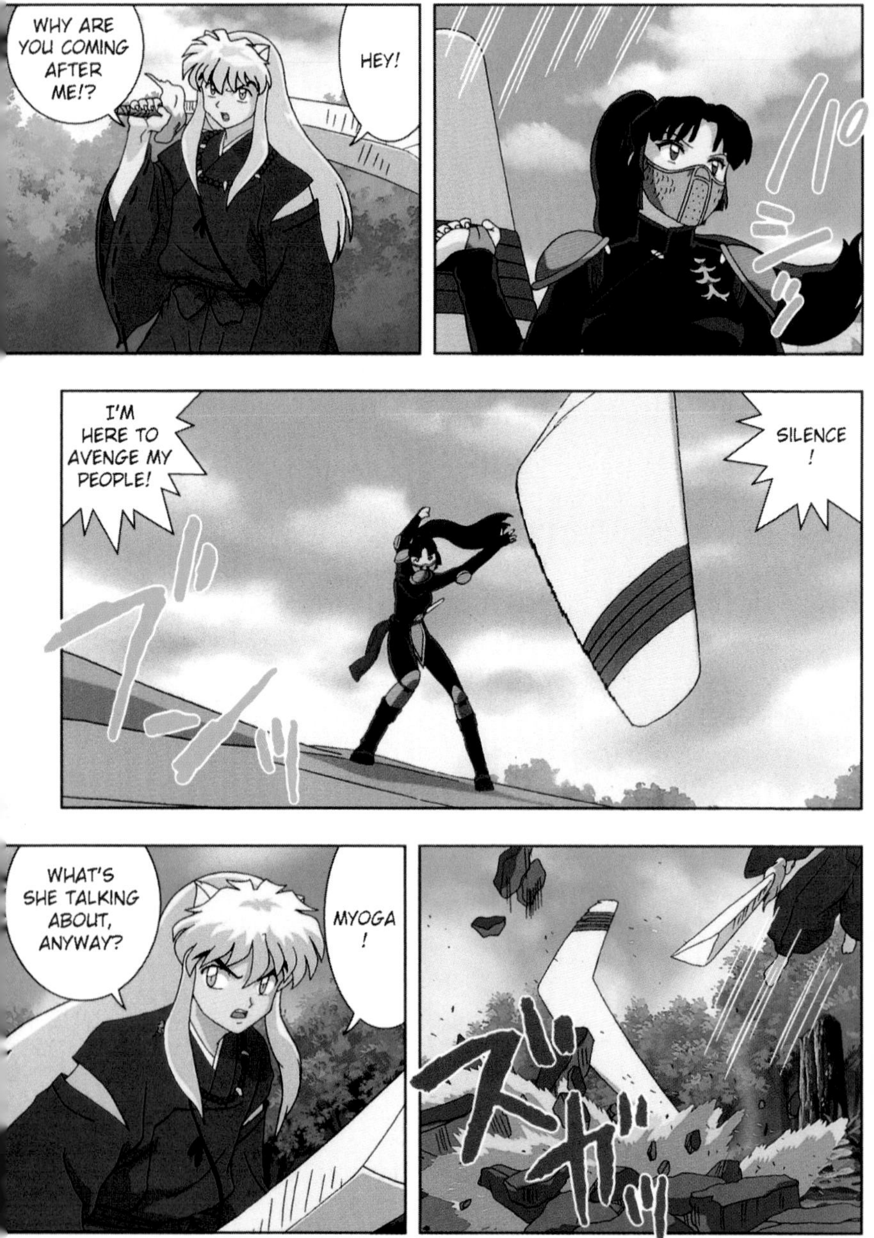
HEY!
WHY ARE YOU COMING AFTER ME!?
SILENCE!
I'M HERE TO AVENGE MY PEOPLE!
MYOGA!
WHAT'S SHE TALKING ABOUT, ANYWAY?

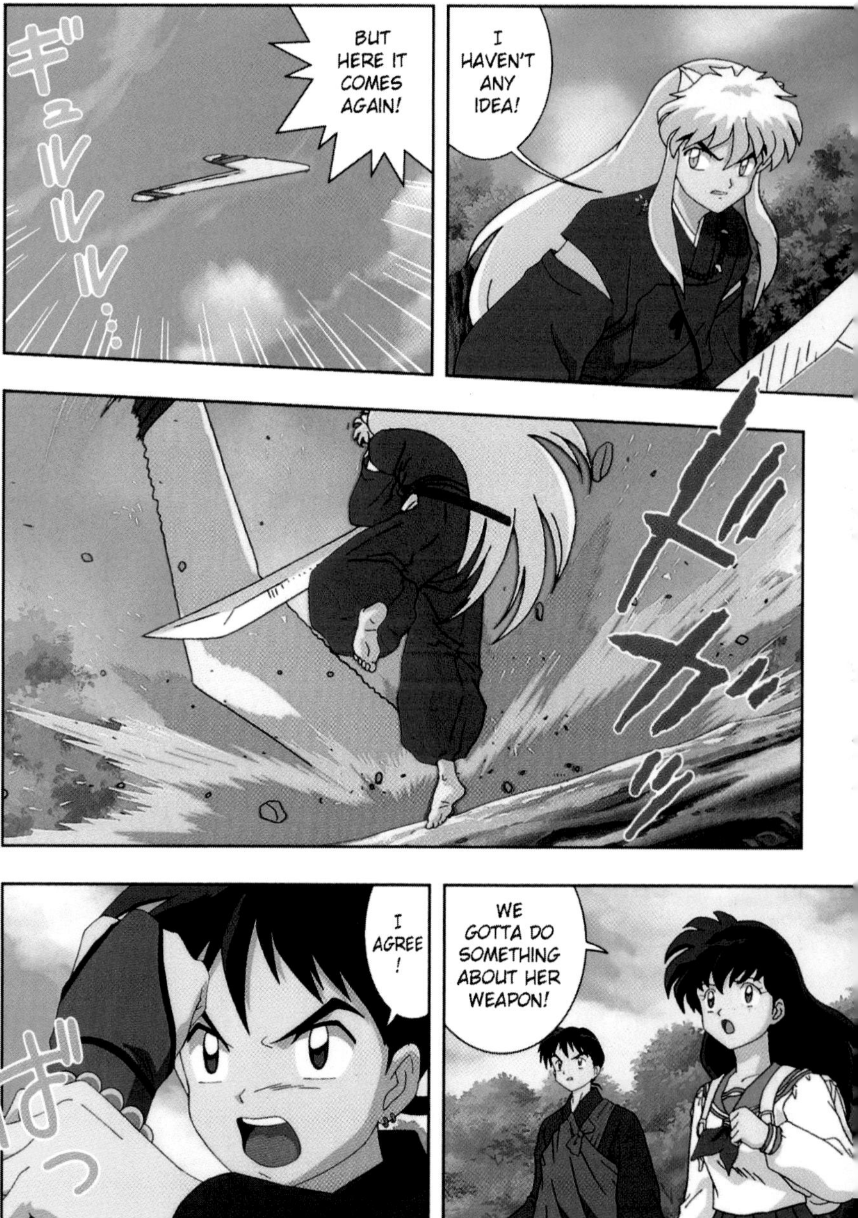
I HAVEN'T ANY IDEA!
BUT HERE IT COMES AGAIN!
ギュルルル…
WE GOTTA DO SOMETHING ABOUT HER WEAPON!
I AGREE!
ばっ

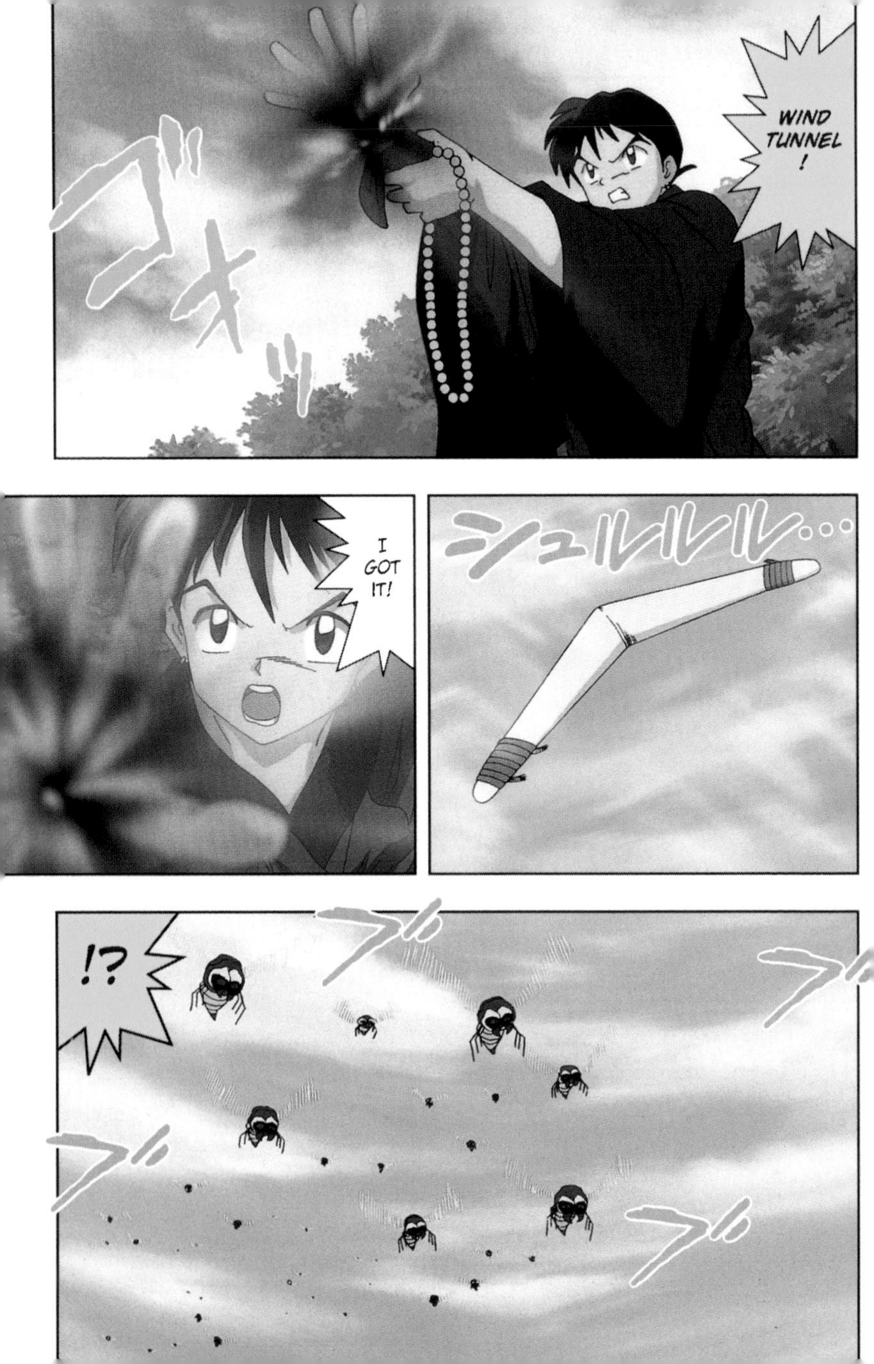
WIND TUNNEL !
ゴオッ
シュルルルル...
I GOT IT!
!?

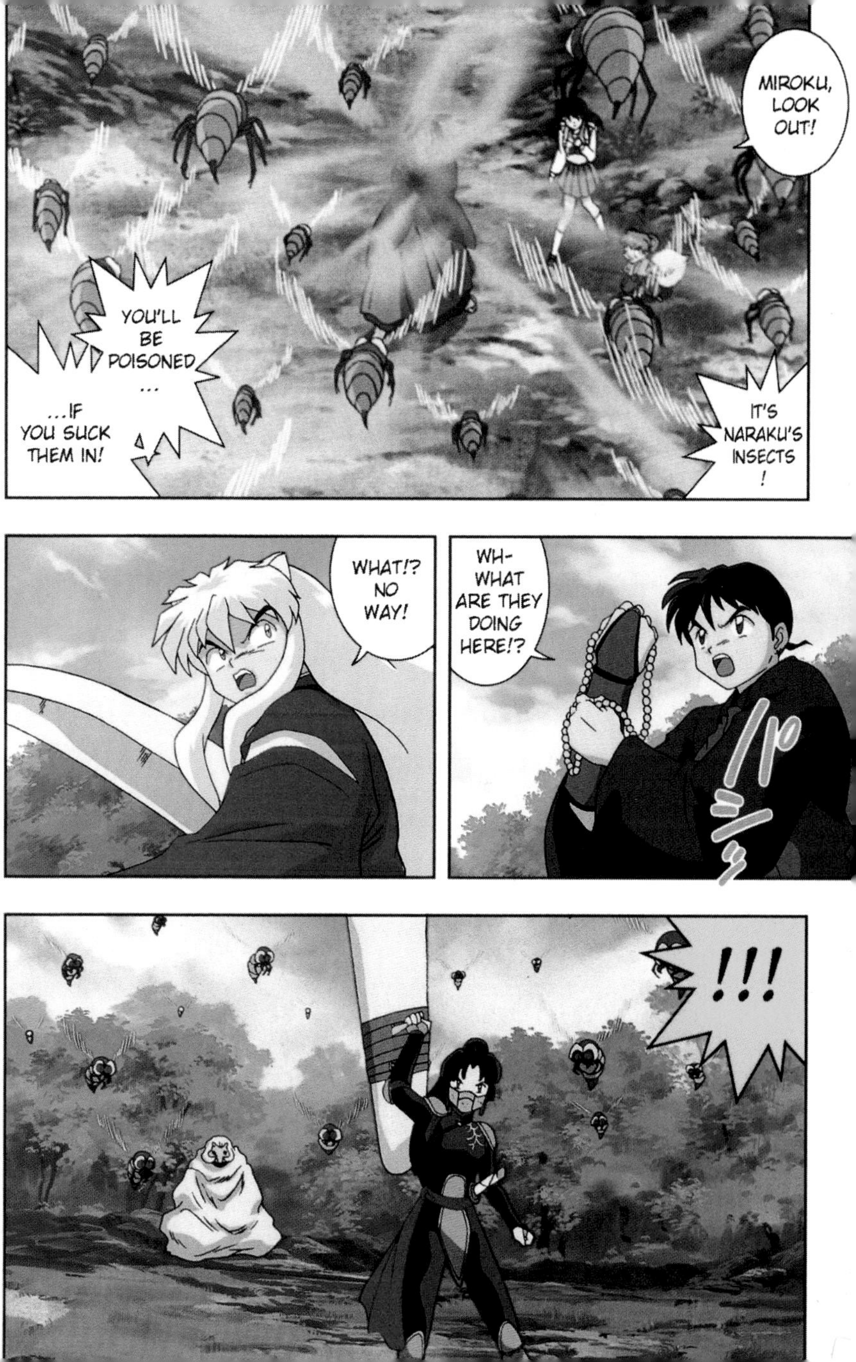
MIROKU, LOOK OUT!
IT'S NARAKU'S INSECTS!
YOU'LL BE POISONED...
...IF YOU SUCK THEM IN!
WH-WHAT ARE THEY DOING HERE!?
パシッ
WHAT!? NO WAY!
!!!

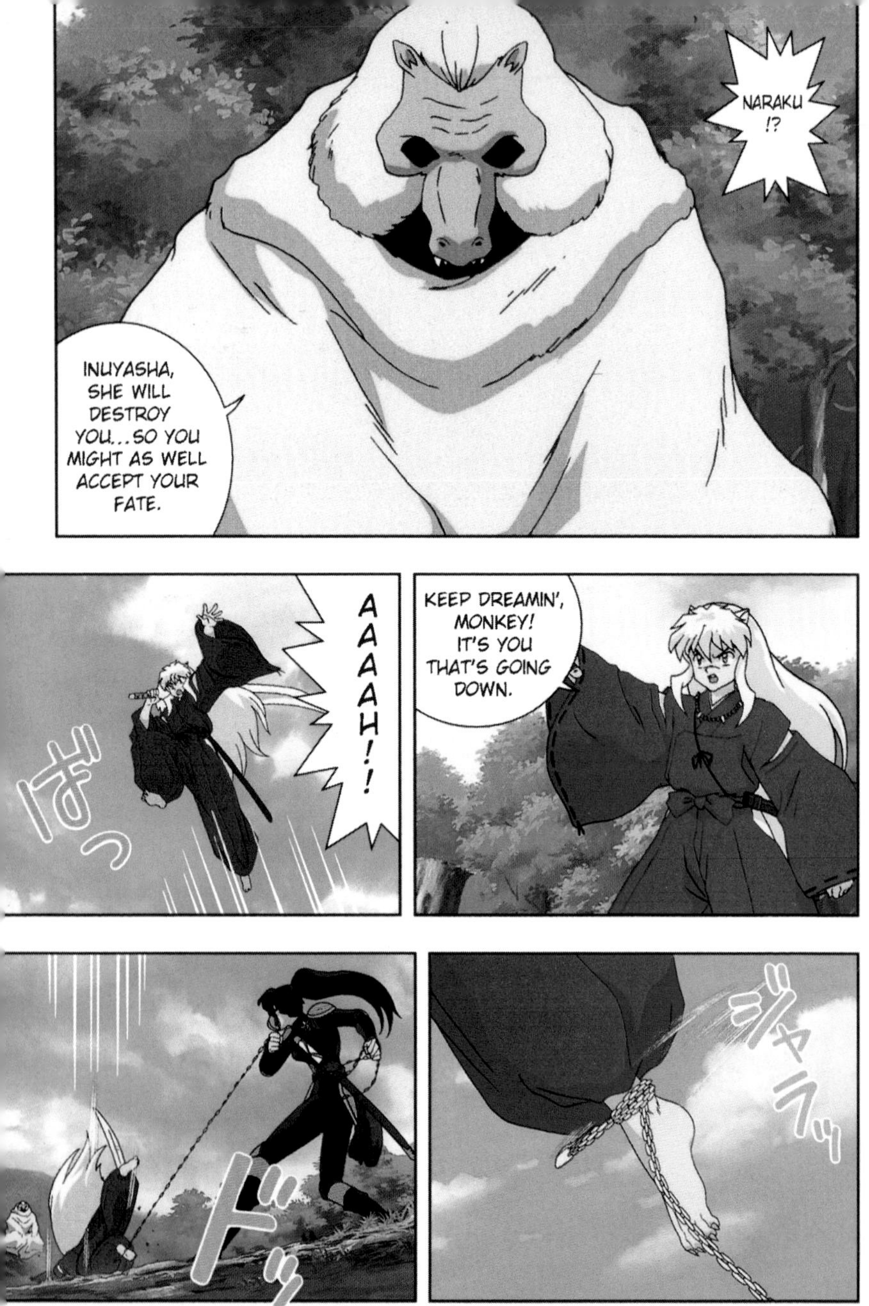
NARAKU !?
INUYASHA, SHE WILL DESTROY YOU...SO YOU MIGHT AS WELL ACCEPT YOUR FATE.
KEEP DREAMIN', MONKEY! IT'S YOU THAT'S GOING DOWN.
AAAAAH!!
ぱっ
ジャラッ
ドッ

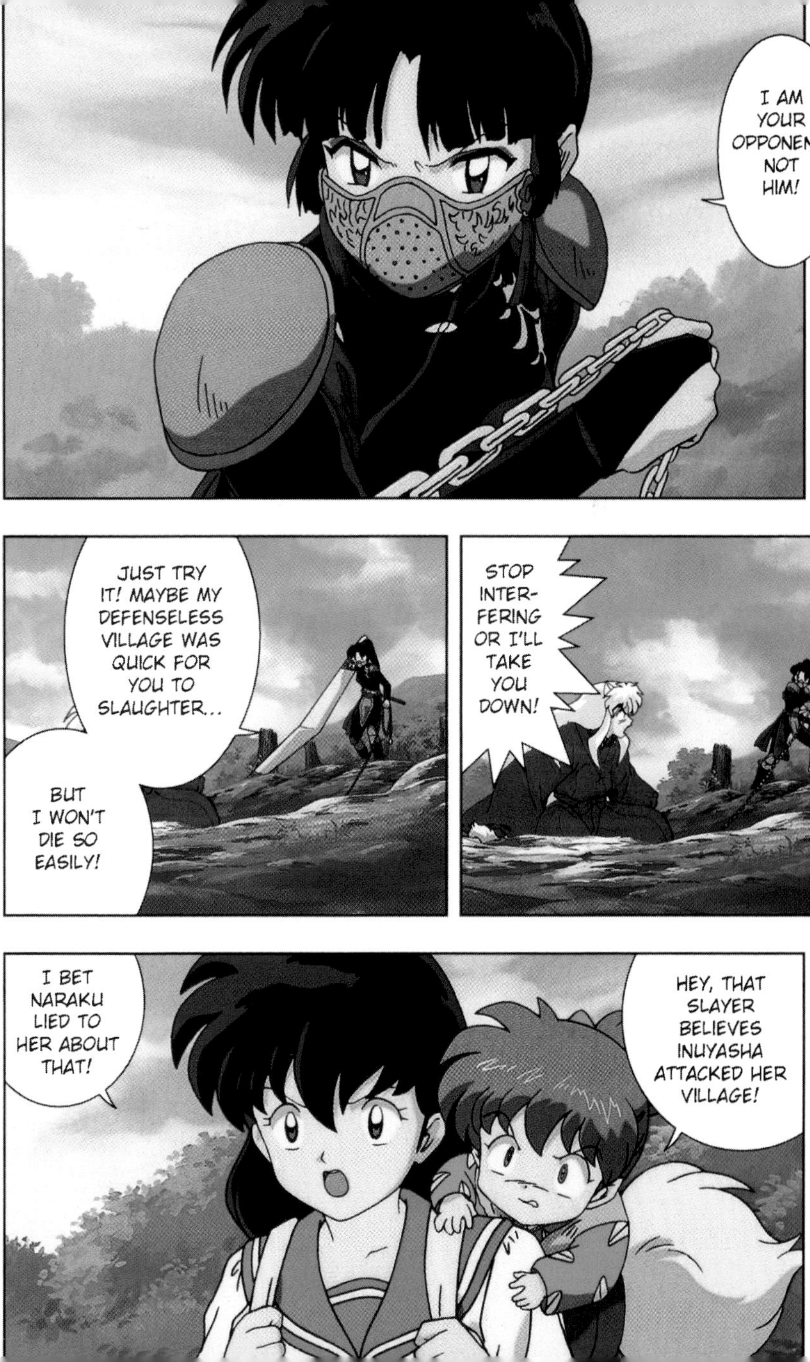
I AM YOUR OPPONENT, NOT HIM!
STOP INTER-FERING OR I'LL TAKE YOU DOWN!
JUST TRY IT! MAYBE MY DEFENSELESS VILLAGE WAS QUICK FOR YOU TO SLAUGHTER...
BUT I WON'T DIE SO EASILY!
HEY, THAT SLAYER BELIEVES INUYASHA ATTACKED HER VILLAGE!
I BET NARAKU LIED TO HER ABOUT THAT!

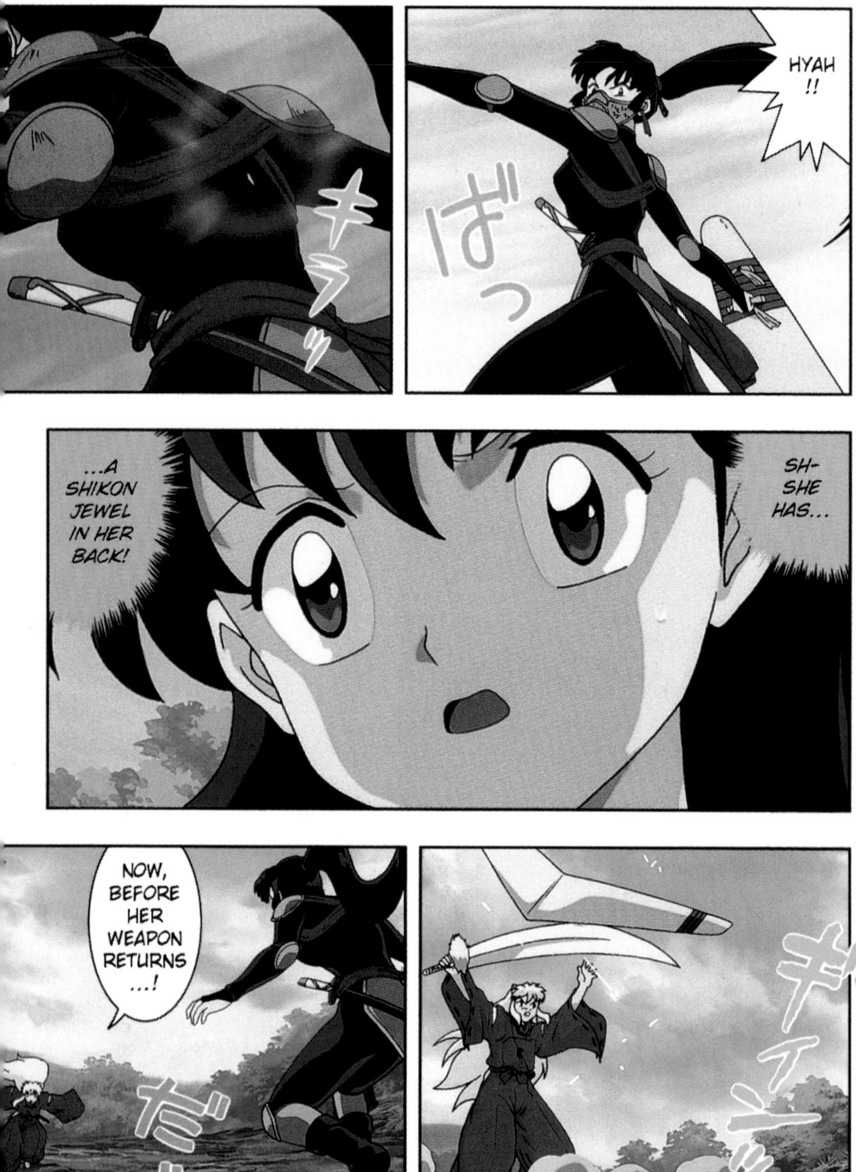
HYAH!!
ばっ
キラッ
SH-SHE HAS...
...A SHIKON JEWEL IN HER BACK!
NOW, BEFORE HER WEAPON RETURNS...!
だッ

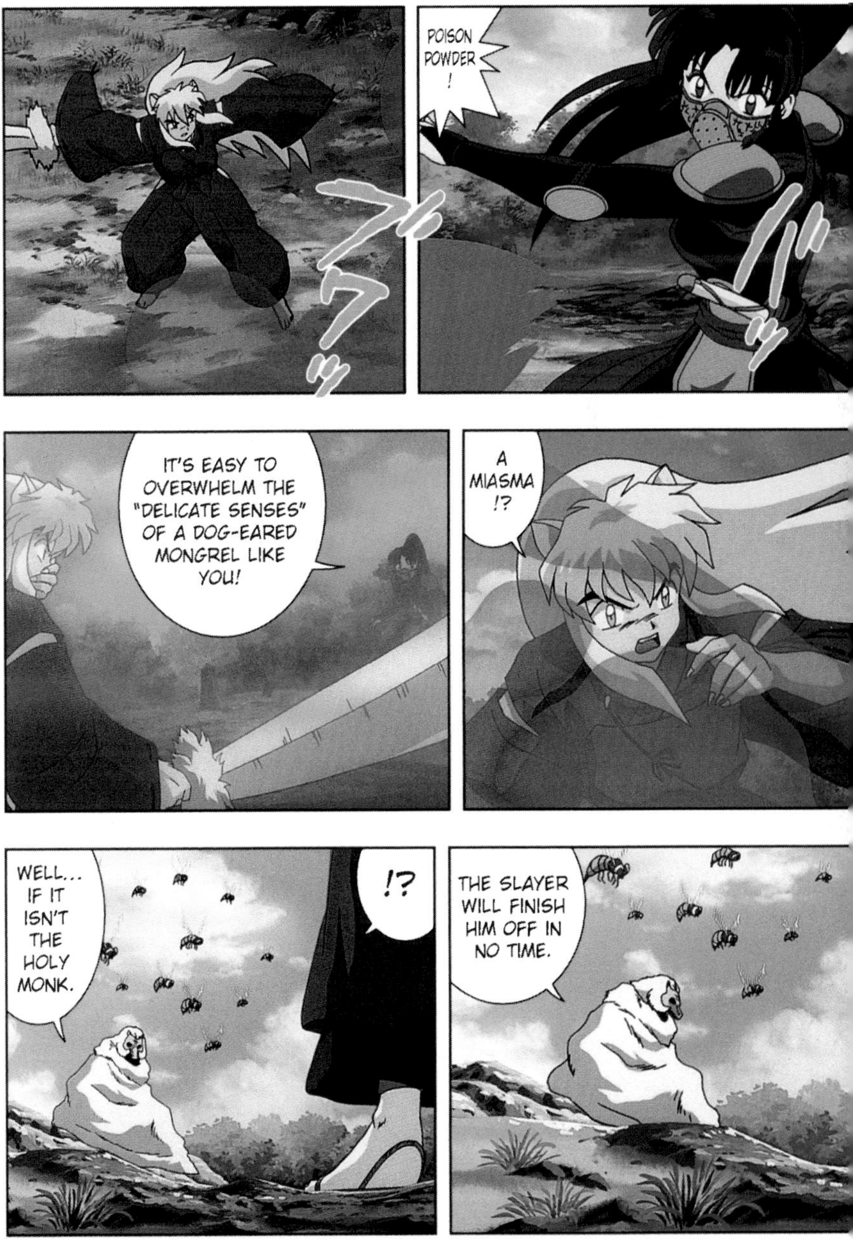
POISON POWDER !
A MIASMA !?
IT'S EASY TO OVERWHELM THE "DELICATE SENSES" OF A DOG-EARED MONGREL LIKE YOU!
THE SLAYER WILL FINISH HIM OFF IN NO TIME.
!?
WELL... IF IT ISN'T THE HOLY MONK.

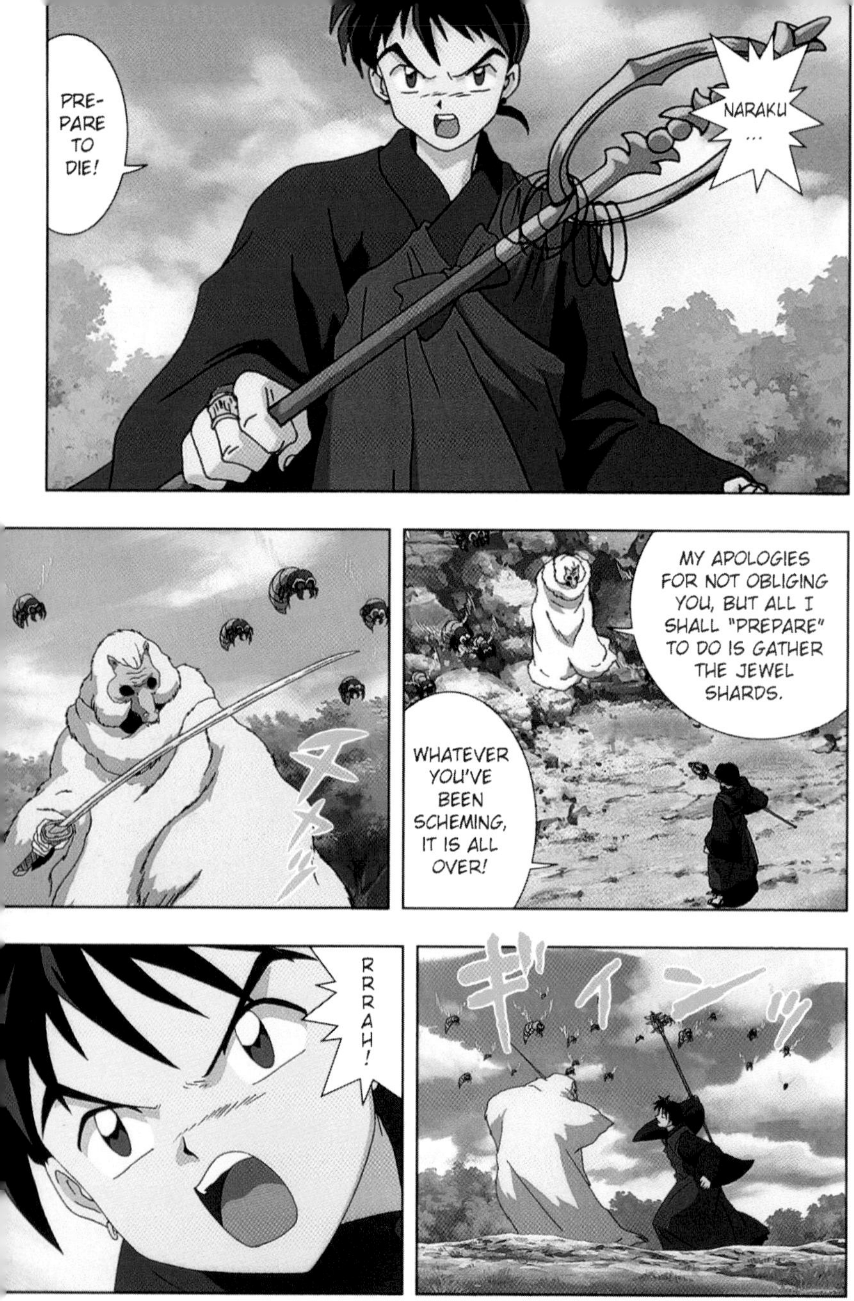
NARAKU ...
PRE-PARE TO DIE!
MY APOLOGIES FOR NOT OBLIGING YOU, BUT ALL I SHALL "PREPARE" TO DO IS GATHER THE JEWEL SHARDS.
WHATEVER YOU'VE BEEN SCHEMING, IT IS ALL OVER!
RRRAH!

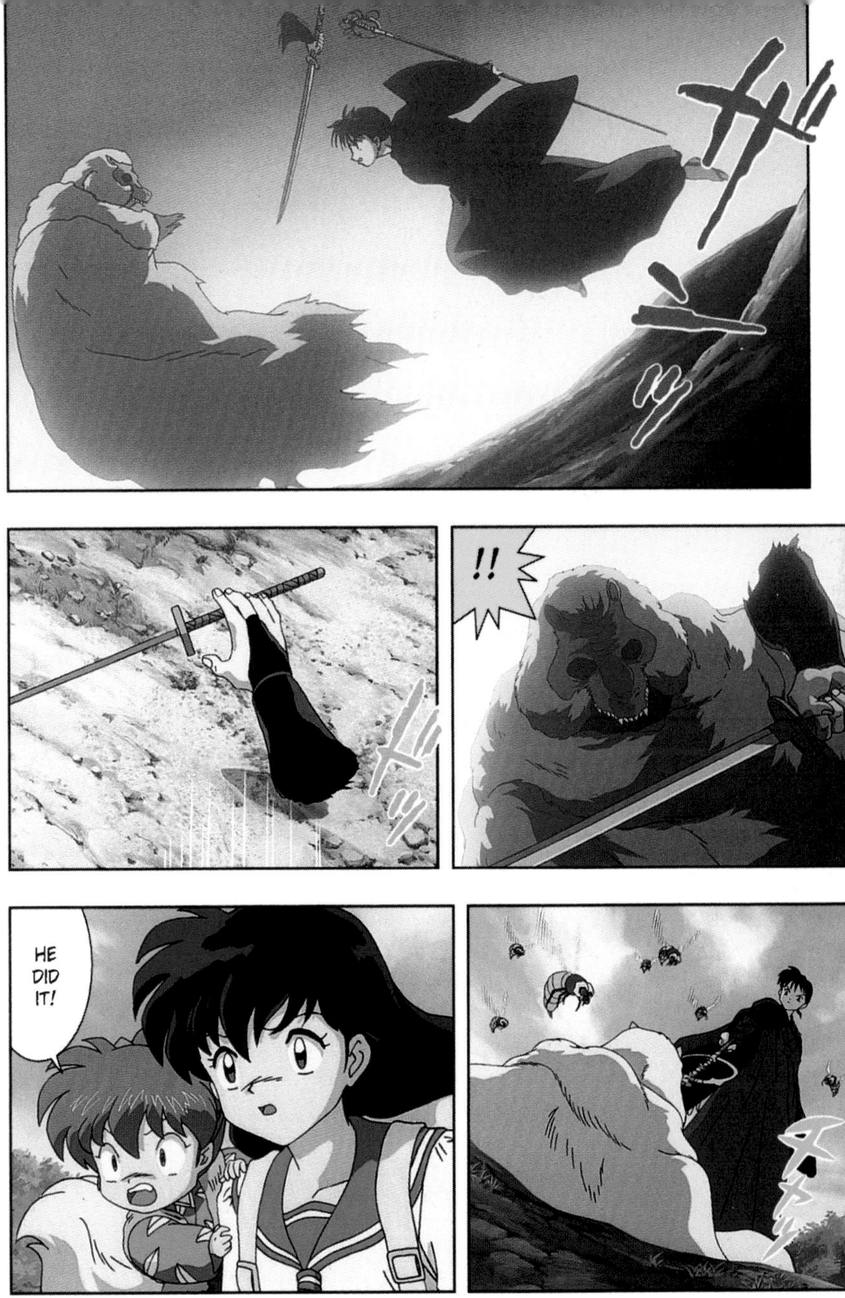
!!
HE DID IT!

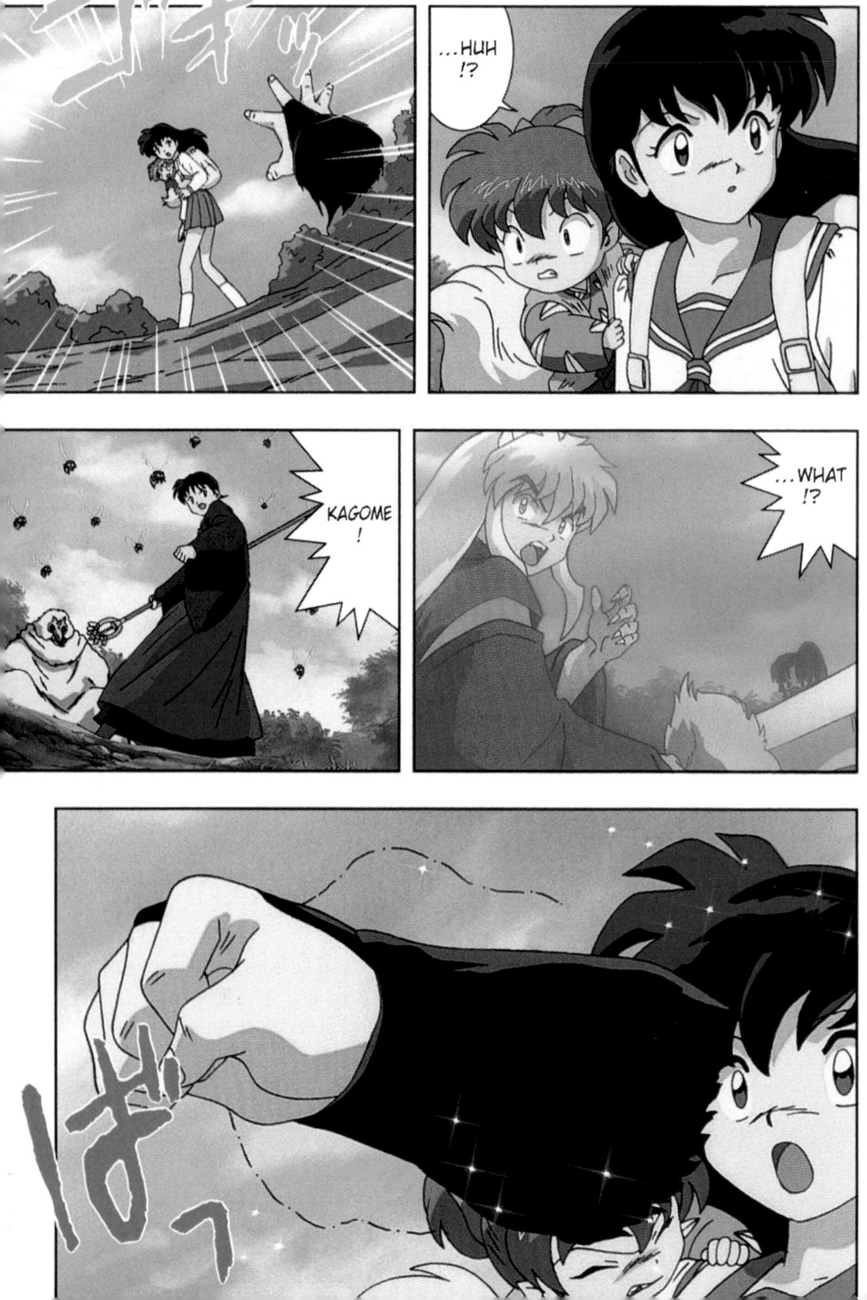
...HUH !?
...WHAT !?
KAGOME !
ばっ

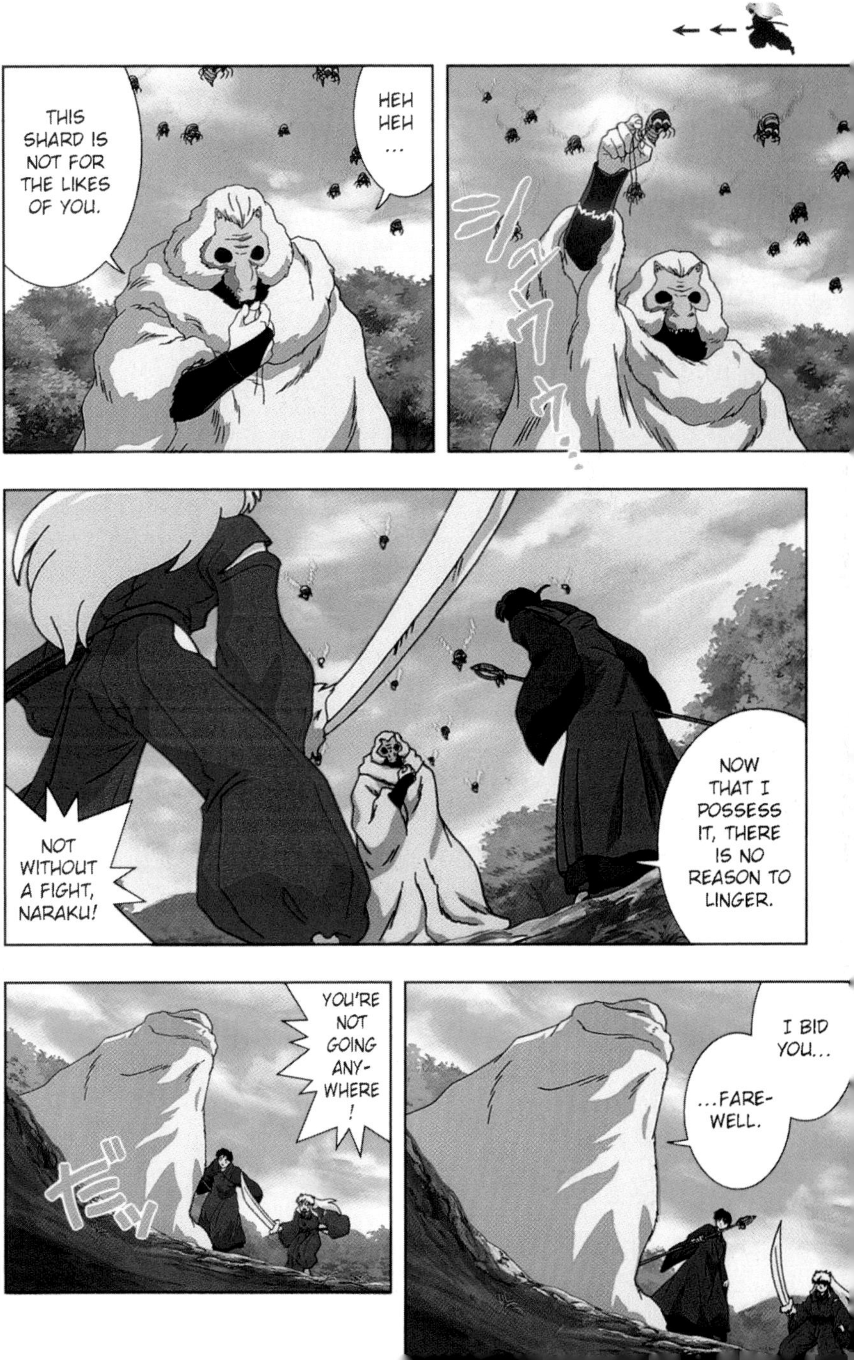
HEH HEH ...
THIS SHARD IS NOT FOR THE LIKES OF YOU.
NOW THAT I POSSESS IT, THERE IS NO REASON TO LINGER.
NOT WITHOUT A FIGHT, NARAKU!
I BID YOU...
...FARE-WELL.
YOU'RE NOT GOING ANY-WHERE!

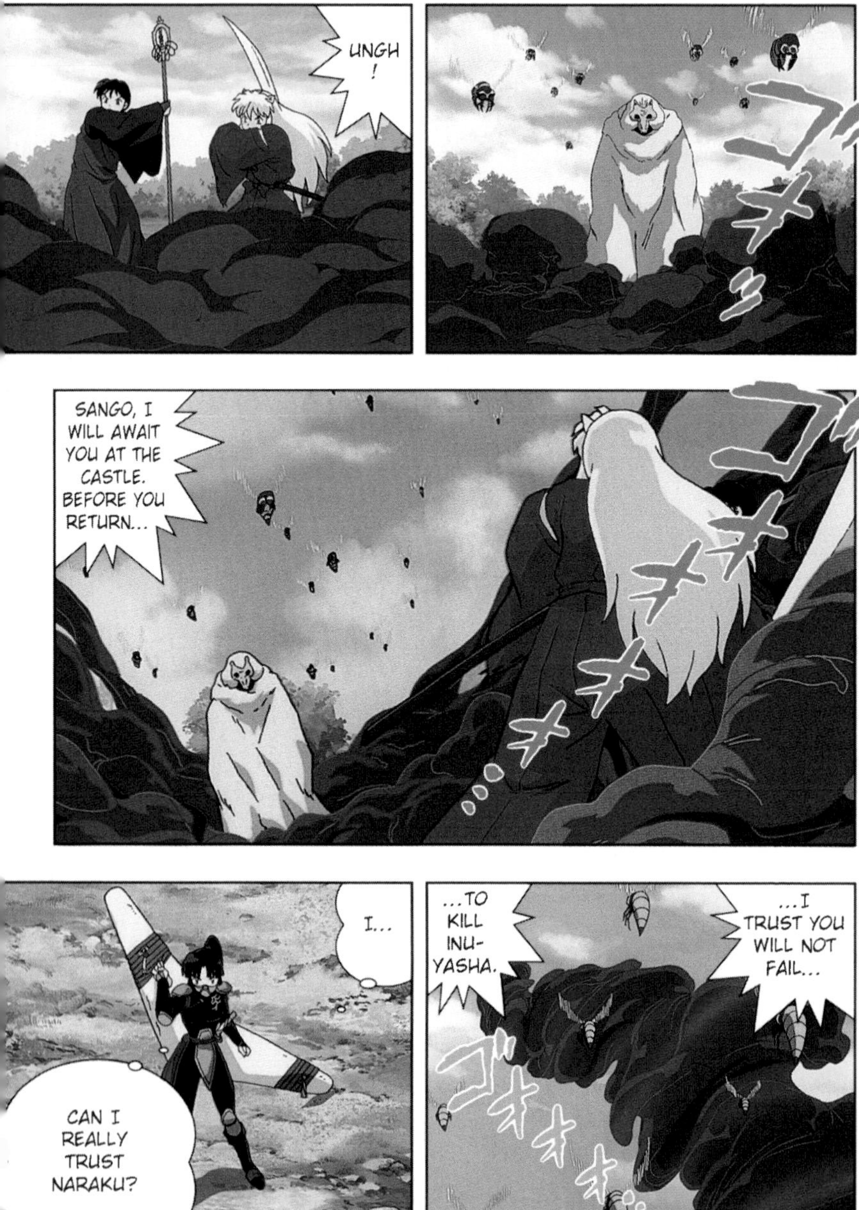
UNGH!
SANGO, I WILL AWAIT YOU AT THE CASTLE. BEFORE YOU RETURN...
...I TRUST YOU WILL NOT FAIL...
...TO KILL INU-YASHA.
I...
CAN I REALLY TRUST NARAKU?

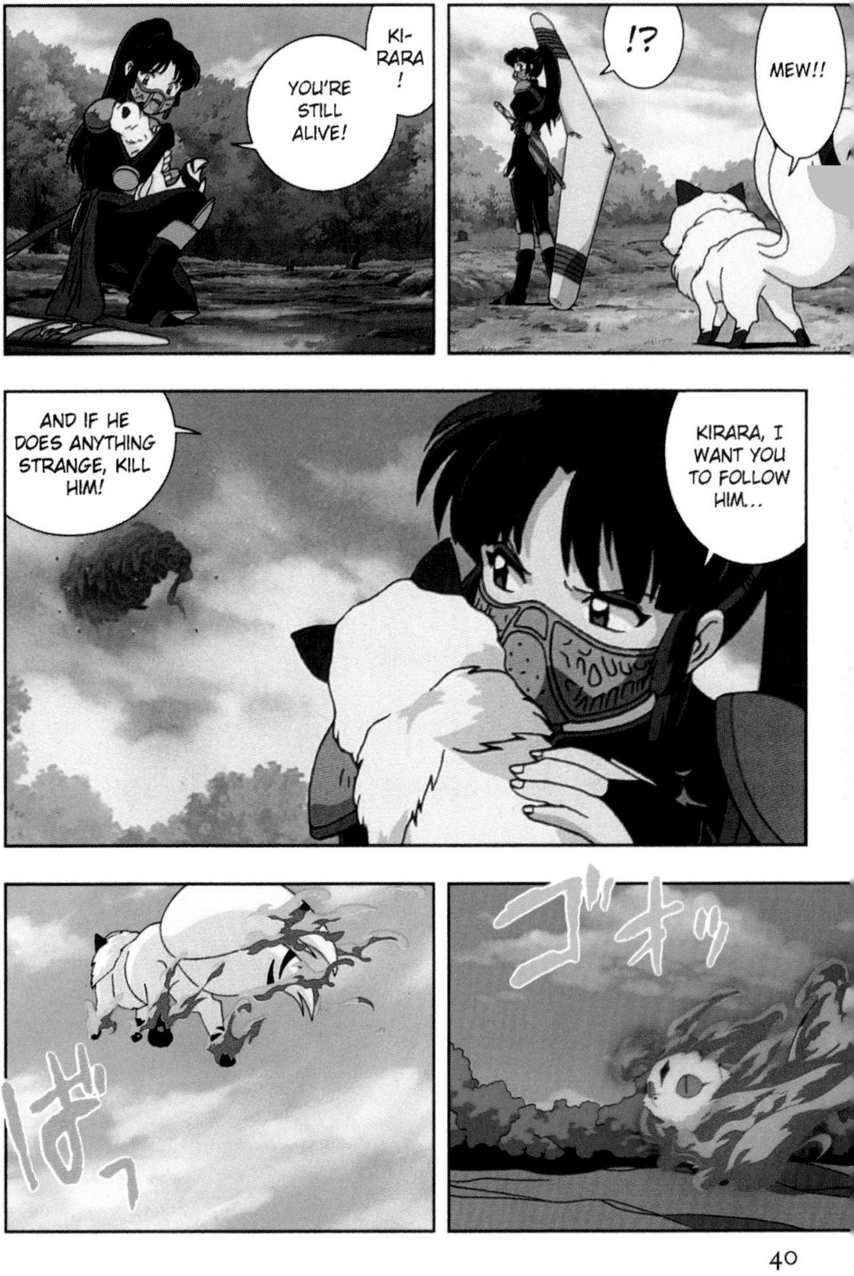
MEW!!
!?
KI-RARA!
YOU'RE STILL ALIVE!
KIRARA, I WANT YOU TO FOLLOW HIM...
AND IF HE DOES ANYTHING STRANGE, KILL HIM!
ゴオッ
ぱっ

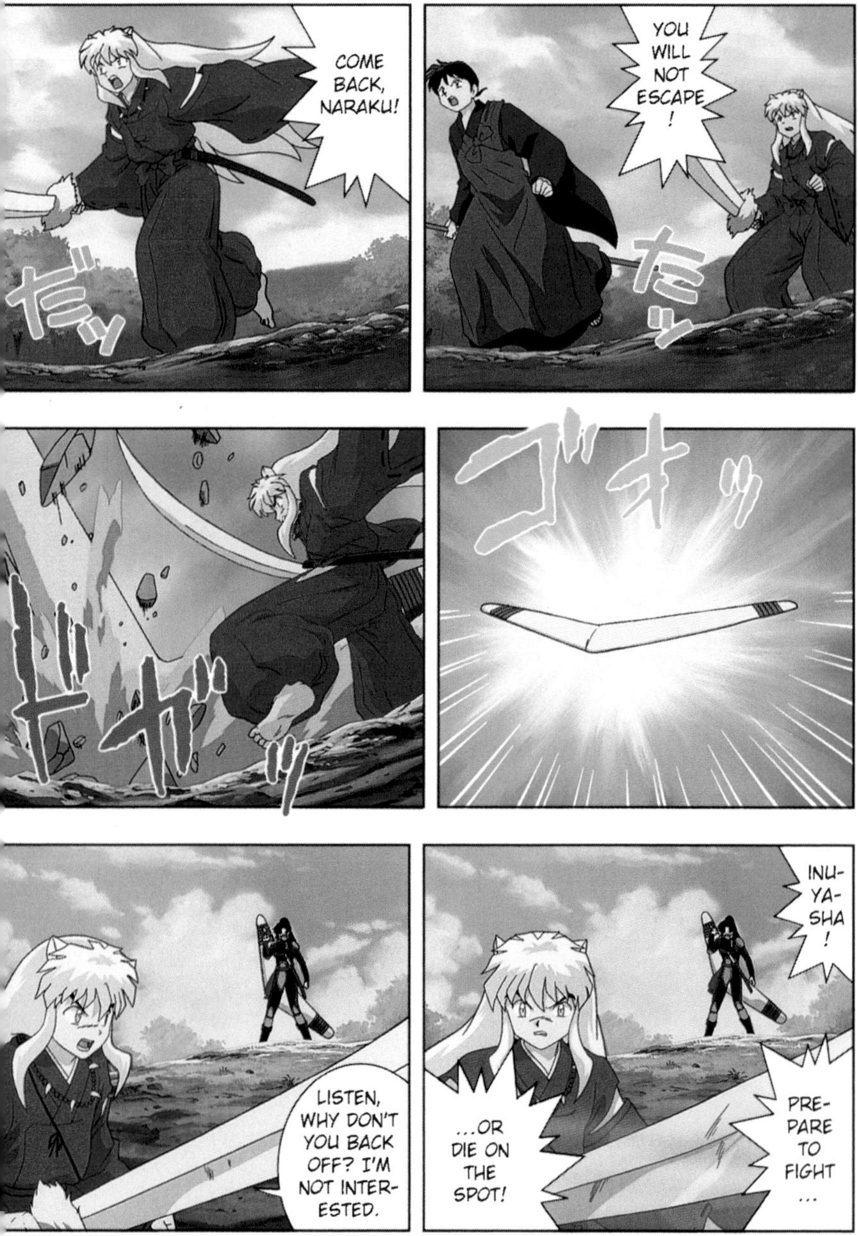
YOU WILL NOT ESCAPE!
たッ
COME BACK, NARAKU!
ダッ
ゴキッ
ドガッ
INU-YASHA!
PREPARE TO FIGHT...
...OR DIE ON THE SPOT!
LISTEN, WHY DON'T YOU BACK OFF? I'M NOT INTERESTED.

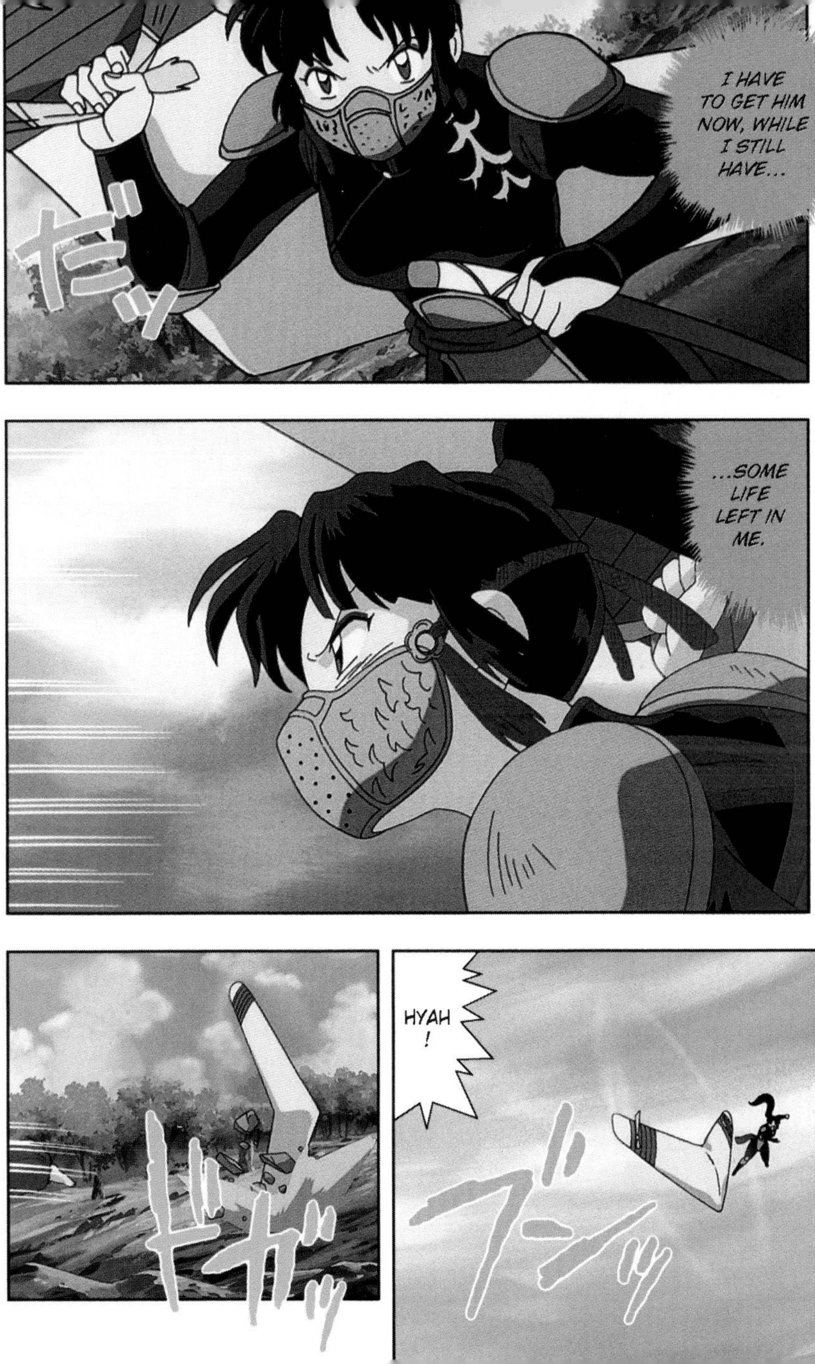
I HAVE TO GET HIM NOW, WHILE I STILL HAVE...
...SOME LIFE LEFT IN ME.
HYAH!

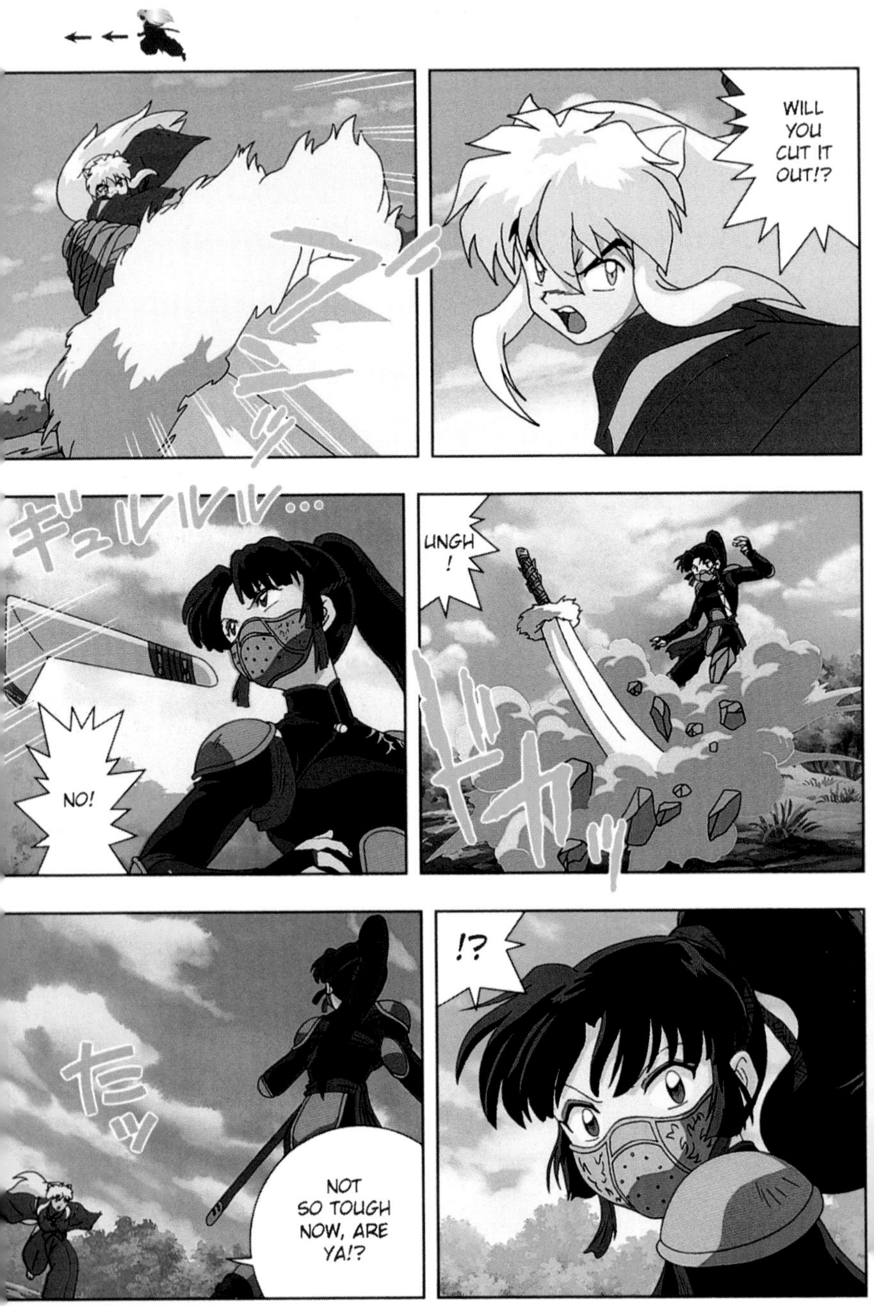
WILL YOU CUT IT OUT!?
UNGH!
ドカッ
ギュルルル...
NO!
!?
たッ
NOT SO TOUGH NOW, ARE YA!?

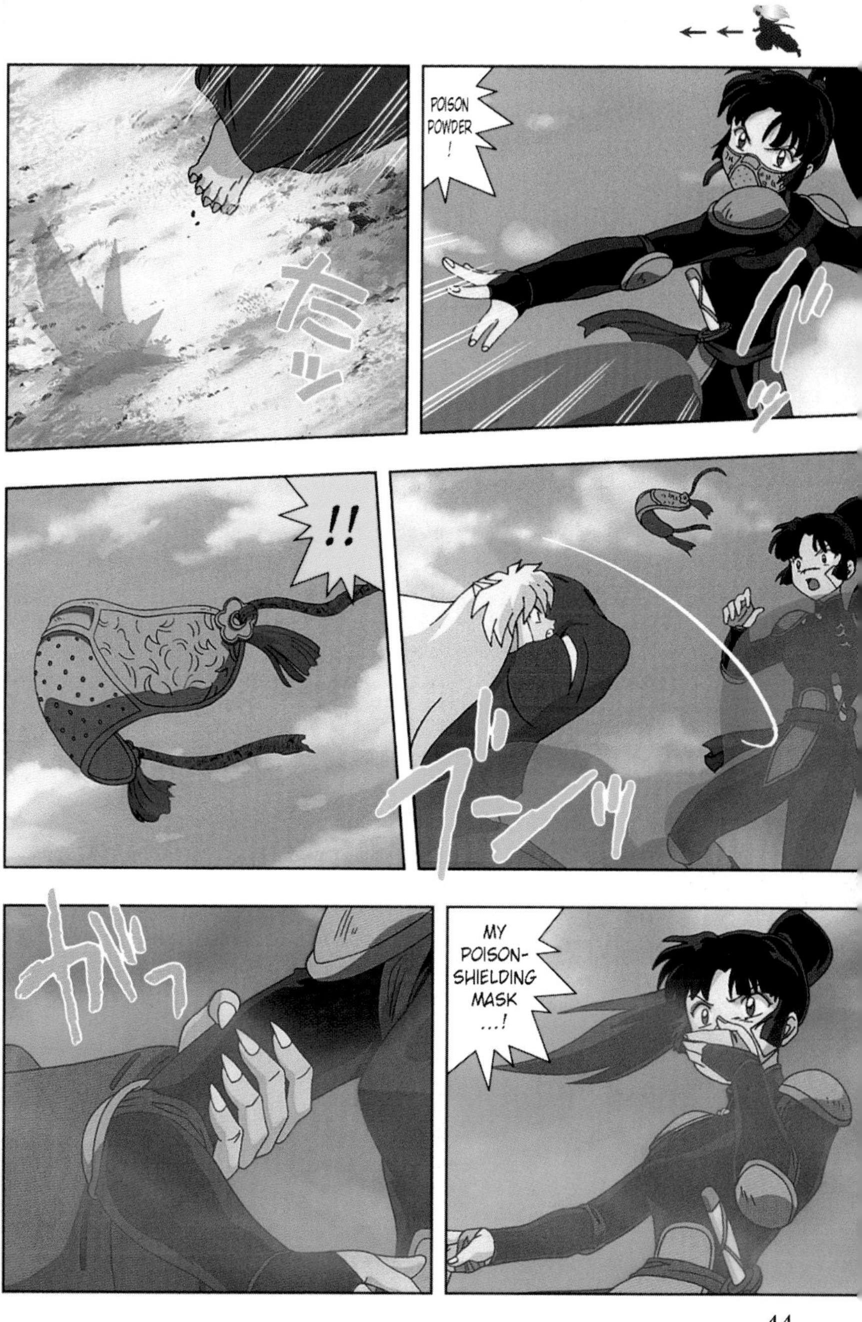

POISON POWDER !
!!
ブーンッ
MY POISON-SHIELDING MASK ...!

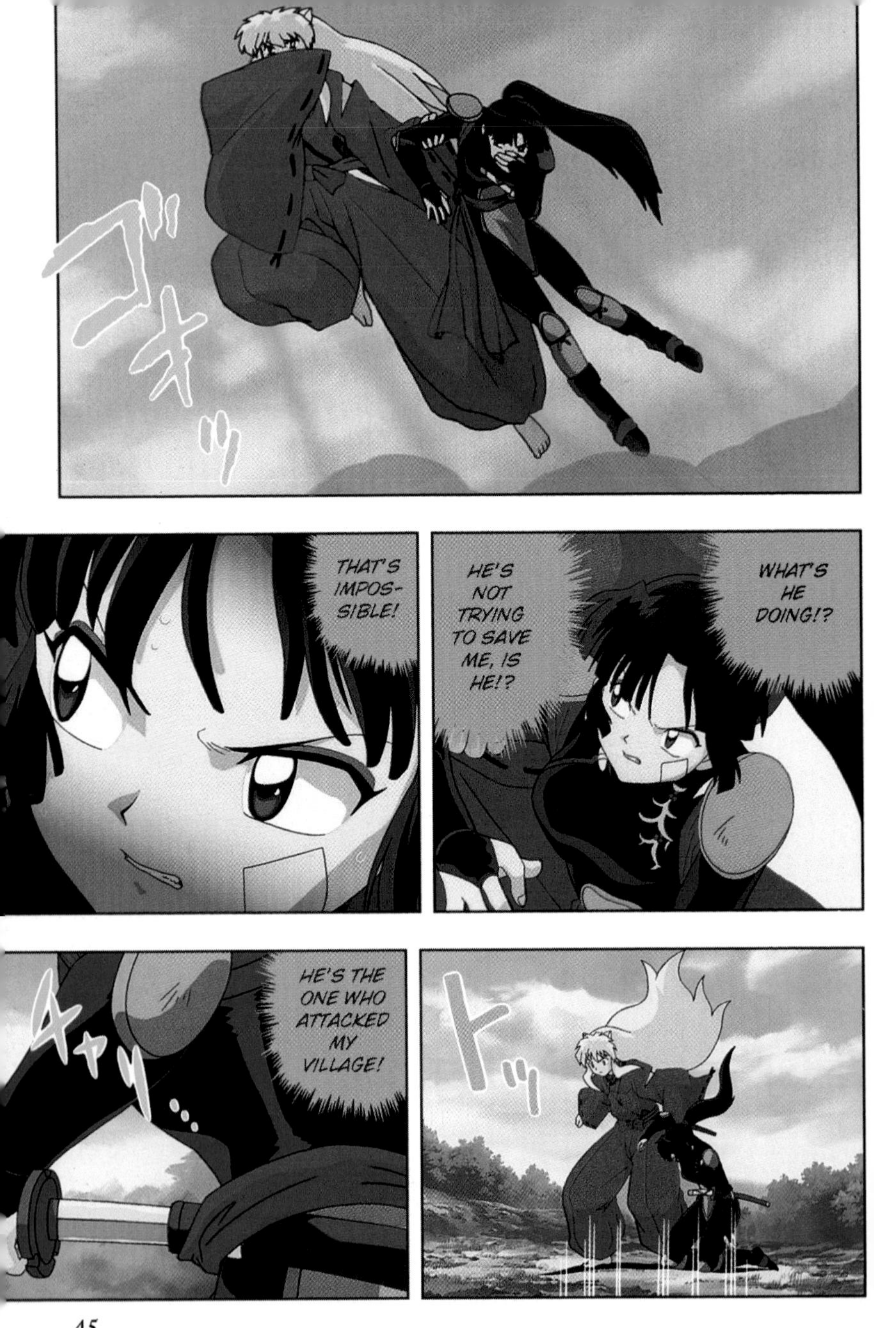
ゴオッ
WHAT'S HE DOING!?
HE'S NOT TRYING TO SAVE ME, IS HE!?
THAT'S IMPOS-SIBLE!
トッ
HE'S THE ONE WHO ATTACKED MY VILLAGE!

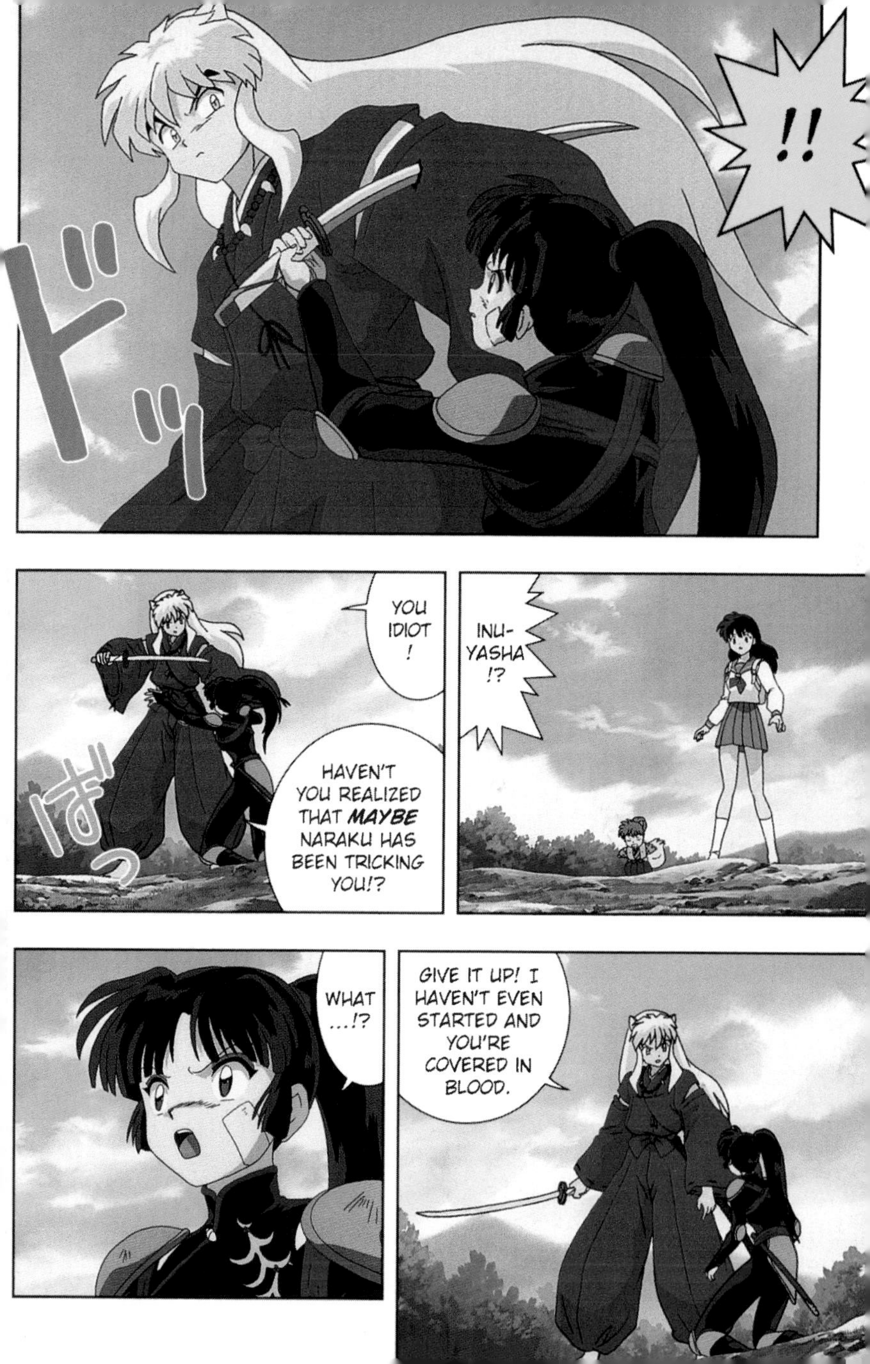
!!
ドッ
INU-YASHA!?
YOU IDIOT!
HAVEN'T YOU REALIZED THAT *MAYBE* NARAKU HAS BEEN TRICKING YOU!?
ばっ
GIVE IT UP! I HAVEN'T EVEN STARTED AND YOU'RE COVERED IN BLOOD.
WHAT...!?

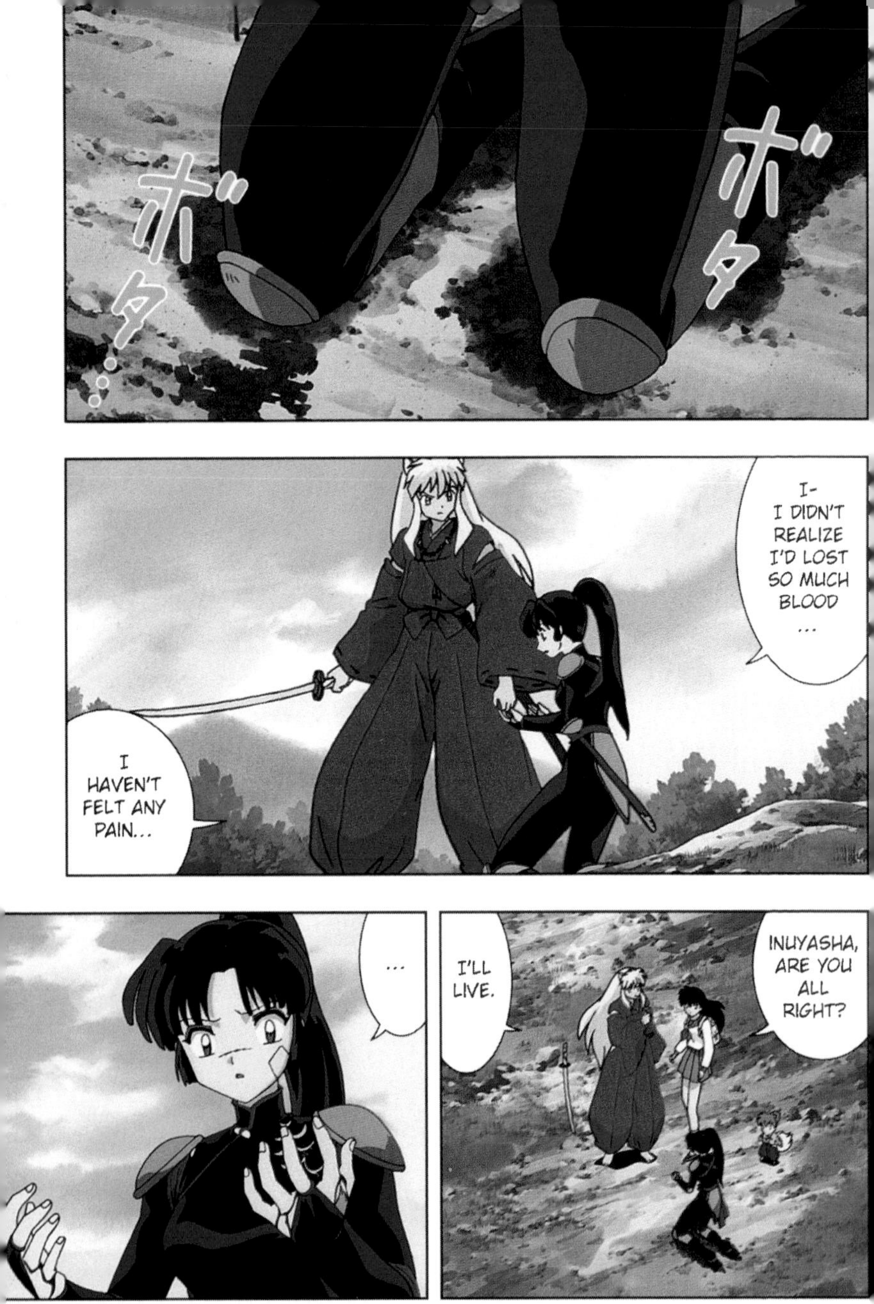
ボタ
ボタ…
I- I DIDN'T REALIZE I'D LOST SO MUCH BLOOD …
I HAVEN'T FELT ANY PAIN…
INUYASHA, ARE YOU ALL RIGHT?
I'LL LIVE.
…

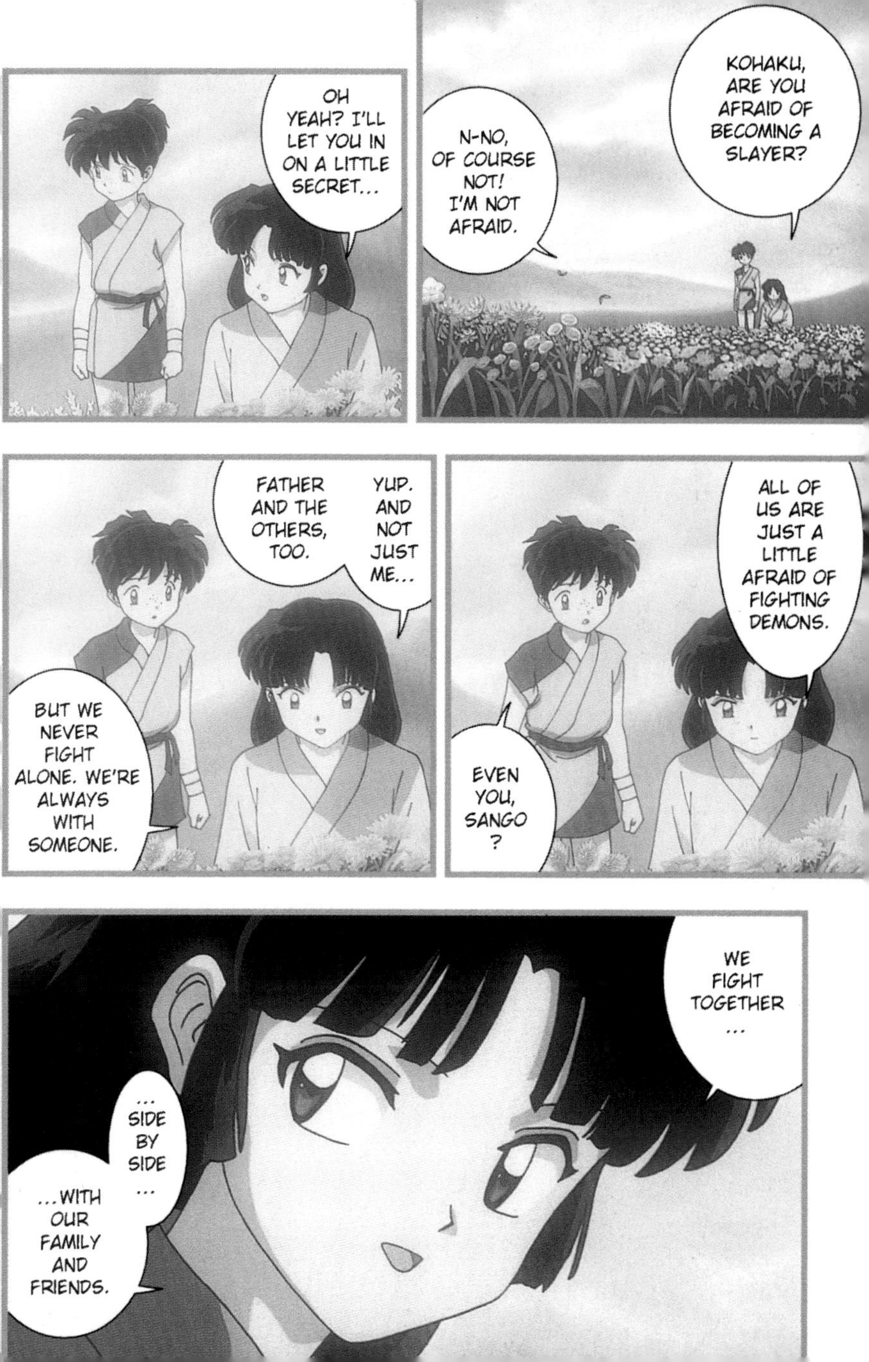
KOHAKU, ARE YOU AFRAID OF BECOMING A SLAYER?
N-NO, OF COURSE NOT! I'M NOT AFRAID.
OH YEAH? I'LL LET YOU IN ON A LITTLE SECRET...
ALL OF US ARE JUST A LITTLE AFRAID OF FIGHTING DEMONS.
EVEN YOU, SANGO?
YUP. AND NOT JUST ME...
FATHER AND THE OTHERS, TOO.
BUT WE NEVER FIGHT ALONE. WE'RE ALWAYS WITH SOMEONE.
WE FIGHT TOGETHER...
...SIDE BY SIDE...
...WITH OUR FAMILY AND FRIENDS.

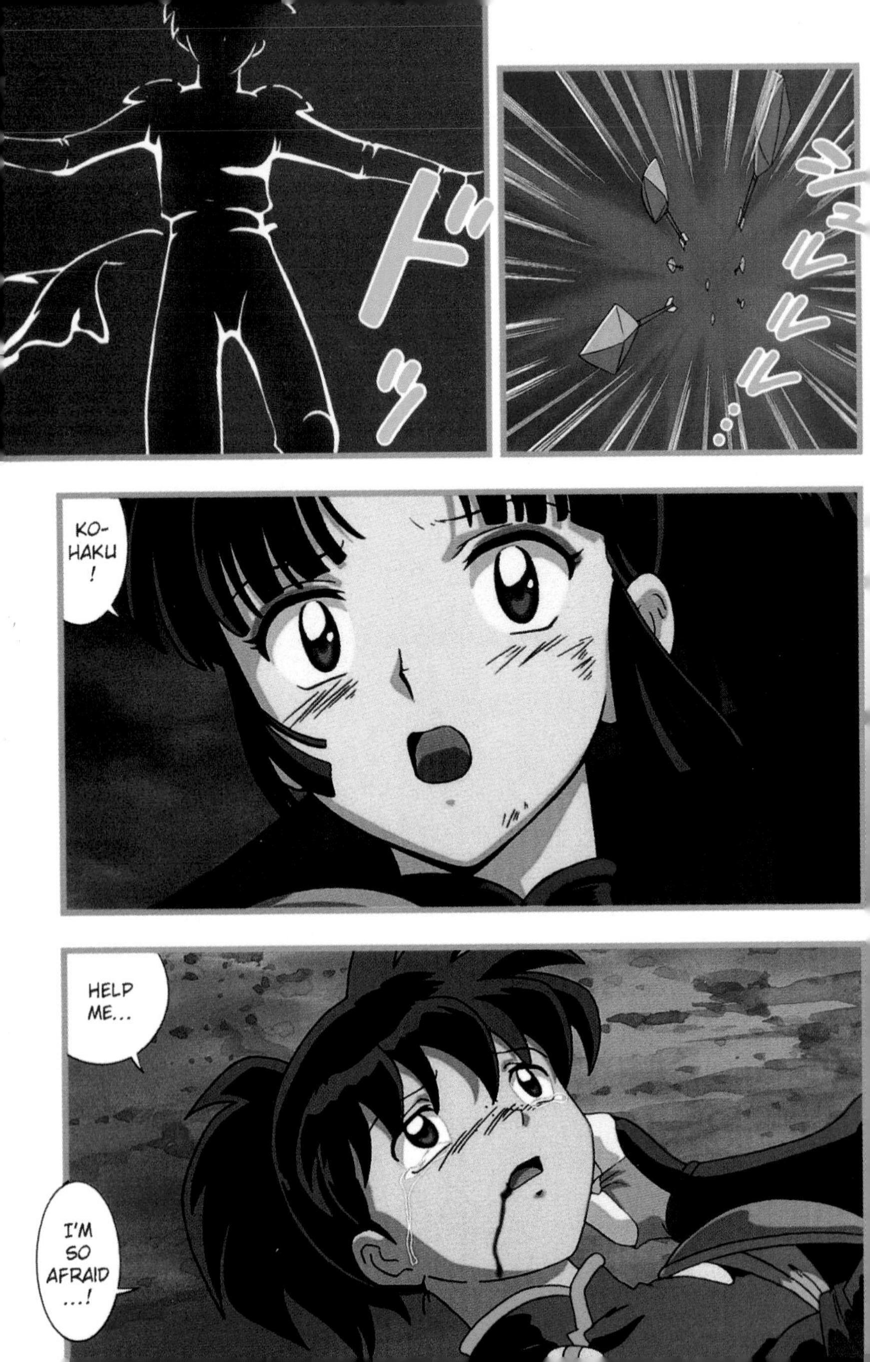
ドッ
KO-HAKU!
HELP ME...
I'M SO AFRAID...!

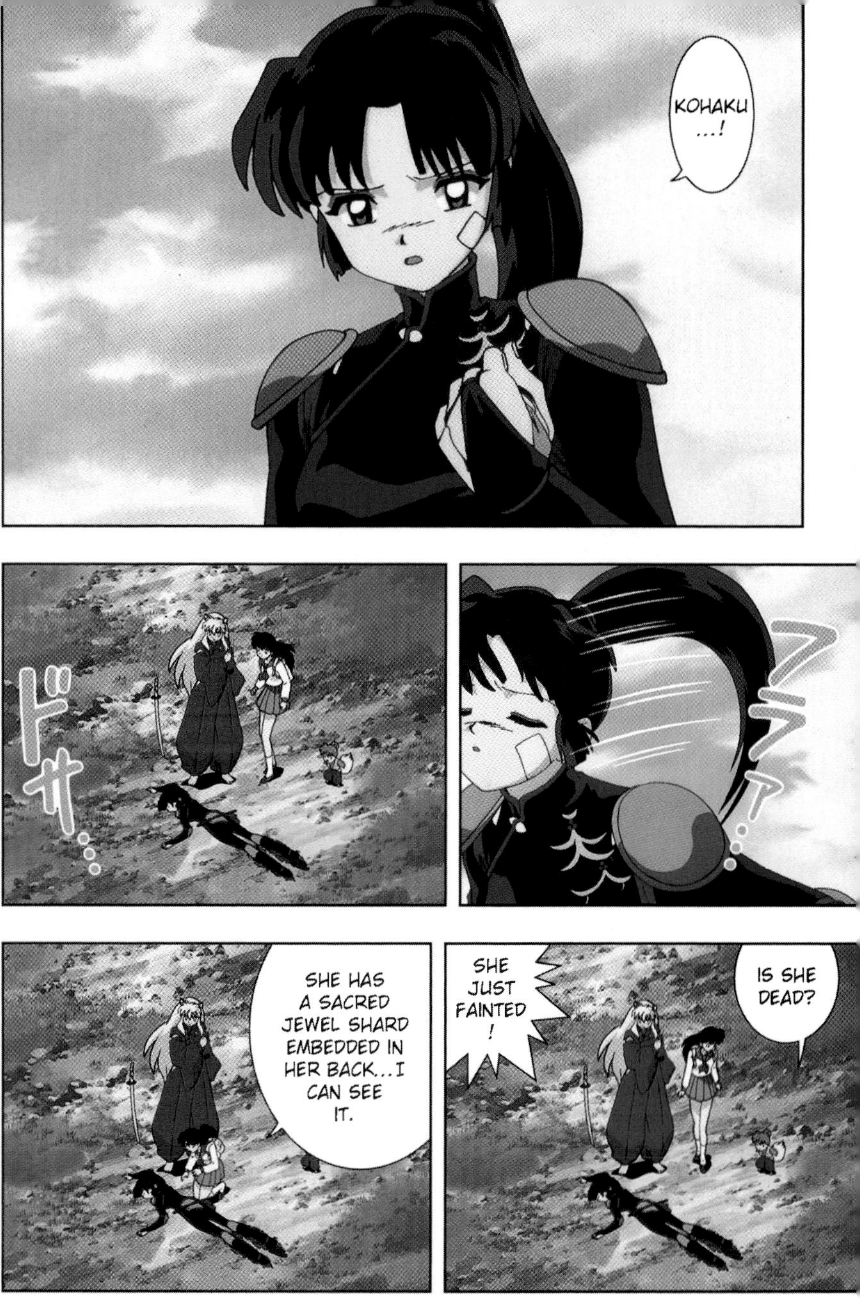
KOHAKU ...!
フラァ...
ドサ...
IS SHE DEAD?
SHE JUST FAINTED!
SHE HAS A SACRED JEWEL SHARD EMBEDDED IN HER BACK...I CAN SEE IT.

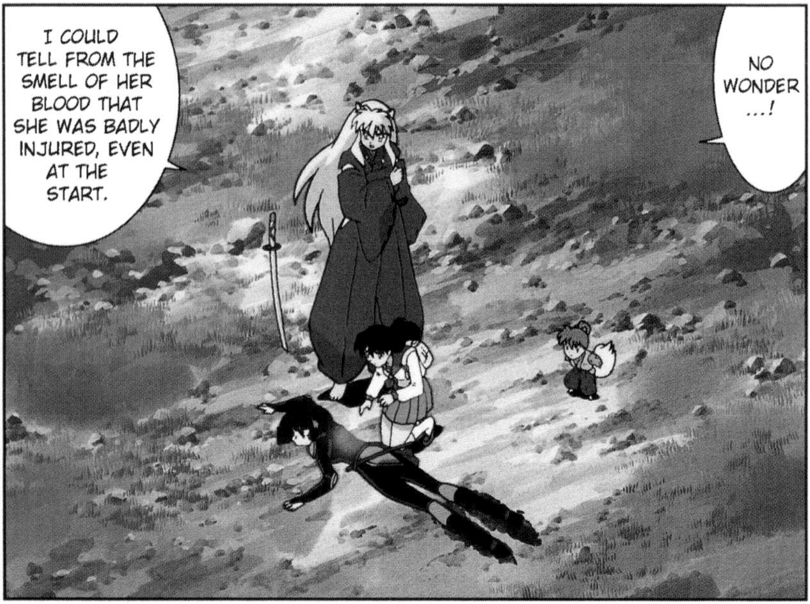
NO WONDER ...!
I COULD TELL FROM THE SMELL OF HER BLOOD THAT SHE WAS BADLY INJURED, EVEN AT THE START.

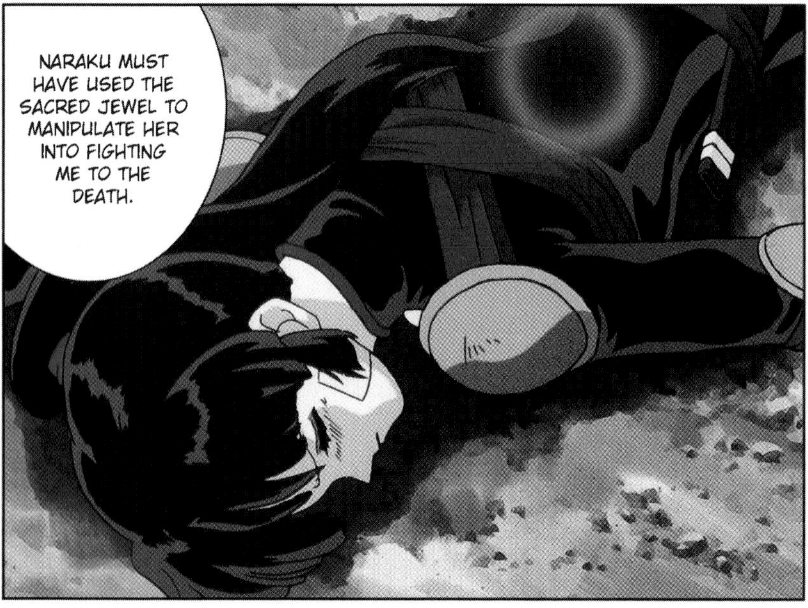
NARAKU MUST HAVE USED THE SACRED JEWEL TO MANIPULATE HER INTO FIGHTING ME TO THE DEATH.

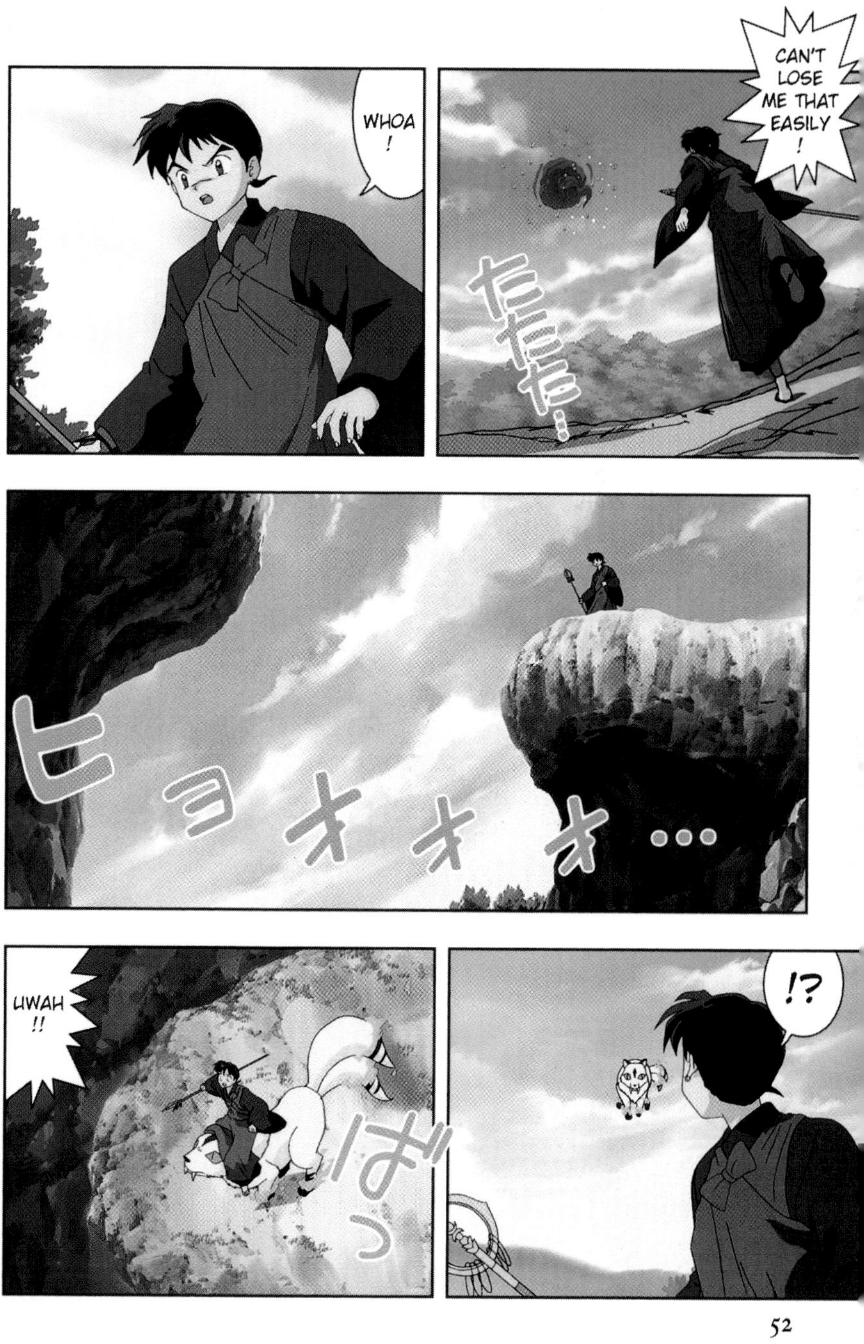
CAN'T LOSE ME THAT EASILY!
たたた…
WHOA!
ヒョオォォ…
!?
UWAH!!
ばっ

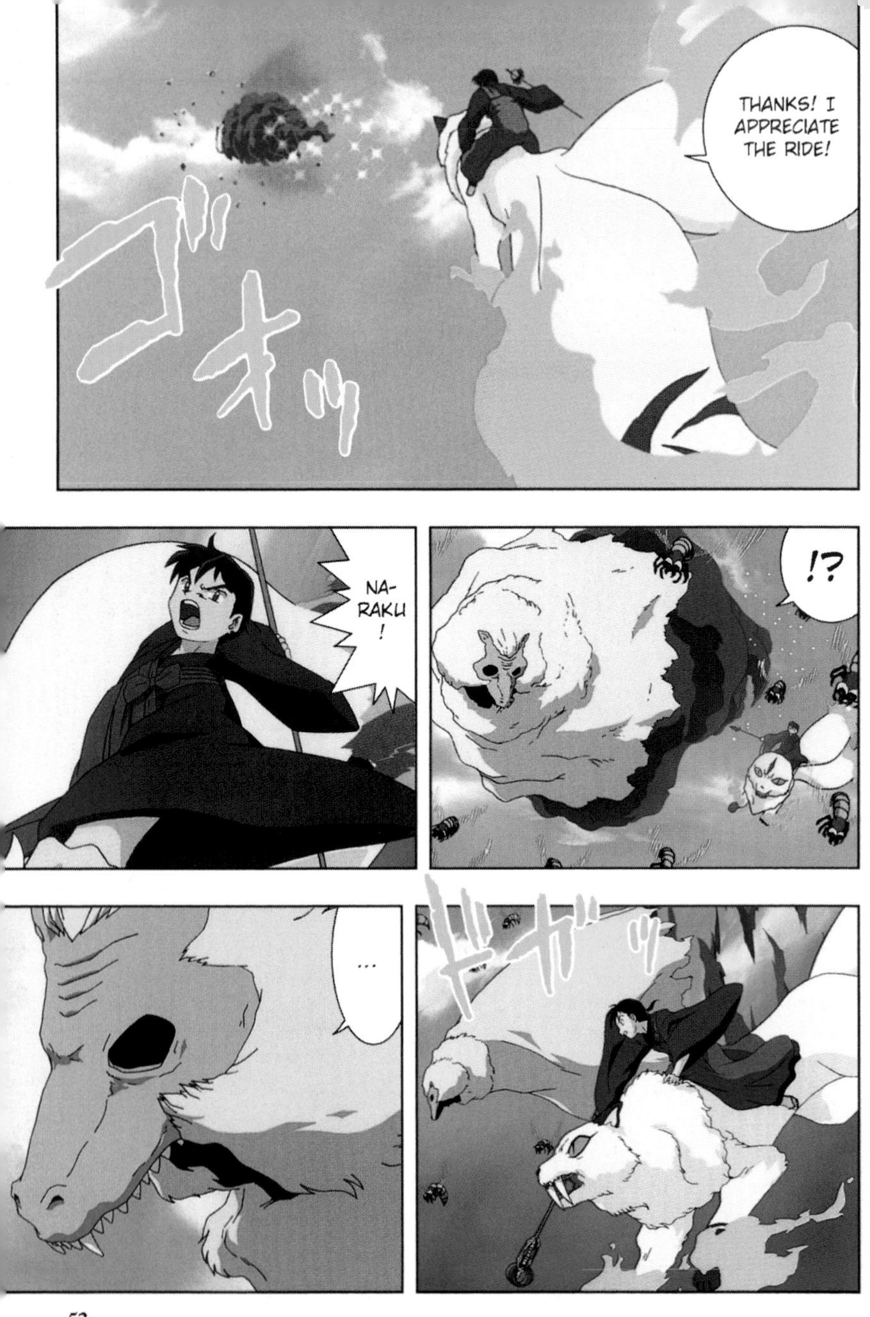
THANKS! I APPRECIATE THE RIDE!
ゴオッ
!?
NA-RAKU!
ドガッ
...

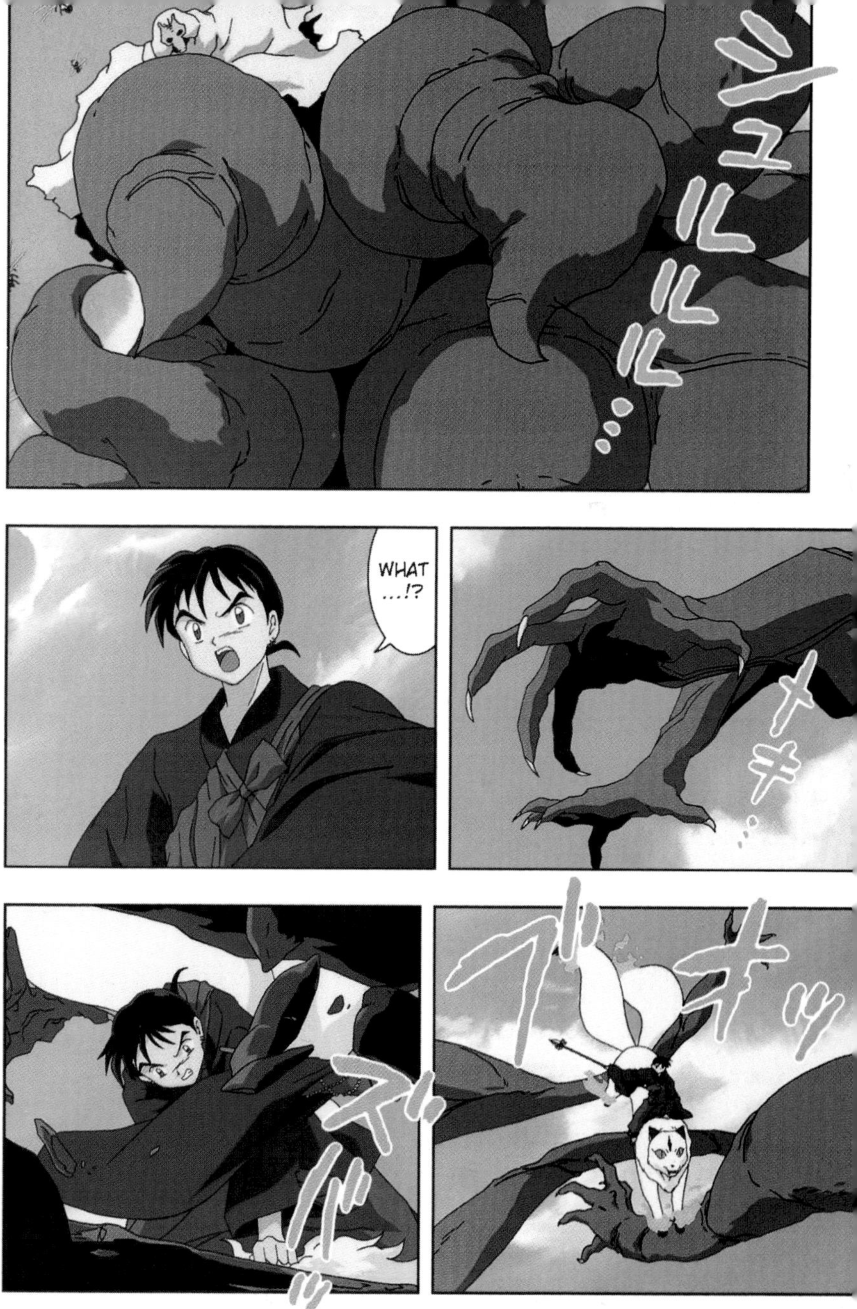
シュルルル…
メキ…
WHAT …!?
ブオッ
ズザッ

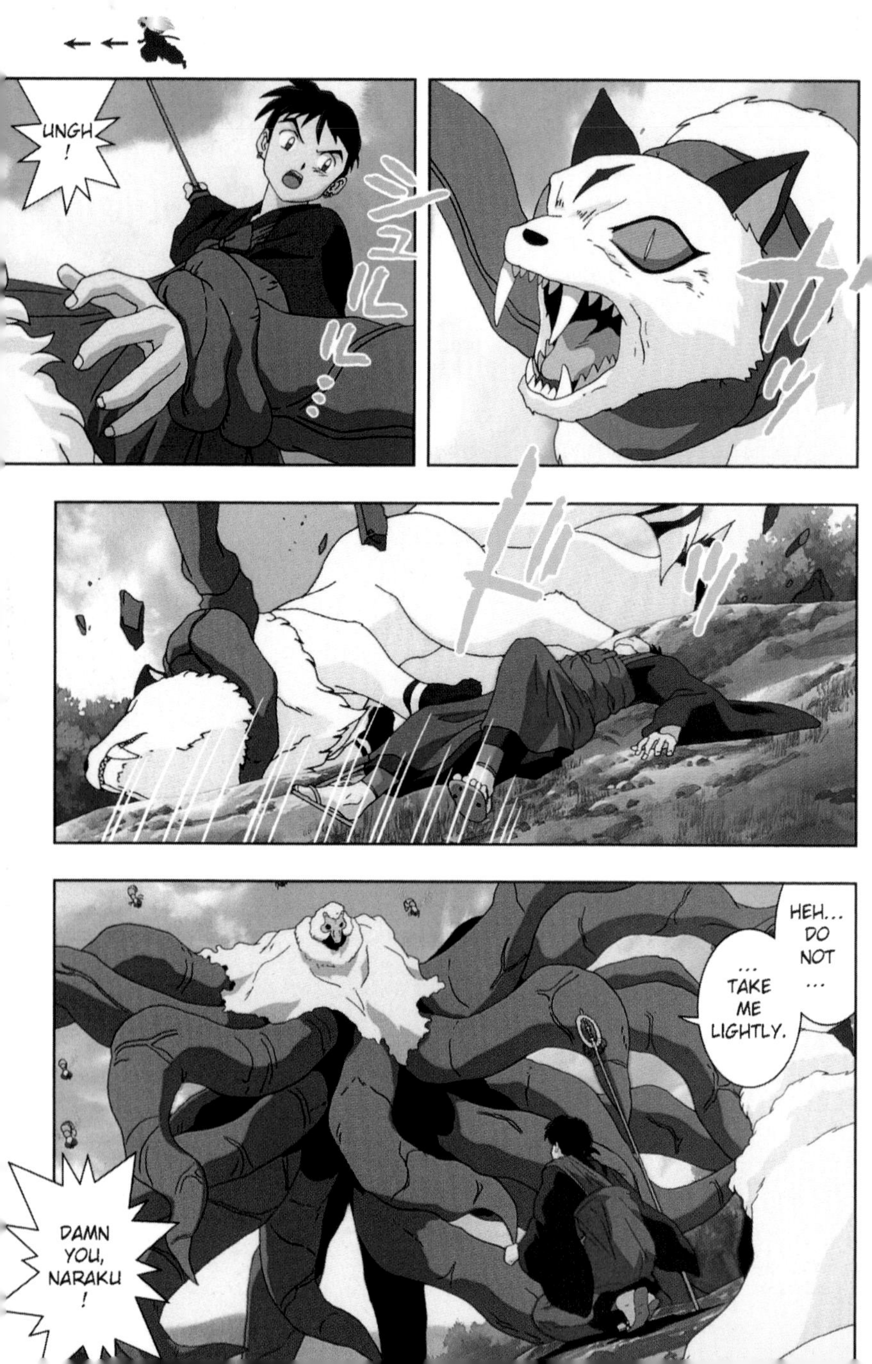
ガッ
UNGH!
ジュルル…
HEH... DO NOT ...
... TAKE ME LIGHTLY.
DAMN YOU, NARAKU!

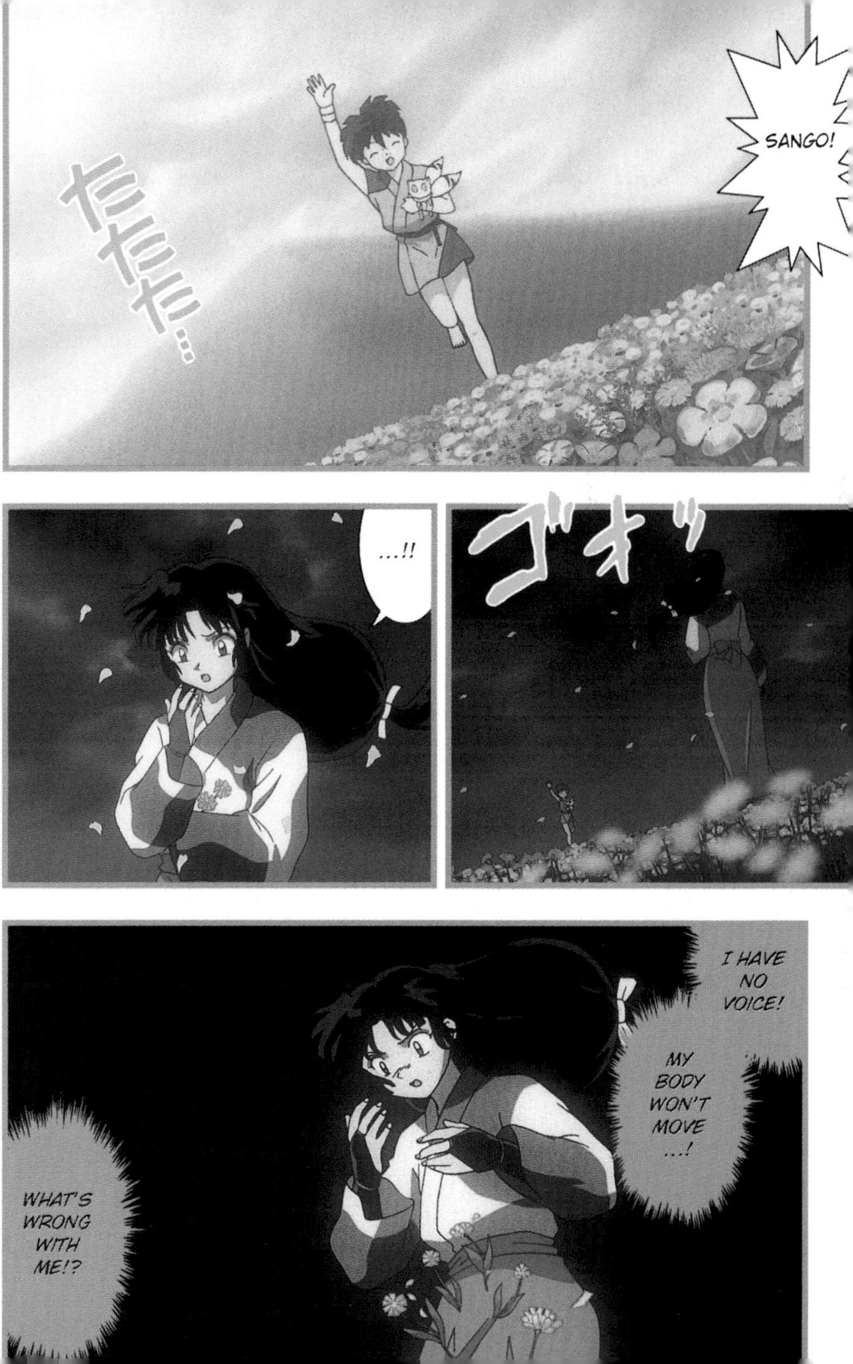
SANGO!
たたた…
ゴオッ
...!!
I HAVE NO VOICE!
MY BODY WON'T MOVE ...!
WHAT'S WRONG WITH ME!?

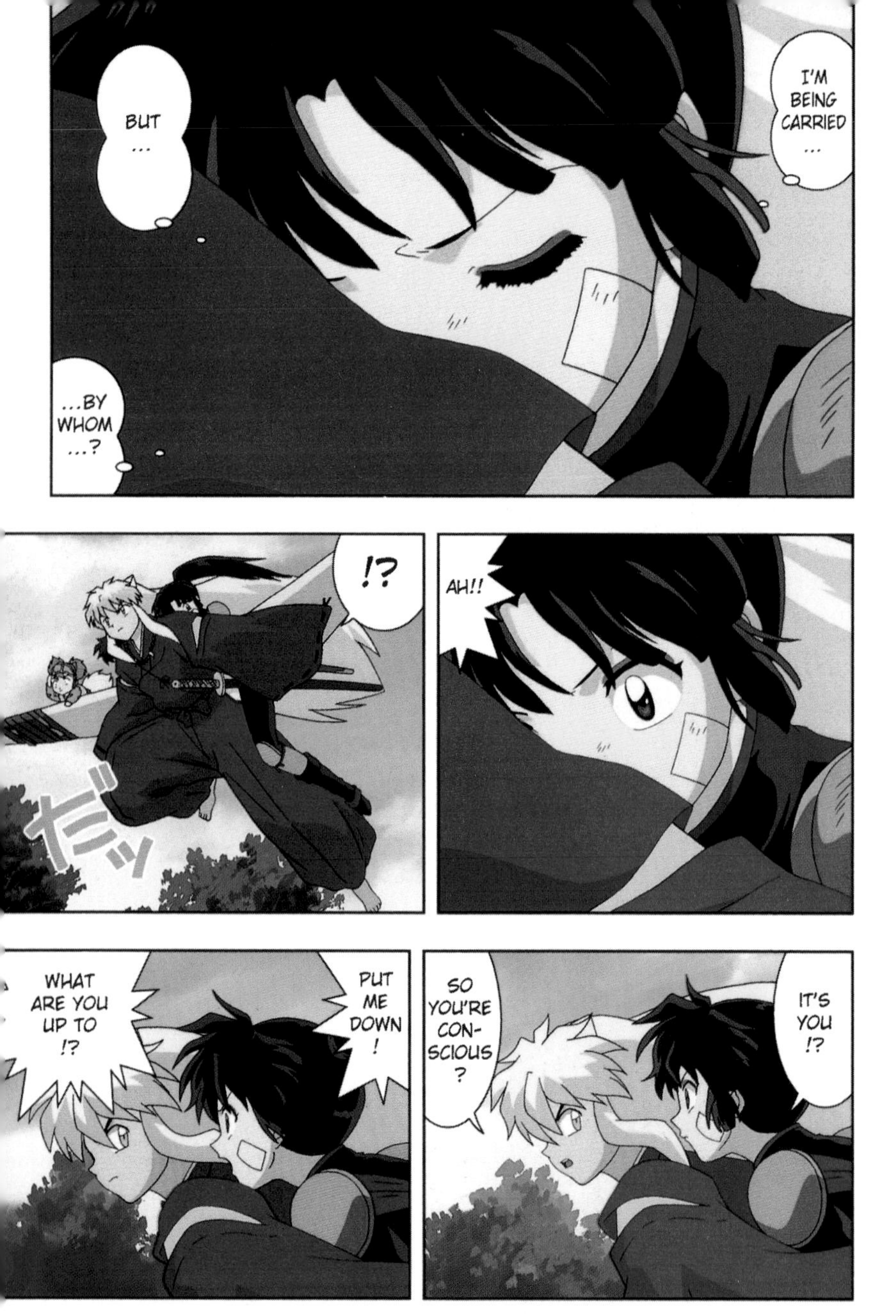
I'M BEING CARRIED ...
BUT ...
...BY WHOM ...?
AH!!
!?
IT'S YOU !?
SO YOU'RE CON- SCIOUS ?
PUT ME DOWN !
WHAT ARE YOU UP TO !?

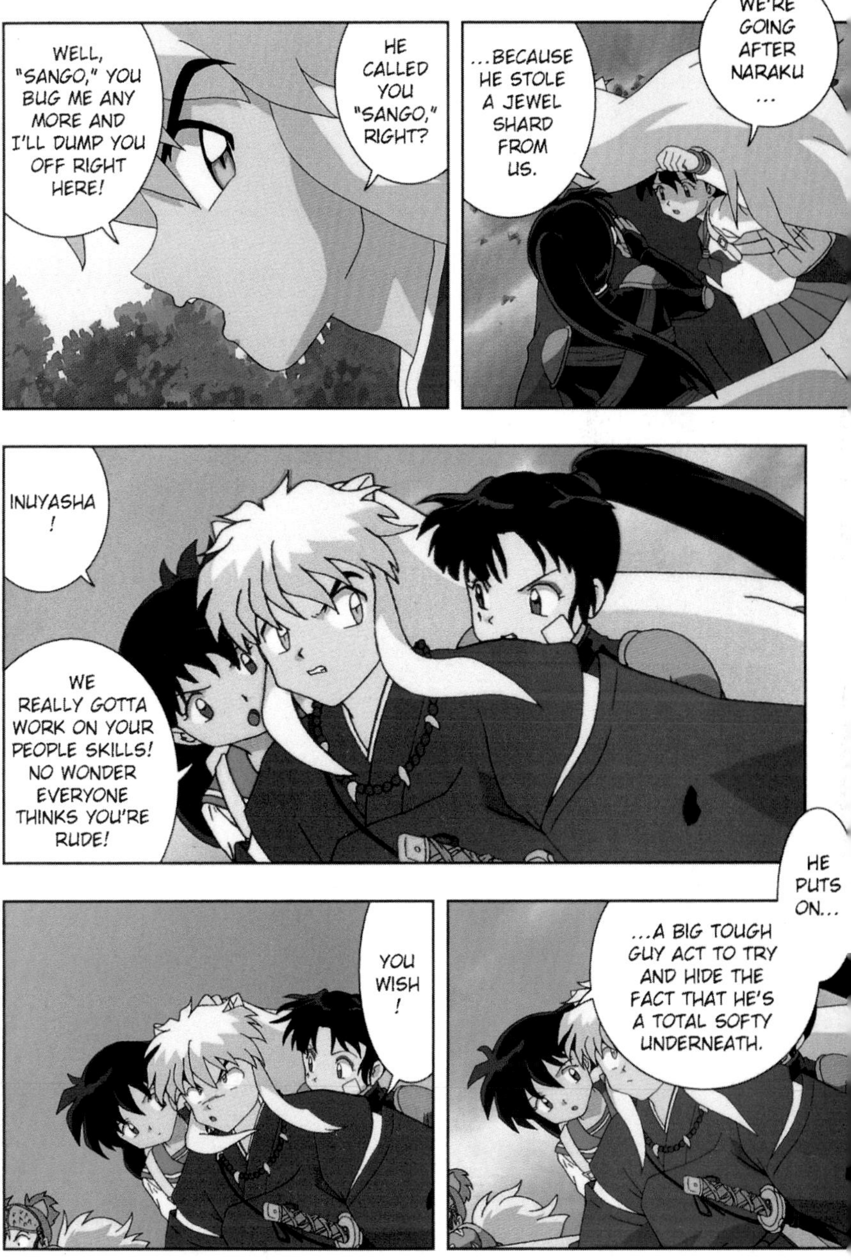
WE'RE GOING AFTER NARAKU ...
...BECAUSE HE STOLE A JEWEL SHARD FROM US.
HE CALLED YOU "SANGO," RIGHT?
WELL, "SANGO," YOU BUG ME ANY MORE AND I'LL DUMP YOU OFF RIGHT HERE!
INUYASHA !
WE REALLY GOTTA WORK ON YOUR PEOPLE SKILLS! NO WONDER EVERYONE THINKS YOU'RE RUDE!
HE PUTS ON...
...A BIG TOUGH GUY ACT TO TRY AND HIDE THE FACT THAT HE'S A TOTAL SOFTY UNDERNEATH.
YOU WISH !

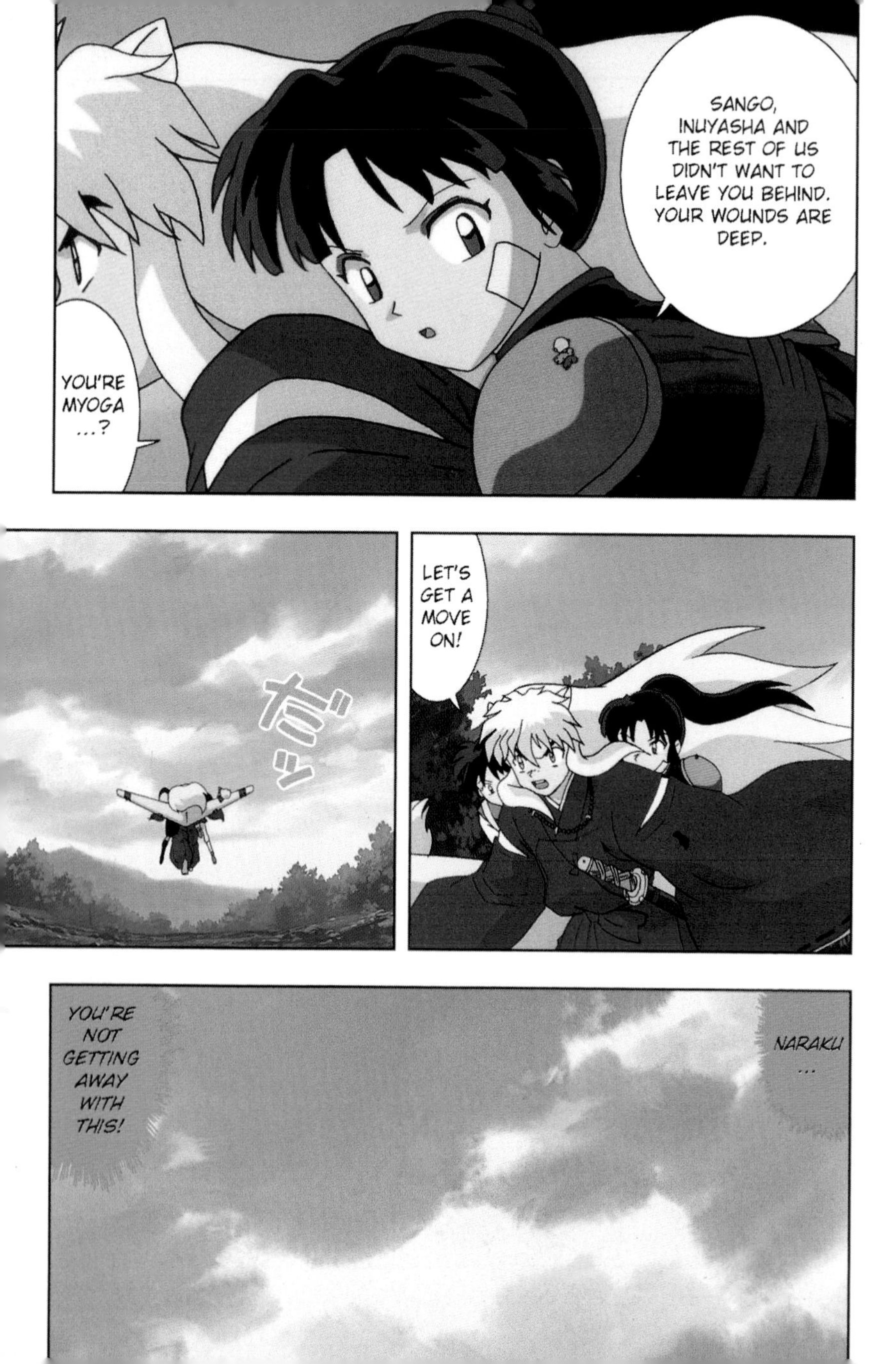
SANGO, INUYASHA AND THE REST OF US DIDN'T WANT TO LEAVE YOU BEHIND. YOUR WOUNDS ARE DEEP.
YOU'RE MYOGA ...?
LET'S GET A MOVE ON!
ダッ
NARAKU ...
YOU'RE NOT GETTING AWAY WITH THIS!

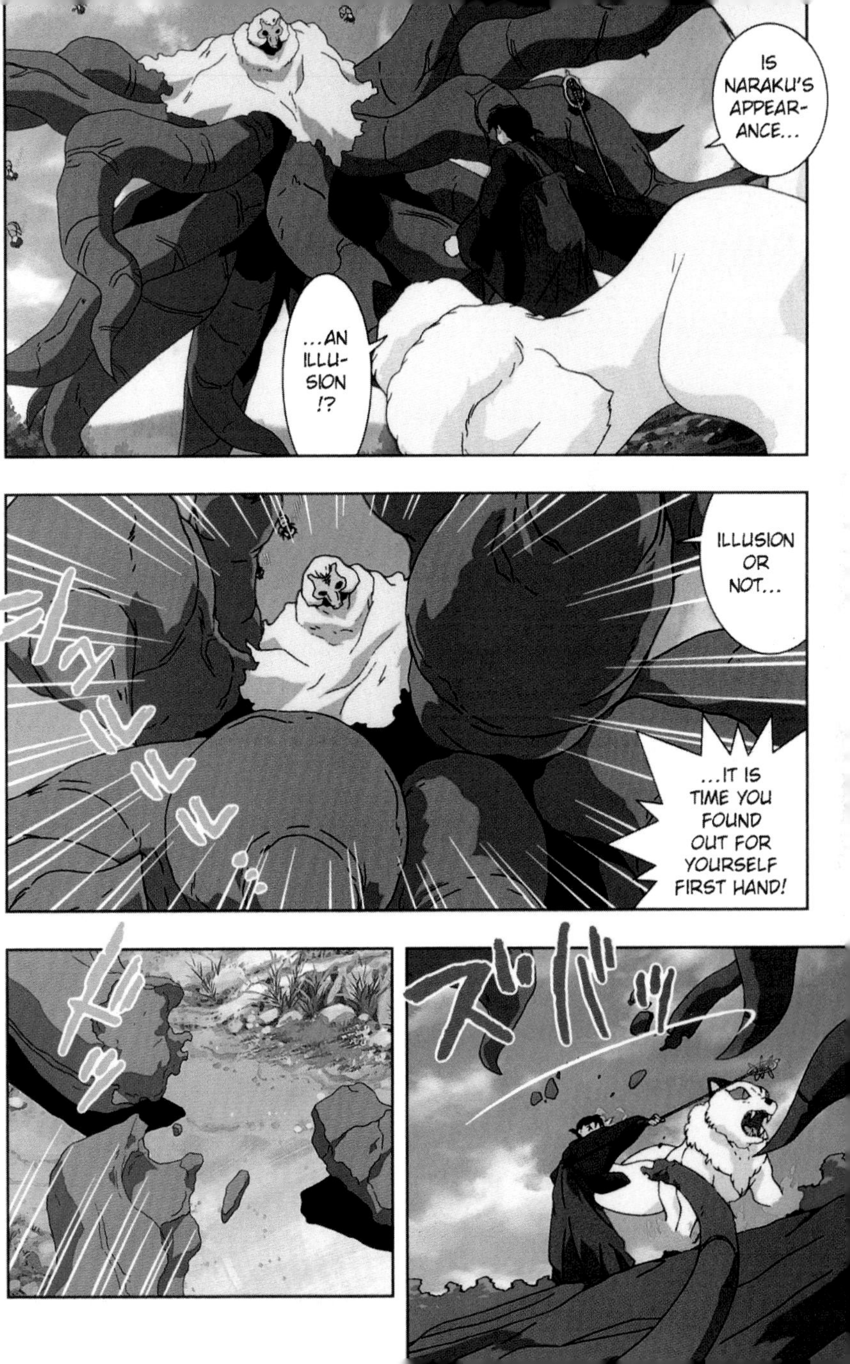
IS NARAKU'S APPEAR-ANCE...
...AN ILLU-SION!?
ILLUSION OR NOT...
...IT IS TIME YOU FOUND OUT FOR YOURSELF FIRST HAND!

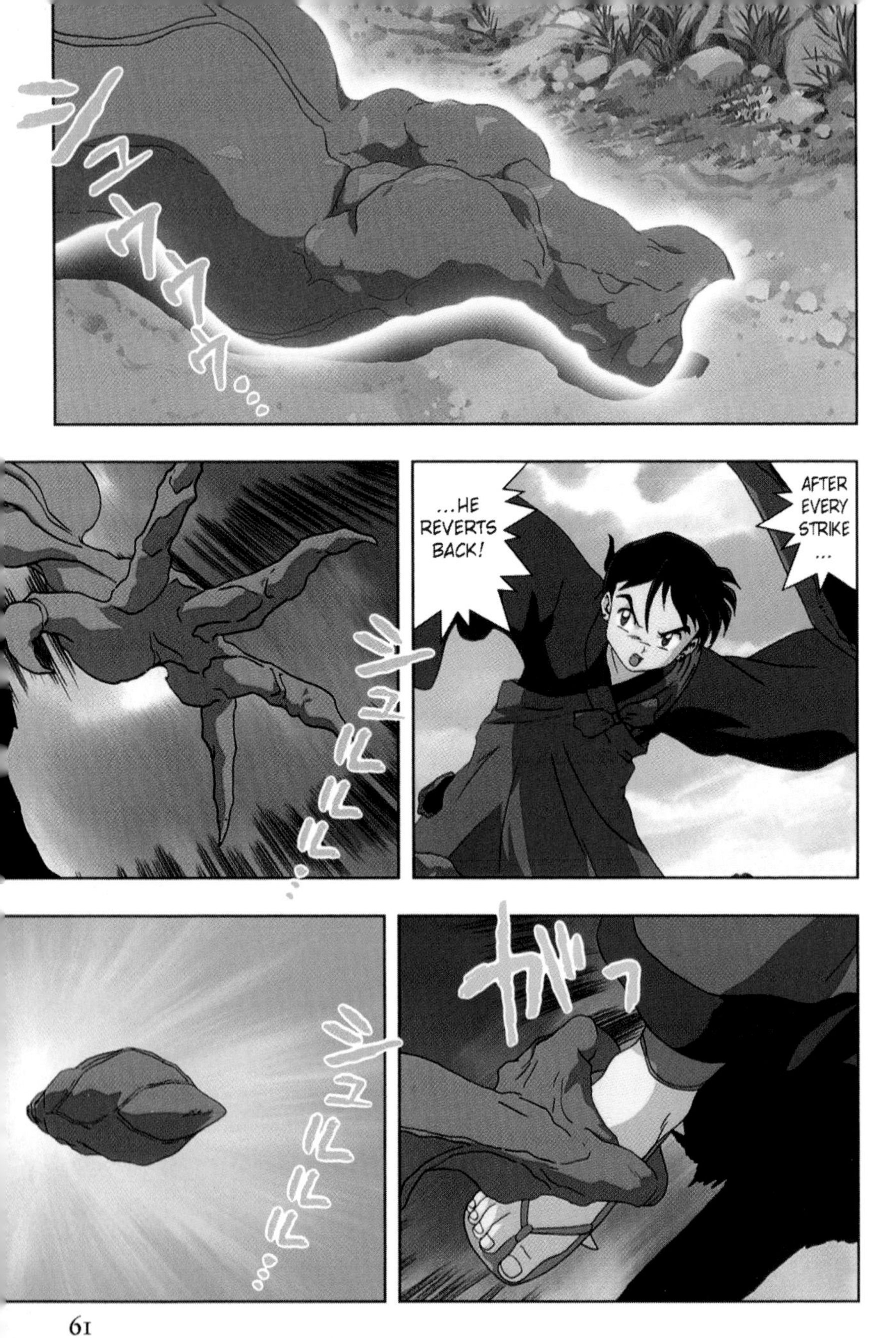
AFTER EVERY STRIKE ...
...HE REVERTS BACK!

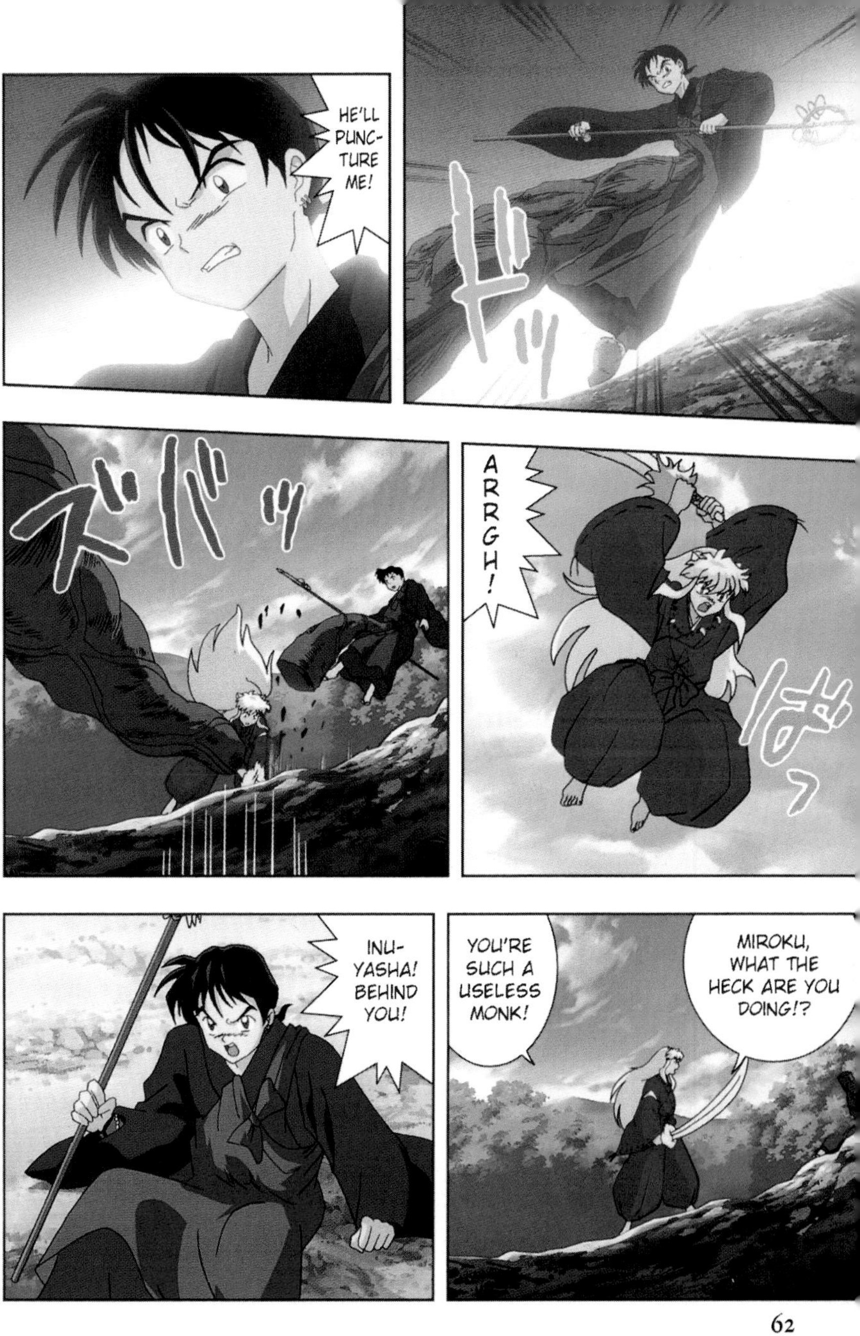
ドッ
HE'LL PUNC-TURE ME!
ARRGH!
ぱっ
ズバッ
MIROKU, WHAT THE HECK ARE YOU DOING!?
YOU'RE SUCH A USELESS MONK!
INU-YASHA! BEHIND YOU!

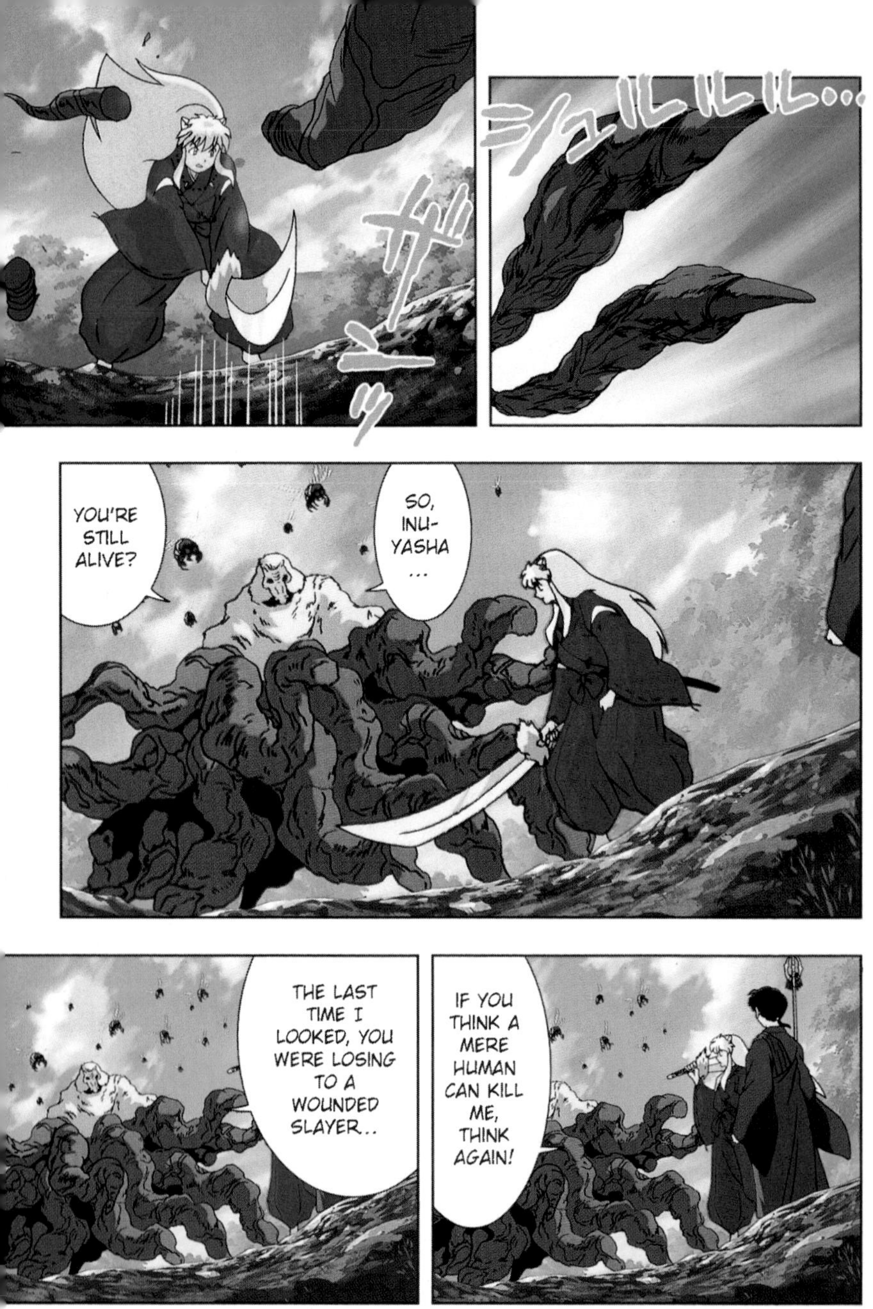
シュルルル…
SO, INU-YASHA...
YOU'RE STILL ALIVE?
IF YOU THINK A MERE HUMAN CAN KILL ME, THINK AGAIN!
THE LAST TIME I LOOKED, YOU WERE LOSING TO A WOUNDED SLAYER..

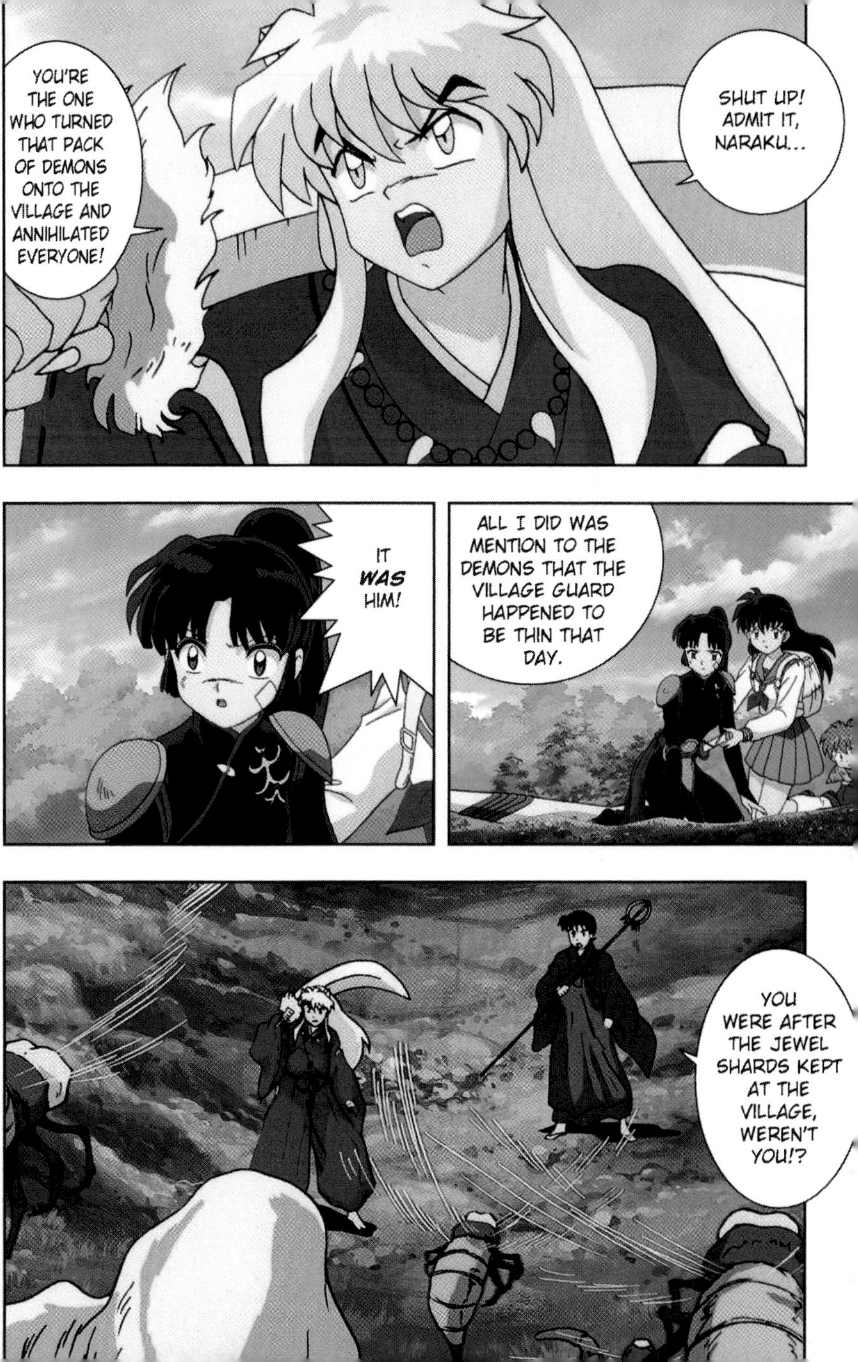
SHUT UP! ADMIT IT, NARAKU...
YOU'RE THE ONE WHO TURNED THAT PACK OF DEMONS ONTO THE VILLAGE AND ANNIHILATED EVERYONE!
ALL I DID WAS MENTION TO THE DEMONS THAT THE VILLAGE GUARD HAPPENED TO BE THIN THAT DAY.
IT *WAS* HIM!
YOU WERE AFTER THE JEWEL SHARDS KEPT AT THE VILLAGE, WEREN'T YOU!?

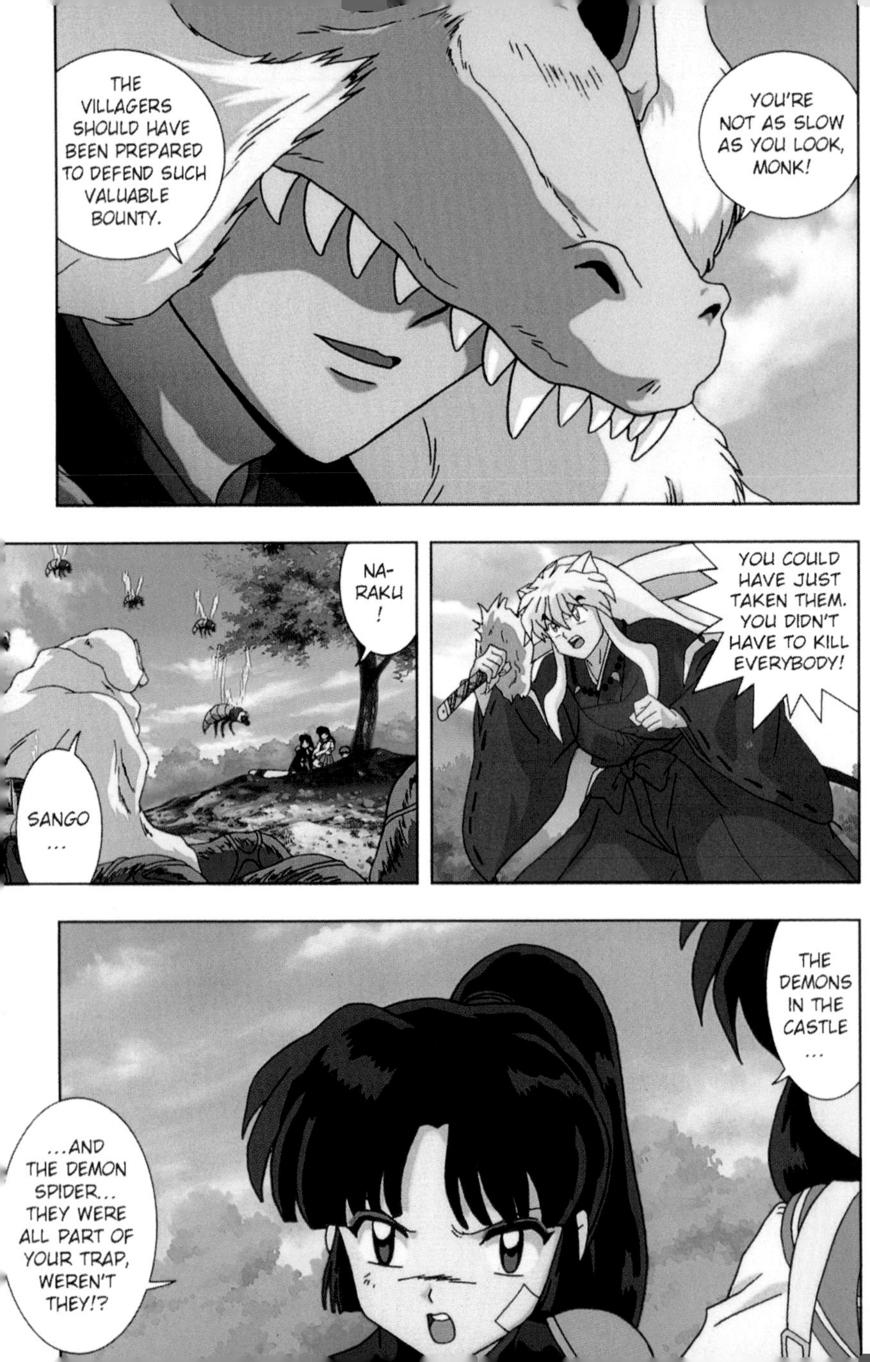
YOU'RE NOT AS SLOW AS YOU LOOK, MONK!
THE VILLAGERS SHOULD HAVE BEEN PREPARED TO DEFEND SUCH VALUABLE BOUNTY.
YOU COULD HAVE JUST TAKEN THEM. YOU DIDN'T HAVE TO KILL EVERYBODY!
NA-RAKU!
SANGO...
THE DEMONS IN THE CASTLE...
...AND THE DEMON SPIDER... THEY WERE ALL PART OF YOUR TRAP, WEREN'T THEY!?

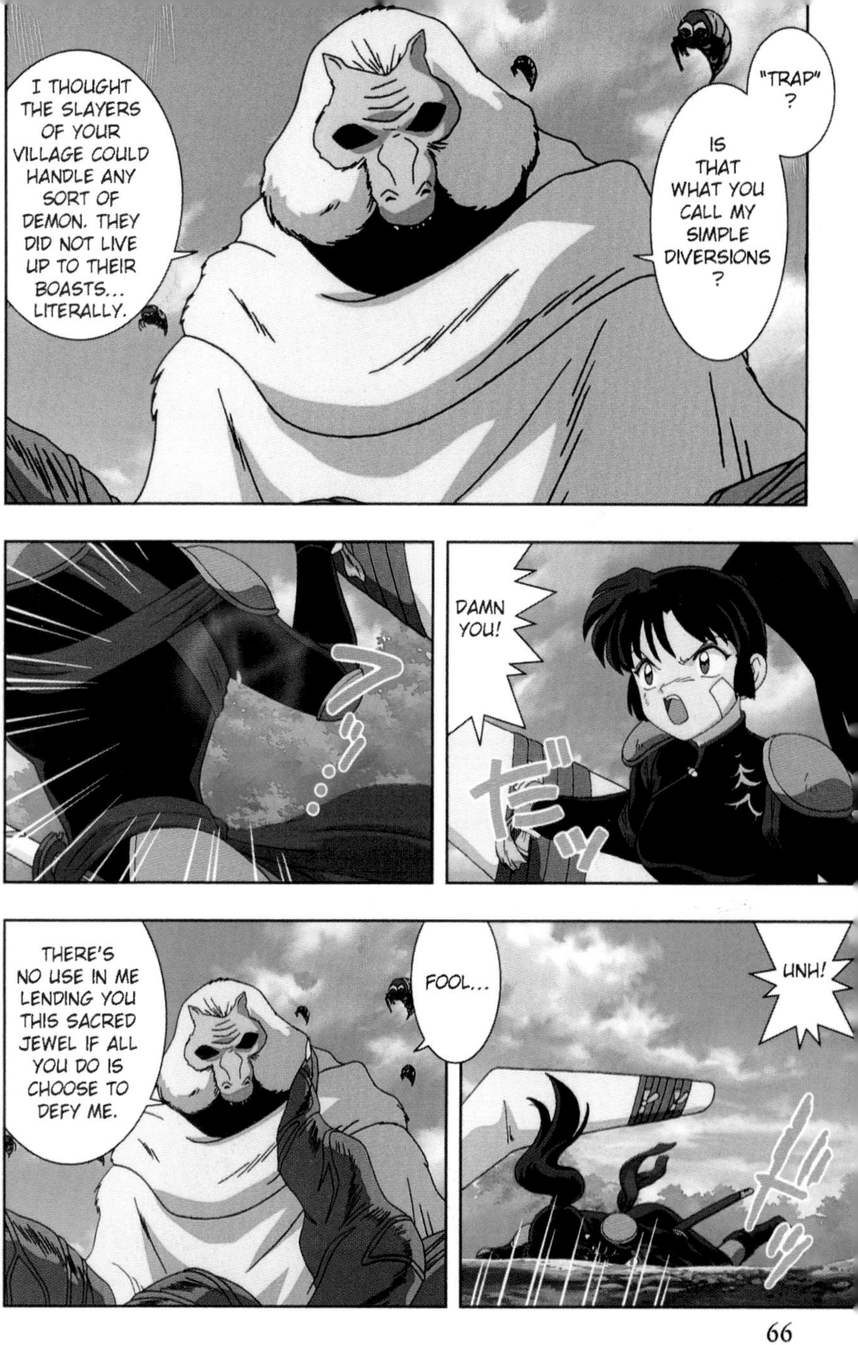
"TRAP"?
IS THAT WHAT YOU CALL MY SIMPLE DIVERSIONS?
I THOUGHT THE SLAYERS OF YOUR VILLAGE COULD HANDLE ANY SORT OF DEMON. THEY DID NOT LIVE UP TO THEIR BOASTS... LITERALLY.
DAMN YOU!
UNH!
FOOL...
THERE'S NO USE IN ME LENDING YOU THIS SACRED JEWEL IF ALL YOU DO IS CHOOSE TO DEFY ME.

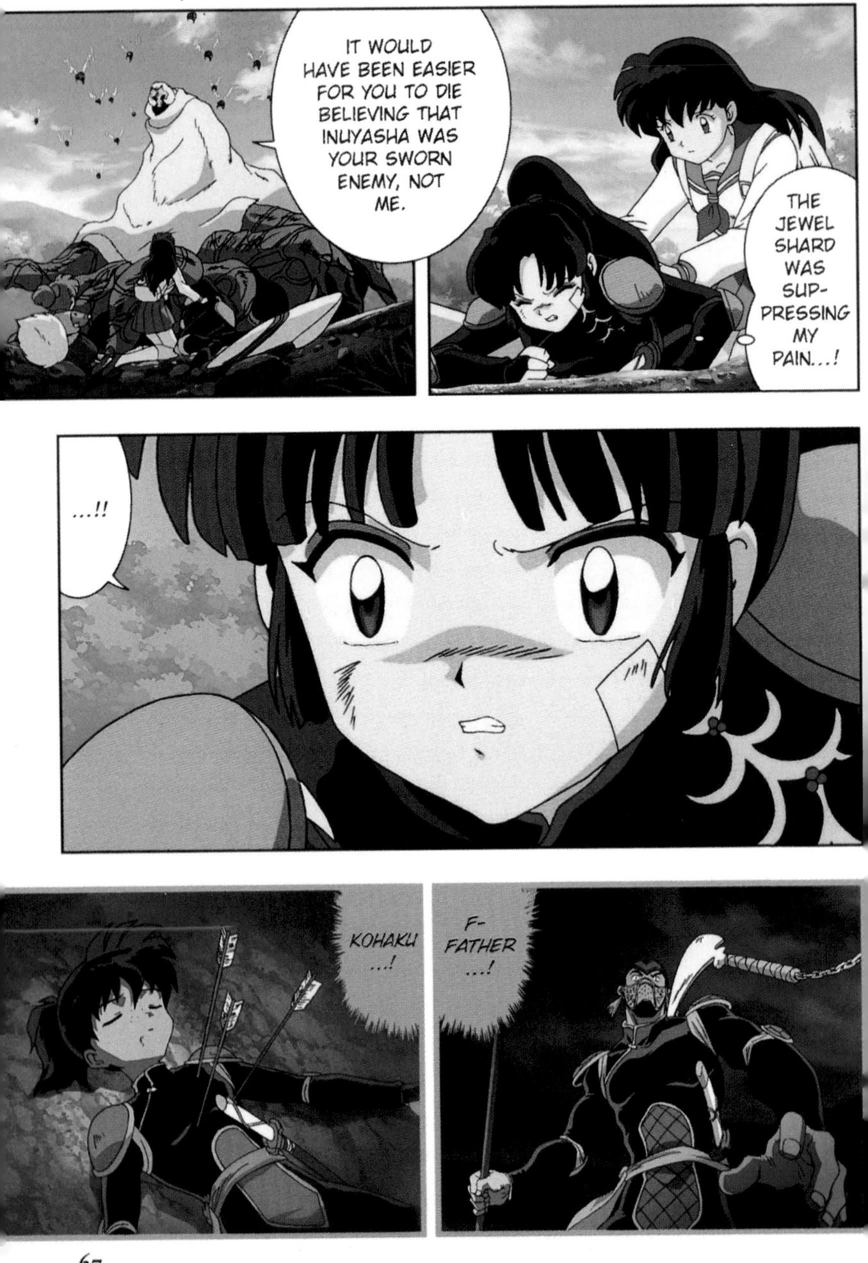
THE JEWEL SHARD WAS SUP-PRESSING MY PAIN...!
IT WOULD HAVE BEEN EASIER FOR YOU TO DIE BELIEVING THAT INUYASHA WAS YOUR SWORN ENEMY, NOT ME.
...!!
F-FATHER ...!
KOHAKU ...!

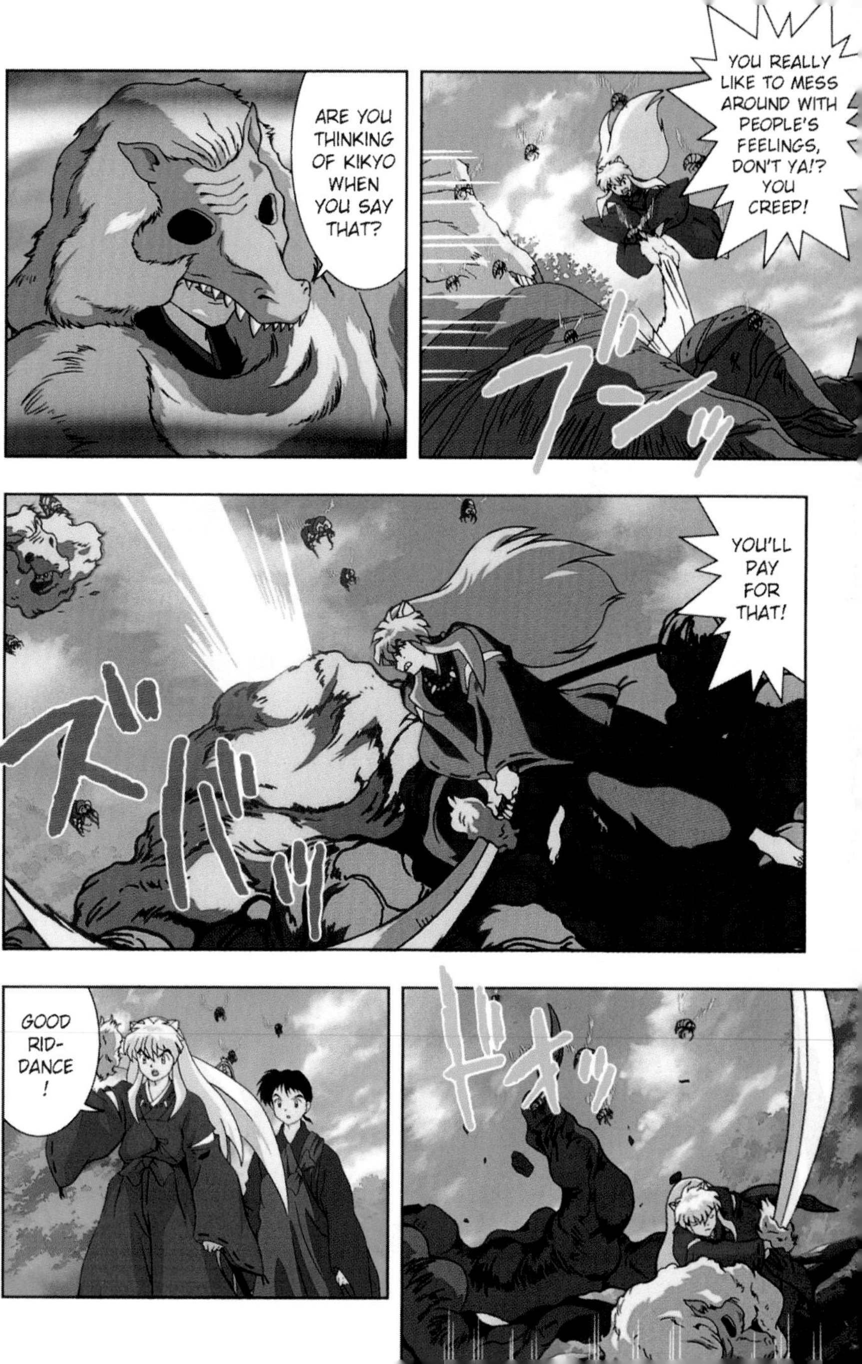
YOU REALLY LIKE TO MESS AROUND WITH PEOPLE'S FEELINGS, DON'T YA!? YOU CREEP!
ブンッ
ARE YOU THINKING OF KIKYO WHEN YOU SAY THAT?
YOU'LL PAY FOR THAT!
ズバッ
ドオッ
GOOD RID-DANCE!

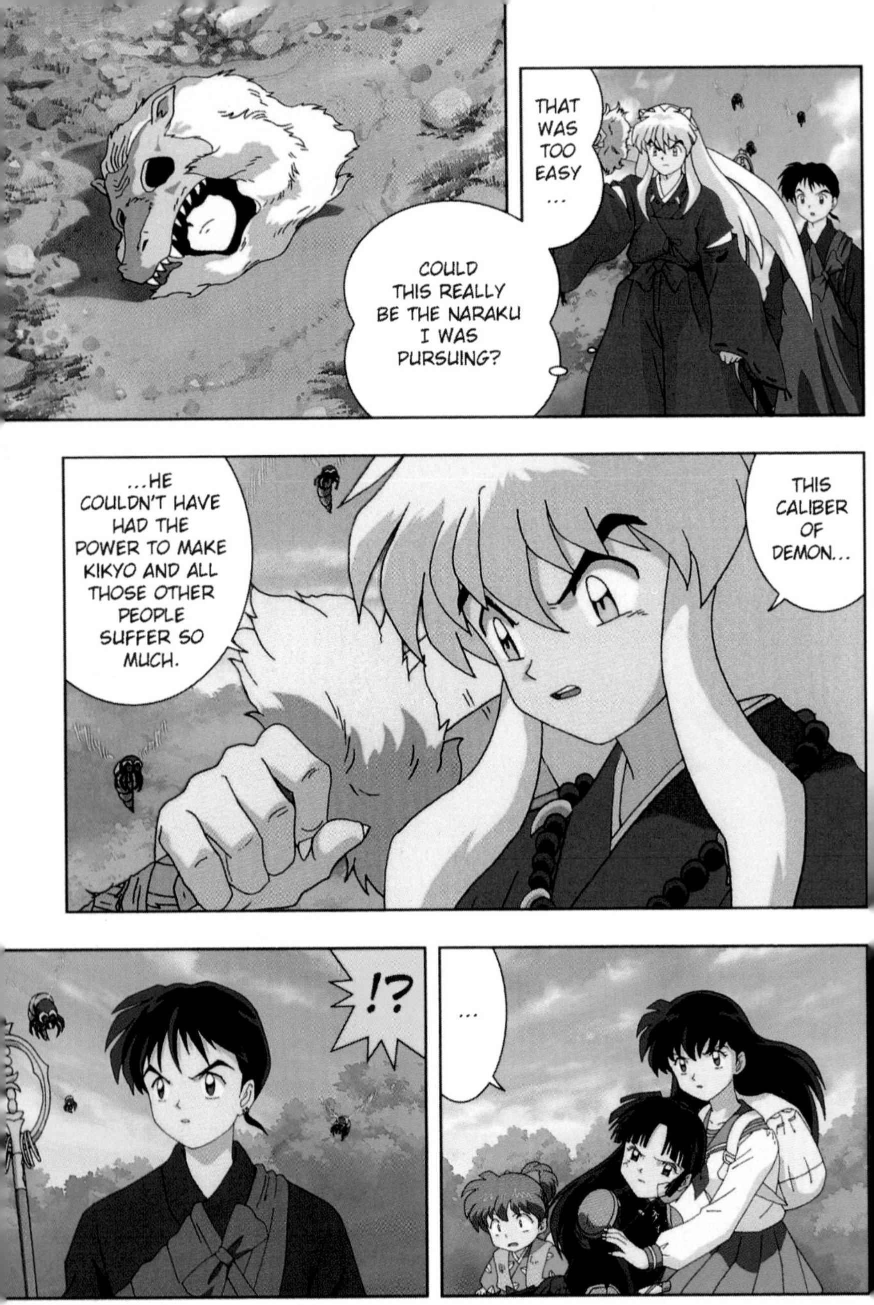
THAT WAS TOO EASY ...
COULD THIS REALLY BE THE NARAKU I WAS PURSUING?
THIS CALIBER OF DEMON...
...HE COULDN'T HAVE HAD THE POWER TO MAKE KIKYO AND ALL THOSE OTHER PEOPLE SUFFER SO MUCH.
...
!?

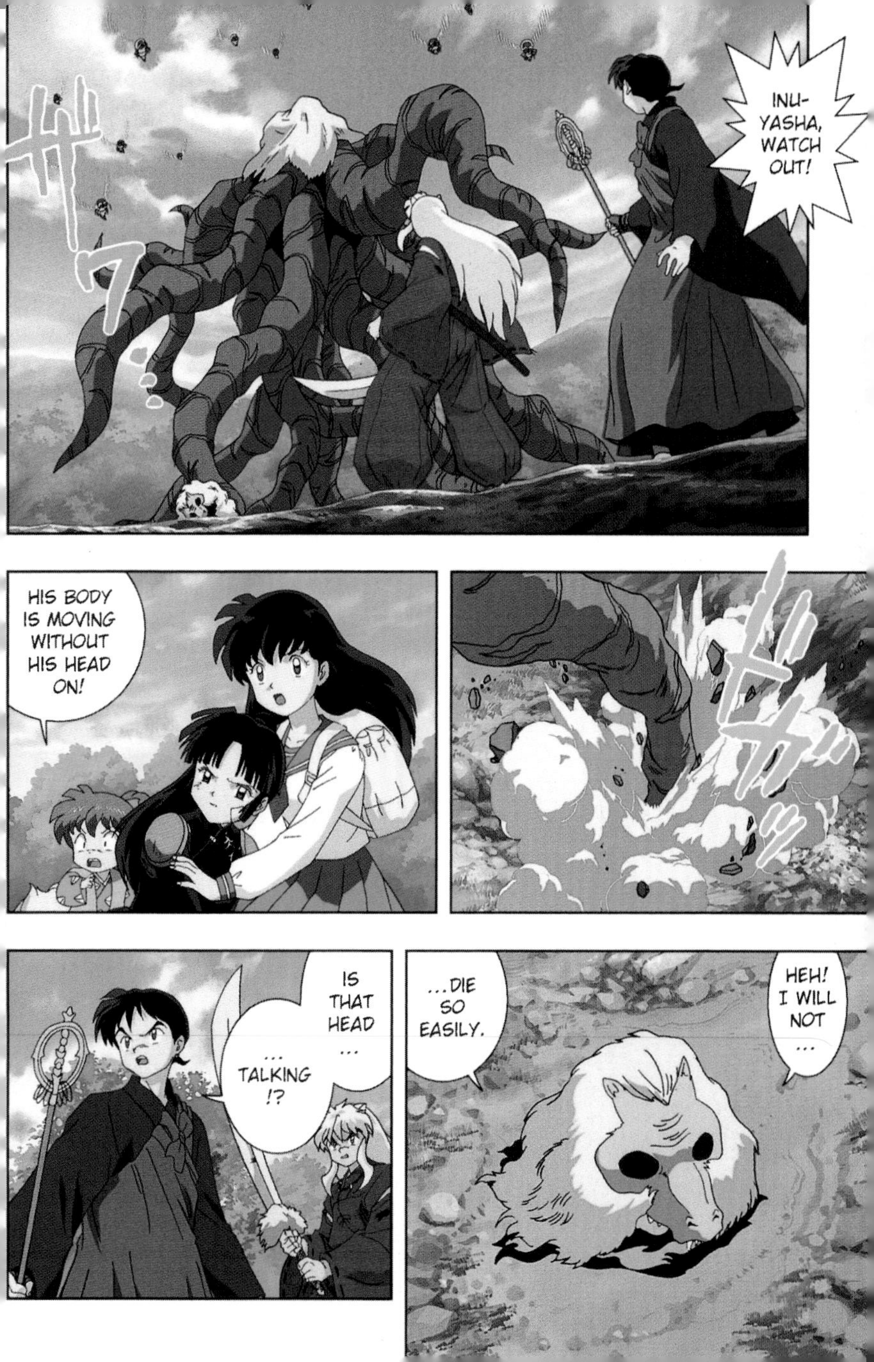
INU-YASHA, WATCH OUT!
HIS BODY IS MOVING WITHOUT HIS HEAD ON!
HEH! I WILL NOT ...
...DIE SO EASILY.
IS THAT HEAD ...
... TALKING !?

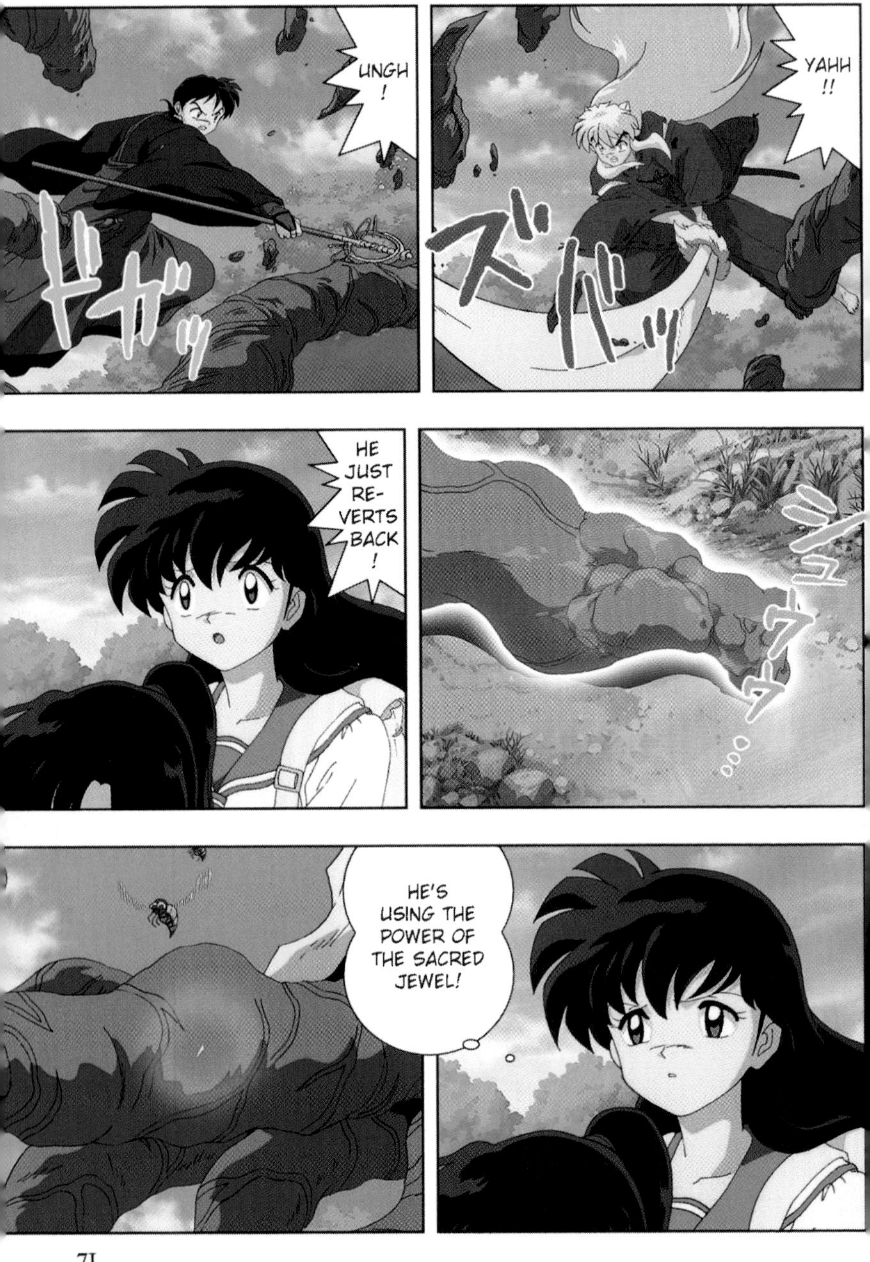
YAHH !!
ズバッ
UNGH !
ドガッ
シュウウ…
HE JUST RE- VERTS BACK !
HE'S USING THE POWER OF THE SACRED JEWEL!

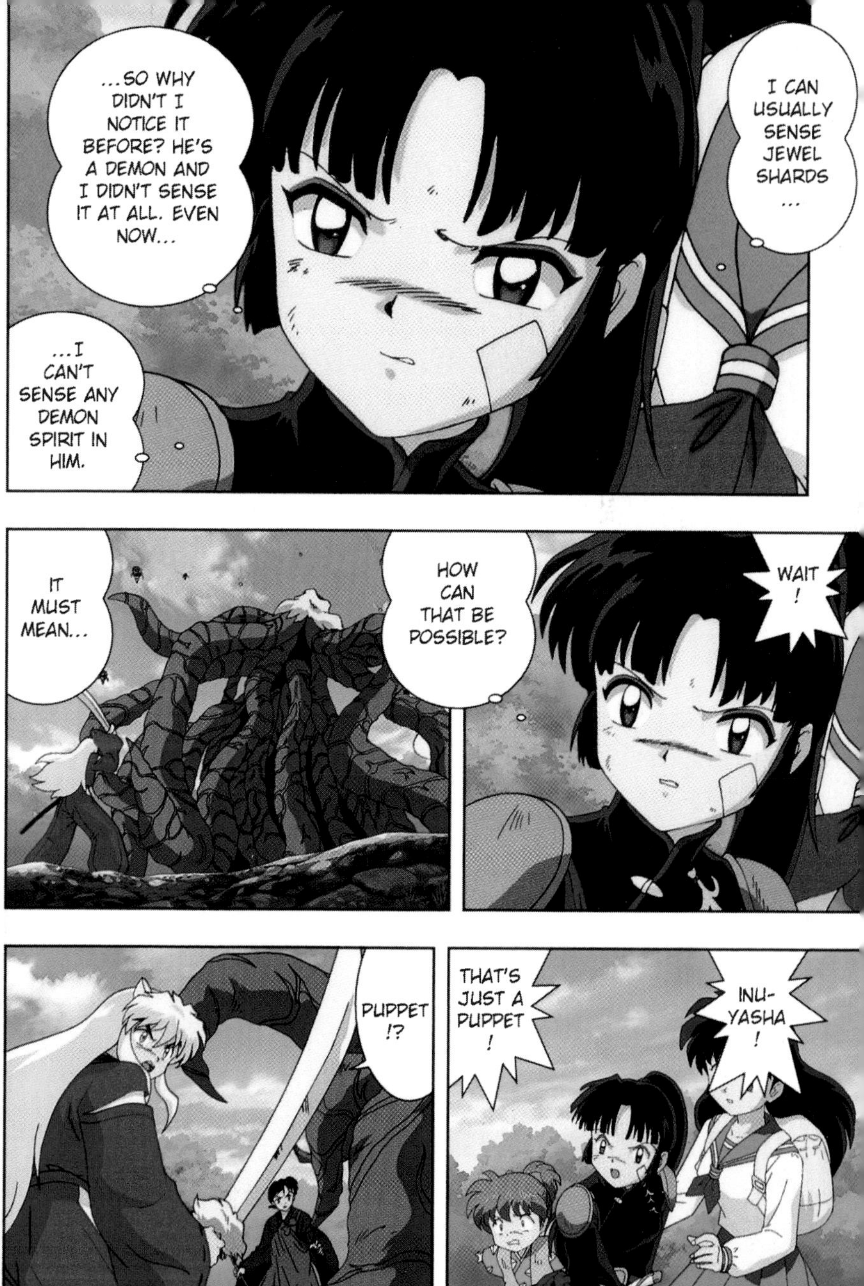
I CAN USUALLY SENSE JEWEL SHARDS...
...SO WHY DIDN'T I NOTICE IT BEFORE? HE'S A DEMON AND I DIDN'T SENSE IT AT ALL. EVEN NOW...
...I CAN'T SENSE ANY DEMON SPIRIT IN HIM.
WAIT!
HOW CAN THAT BE POSSIBLE?
IT MUST MEAN...
INU-YASHA!
THAT'S JUST A PUPPET!
PUPPET!?

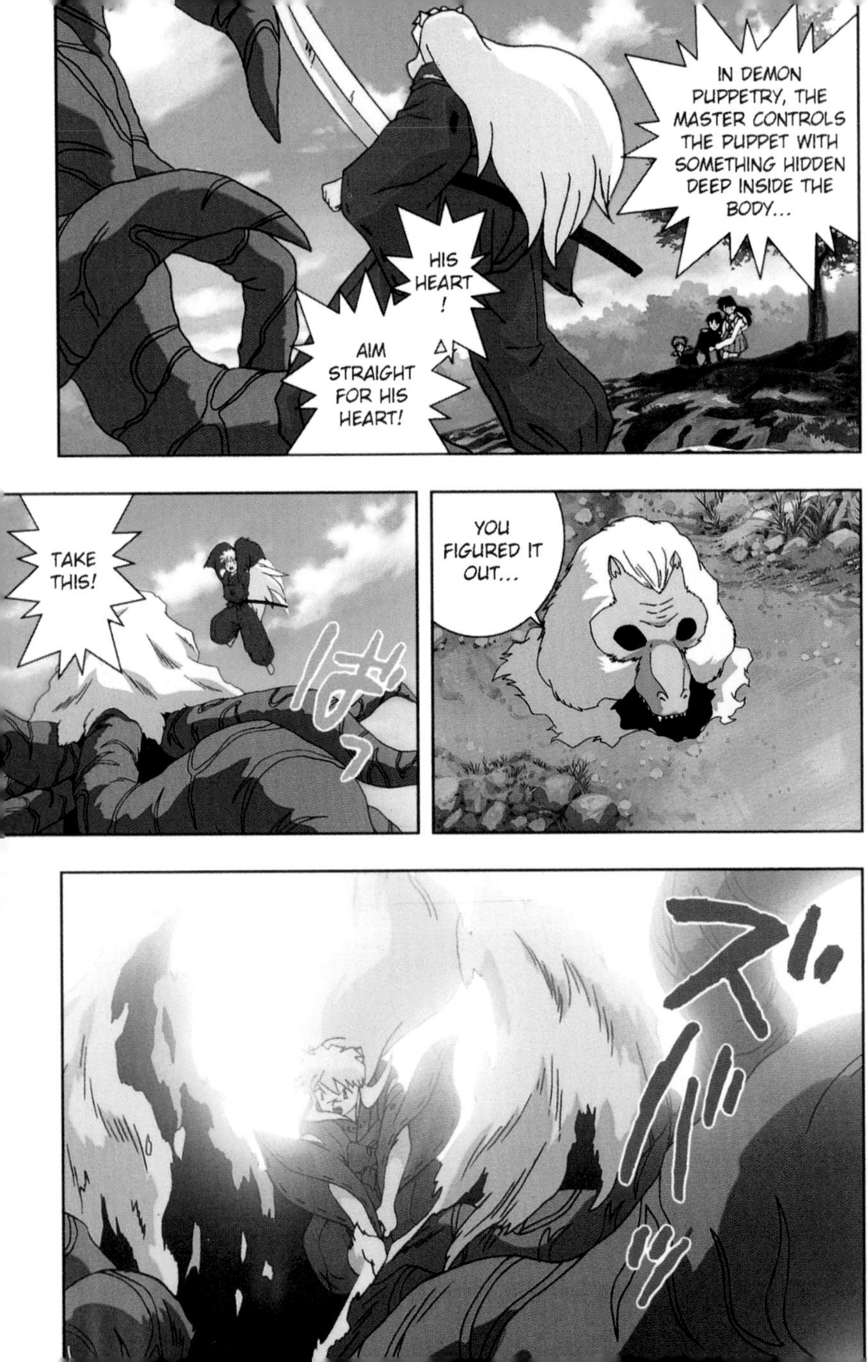
IN DEMON PUPPETRY, THE MASTER CONTROLS THE PUPPET WITH SOMETHING HIDDEN DEEP INSIDE THE BODY...
HIS HEART!
AIM STRAIGHT FOR HIS HEART!
YOU FIGURED IT OUT...
TAKE THIS!
ばっ

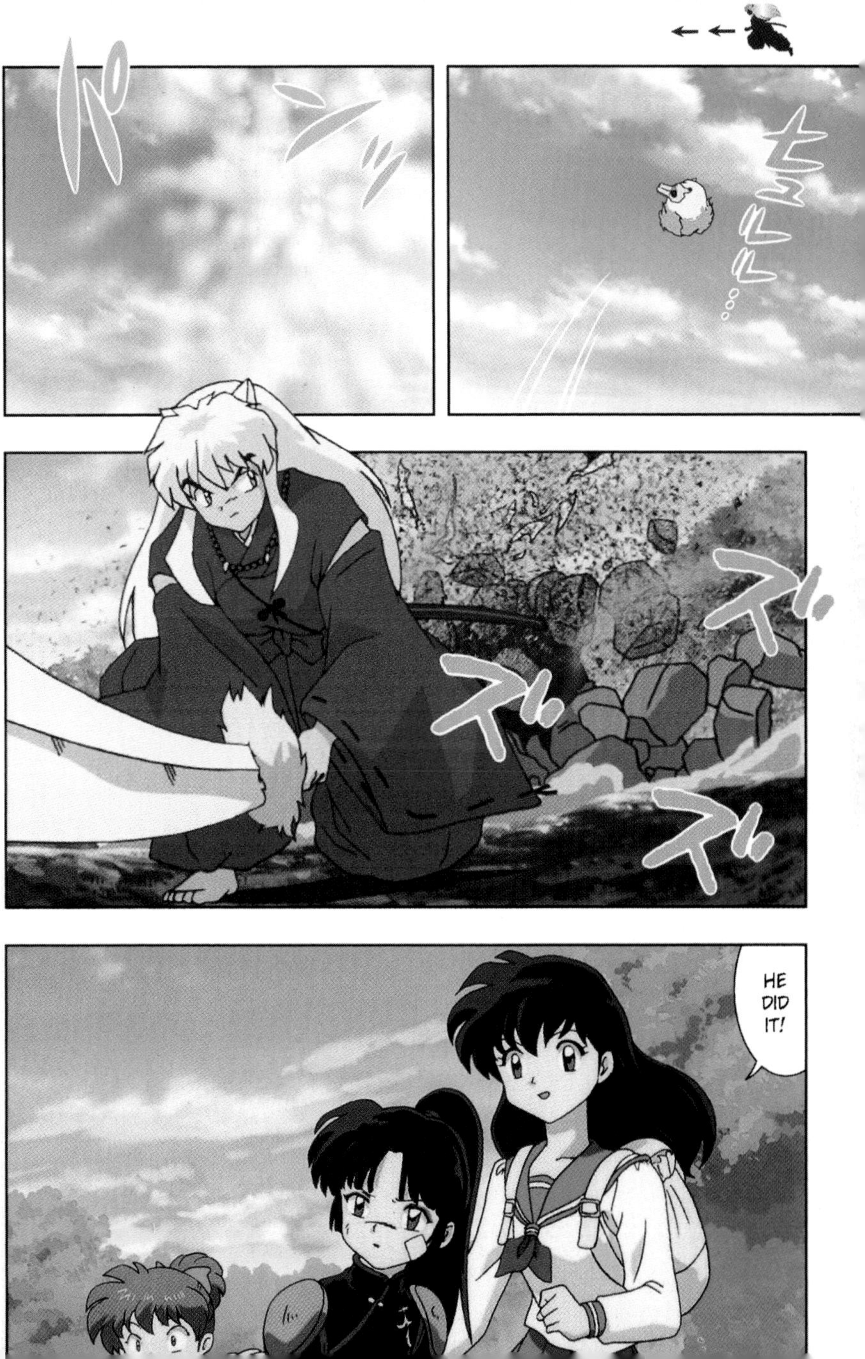
HE DID IT!

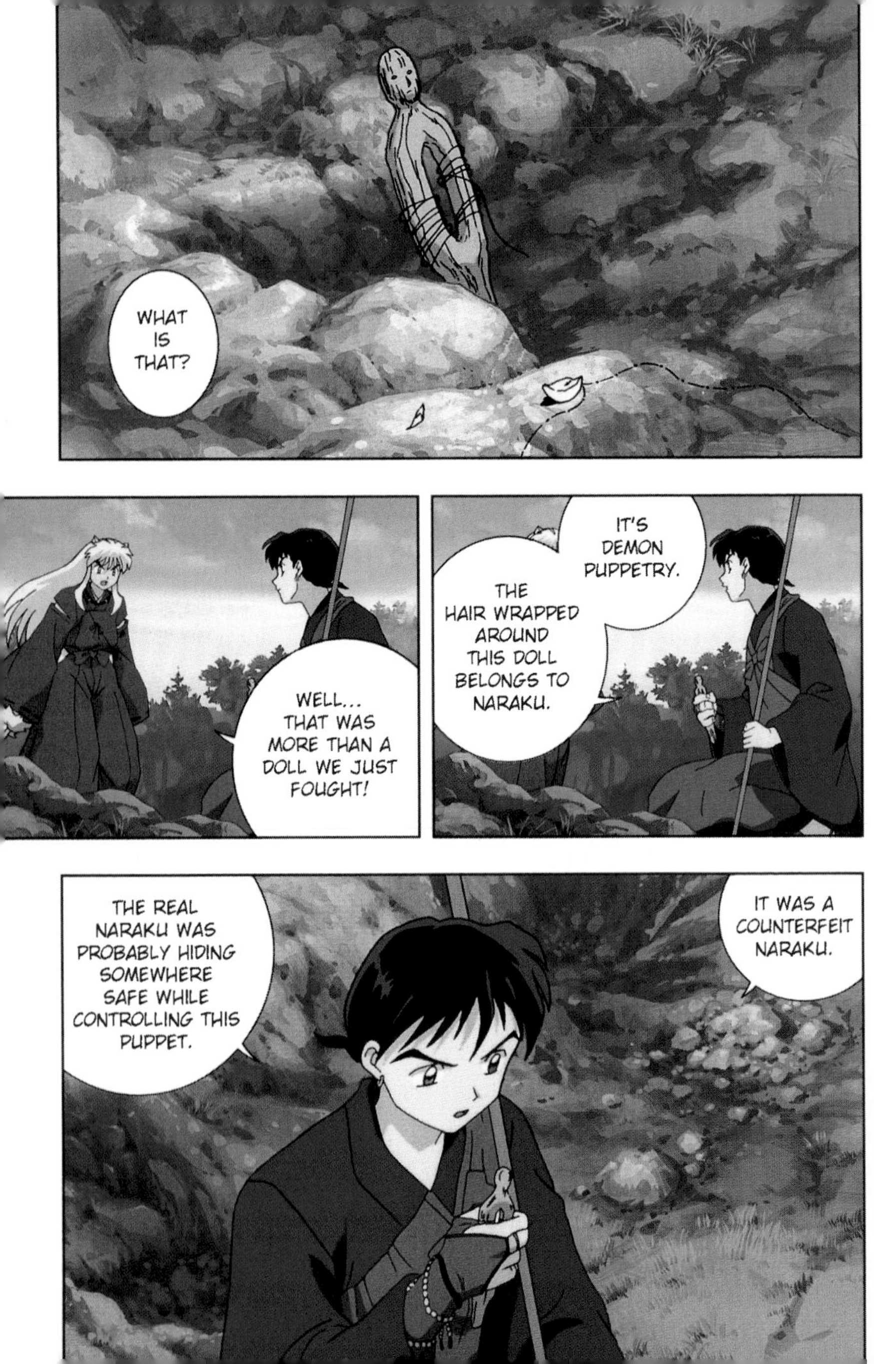
WHAT IS THAT?
IT'S DEMON PUPPETRY.
THE HAIR WRAPPED AROUND THIS DOLL BELONGS TO NARAKU.
WELL... THAT WAS MORE THAN A DOLL WE JUST FOUGHT!
IT WAS A COUNTERFEIT NARAKU.
THE REAL NARAKU WAS PROBABLY HIDING SOMEWHERE SAFE WHILE CONTROLLING THIS PUPPET.

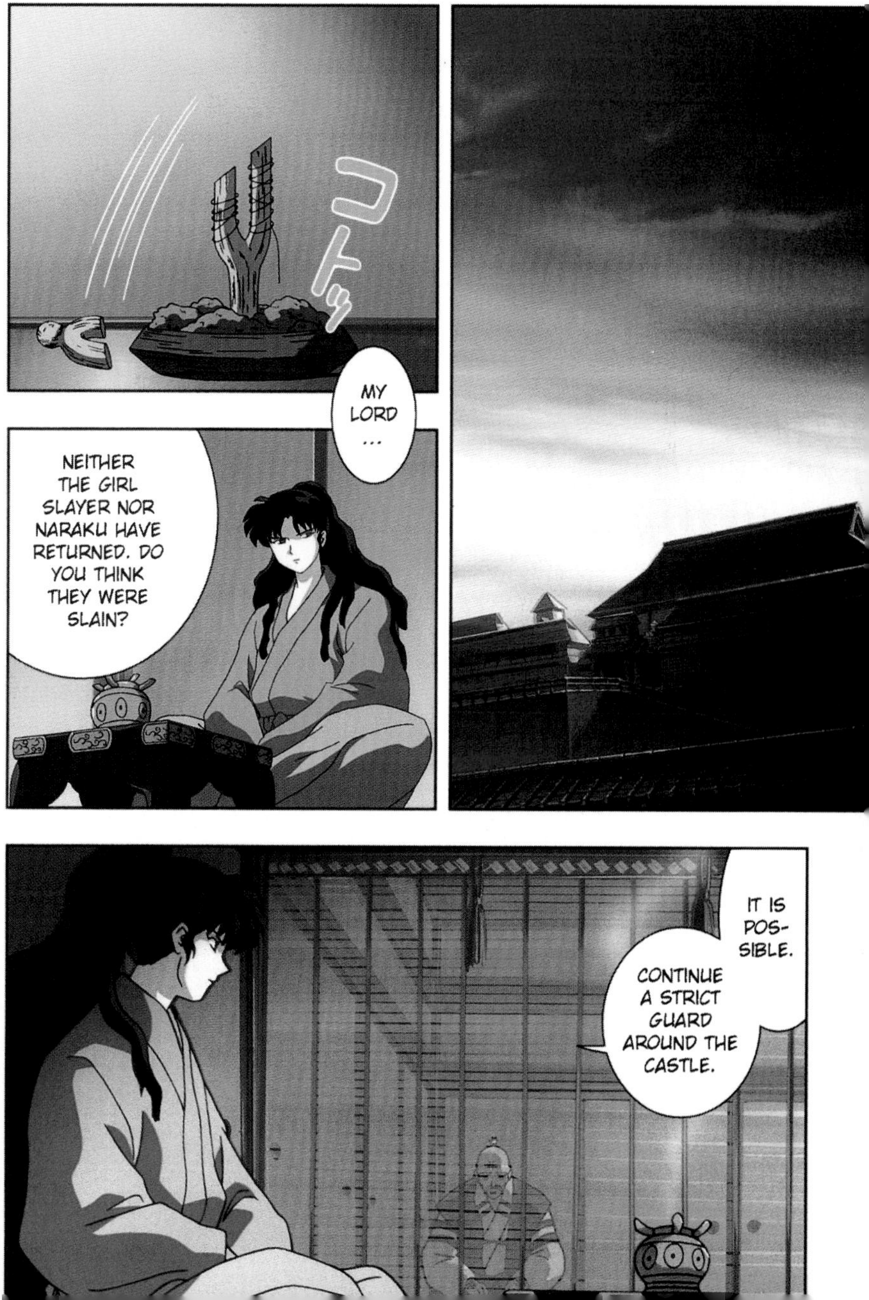
コトッ
MY LORD ...
NEITHER THE GIRL SLAYER NOR NARAKU HAVE RETURNED. DO YOU THINK THEY WERE SLAIN?
IT IS POS-SIBLE.
CONTINUE A STRICT GUARD AROUND THE CASTLE.

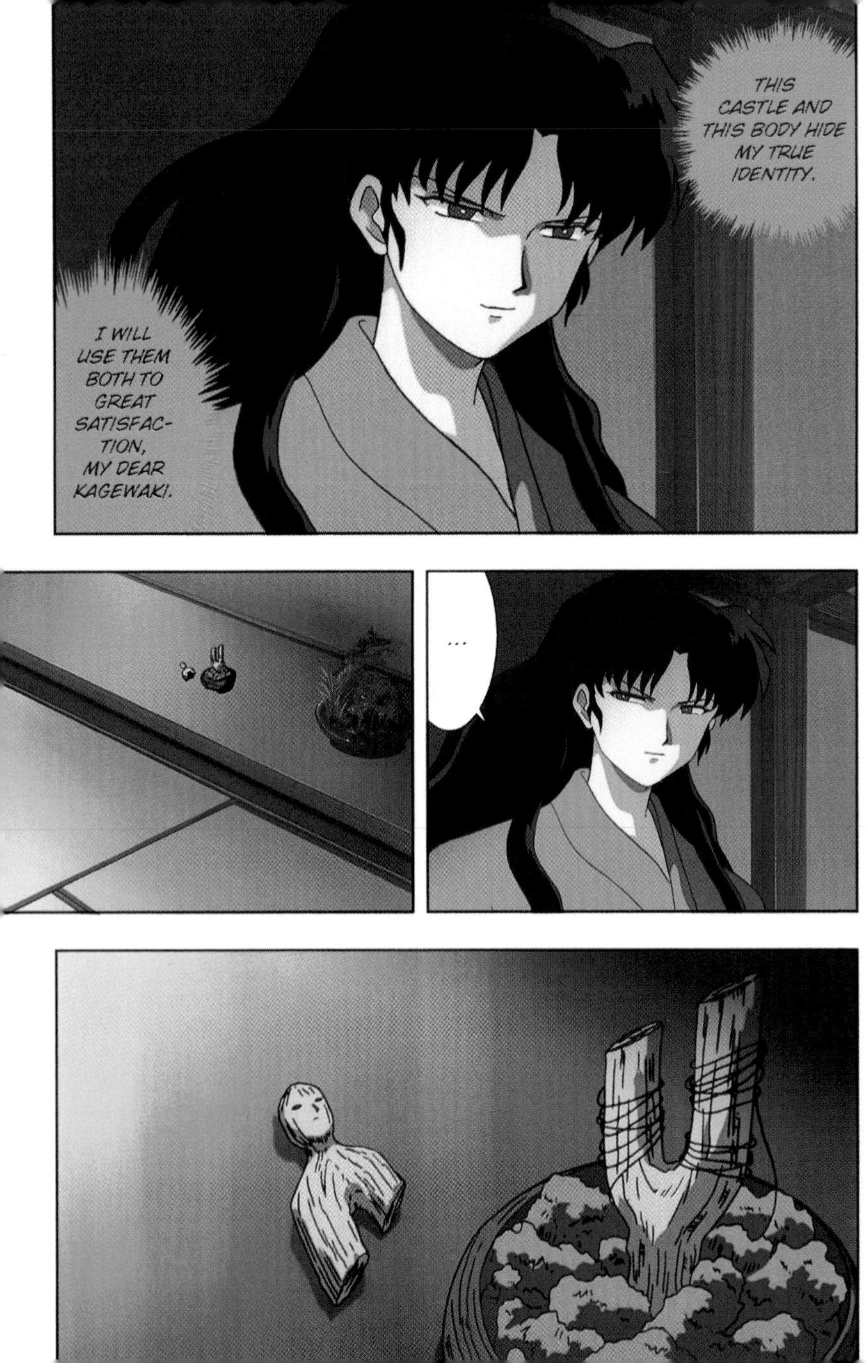
THIS CASTLE AND THIS BODY HIDE MY TRUE IDENTITY.
I WILL USE THEM BOTH TO GREAT SATISFACTION, MY DEAR KAGEWAKI.
...

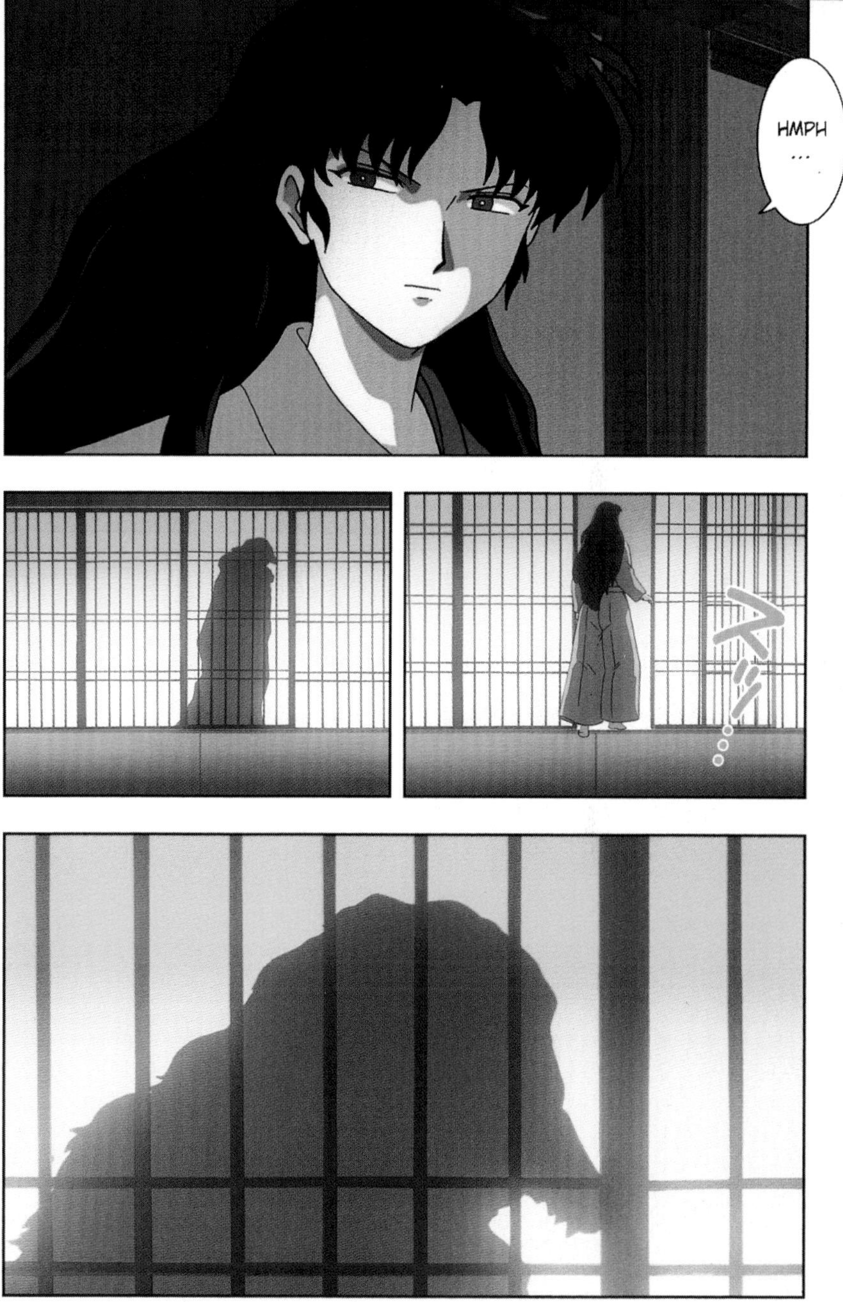
HMPH
...
スッ

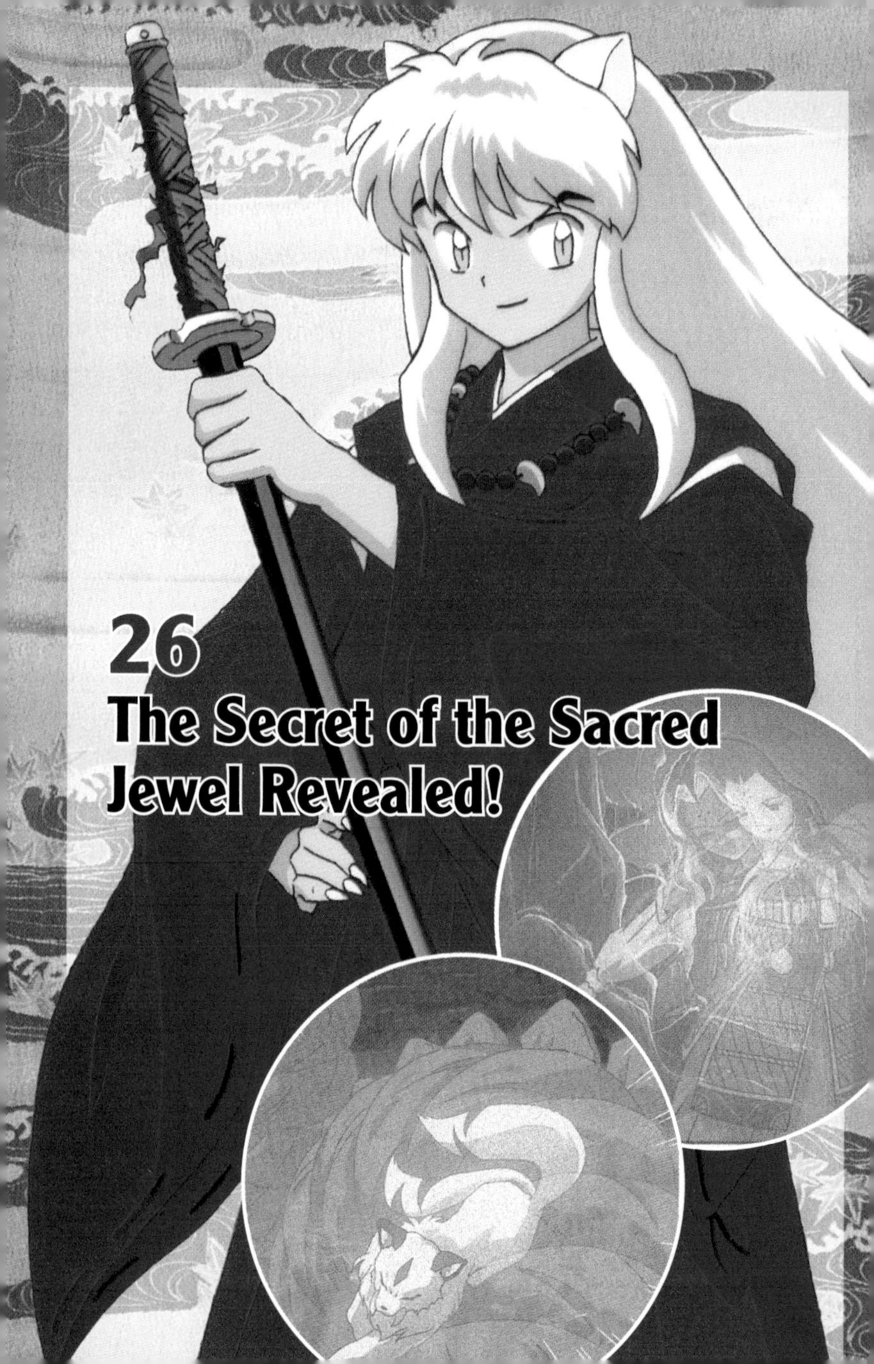
26
The Secret of the Sacred Jewel Revealed!

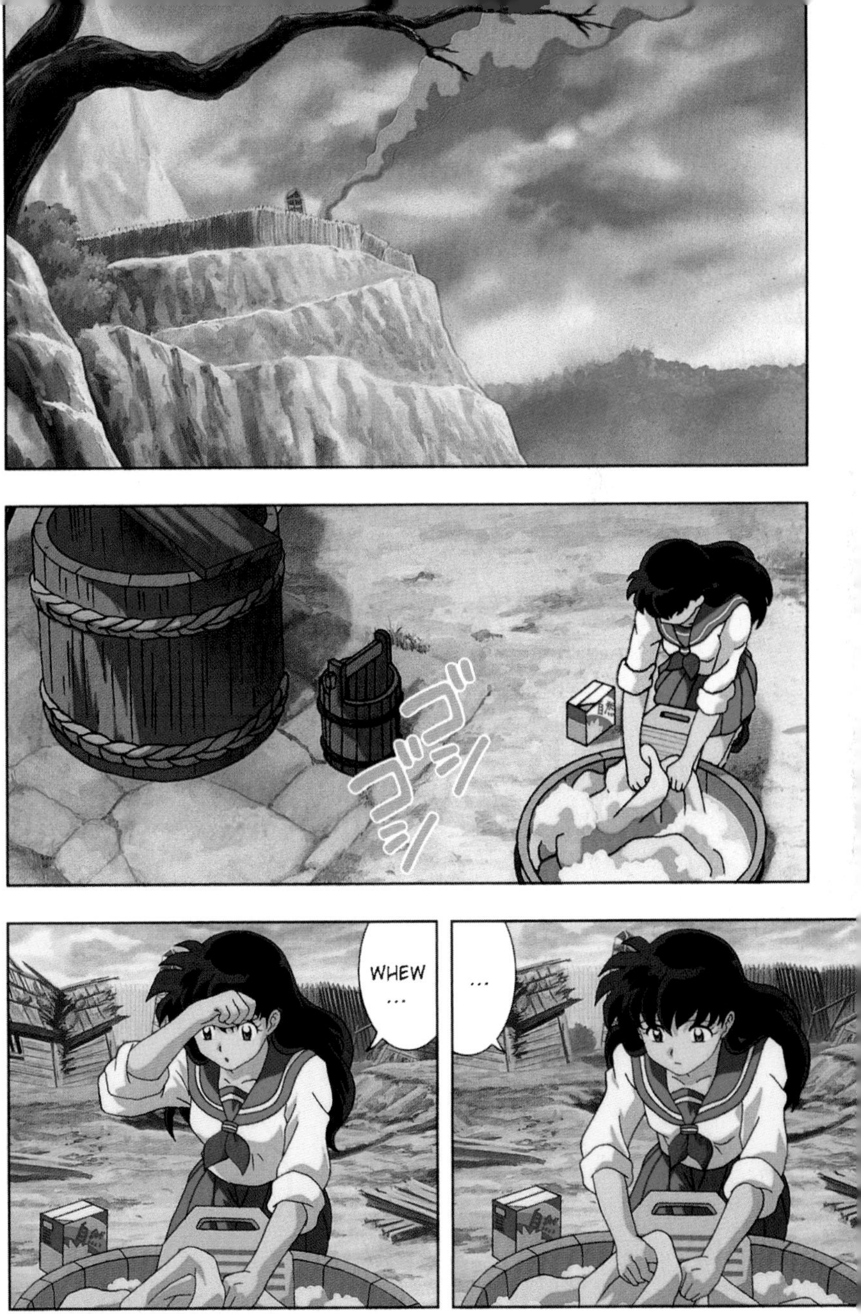
ゴシッ
ゴシッ
...
WHEW ...

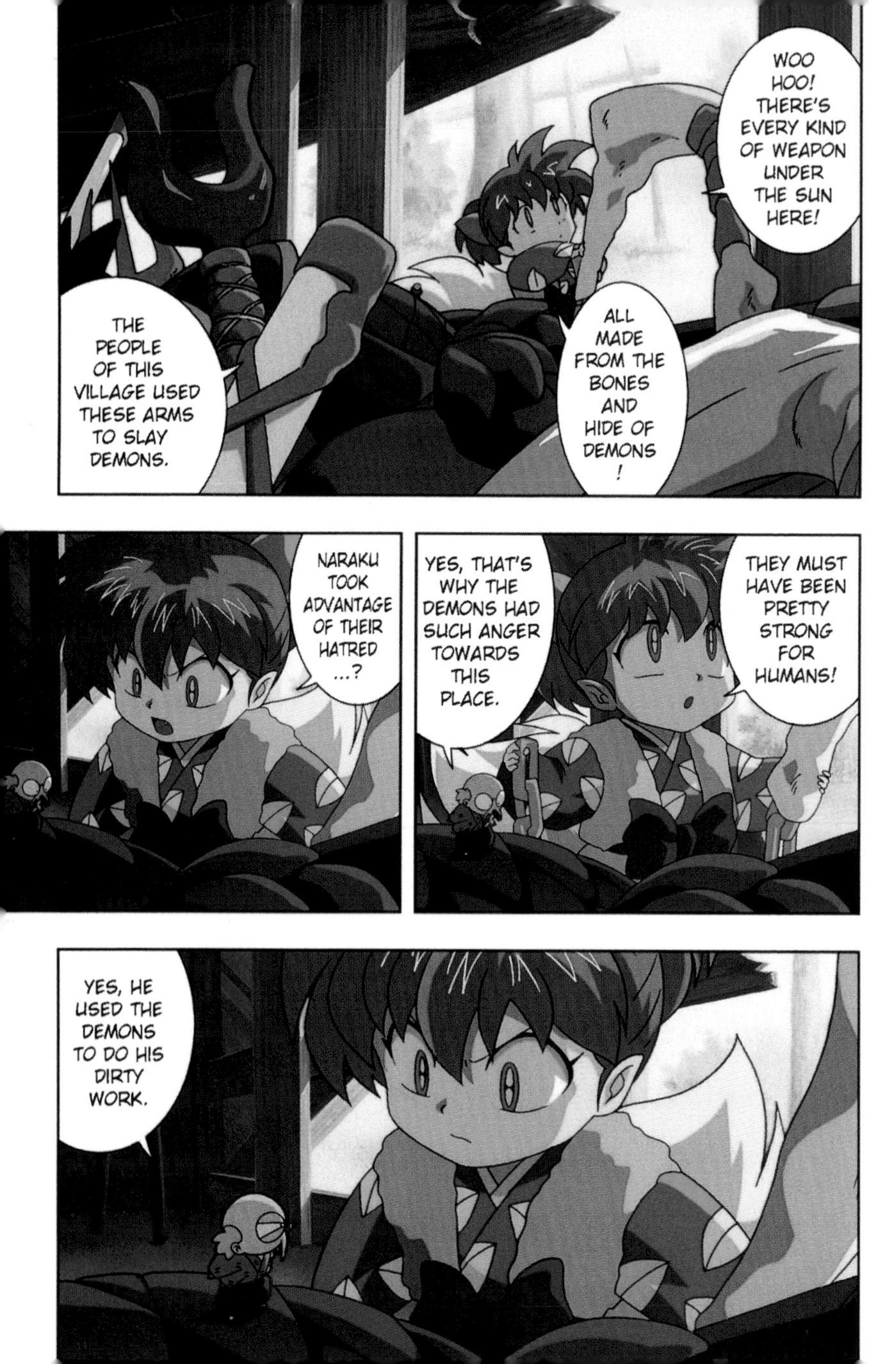
WOO HOO! THERE'S EVERY KIND OF WEAPON UNDER THE SUN HERE!
ALL MADE FROM THE BONES AND HIDE OF DEMONS!
THE PEOPLE OF THIS VILLAGE USED THESE ARMS TO SLAY DEMONS.
THEY MUST HAVE BEEN PRETTY STRONG FOR HUMANS!
YES, THAT'S WHY THE DEMONS HAD SUCH ANGER TOWARDS THIS PLACE.
NARAKU TOOK ADVANTAGE OF THEIR HATRED ...?
YES, HE USED THE DEMONS TO DO HIS DIRTY WORK.

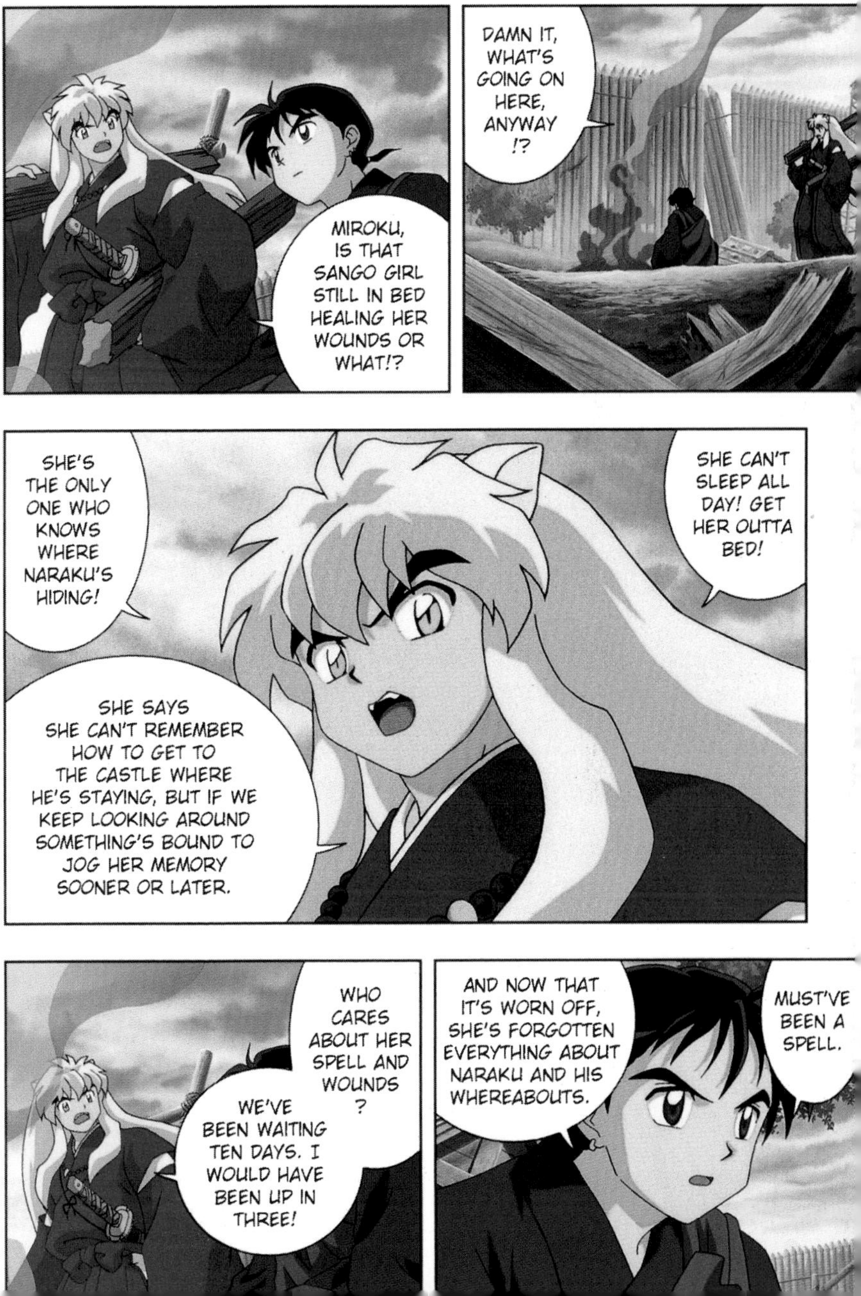
DAMN IT, WHAT'S GOING ON HERE, ANYWAY !?
MIROKU, IS THAT SANGO GIRL STILL IN BED HEALING HER WOUNDS OR WHAT!?
SHE CAN'T SLEEP ALL DAY! GET HER OUTTA BED!
SHE'S THE ONLY ONE WHO KNOWS WHERE NARAKU'S HIDING!
SHE SAYS SHE CAN'T REMEMBER HOW TO GET TO THE CASTLE WHERE HE'S STAYING, BUT IF WE KEEP LOOKING AROUND SOMETHING'S BOUND TO JOG HER MEMORY SOONER OR LATER.
MUST'VE BEEN A SPELL.
AND NOW THAT IT'S WORN OFF, SHE'S FORGOTTEN EVERYTHING ABOUT NARAKU AND HIS WHEREABOUTS.
WHO CARES ABOUT HER SPELL AND WOUNDS ?
WE'VE BEEN WAITING TEN DAYS. I WOULD HAVE BEEN UP IN THREE!

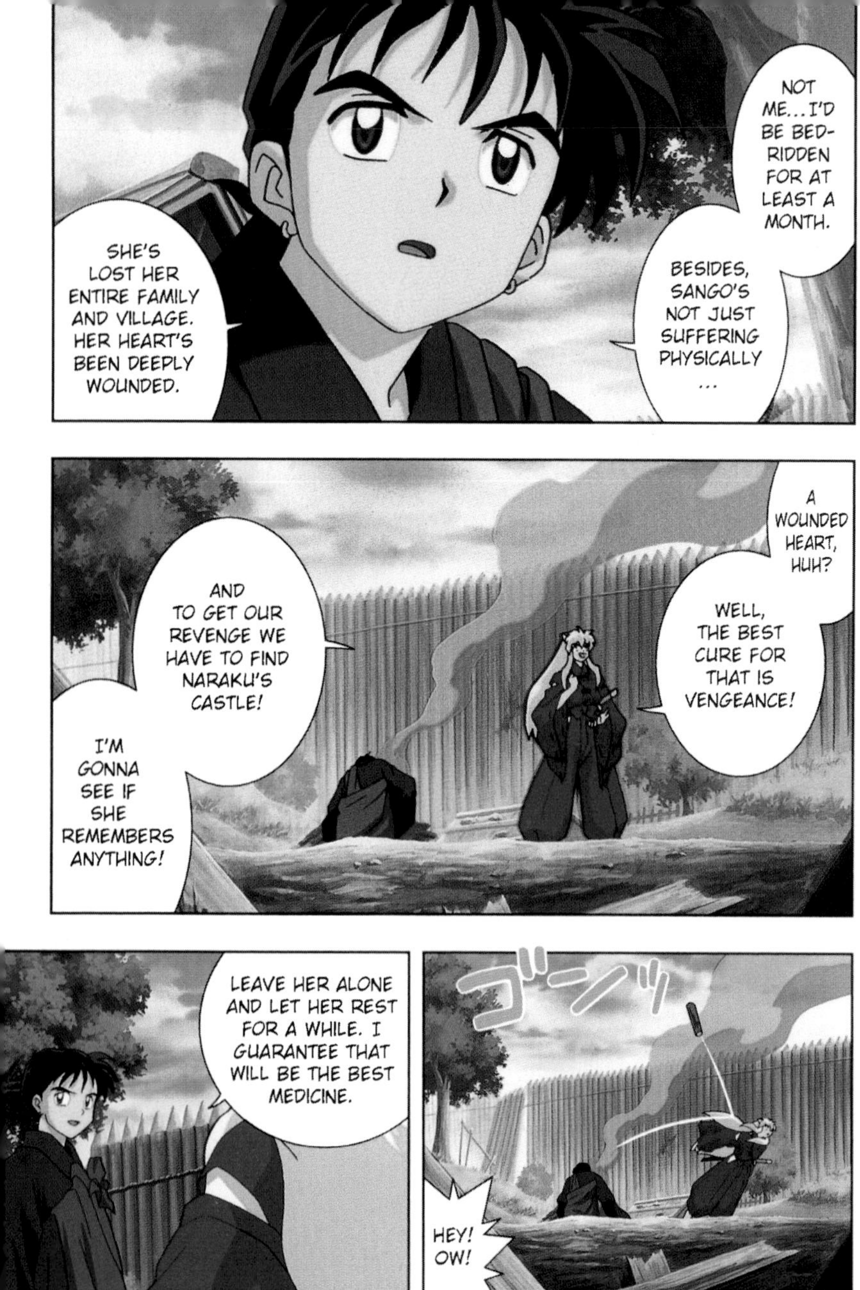
NOT ME...I'D BE BED-RIDDEN FOR AT LEAST A MONTH.
BESIDES, SANGO'S NOT JUST SUFFERING PHYSICALLY ...
SHE'S LOST HER ENTIRE FAMILY AND VILLAGE. HER HEART'S BEEN DEEPLY WOUNDED.
A WOUNDED HEART, HUH?
WELL, THE BEST CURE FOR THAT IS VENGEANCE!
AND TO GET OUR REVENGE WE HAVE TO FIND NARAKU'S CASTLE!
I'M GONNA SEE IF SHE REMEMBERS ANYTHING!
ゴーンッ
HEY! OW!
LEAVE HER ALONE AND LET HER REST FOR A WHILE. I GUARANTEE THAT WILL BE THE BEST MEDICINE.

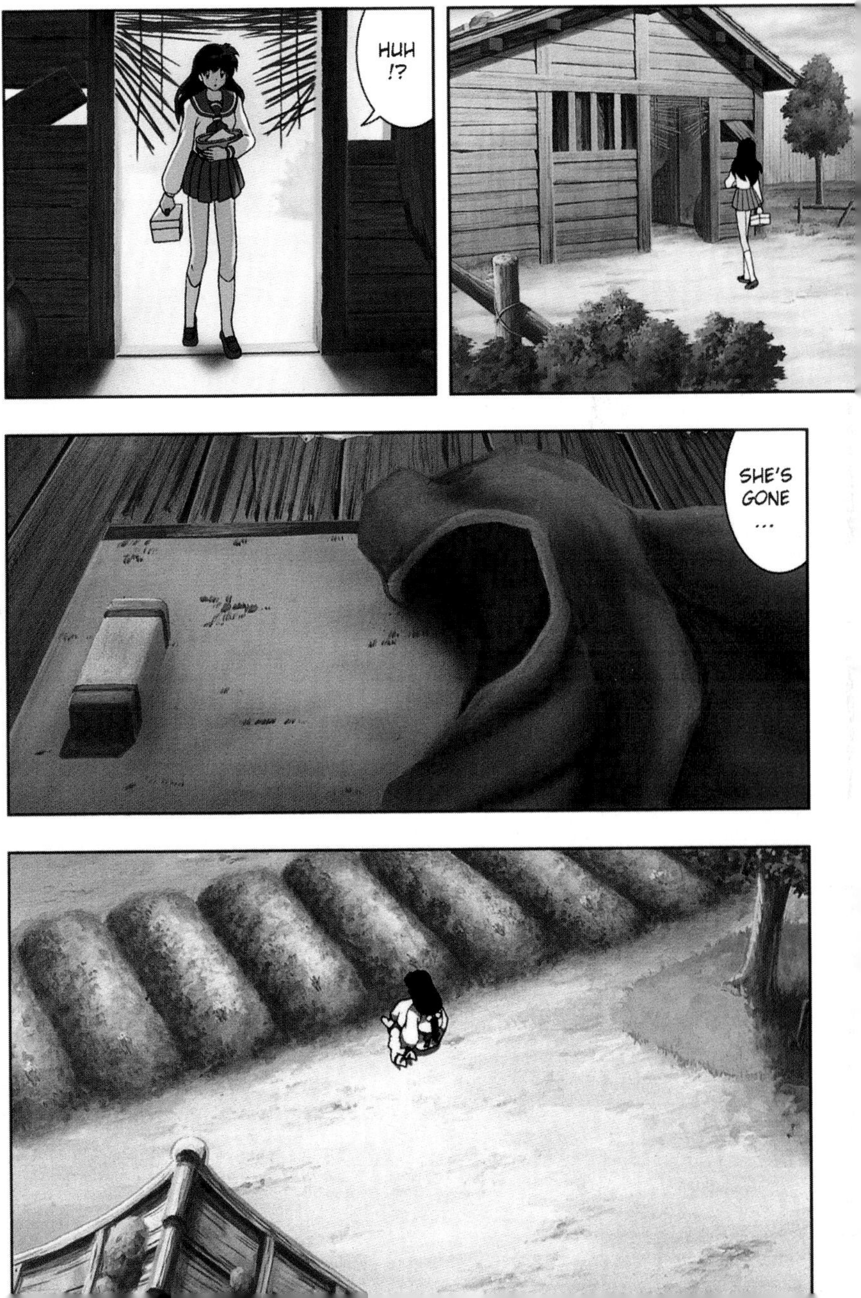
HUH !?
SHE'S GONE ...

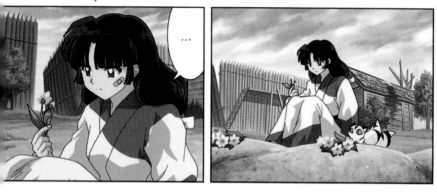

...

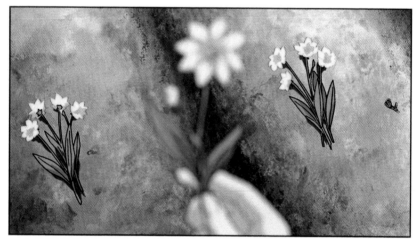

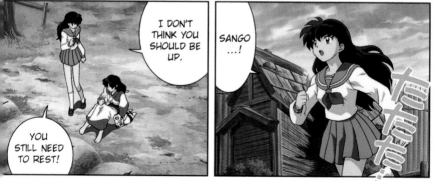

I DON'T THINK YOU SHOULD BE UP.

YOU STILL NEED TO REST!

SANGO ...!

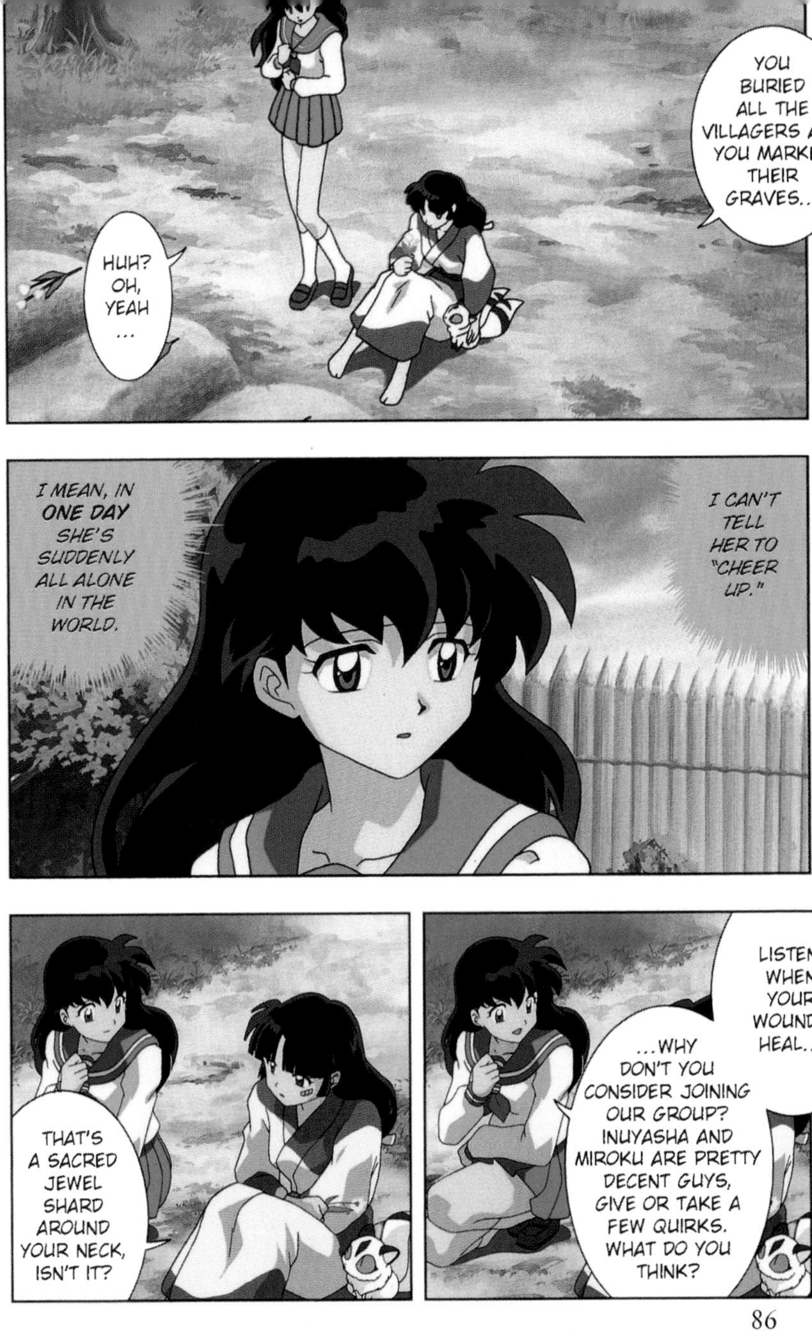
YOU BURIED ALL THE VILLAGERS AND YOU MARKED THEIR GRAVES...
HUH? OH, YEAH...
I CAN'T TELL HER TO "CHEER UP."
I MEAN, IN **ONE DAY** SHE'S SUDDENLY ALL ALONE IN THE WORLD.
LISTEN, WHEN YOUR WOUNDS HEAL...
...WHY DON'T YOU CONSIDER JOINING OUR GROUP? INUYASHA AND MIROKU ARE PRETTY DECENT GUYS, GIVE OR TAKE A FEW QUIRKS. WHAT DO YOU THINK?
THAT'S A SACRED JEWEL SHARD AROUND YOUR NECK, ISN'T IT?

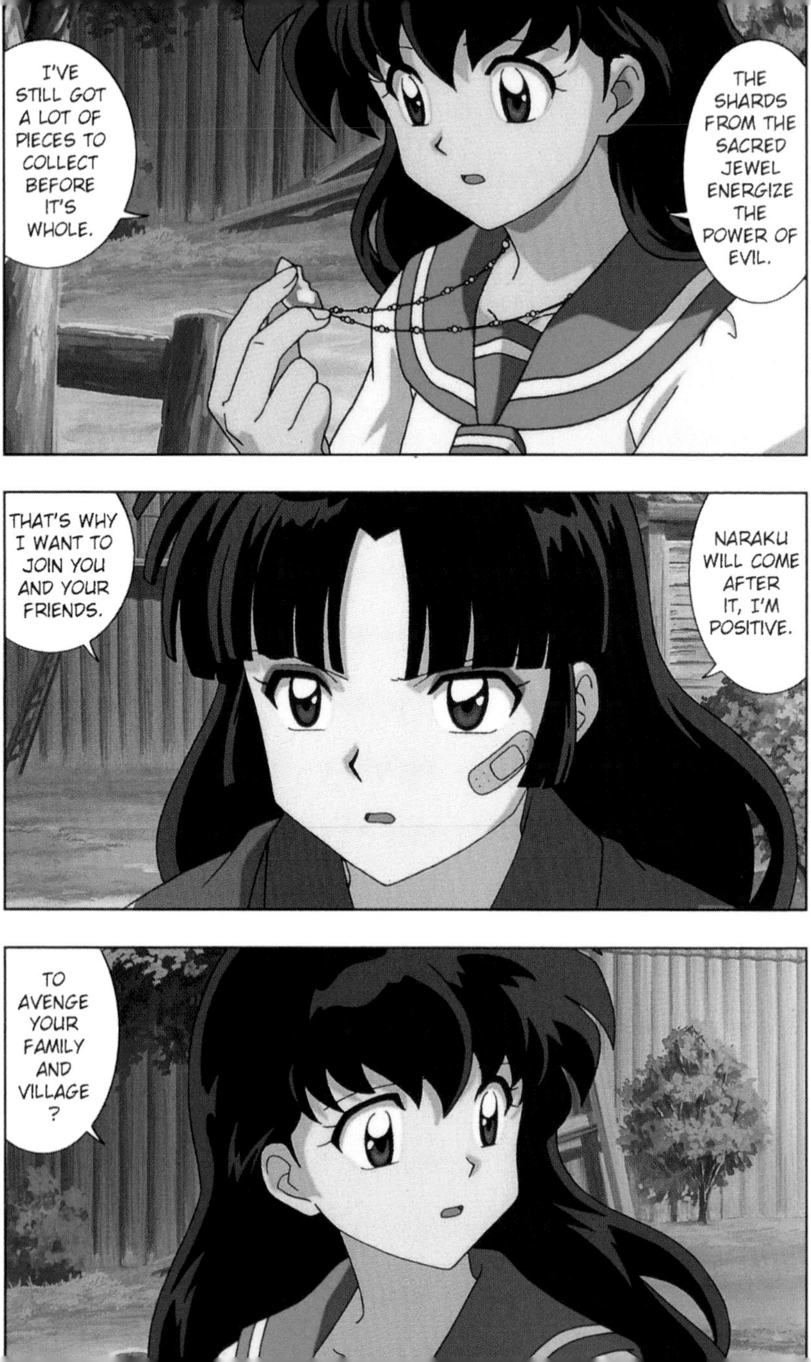
THE SHARDS FROM THE SACRED JEWEL ENERGIZE THE POWER OF EVIL.
I'VE STILL GOT A LOT OF PIECES TO COLLECT BEFORE IT'S WHOLE.
NARAKU WILL COME AFTER IT, I'M POSITIVE.
THAT'S WHY I WANT TO JOIN YOU AND YOUR FRIENDS.
TO AVENGE YOUR FAMILY AND VILLAGE?

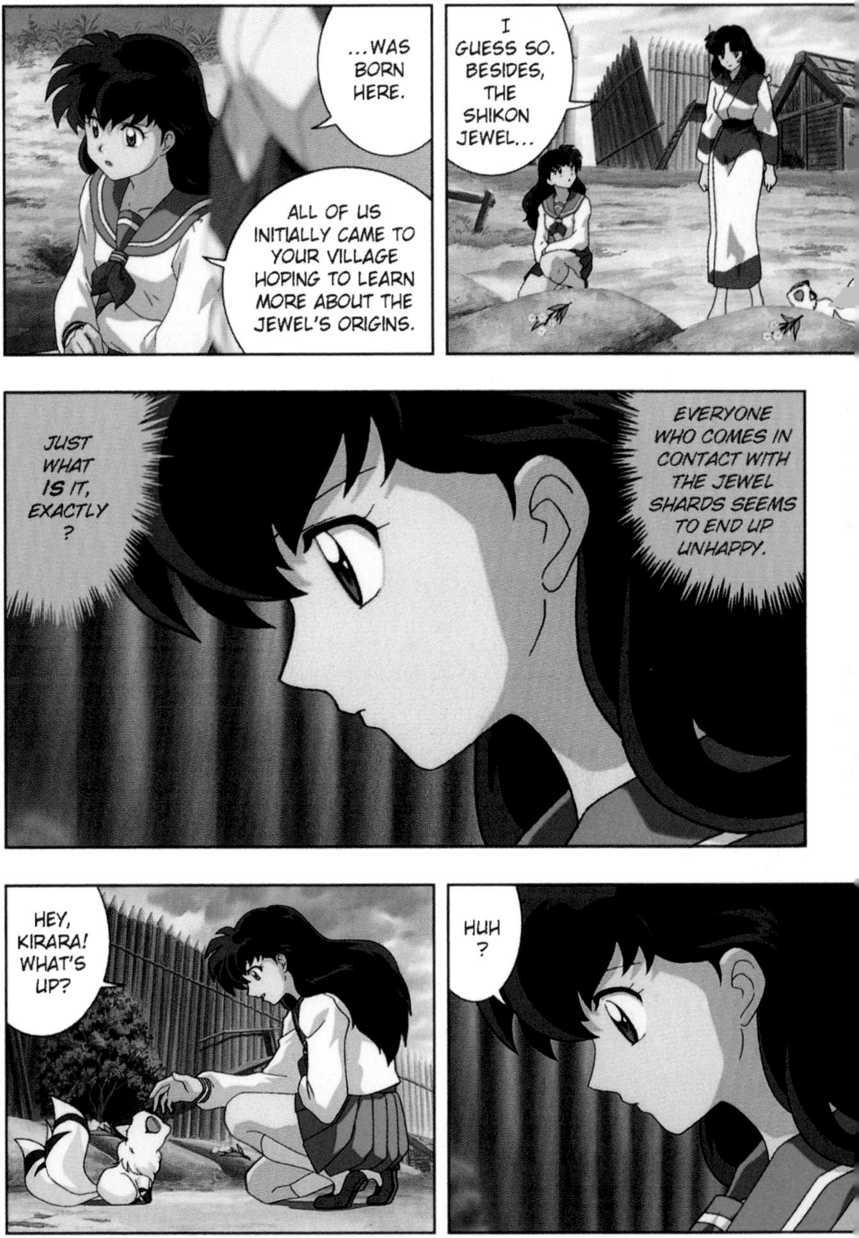
I GUESS SO. BESIDES, THE SHIKON JEWEL...
...WAS BORN HERE.
ALL OF US INITIALLY CAME TO YOUR VILLAGE HOPING TO LEARN MORE ABOUT THE JEWEL'S ORIGINS.
EVERYONE WHO COMES IN CONTACT WITH THE JEWEL SHARDS SEEMS TO END UP UNHAPPY.
JUST WHAT IS IT, EXACTLY?
HUH?
HEY, KIRARA! WHAT'S UP?

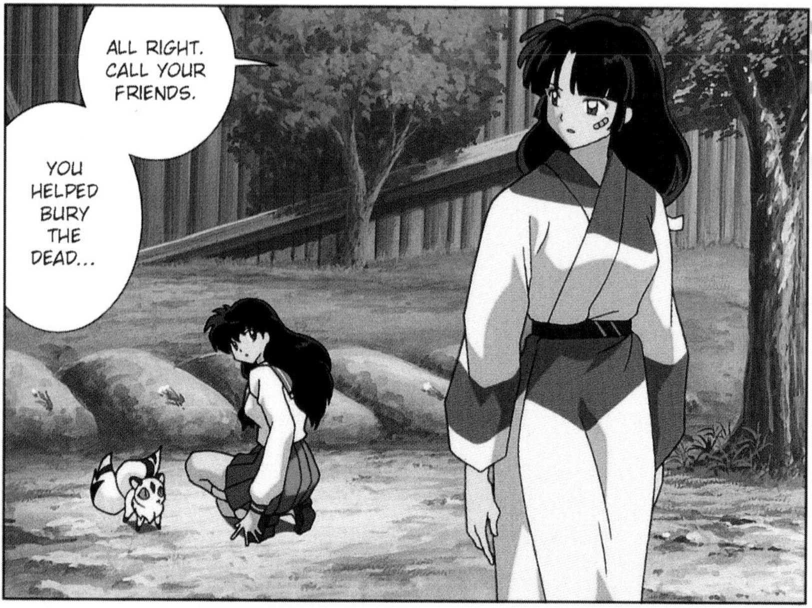
ALL RIGHT. CALL YOUR FRIENDS.
YOU HELPED BURY THE DEAD...

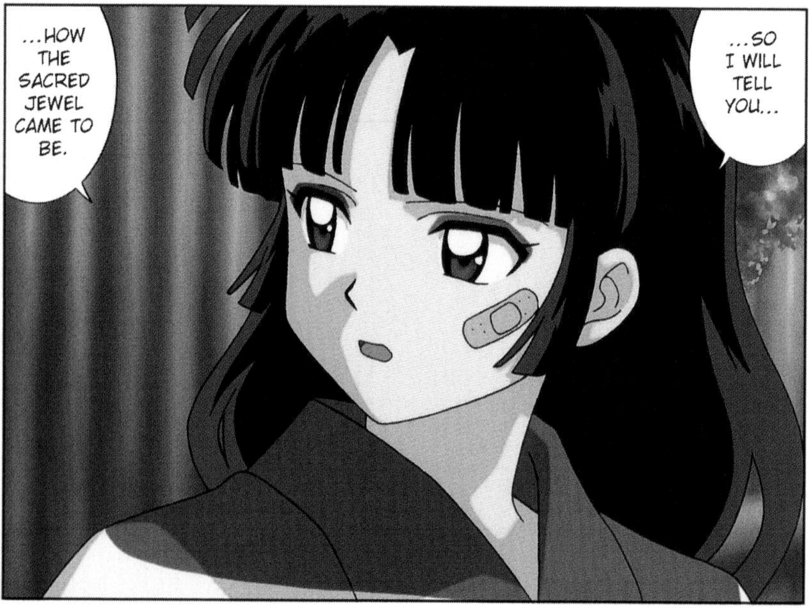
...SO I WILL TELL YOU...
...HOW THE SACRED JEWEL CAME TO BE.

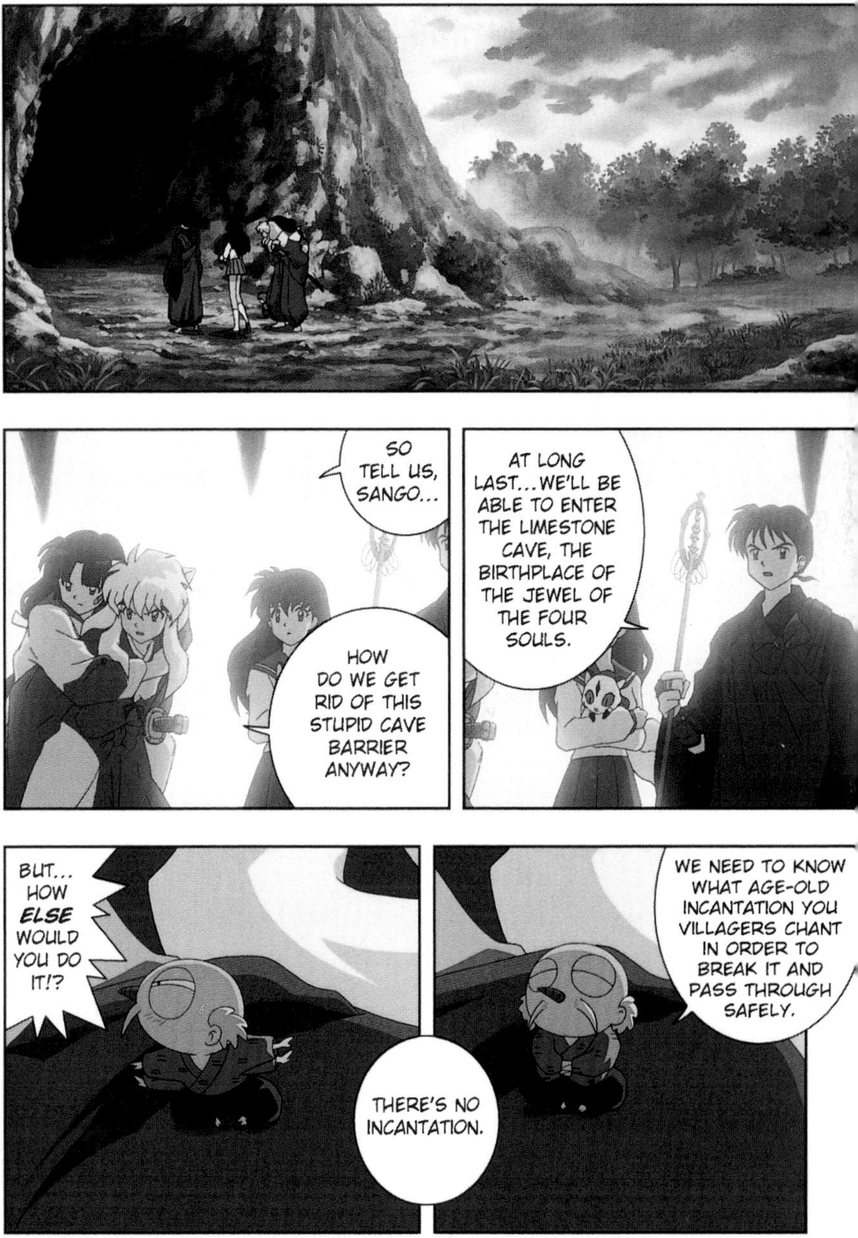
AT LONG LAST...WE'LL BE ABLE TO ENTER THE LIMESTONE CAVE, THE BIRTHPLACE OF THE JEWEL OF THE FOUR SOULS.
SO TELL US, SANGO...
HOW DO WE GET RID OF THIS STUPID CAVE BARRIER ANYWAY?
WE NEED TO KNOW WHAT AGE-OLD INCANTATION YOU VILLAGERS CHANT IN ORDER TO BREAK IT AND PASS THROUGH SAFELY.
THERE'S NO INCANTATION.
BUT... HOW *ELSE* WOULD YOU DO IT!?

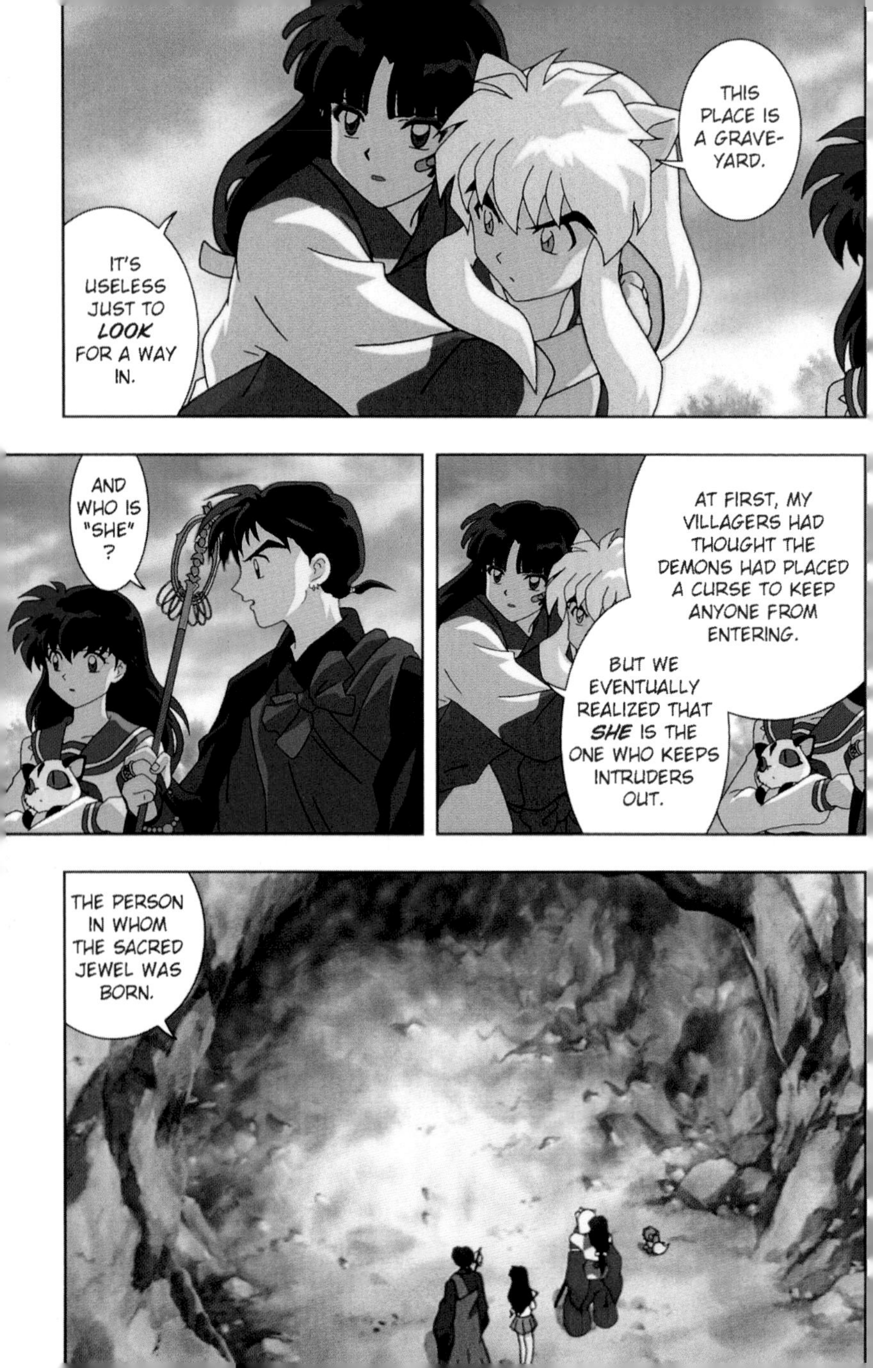
THIS PLACE IS A GRAVE-YARD.
IT'S USELESS JUST TO **LOOK** FOR A WAY IN.
AT FIRST, MY VILLAGERS HAD THOUGHT THE DEMONS HAD PLACED A CURSE TO KEEP ANYONE FROM ENTERING.
BUT WE EVENTUALLY REALIZED THAT **SHE** IS THE ONE WHO KEEPS INTRUDERS OUT.
AND WHO IS "SHE" ?
THE PERSON IN WHOM THE SACRED JEWEL WAS BORN.

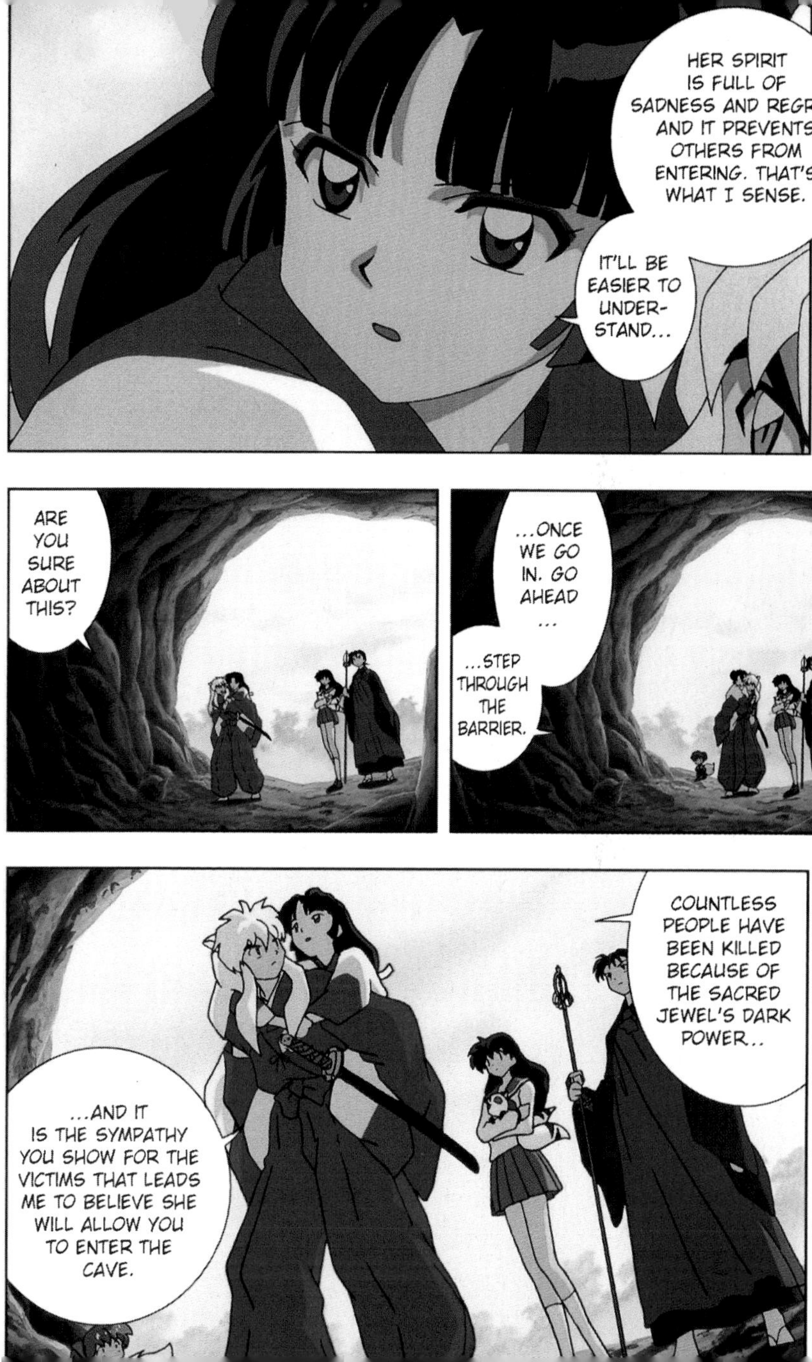
HER SPIRIT IS FULL OF SADNESS AND REGRET, AND IT PREVENTS OTHERS FROM ENTERING. THAT'S WHAT I SENSE.
IT'LL BE EASIER TO UNDER-STAND...
...ONCE WE GO IN. GO AHEAD ...
...STEP THROUGH THE BARRIER.
ARE YOU SURE ABOUT THIS?
COUNTLESS PEOPLE HAVE BEEN KILLED BECAUSE OF THE SACRED JEWEL'S DARK POWER..
...AND IT IS THE SYMPATHY YOU SHOW FOR THE VICTIMS THAT LEADS ME TO BELIEVE SHE WILL ALLOW YOU TO ENTER THE CAVE.

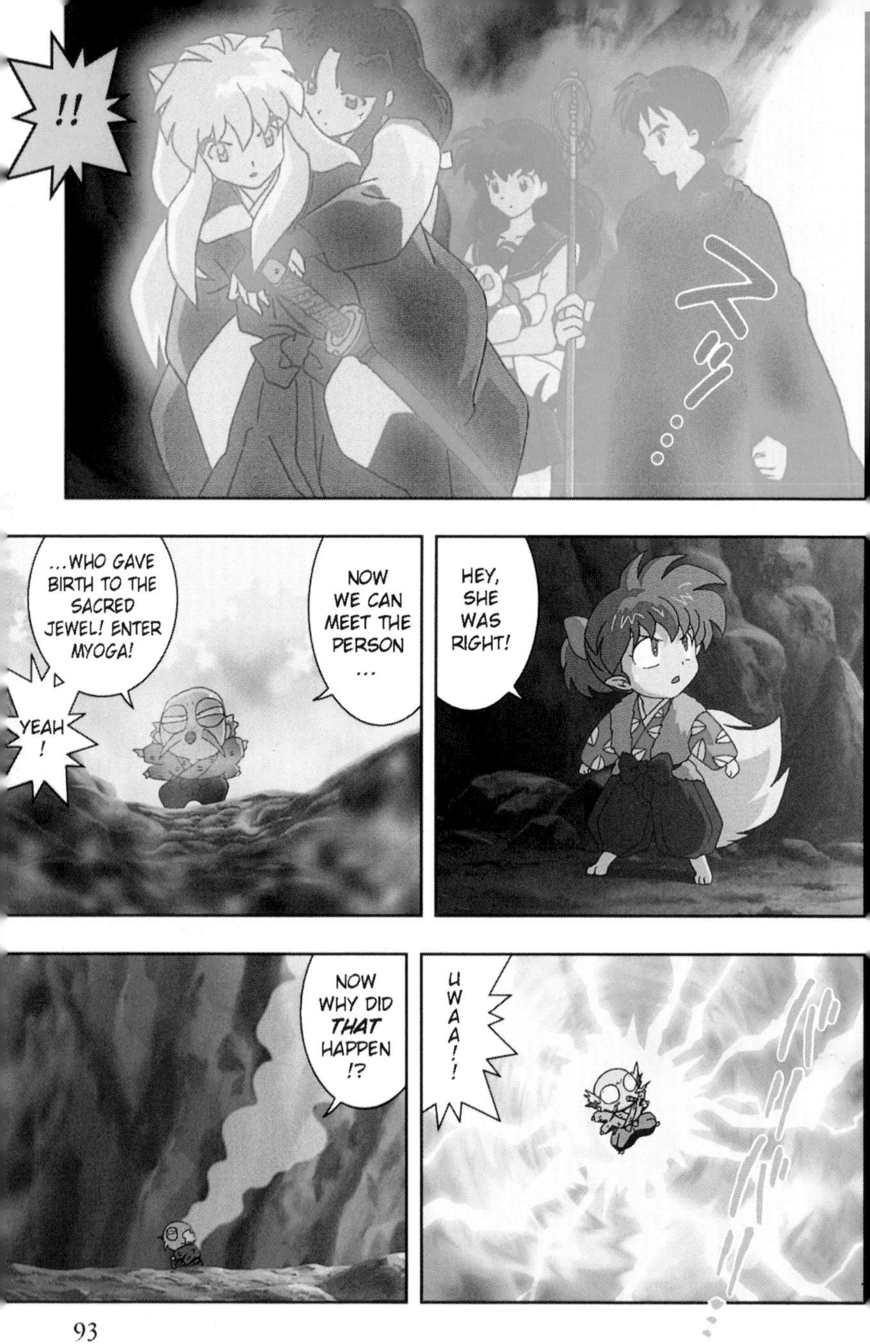
!!
スッ…
HEY, SHE WAS RIGHT!
NOW WE CAN MEET THE PERSON ...
...WHO GAVE BIRTH TO THE SACRED JEWEL! ENTER MYOGA!
YEAH!
UWAAA!!
NOW WHY DID ***THAT*** HAPPEN!?

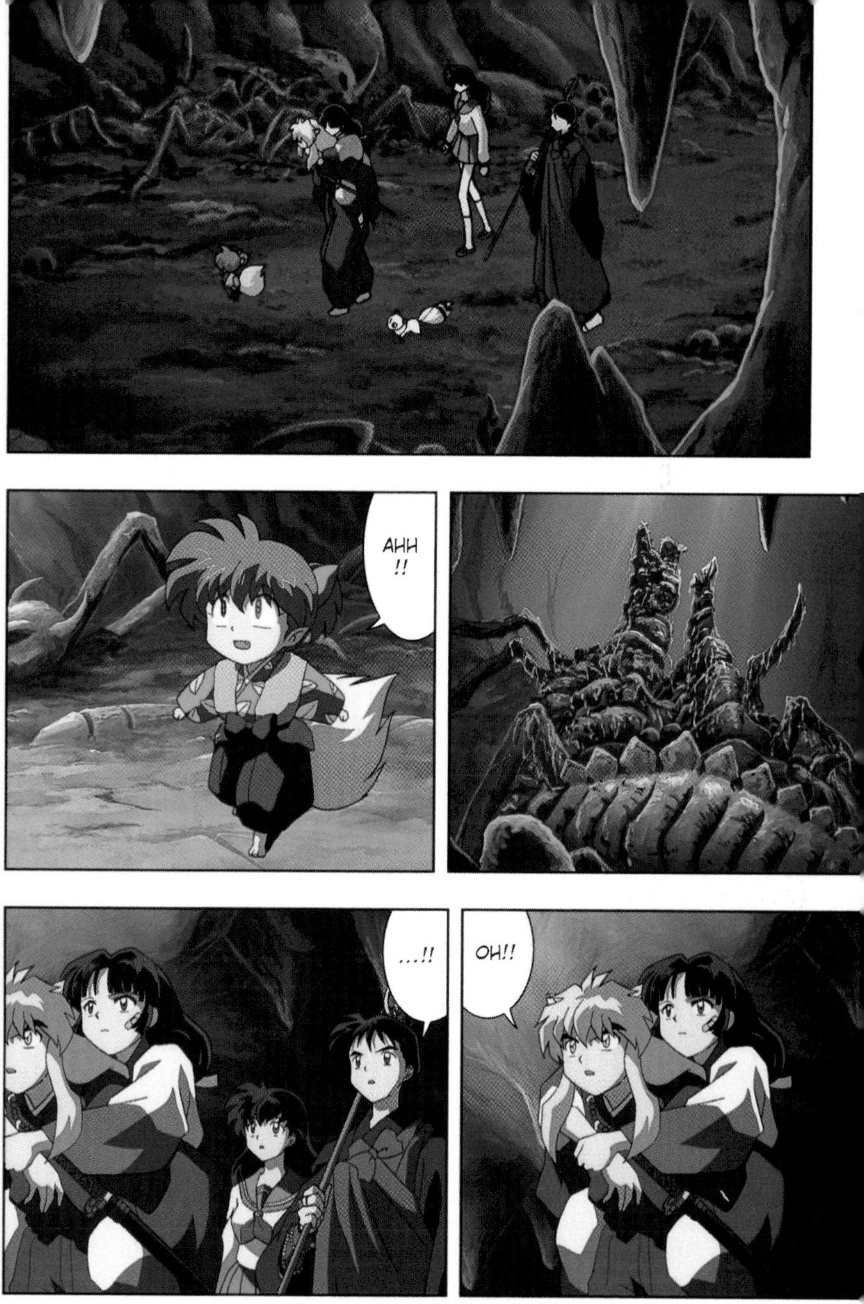
AHH !!
OH!!
...!!

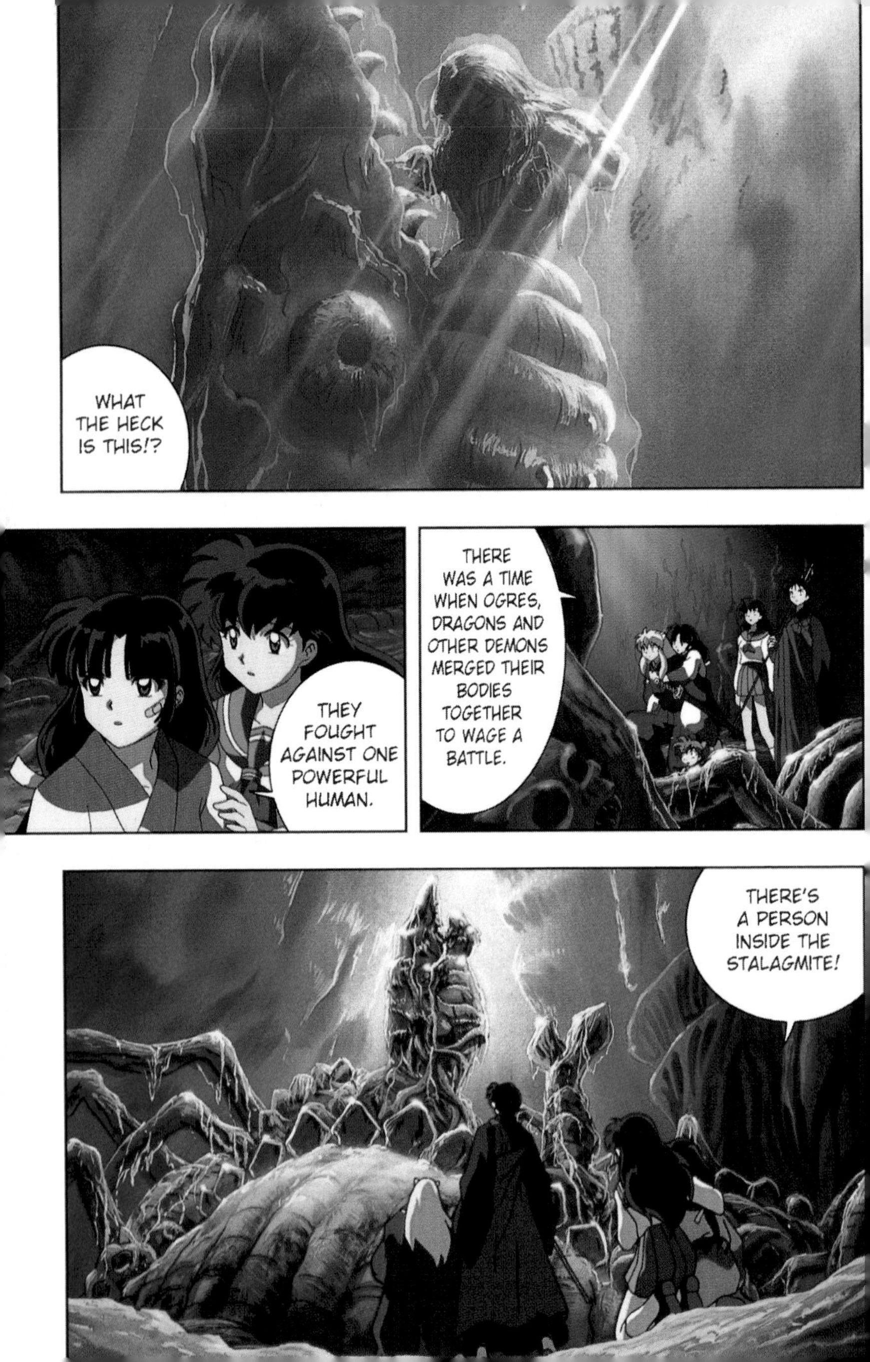
WHAT THE HECK IS THIS!?
THERE WAS A TIME WHEN OGRES, DRAGONS AND OTHER DEMONS MERGED THEIR BODIES TOGETHER TO WAGE A BATTLE.
THEY FOUGHT AGAINST ONE POWERFUL HUMAN.
THERE'S A PERSON INSIDE THE STALAGMITE!

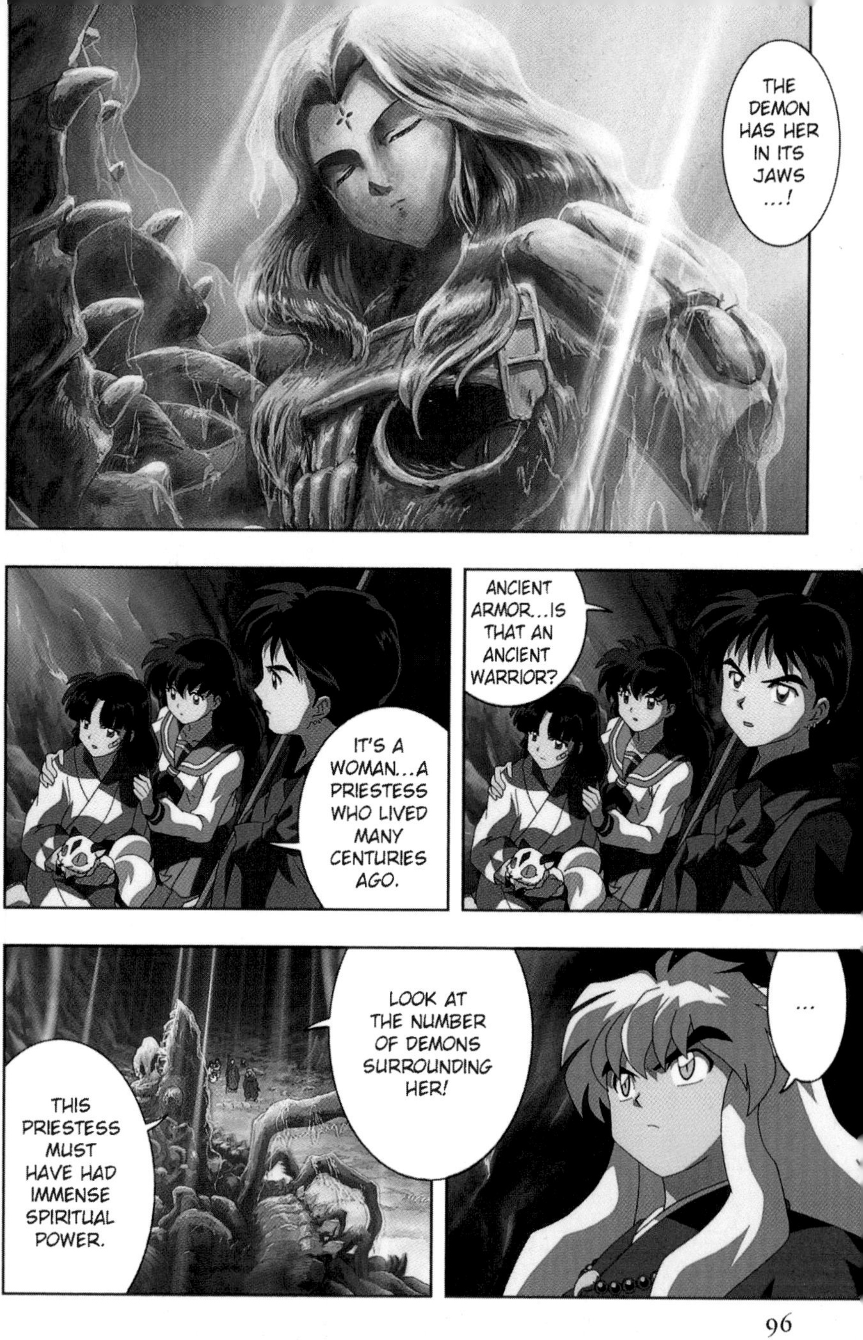
THE DEMON HAS HER IN ITS JAWS ...!
ANCIENT ARMOR...IS THAT AN ANCIENT WARRIOR?
IT'S A WOMAN...A PRIESTESS WHO LIVED MANY CENTURIES AGO.
...
LOOK AT THE NUMBER OF DEMONS SURROUNDING HER!
THIS PRIESTESS MUST HAVE HAD IMMENSE SPIRITUAL POWER.

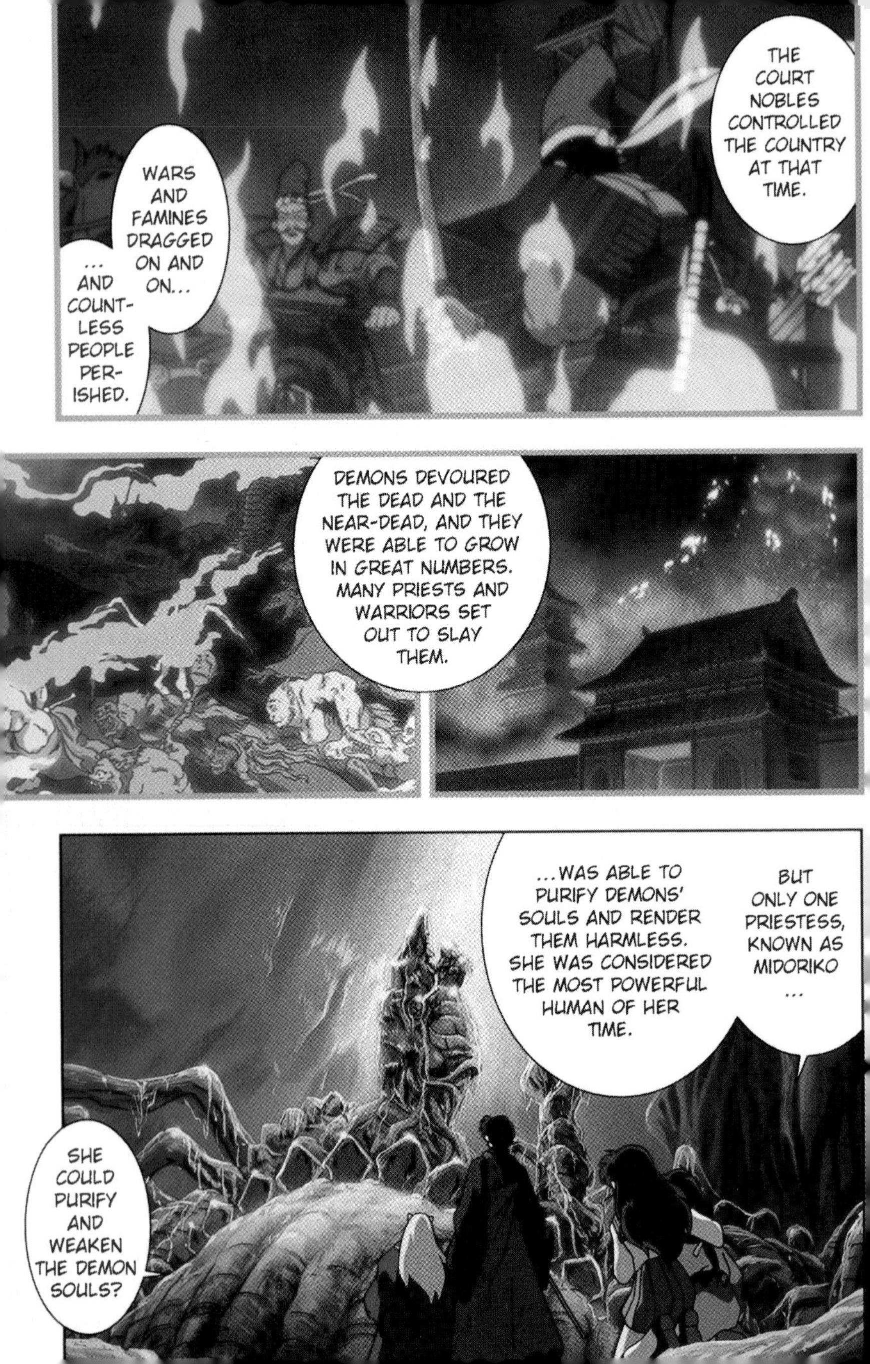
THE COURT NOBLES CONTROLLED THE COUNTRY AT THAT TIME.
WARS AND FAMINES DRAGGED ON AND ON...
...AND COUNT-LESS PEOPLE PER-ISHED.
DEMONS DEVOURED THE DEAD AND THE NEAR-DEAD, AND THEY WERE ABLE TO GROW IN GREAT NUMBERS. MANY PRIESTS AND WARRIORS SET OUT TO SLAY THEM.
BUT ONLY ONE PRIESTESS, KNOWN AS MIDORIKO...
...WAS ABLE TO PURIFY DEMONS' SOULS AND RENDER THEM HARMLESS. SHE WAS CONSIDERED THE MOST POWERFUL HUMAN OF HER TIME.
SHE COULD PURIFY AND WEAKEN THE DEMON SOULS?

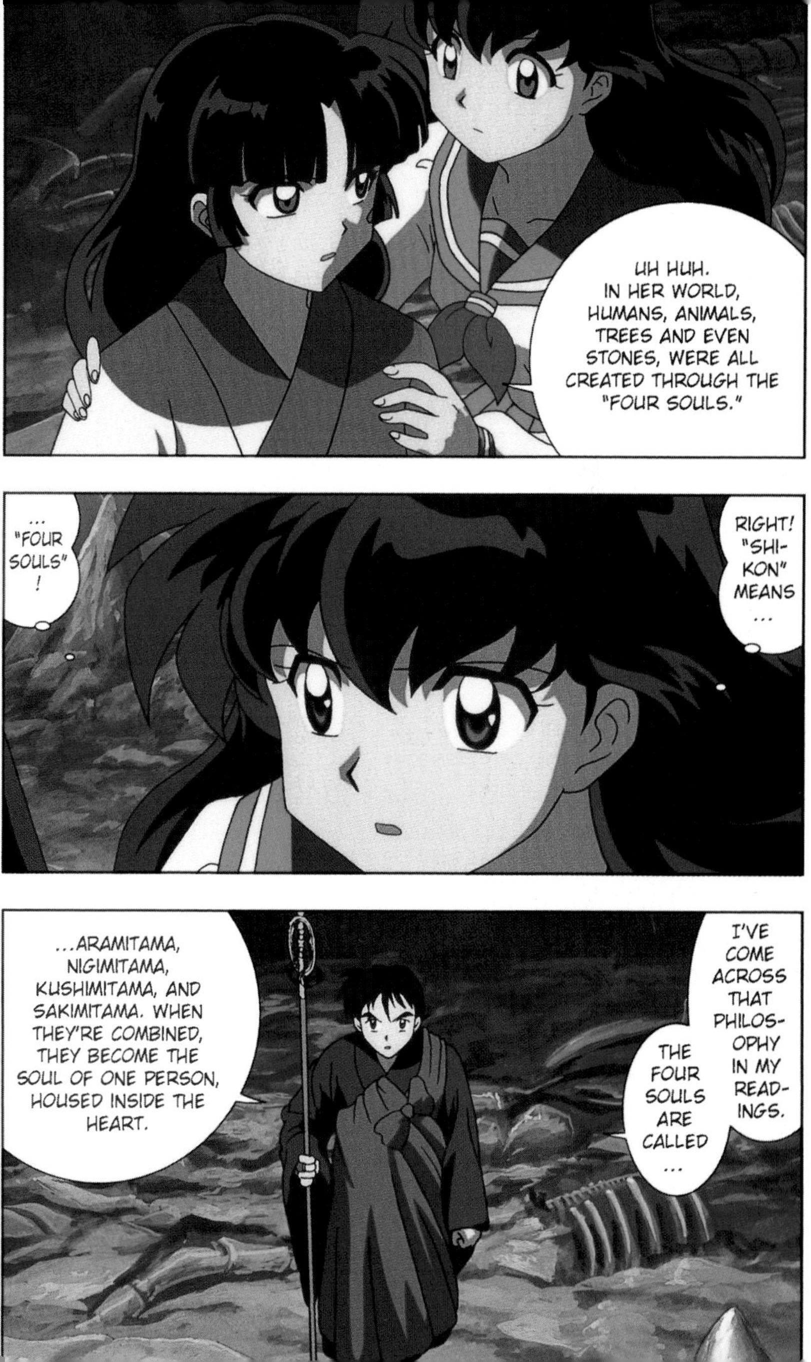
UH HUH. IN HER WORLD, HUMANS, ANIMALS, TREES AND EVEN STONES, WERE ALL CREATED THROUGH THE "FOUR SOULS."
RIGHT! "SHI-KON" MEANS...
..."FOUR SOULS"!
I'VE COME ACROSS THAT PHILOSOPHY IN MY READINGS.
THE FOUR SOULS ARE CALLED...
...ARAMITAMA, NIGIMITAMA, KUSHIMITAMA, AND SAKIMITAMA. WHEN THEY'RE COMBINED, THEY BECOME THE SOUL OF ONE PERSON, HOUSED INSIDE THE HEART.

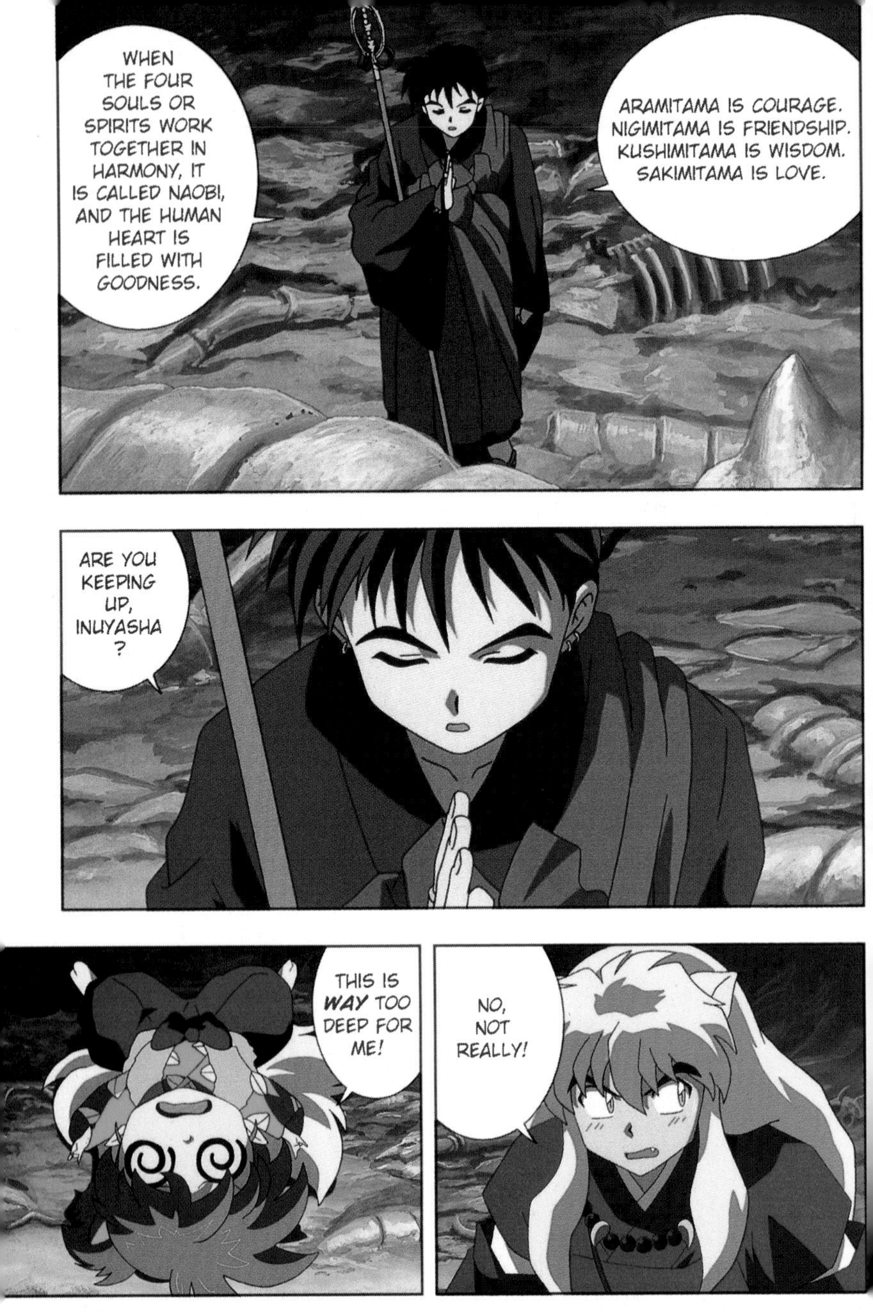
ARAMITAMA IS COURAGE. NIGIMITAMA IS FRIENDSHIP. KUSHIMITAMA IS WISDOM. SAKIMITAMA IS LOVE.
WHEN THE FOUR SOULS OR SPIRITS WORK TOGETHER IN HARMONY, IT IS CALLED NAOBI, AND THE HUMAN HEART IS FILLED WITH GOODNESS.
ARE YOU KEEPING UP, INUYASHA?
NO, NOT REALLY!
THIS IS WAY TOO DEEP FOR ME!

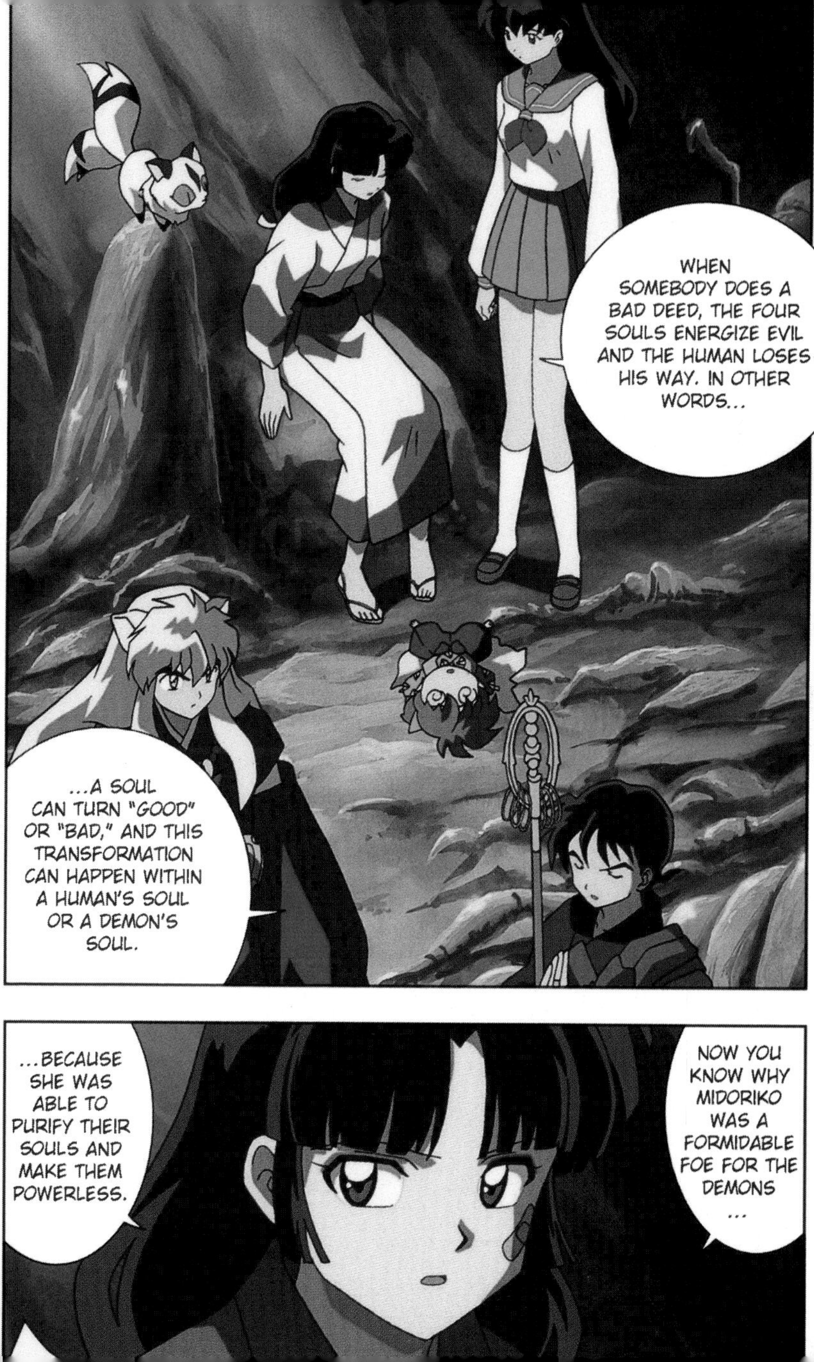
WHEN SOMEBODY DOES A BAD DEED, THE FOUR SOULS ENERGIZE EVIL AND THE HUMAN LOSES HIS WAY. IN OTHER WORDS...
...A SOUL CAN TURN "GOOD" OR "BAD," AND THIS TRANSFORMATION CAN HAPPEN WITHIN A HUMAN'S SOUL OR A DEMON'S SOUL.
NOW YOU KNOW WHY MIDORIKO WAS A FORMIDABLE FOE FOR THE DEMONS ...
...BECAUSE SHE WAS ABLE TO PURIFY THEIR SOULS AND MAKE THEM POWERLESS.

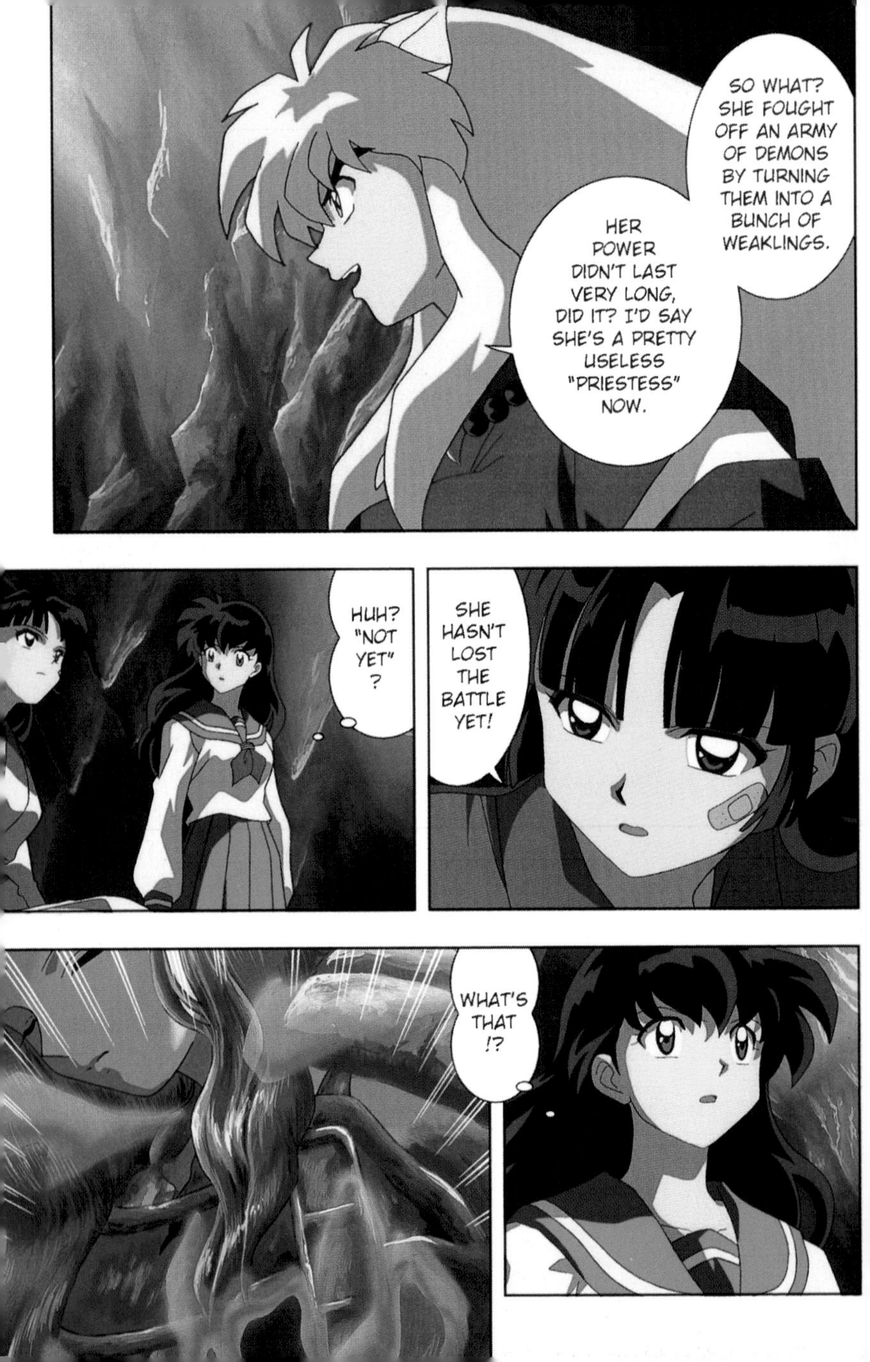
SO WHAT? SHE FOUGHT OFF AN ARMY OF DEMONS BY TURNING THEM INTO A BUNCH OF WEAKLINGS.
HER POWER DIDN'T LAST VERY LONG, DID IT? I'D SAY SHE'S A PRETTY USELESS "PRIESTESS" NOW.
SHE HASN'T LOST THE BATTLE YET!
HUH? "NOT YET" ?
WHAT'S THAT !?

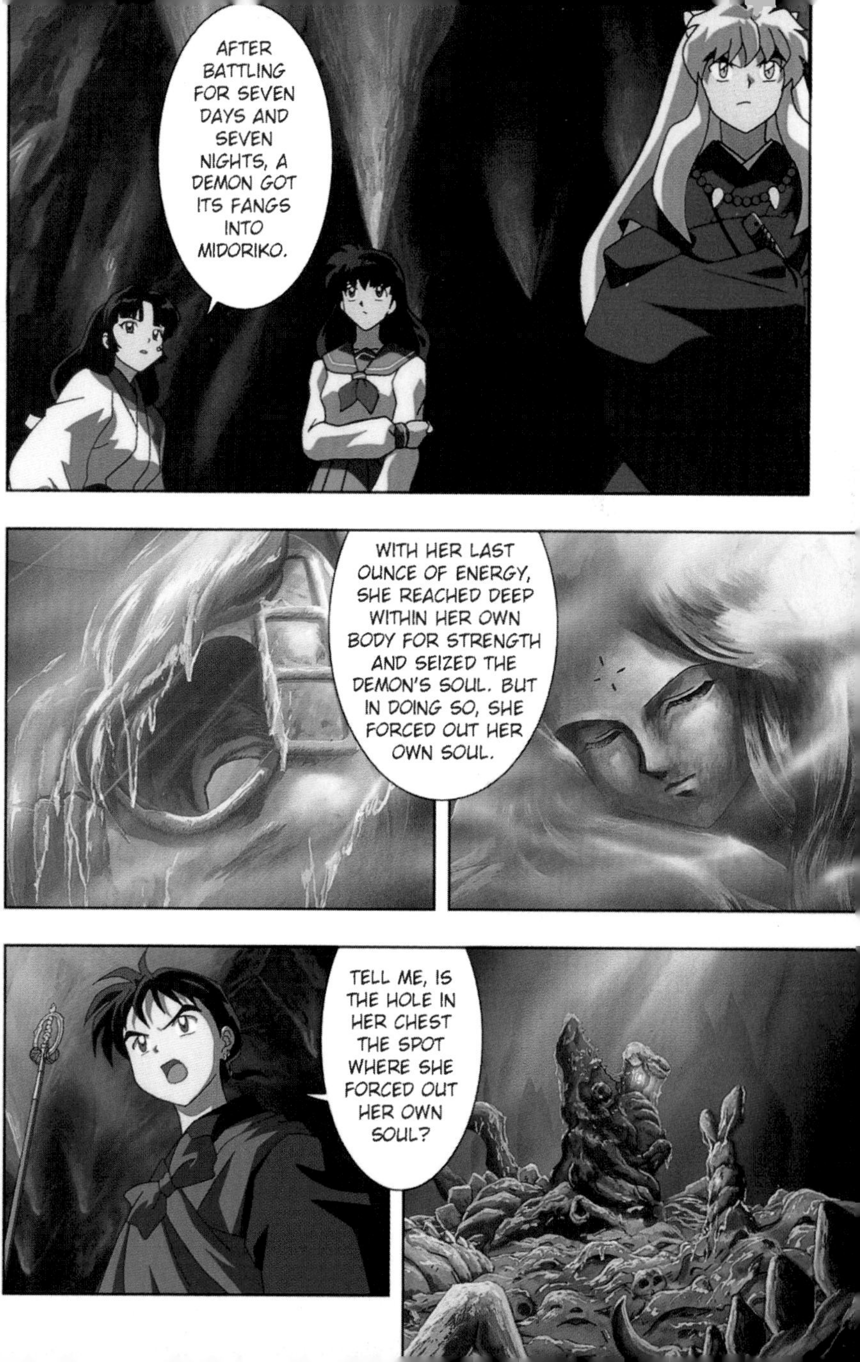
AFTER BATTLING FOR SEVEN DAYS AND SEVEN NIGHTS, A DEMON GOT ITS FANGS INTO MIDORIKO.
WITH HER LAST OUNCE OF ENERGY, SHE REACHED DEEP WITHIN HER OWN BODY FOR STRENGTH AND SEIZED THE DEMON'S SOUL. BUT IN DOING SO, SHE FORCED OUT HER OWN SOUL.
TELL ME, IS THE HOLE IN HER CHEST THE SPOT WHERE SHE FORCED OUT HER OWN SOUL?

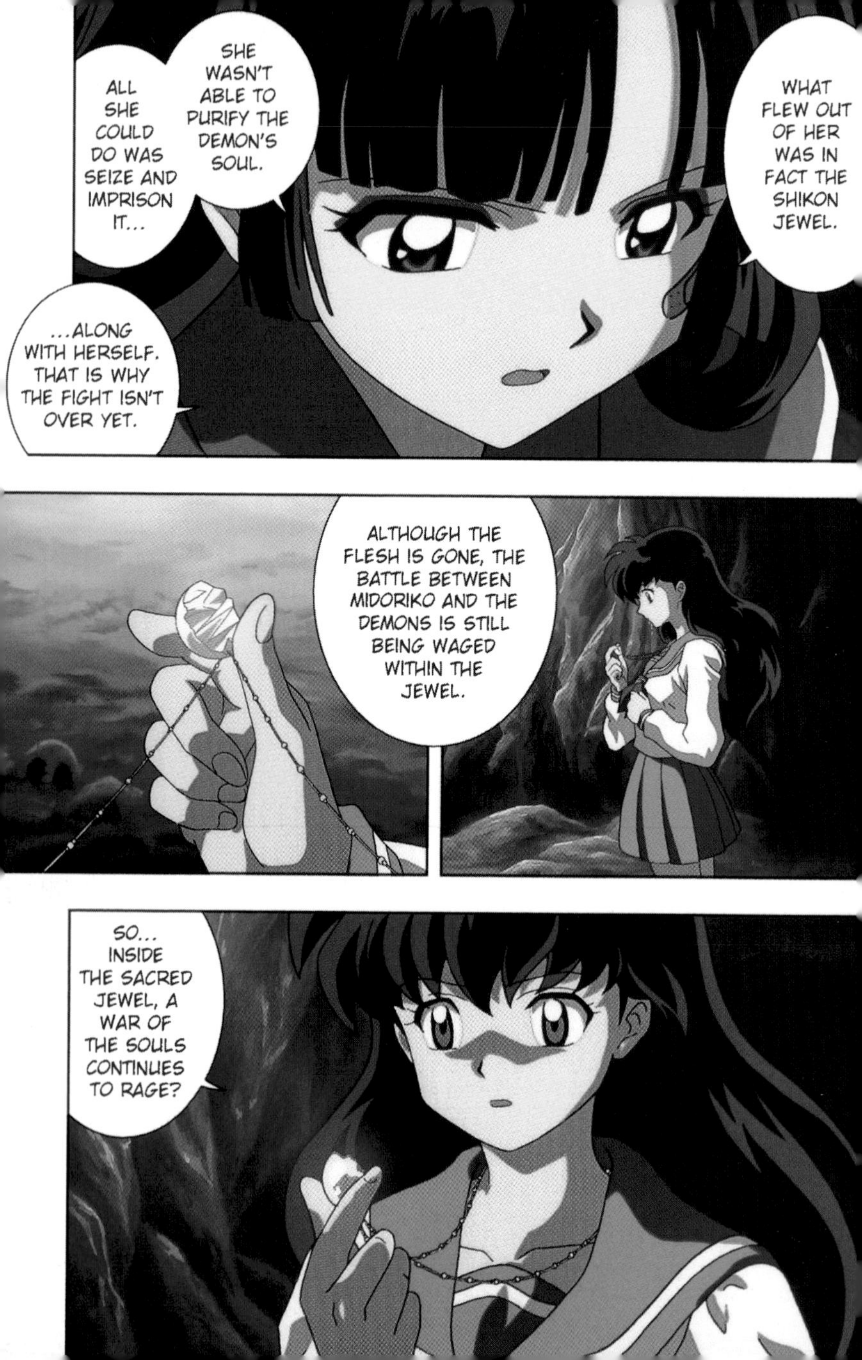
WHAT FLEW OUT OF HER WAS IN FACT THE SHIKON JEWEL.
SHE WASN'T ABLE TO PURIFY THE DEMON'S SOUL.
ALL SHE COULD DO WAS SEIZE AND IMPRISON IT...
...ALONG WITH HERSELF. THAT IS WHY THE FIGHT ISN'T OVER YET.
ALTHOUGH THE FLESH IS GONE, THE BATTLE BETWEEN MIDORIKO AND THE DEMONS IS STILL BEING WAGED WITHIN THE JEWEL.
SO... INSIDE THE SACRED JEWEL, A WAR OF THE SOULS CONTINUES TO RAGE?

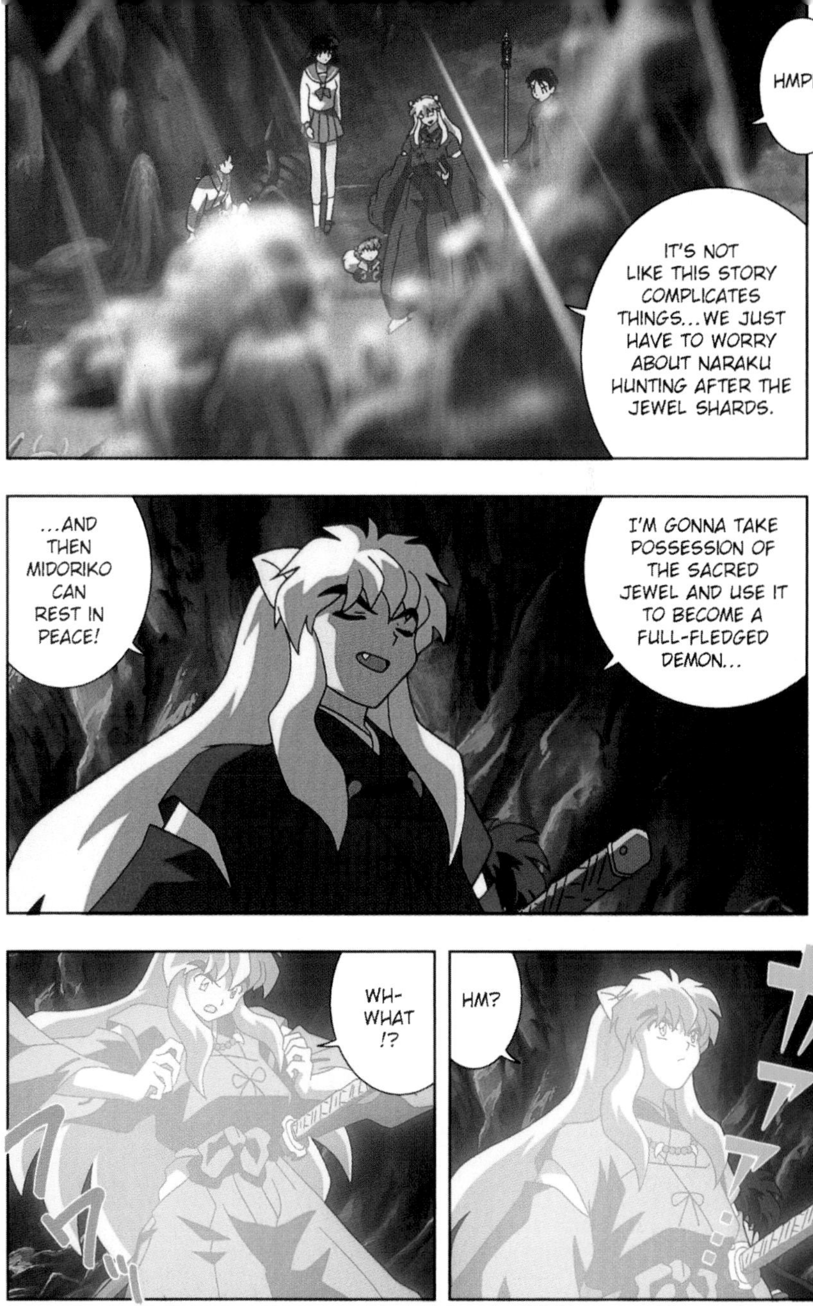
HMPH!
IT'S NOT LIKE THIS STORY COMPLICATES THINGS...WE JUST HAVE TO WORRY ABOUT NARAKU HUNTING AFTER THE JEWEL SHARDS.
I'M GONNA TAKE POSSESSION OF THE SACRED JEWEL AND USE IT TO BECOME A FULL-FLEDGED DEMON...
...AND THEN MIDORIKO CAN REST IN PEACE!
HM?
WH- WHAT !?

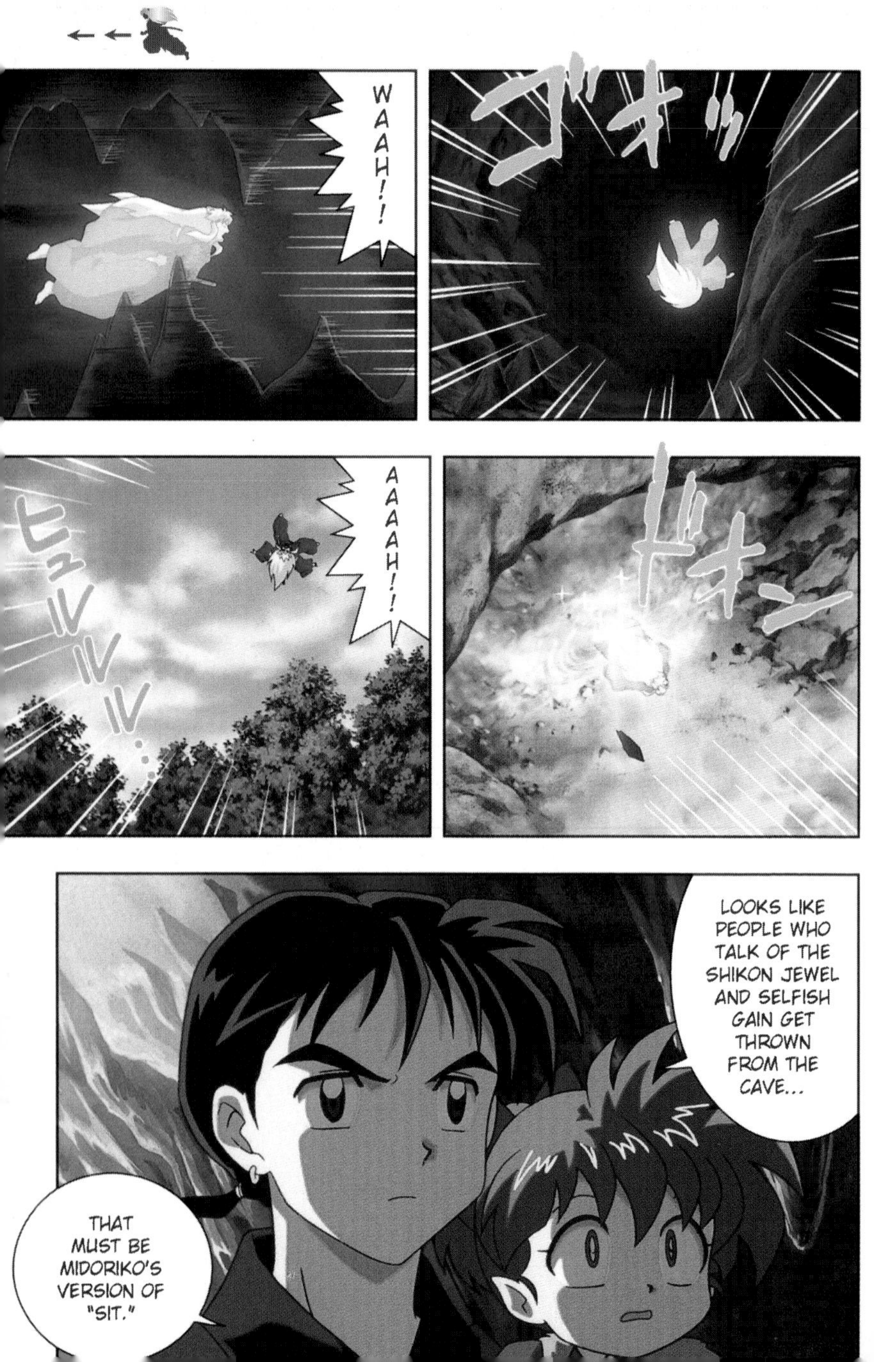
ゴキッ
WAAAH!!
ドォン
AAAAH!!
ヒュルルル…
LOOKS LIKE PEOPLE WHO TALK OF THE SHIKON JEWEL AND SELFISH GAIN GET THROWN FROM THE CAVE...
THAT MUST BE MIDORIKO'S VERSION OF "SIT."

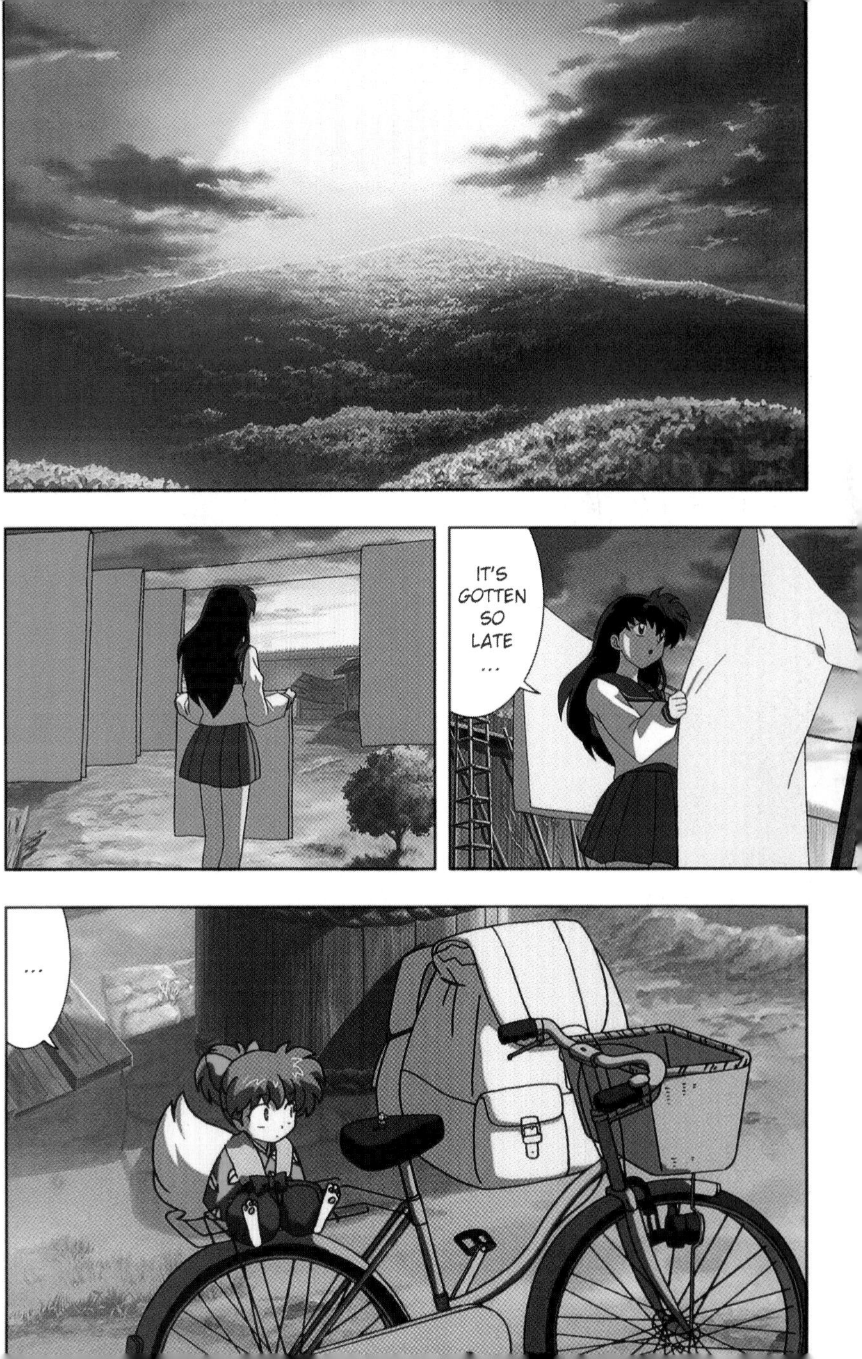
IT'S GOTTEN SO LATE ...
...

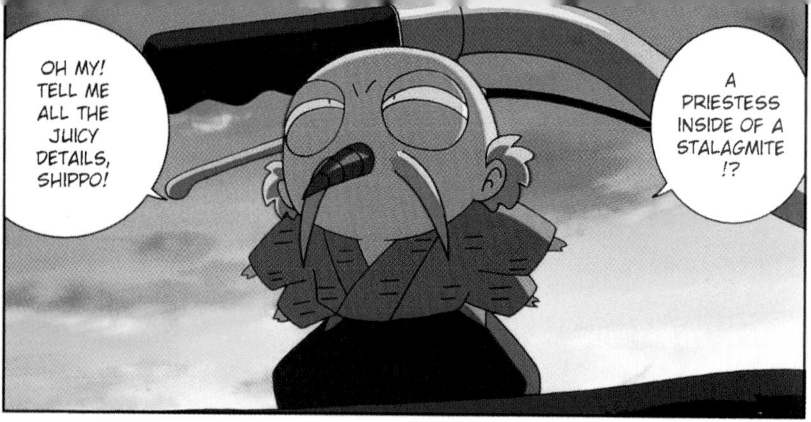
A PRIESTESS INSIDE OF A STALAGMITE !?
OH MY! TELL ME ALL THE JUICY DETAILS, SHIPPO!
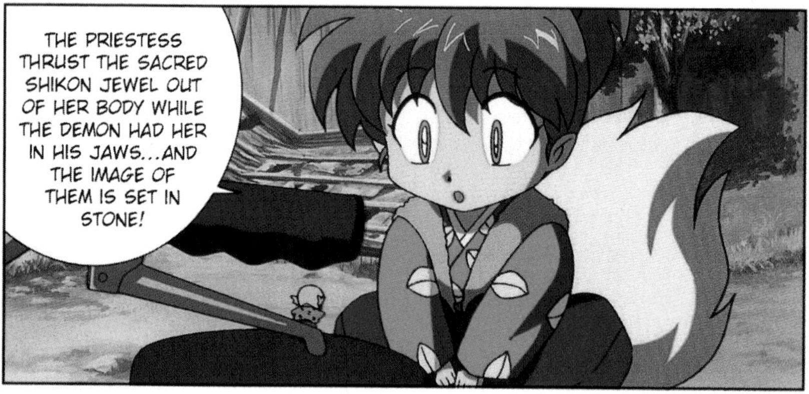
THE PRIESTESS THRUST THE SACRED SHIKON JEWEL OUT OF HER BODY WHILE THE DEMON HAD HER IN HIS JAWS...AND THE IMAGE OF THEM IS SET IN STONE!
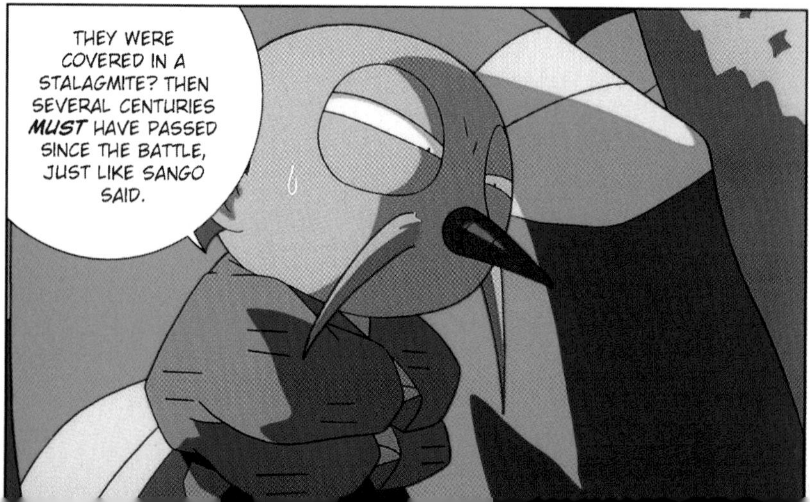
THEY WERE COVERED IN A STALAGMITE? THEN SEVERAL CENTURIES ***MUST*** HAVE PASSED SINCE THE BATTLE, JUST LIKE SANGO SAID.

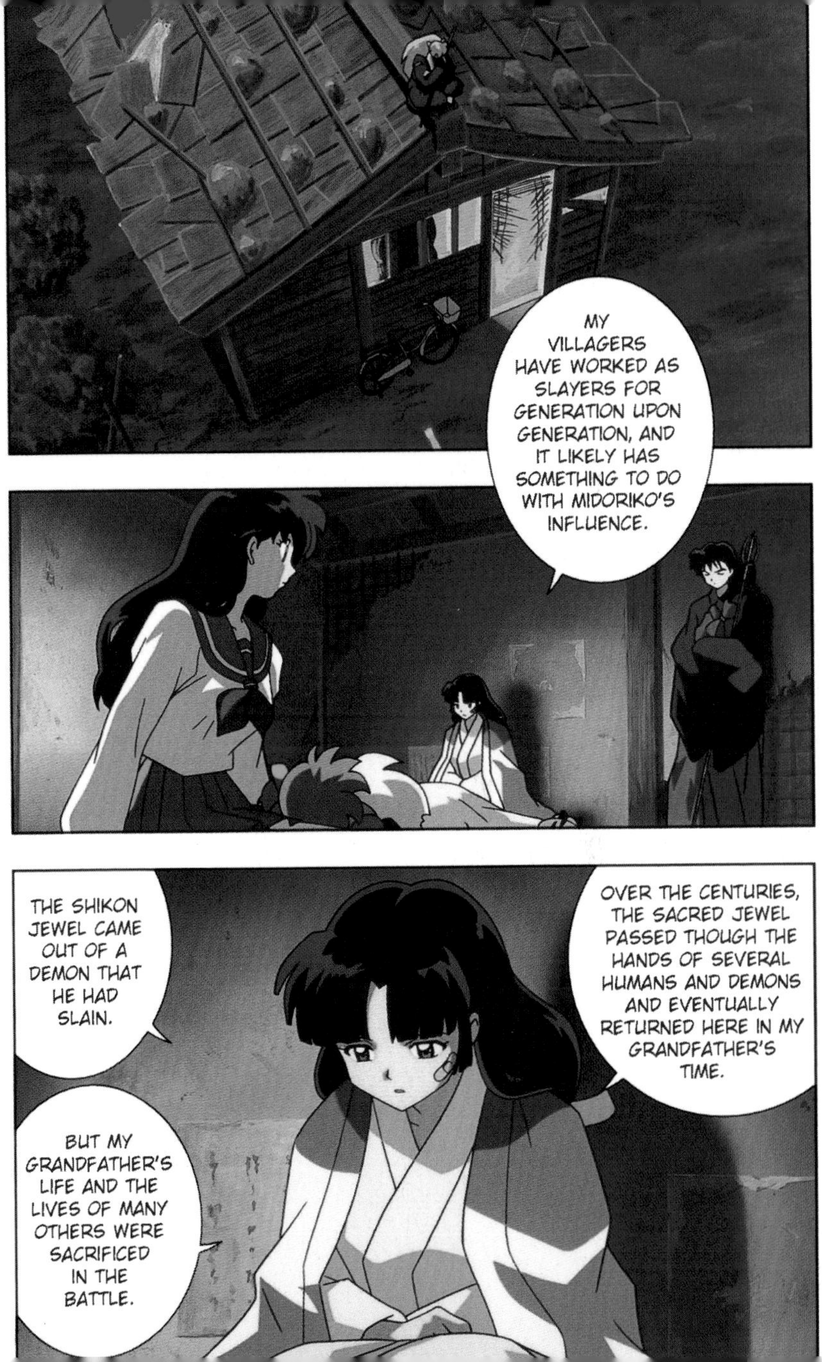
MY VILLAGERS HAVE WORKED AS SLAYERS FOR GENERATION UPON GENERATION, AND IT LIKELY HAS SOMETHING TO DO WITH MIDORIKO'S INFLUENCE.
OVER THE CENTURIES, THE SACRED JEWEL PASSED THOUGH THE HANDS OF SEVERAL HUMANS AND DEMONS AND EVENTUALLY RETURNED HERE IN MY GRANDFATHER'S TIME.
THE SHIKON JEWEL CAME OUT OF A DEMON THAT HE HAD SLAIN.
BUT MY GRANDFATHER'S LIFE AND THE LIVES OF MANY OTHERS WERE SACRIFICED IN THE BATTLE.

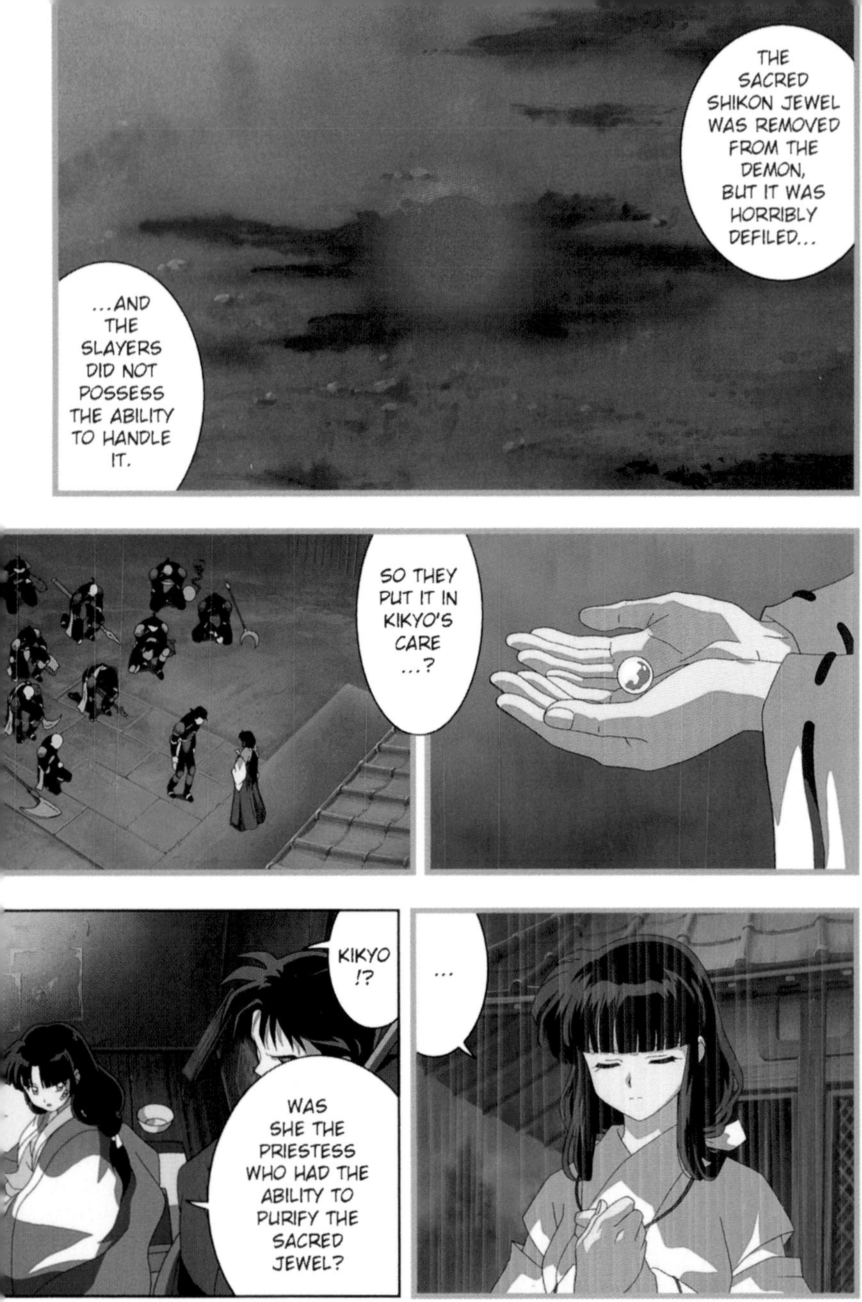
THE SACRED SHIKON JEWEL WAS REMOVED FROM THE DEMON, BUT IT WAS HORRIBLY DEFILED...
...AND THE SLAYERS DID NOT POSSESS THE ABILITY TO HANDLE IT.
SO THEY PUT IT IN KIKYO'S CARE ...?
...
KIKYO !?
WAS SHE THE PRIESTESS WHO HAD THE ABILITY TO PURIFY THE SACRED JEWEL?

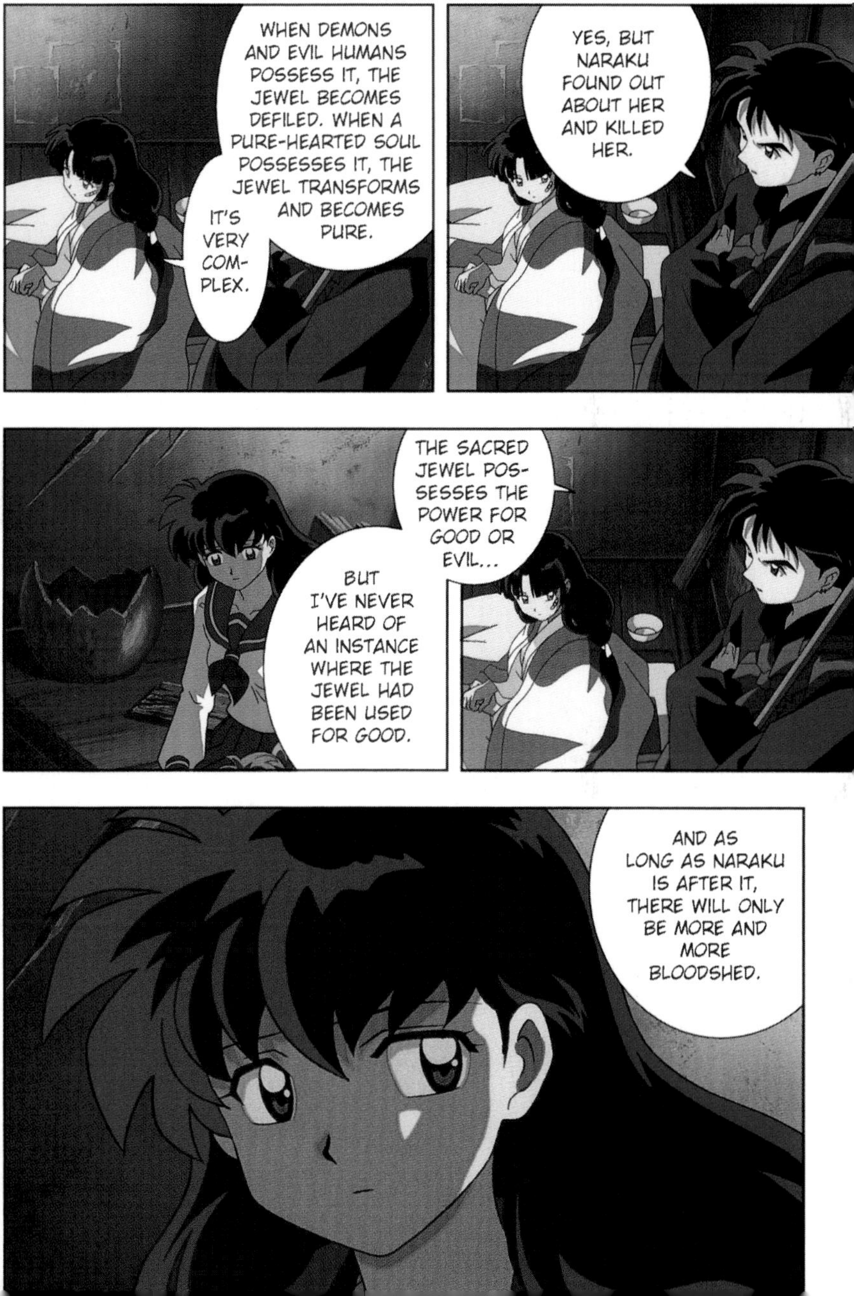
YES, BUT NARAKU FOUND OUT ABOUT HER AND KILLED HER.
WHEN DEMONS AND EVIL HUMANS POSSESS IT, THE JEWEL BECOMES DEFILED. WHEN A PURE-HEARTED SOUL POSSESSES IT, THE JEWEL TRANSFORMS AND BECOMES PURE.
IT'S VERY COM-PLEX.
THE SACRED JEWEL POS-SESSES THE POWER FOR GOOD OR EVIL...
BUT I'VE NEVER HEARD OF AN INSTANCE WHERE THE JEWEL HAD BEEN USED FOR GOOD.
AND AS LONG AS NARAKU IS AFTER IT, THERE WILL ONLY BE MORE AND MORE BLOODSHED.

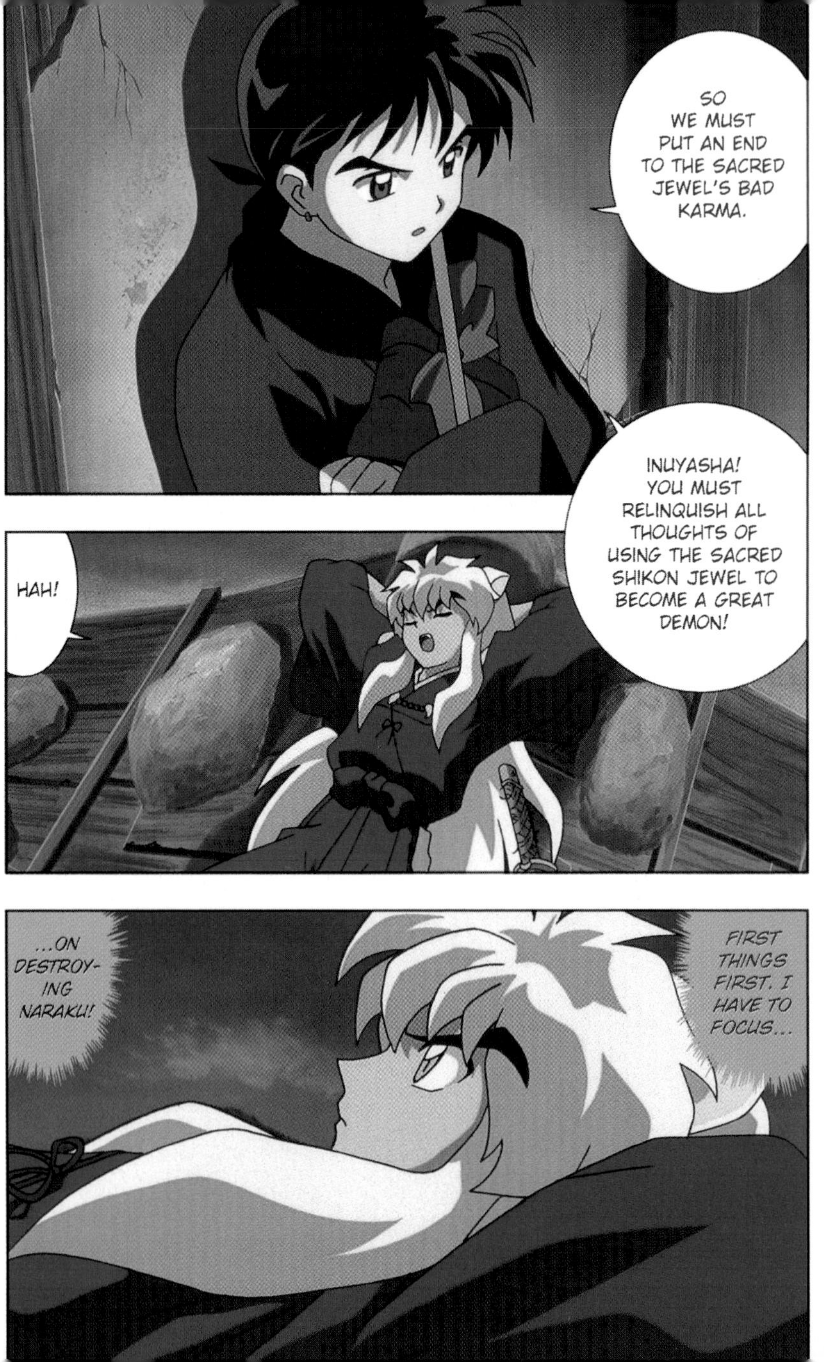
SO WE MUST PUT AN END TO THE SACRED JEWEL'S BAD KARMA.
INUYASHA! YOU MUST RELINQUISH ALL THOUGHTS OF USING THE SACRED SHIKON JEWEL TO BECOME A GREAT DEMON!
HAH!
FIRST THINGS FIRST. I HAVE TO FOCUS...
...ON DESTROYING NARAKU!

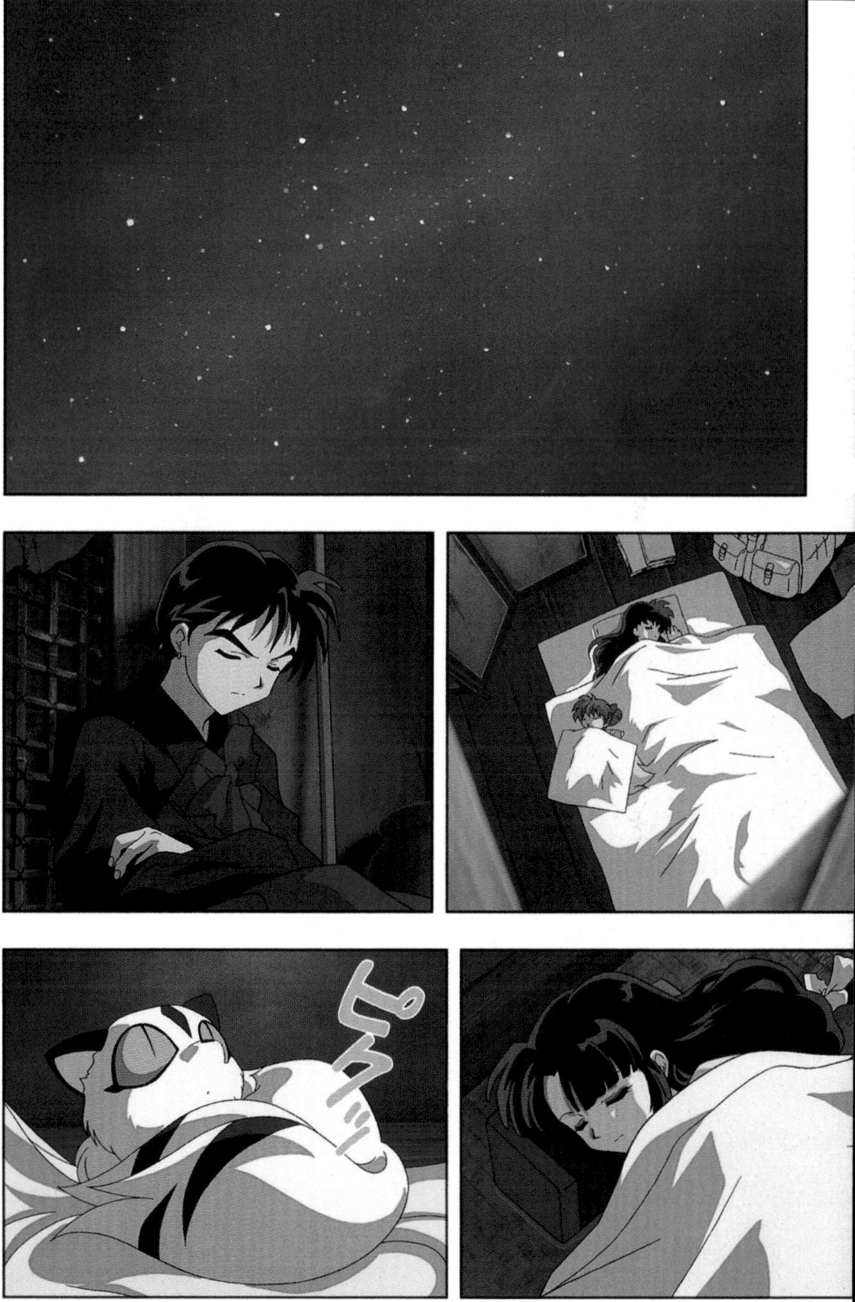
ピク…

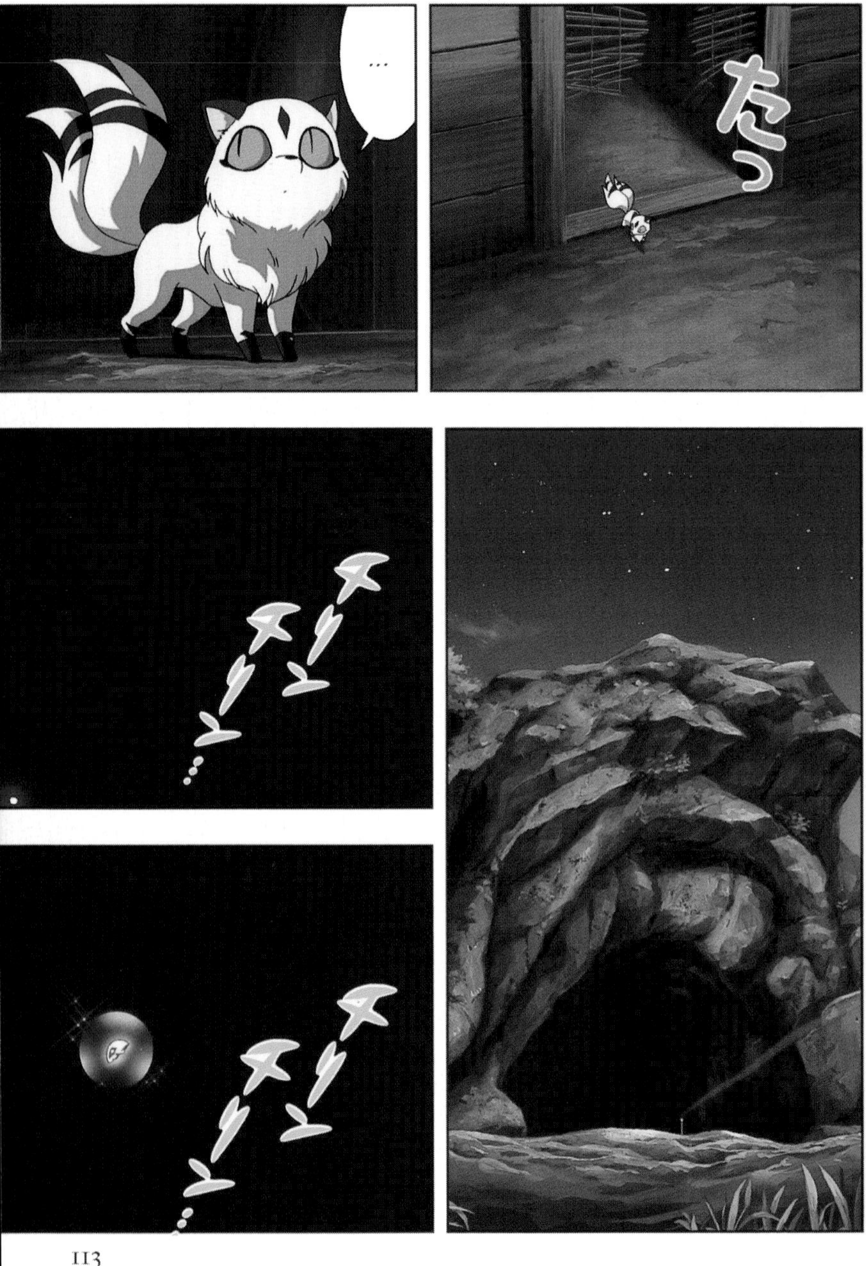
たっ
…

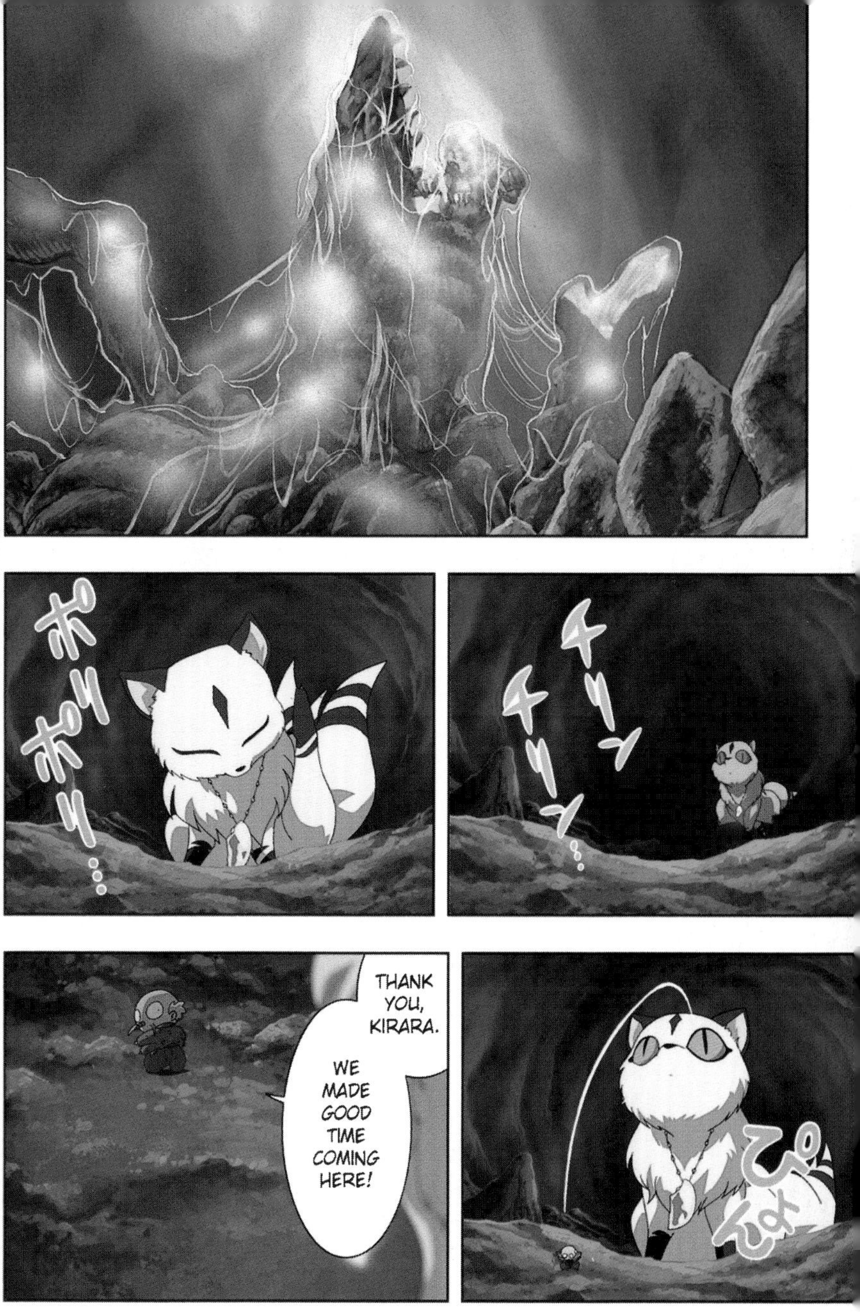
チーン チーン…
ポリポリ…
ぴょん
THANK YOU, KIRARA.
WE MADE GOOD TIME COMING HERE!

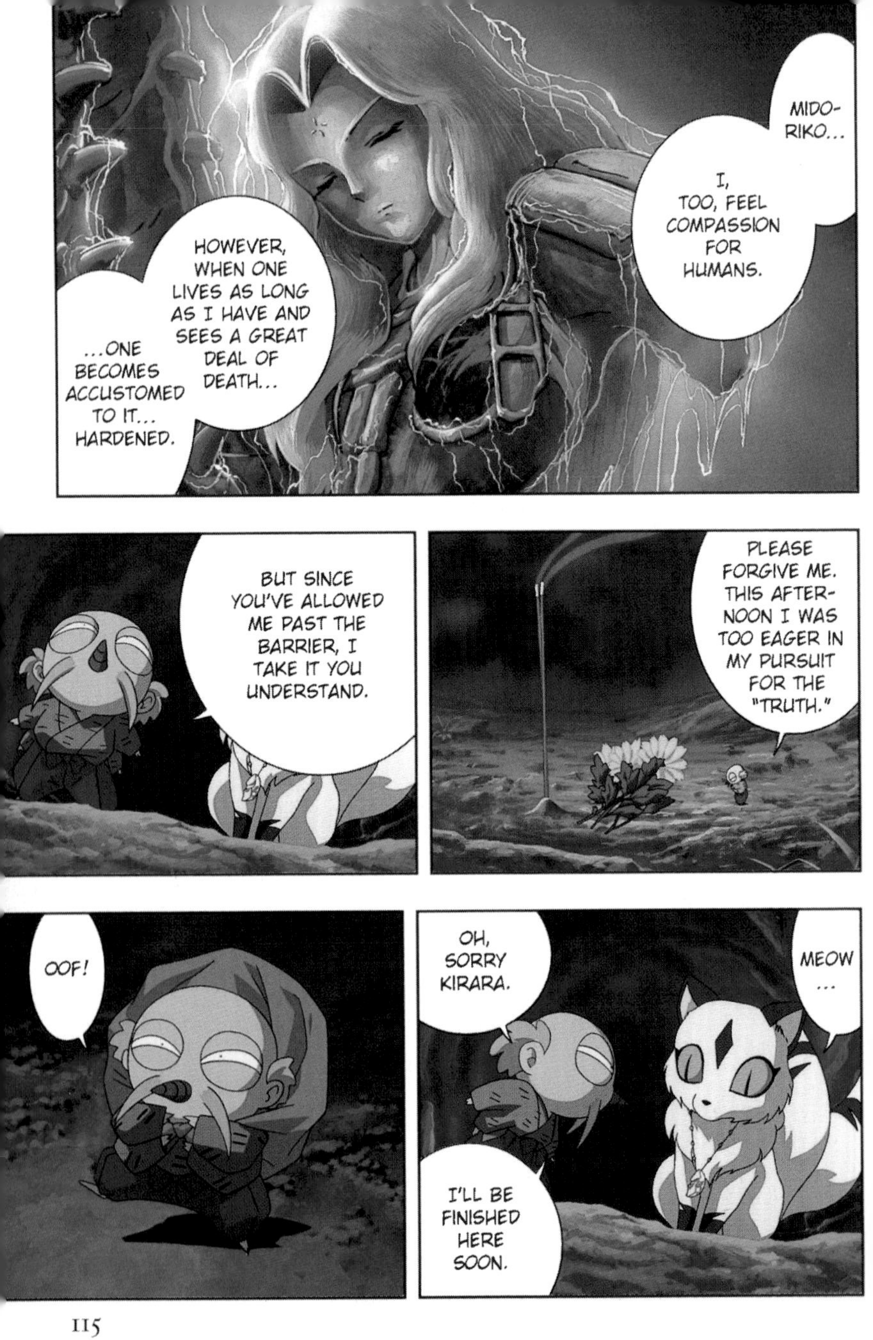
MIDO-RIKO...
I, TOO, FEEL COMPASSION FOR HUMANS.
HOWEVER, WHEN ONE LIVES AS LONG AS I HAVE AND SEES A GREAT DEAL OF DEATH...
...ONE BECOMES ACCUSTOMED TO IT... HARDENED.
PLEASE FORGIVE ME. THIS AFTER-NOON I WAS TOO EAGER IN MY PURSUIT FOR THE "TRUTH."
BUT SINCE YOU'VE ALLOWED ME PAST THE BARRIER, I TAKE IT YOU UNDERSTAND.
MEOW ...
OH, SORRY KIRARA.
I'LL BE FINISHED HERE SOON.
OOF!

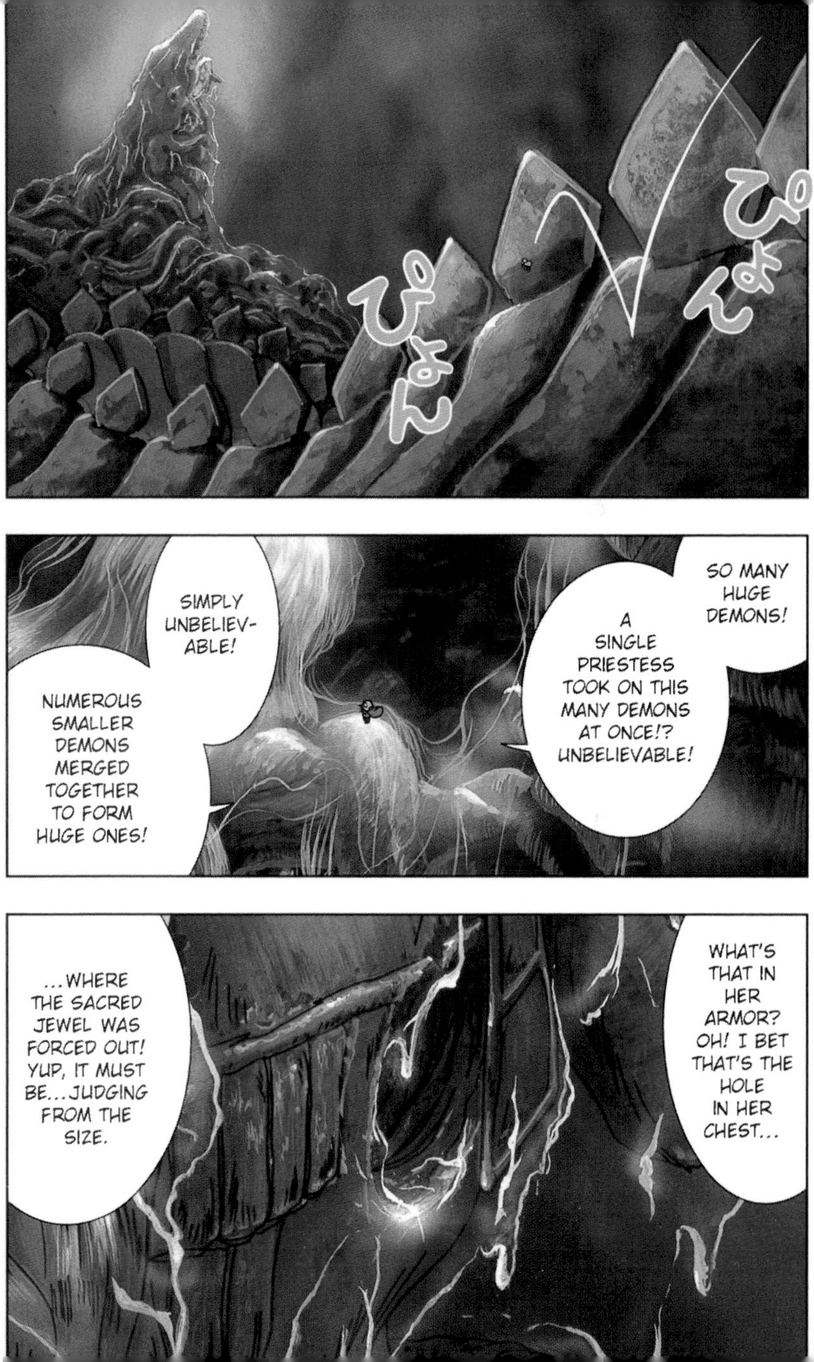
ぴょん
ぴょん
SO MANY HUGE DEMONS!
A SINGLE PRIESTESS TOOK ON THIS MANY DEMONS AT ONCE!? UNBELIEVABLE!
SIMPLY UNBELIEV-ABLE!
NUMEROUS SMALLER DEMONS MERGED TOGETHER TO FORM HUGE ONES!
WHAT'S THAT IN HER ARMOR? OH! I BET THAT'S THE HOLE IN HER CHEST...
...WHERE THE SACRED JEWEL WAS FORCED OUT! YUP, IT MUST BE...JUDGING FROM THE SIZE.

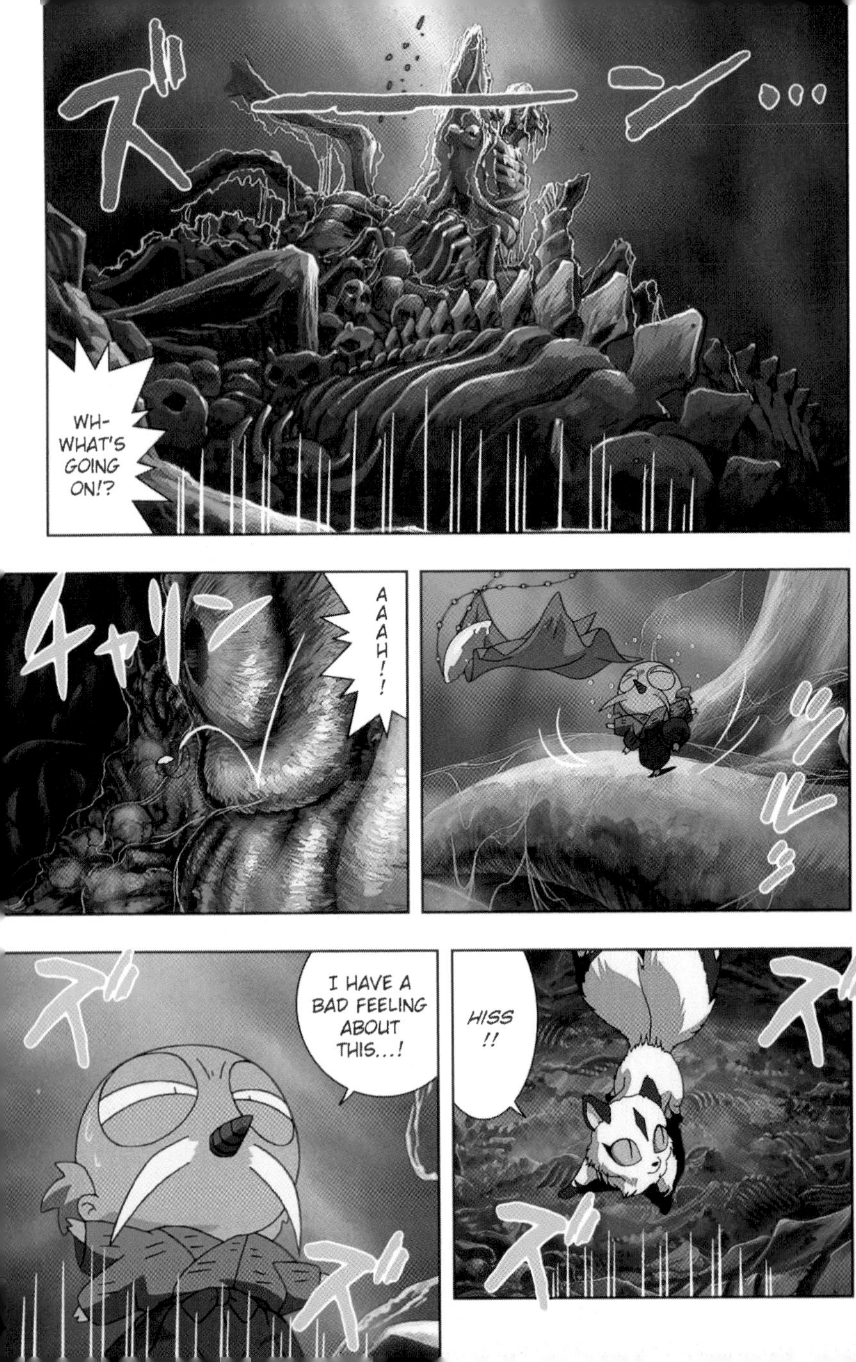
WH- WHAT'S GOING ON!?
AAAAH!!
HISS !!
I HAVE A BAD FEELING ABOUT THIS...!

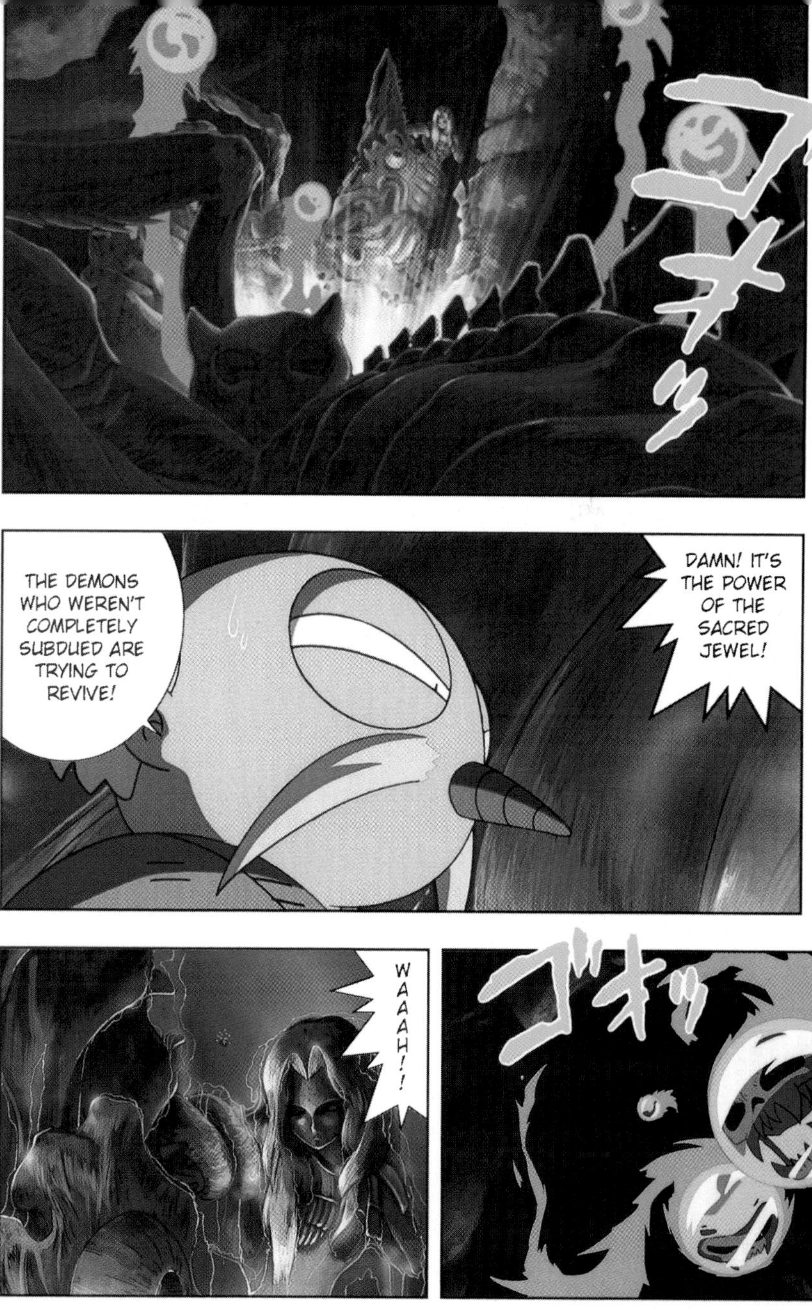
DAMN! IT'S THE POWER OF THE SACRED JEWEL!
THE DEMONS WHO WEREN'T COMPLETELY SUBDUED ARE TRYING TO REVIVE!
WAAAAH!!

ドオッ
ストッ
ゴオッ
GRRR...

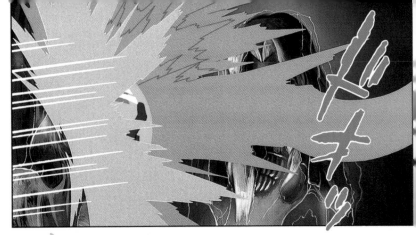

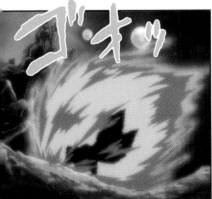

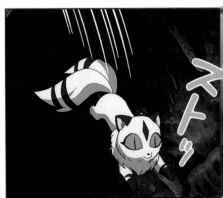

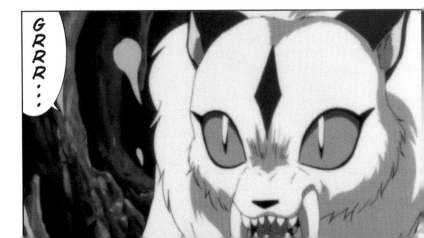

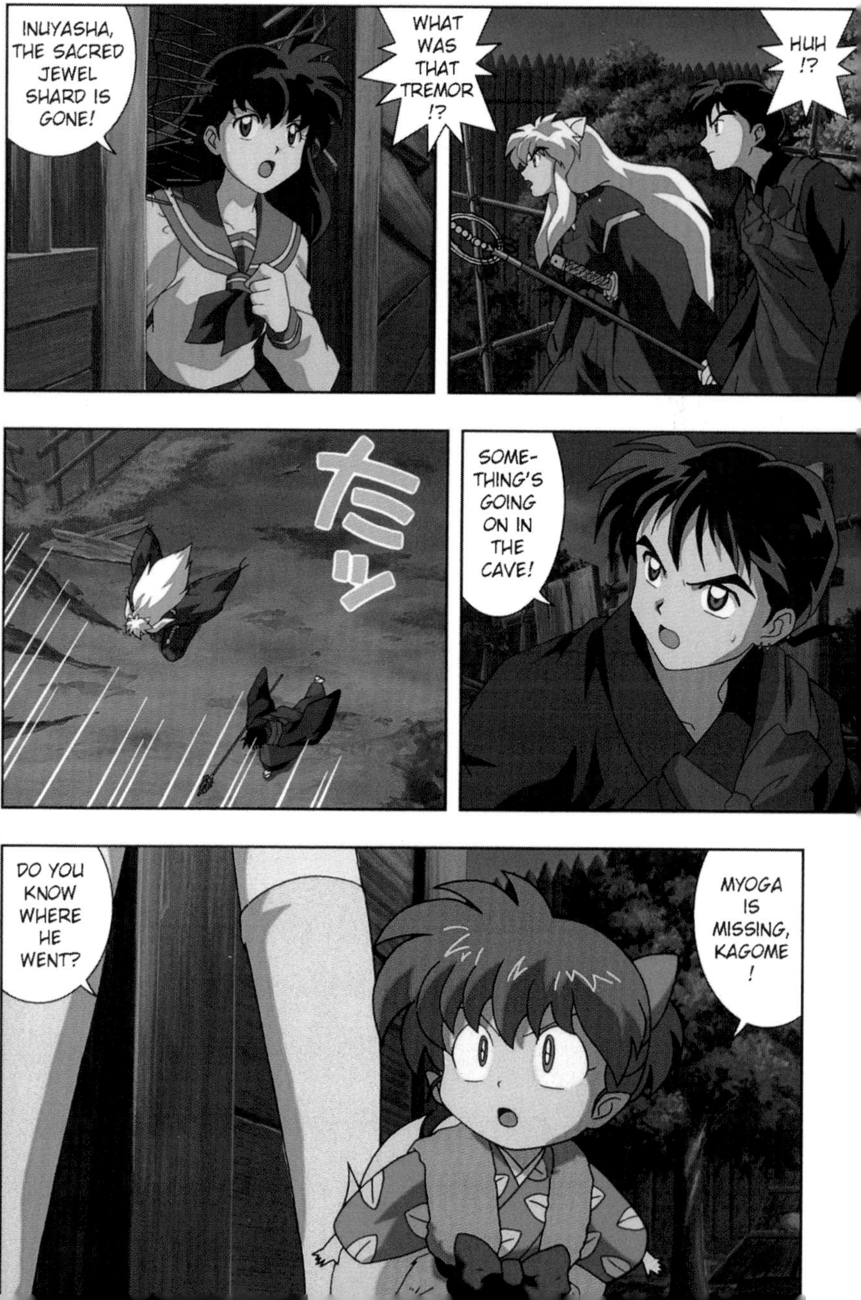
HUH !?
WHAT WAS THAT TREMOR !?
INUYASHA, THE SACRED JEWEL SHARD IS GONE!
SOME-THING'S GOING ON IN THE CAVE!
たッ
MYOGA IS MISSING, KAGOME !
DO YOU KNOW WHERE HE WENT?

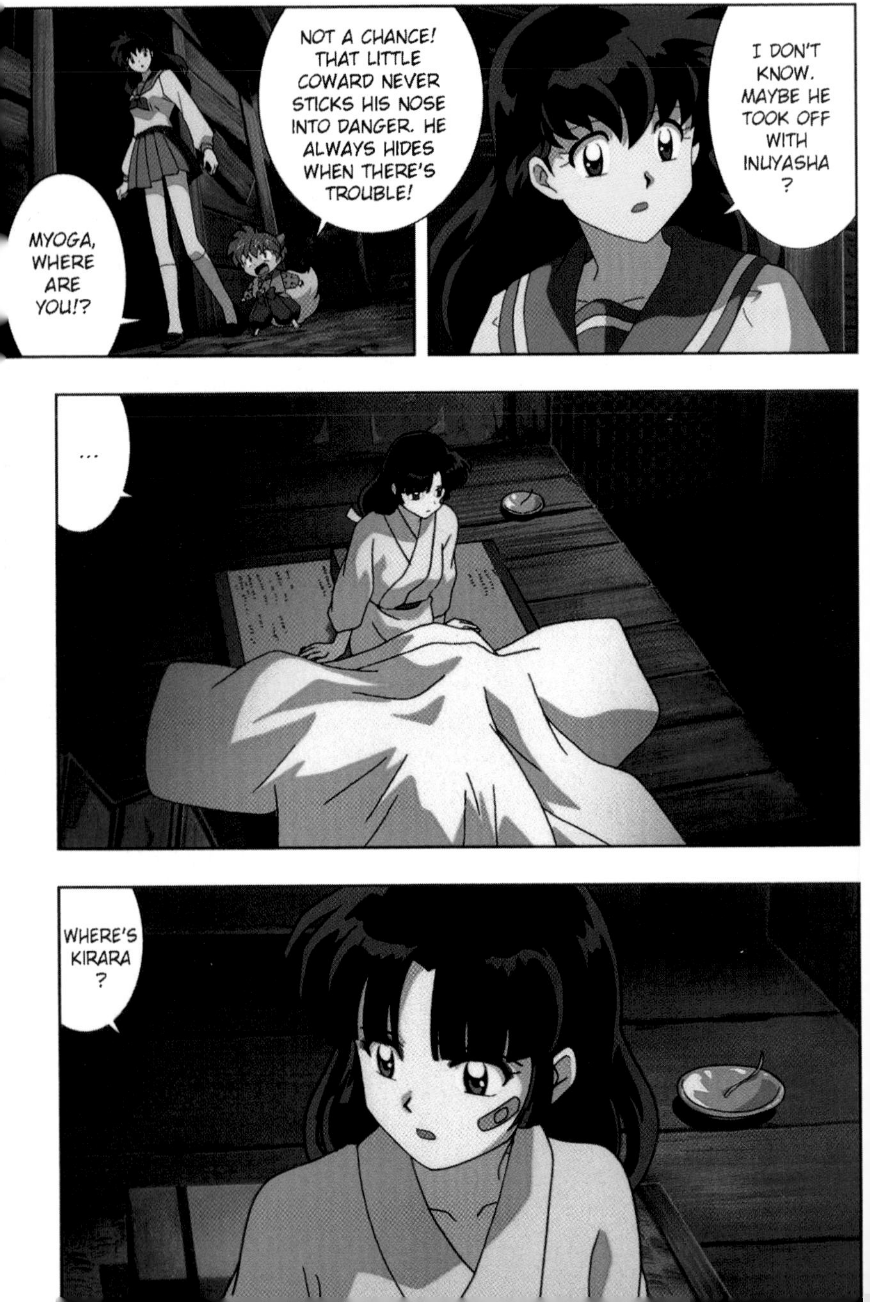
I DON'T KNOW. MAYBE HE TOOK OFF WITH INUYASHA?
NOT A CHANCE! THAT LITTLE COWARD NEVER STICKS HIS NOSE INTO DANGER. HE ALWAYS HIDES WHEN THERE'S TROUBLE!
MYOGA, WHERE ARE YOU!?
...
WHERE'S KIRARA?

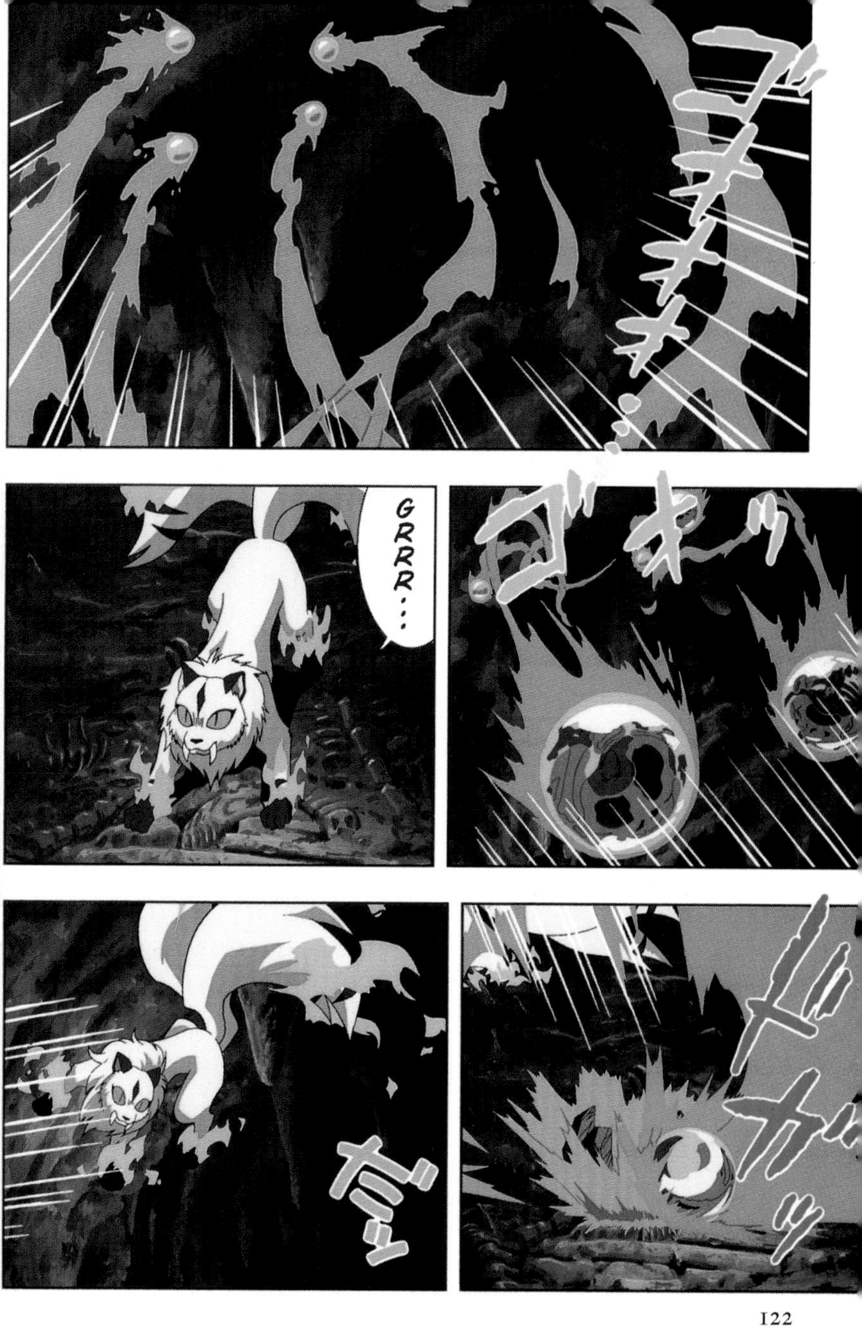
GRRR...

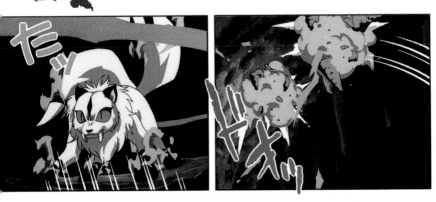

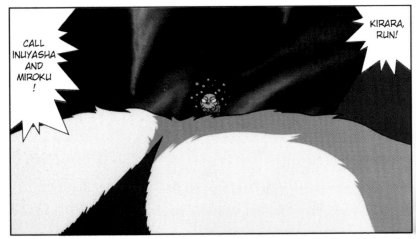

CALL
INUYASHA
AND
MIROKU
!

KIRARA,
RUN!

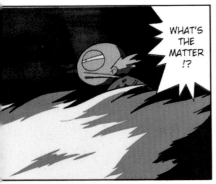

WHAT'S
THE
MATTER
!?

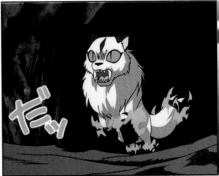

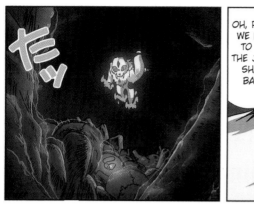

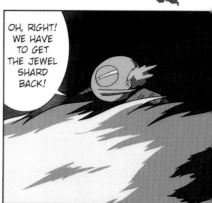

OH, RIGHT! WE HAVE TO GET THE JEWEL SHARD BACK!

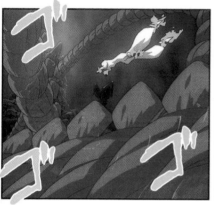

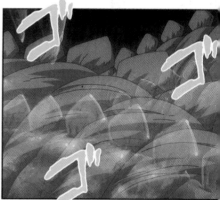

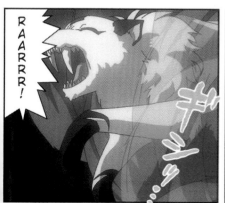

RAARRR!

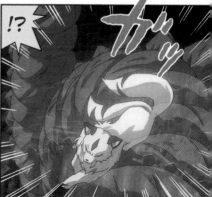

!?

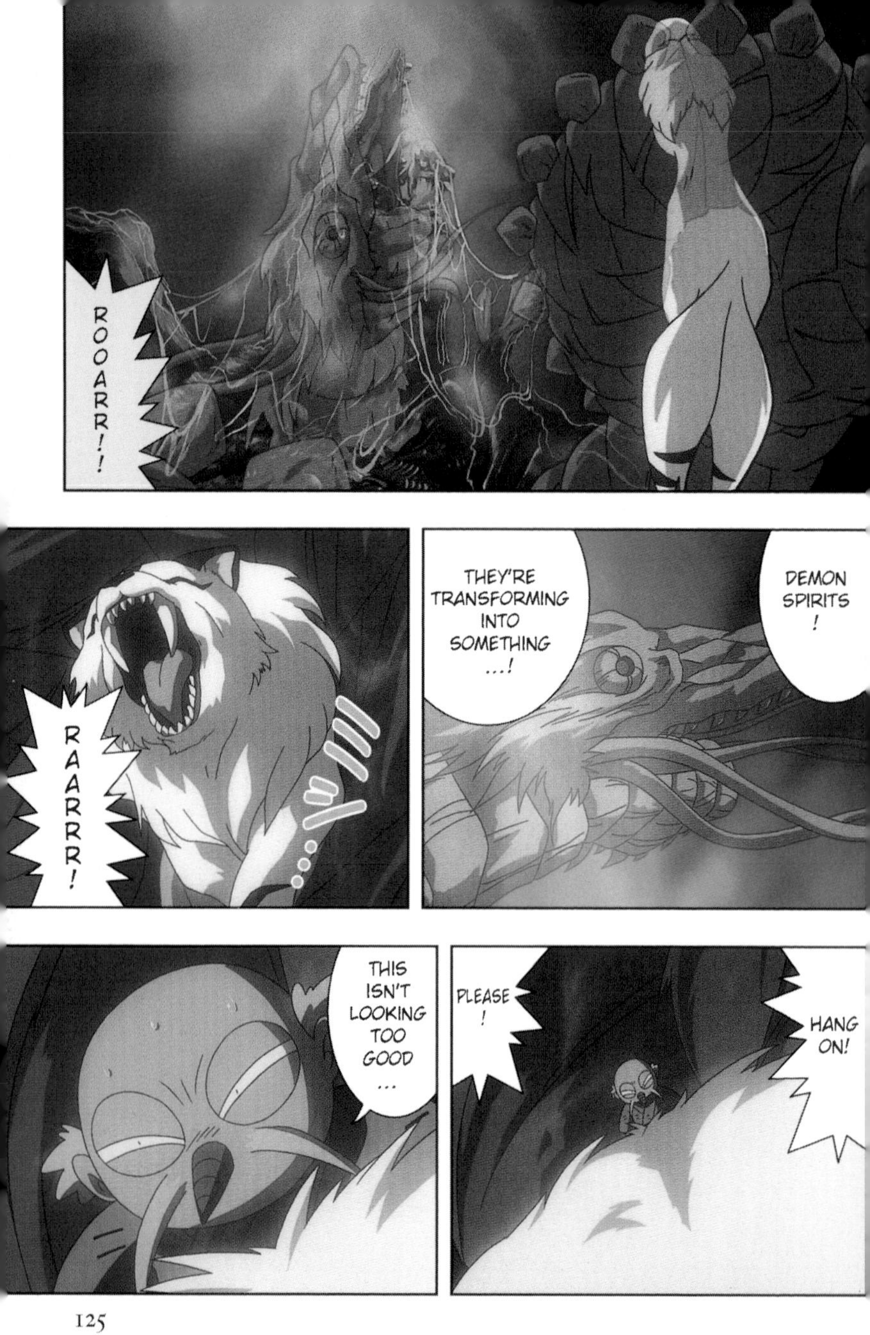
ROOARR!!
DEMON SPIRITS!
THEY'RE TRANSFORMING INTO SOMETHING...!
RAARRR!
HANG ON!
PLEASE!
THIS ISN'T LOOKING TOO GOOD...

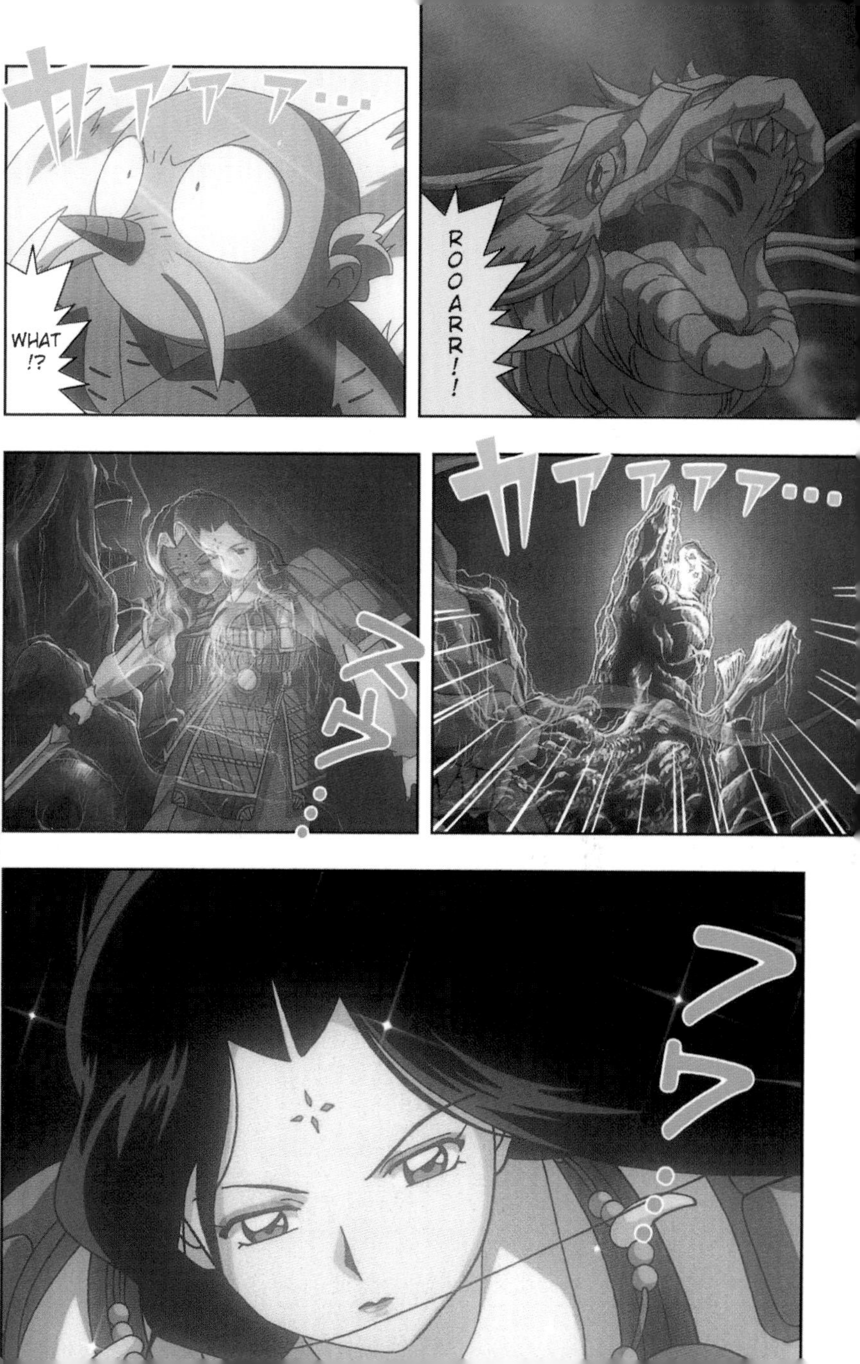

ROOARR!!
カァァァ...
WHAT !?
カァァァァァ...

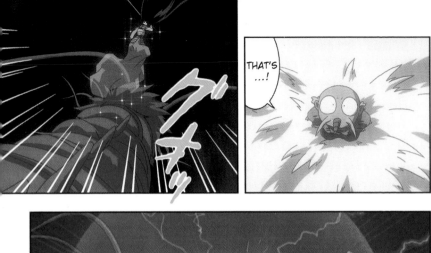

THAT'S
...!

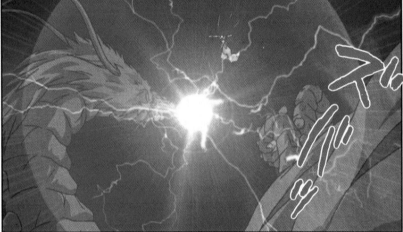

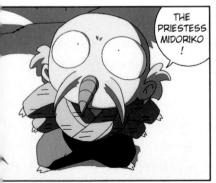

THE PRIESTESS MIDORIKO!

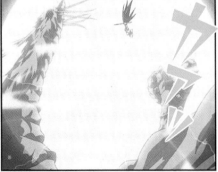

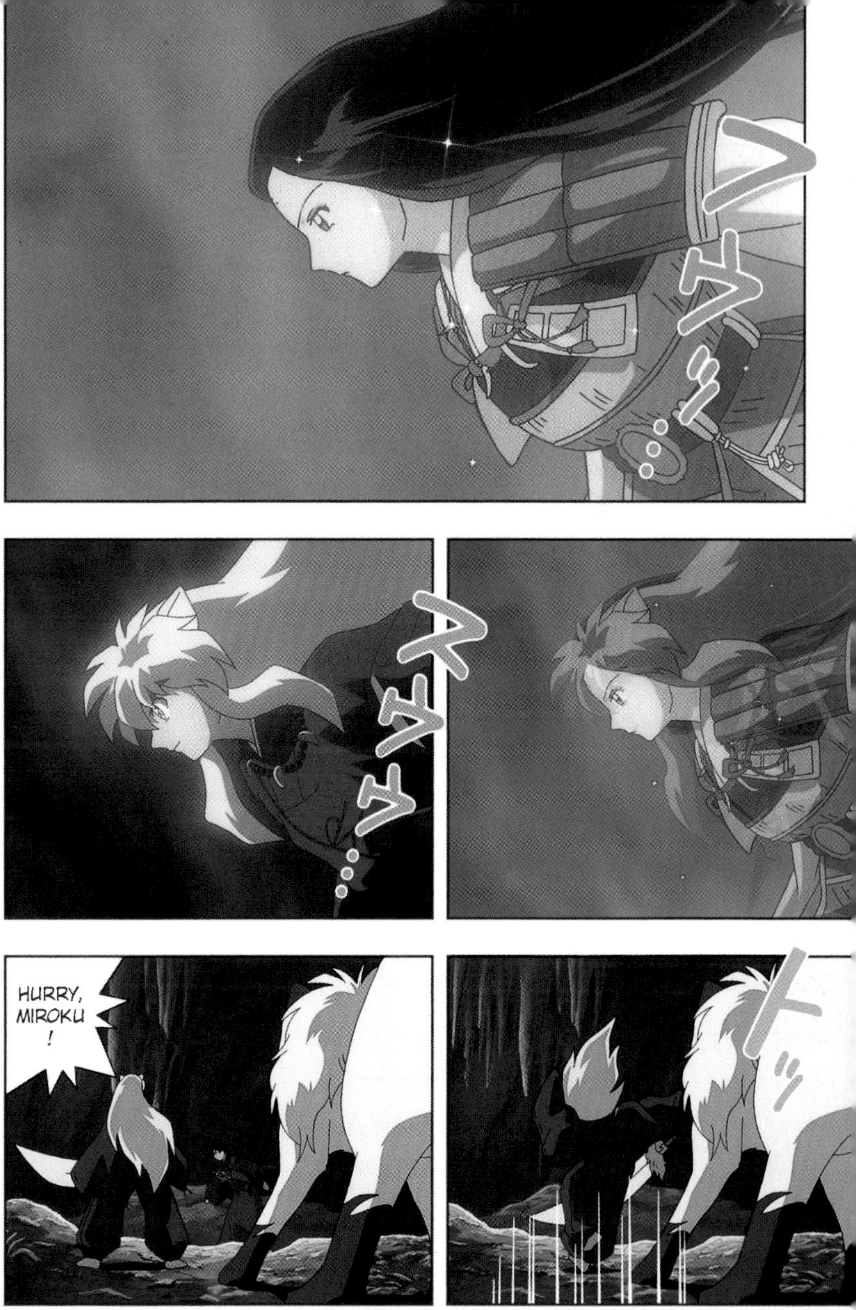
HURRY, MIROKU!

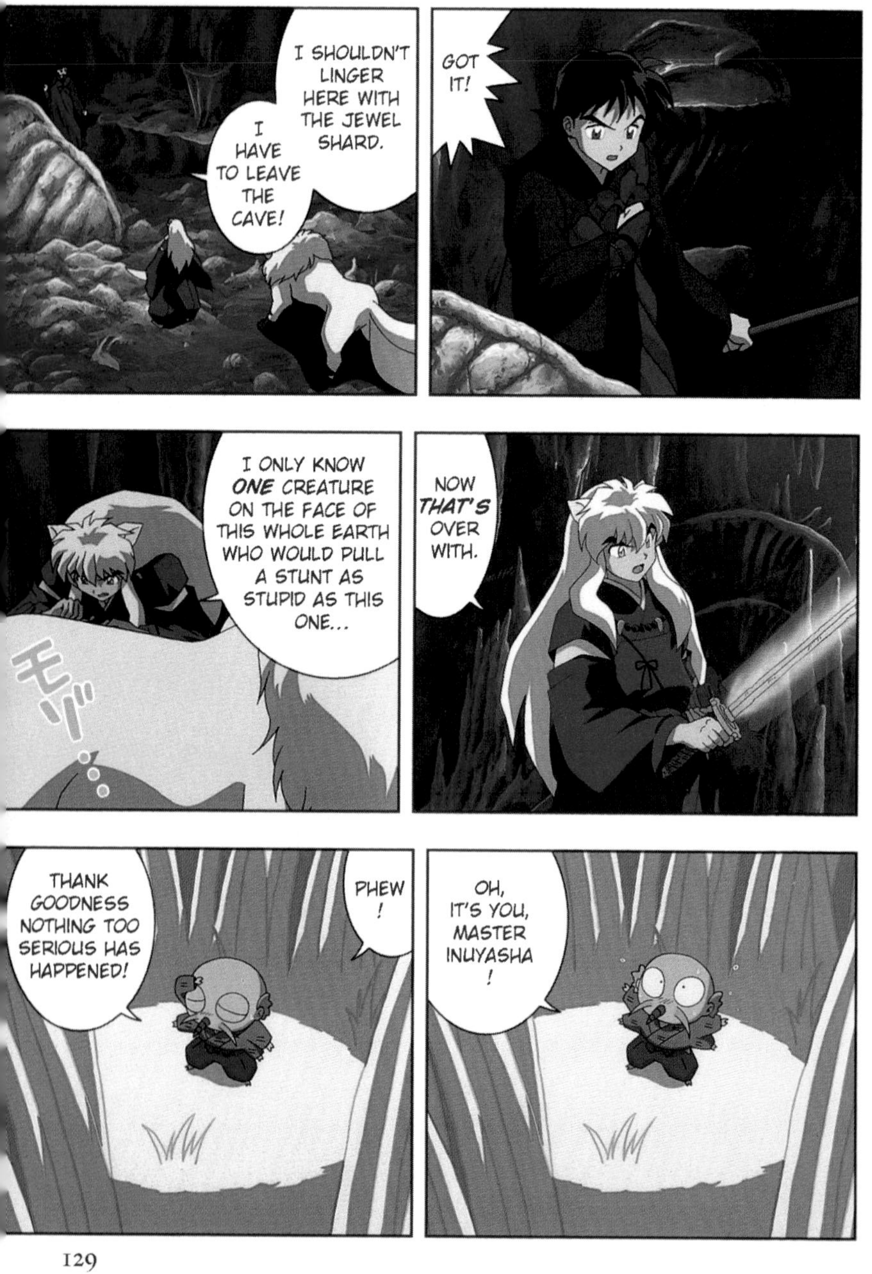
GOT IT!
I SHOULDN'T LINGER HERE WITH THE JEWEL SHARD.
I HAVE TO LEAVE THE CAVE!
NOW *THAT'S* OVER WITH.
I ONLY KNOW *ONE* CREATURE ON THE FACE OF THIS WHOLE EARTH WHO WOULD PULL A STUNT AS STUPID AS THIS ONE...
モゾ
OH, IT'S YOU, MASTER INUYASHA!
PHEW!
THANK GOODNESS NOTHING TOO SERIOUS HAS HAPPENED!

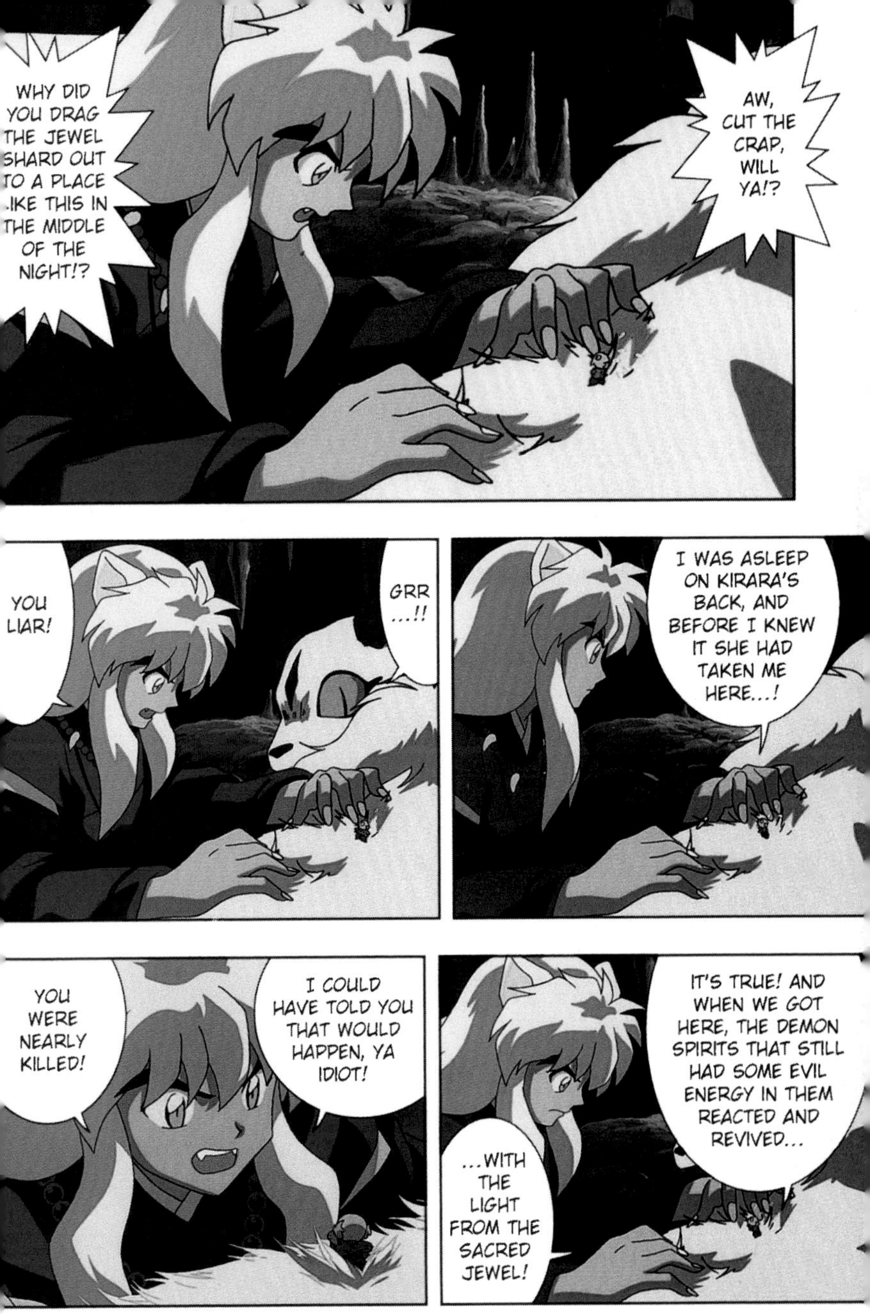
AW, CUT THE CRAP, WILL YA!?
WHY DID YOU DRAG THE JEWEL SHARD OUT TO A PLACE LIKE THIS IN THE MIDDLE OF THE NIGHT!?
I WAS ASLEEP ON KIRARA'S BACK, AND BEFORE I KNEW IT SHE HAD TAKEN ME HERE...!
GRR ...!!
YOU LIAR!
IT'S TRUE! AND WHEN WE GOT HERE, THE DEMON SPIRITS THAT STILL HAD SOME EVIL ENERGY IN THEM REACTED AND REVIVED...
...WITH THE LIGHT FROM THE SACRED JEWEL!
I COULD HAVE TOLD YOU THAT WOULD HAPPEN, YA IDIOT!
YOU WERE NEARLY KILLED!

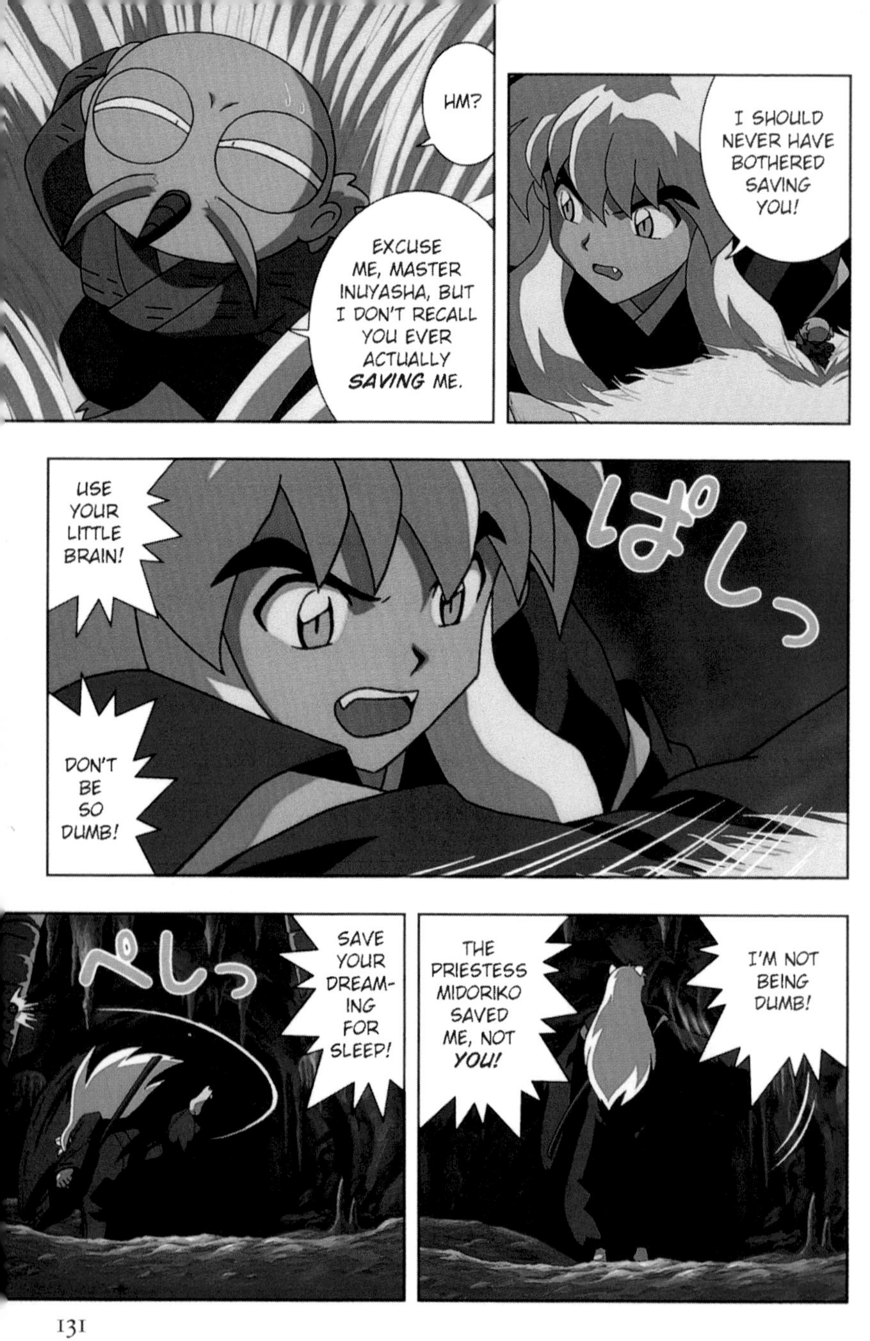
I SHOULD NEVER HAVE BOTHERED SAVING YOU!
HM?
EXCUSE ME, MASTER INUYASHA, BUT I DON'T RECALL YOU EVER ACTUALLY *SAVING* ME.
ぱしっ
USE YOUR LITTLE BRAIN!
DON'T BE SO DUMB!
I'M NOT BEING DUMB!
THE PRIESTESS MIDORIKO SAVED ME, NOT *YOU!*
SAVE YOUR DREAM-ING FOR SLEEP!
ぺしっ

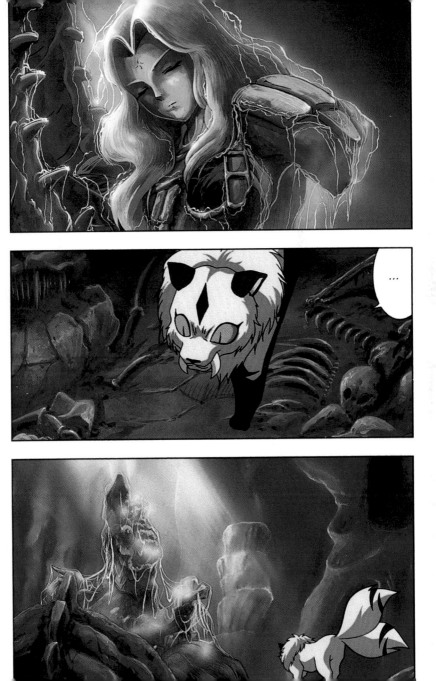

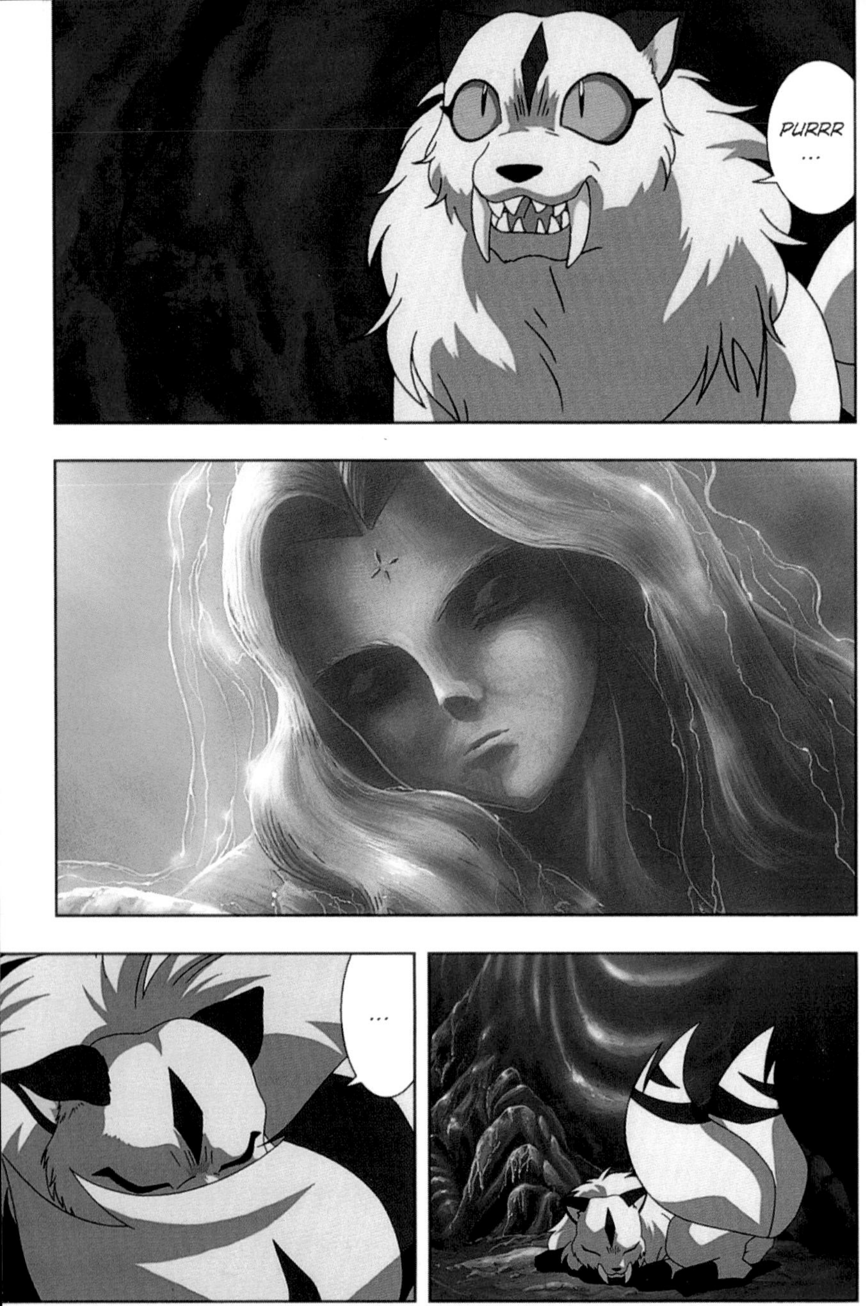
PURRR
...
...

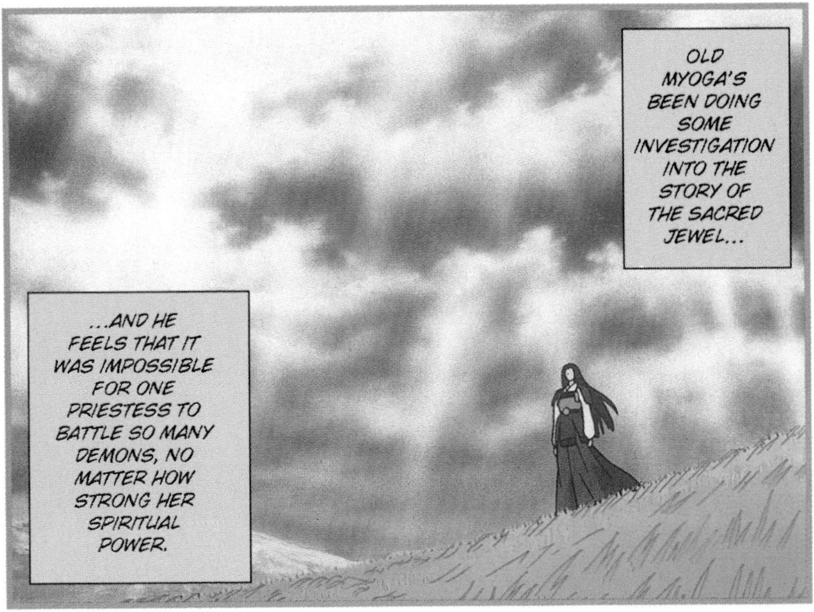
OLD MYOGA'S BEEN DOING SOME INVESTIGATION INTO THE STORY OF THE SACRED JEWEL...
...AND HE FEELS THAT IT WAS IMPOSSIBLE FOR ONE PRIESTESS TO BATTLE SO MANY DEMONS, NO MATTER HOW STRONG HER SPIRITUAL POWER.

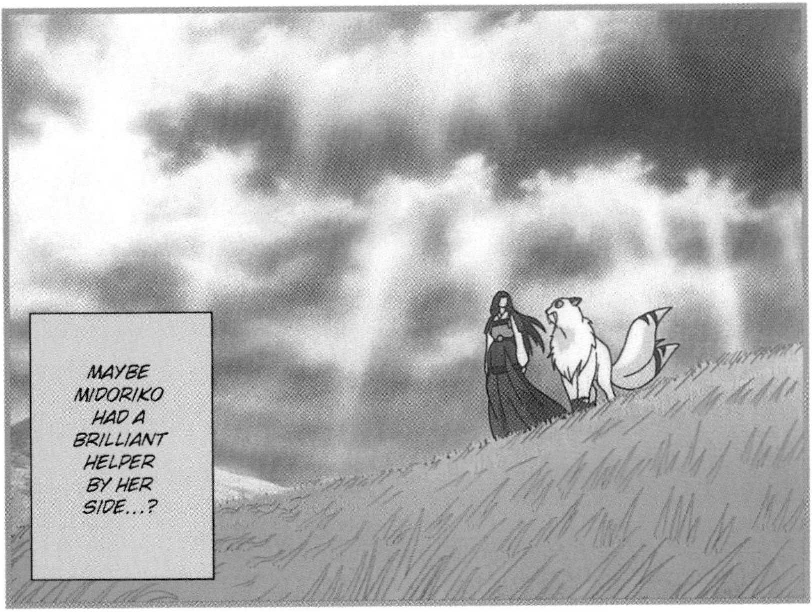
MAYBE MIDORIKO HAD A BRILLIANT HELPER BY HER SIDE...?

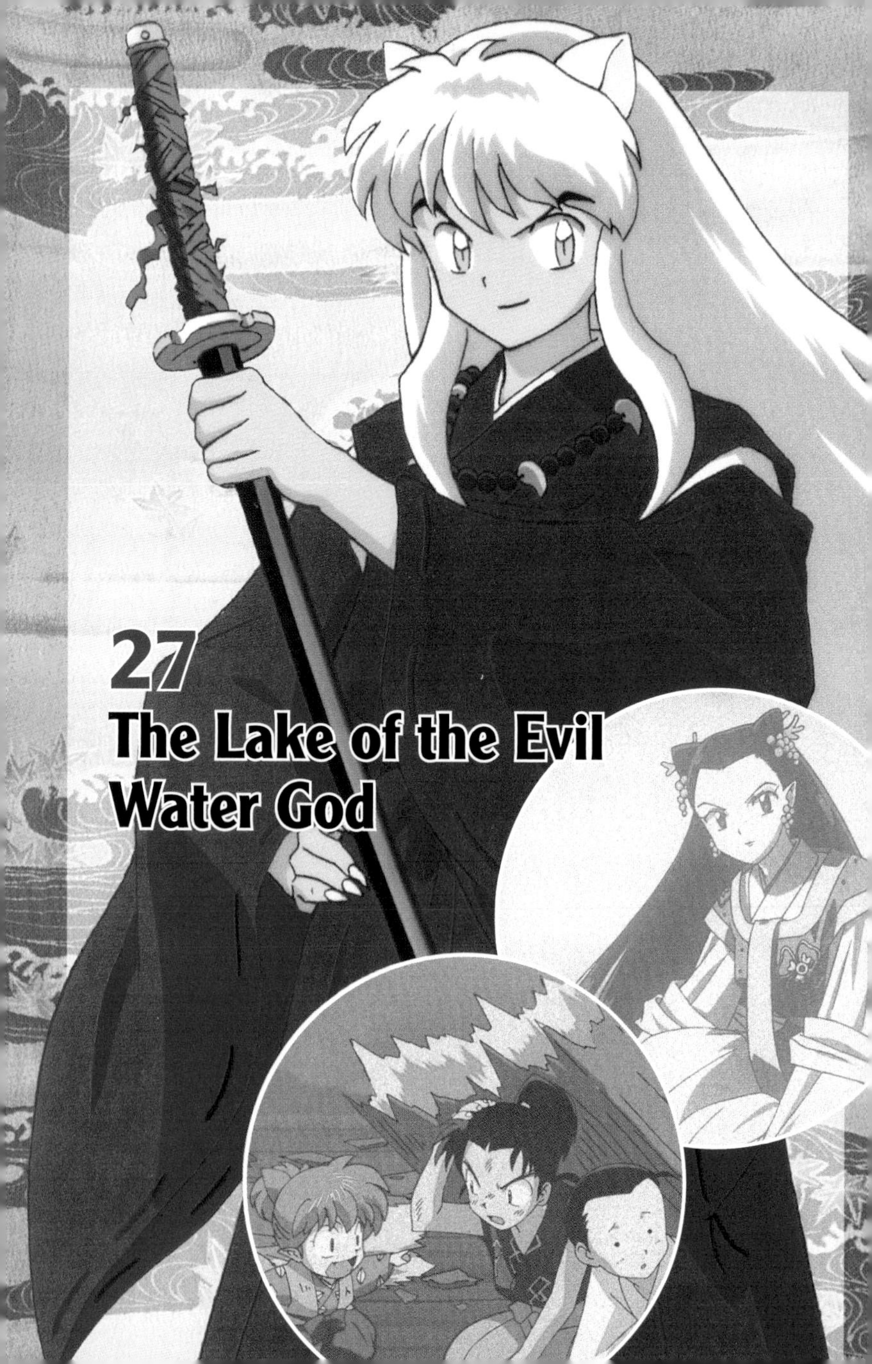
27
The Lake of the Evil Water God

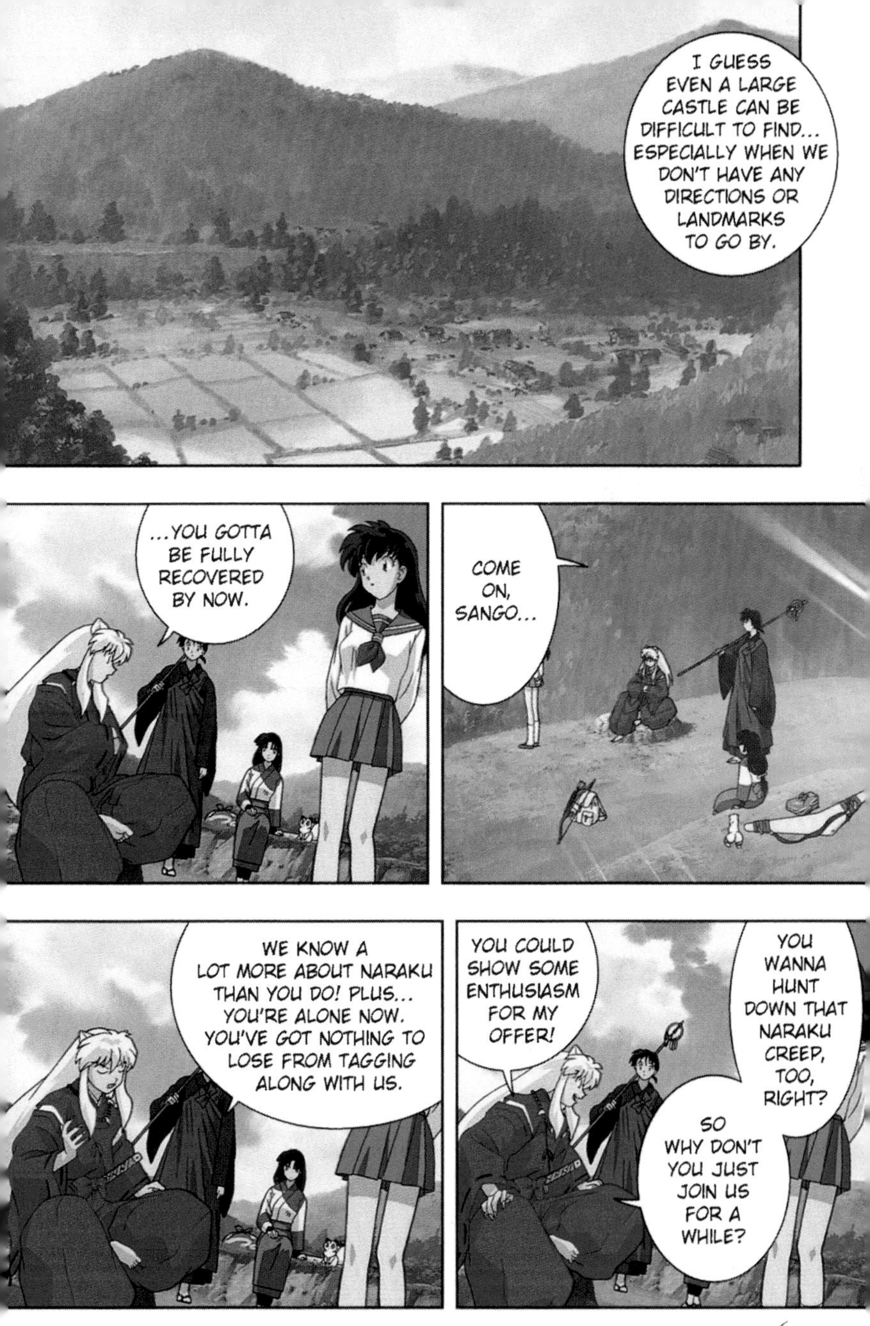
I GUESS EVEN A LARGE CASTLE CAN BE DIFFICULT TO FIND... ESPECIALLY WHEN WE DON'T HAVE ANY DIRECTIONS OR LANDMARKS TO GO BY.
COME ON, SANGO...
...YOU GOTTA BE FULLY RECOVERED BY NOW.
YOU WANNA HUNT DOWN THAT NARAKU CREEP, TOO, RIGHT?
SO WHY DON'T YOU JUST JOIN US FOR A WHILE?
YOU COULD SHOW SOME ENTHUSIASM FOR MY OFFER!
WE KNOW A LOT MORE ABOUT NARAKU THAN YOU DO! PLUS... YOU'RE ALONE NOW. YOU'VE GOT NOTHING TO LOSE FROM TAGGING ALONG WITH US.

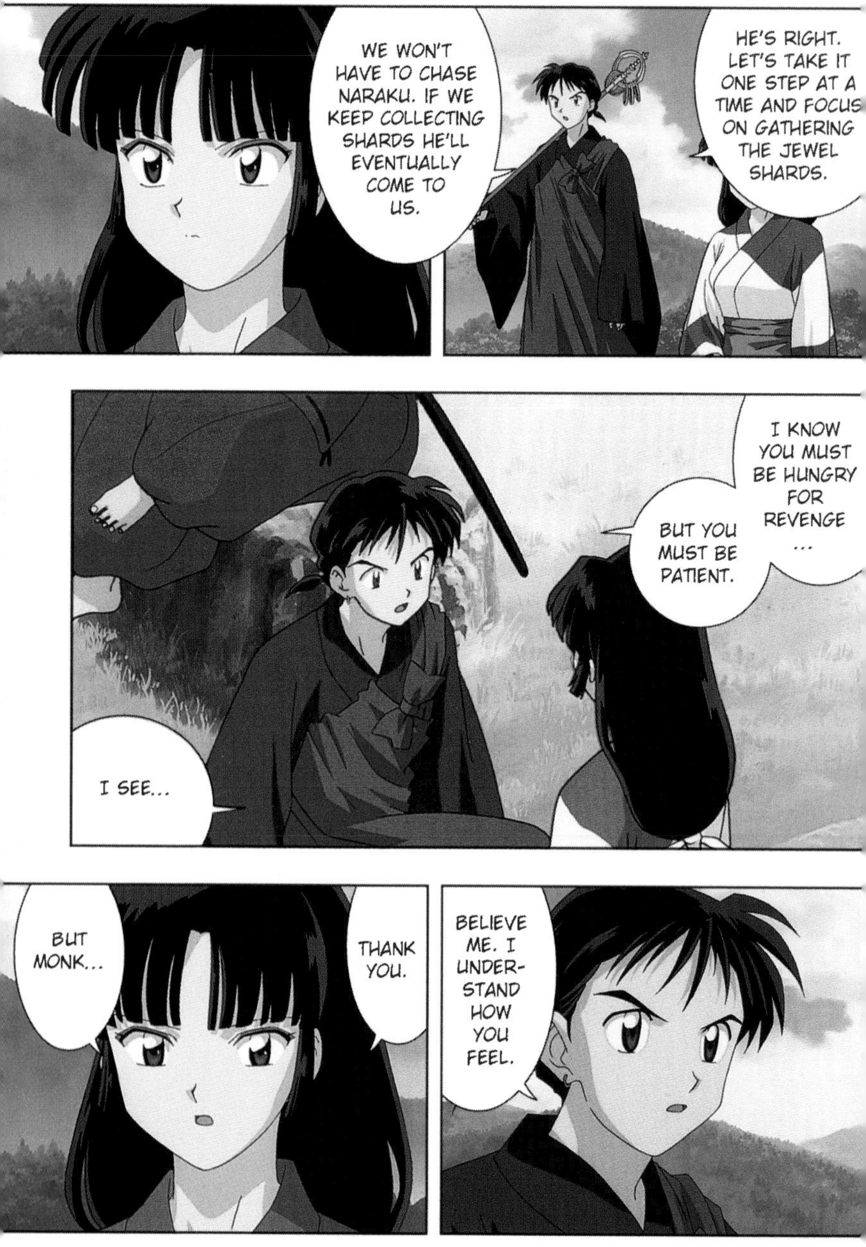
HE'S RIGHT. LET'S TAKE IT ONE STEP AT A TIME AND FOCUS ON GATHERING THE JEWEL SHARDS.
WE WON'T HAVE TO CHASE NARAKU. IF WE KEEP COLLECTING SHARDS HE'LL EVENTUALLY COME TO US.
I KNOW YOU MUST BE HUNGRY FOR REVENGE ...
BUT YOU MUST BE PATIENT.
I SEE...
BELIEVE ME. I UNDER-STAND HOW YOU FEEL.
THANK YOU.
BUT MONK...

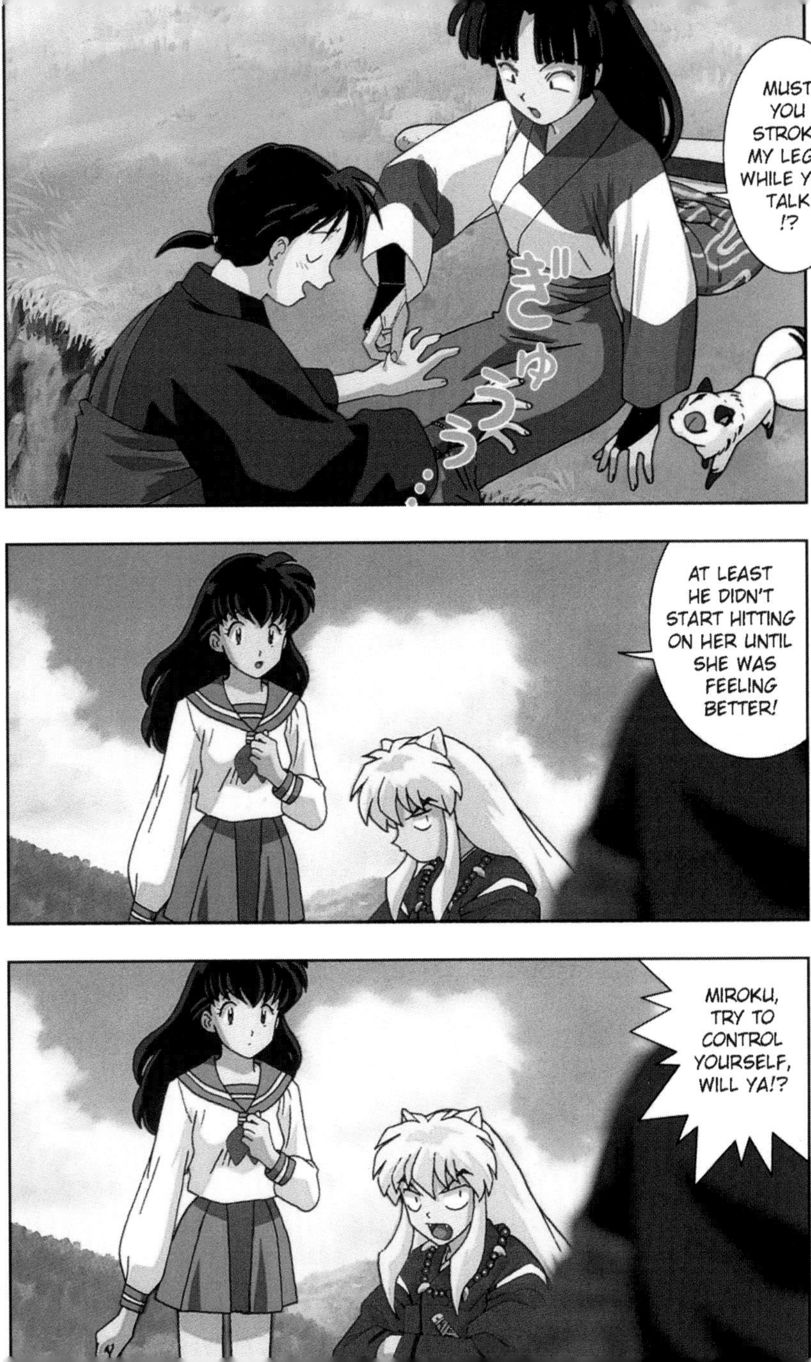
MUST YOU STROKE MY LEGS WHILE YOU TALK !?
ぎゅうう…
AT LEAST HE DIDN'T START HITTING ON HER UNTIL SHE WAS FEELING BETTER!
MIROKU, TRY TO CONTROL YOURSELF, WILL YA!?

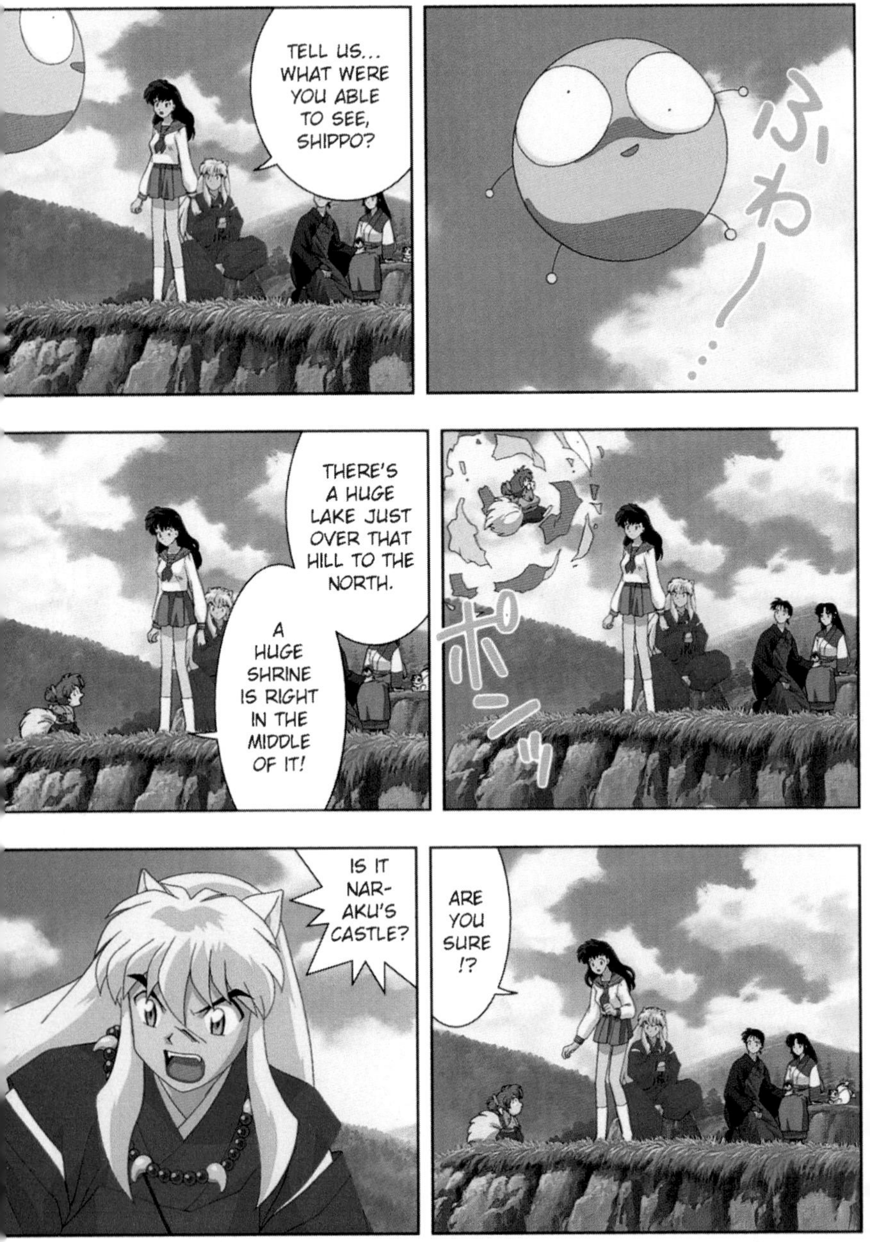
ふわ〜…
TELL US... WHAT WERE YOU ABLE TO SEE, SHIPPO?
ポンッ
THERE'S A HUGE LAKE JUST OVER THAT HILL TO THE NORTH.
A HUGE SHRINE IS RIGHT IN THE MIDDLE OF IT!
ARE YOU SURE !?
IS IT NAR-AKU'S CASTLE?

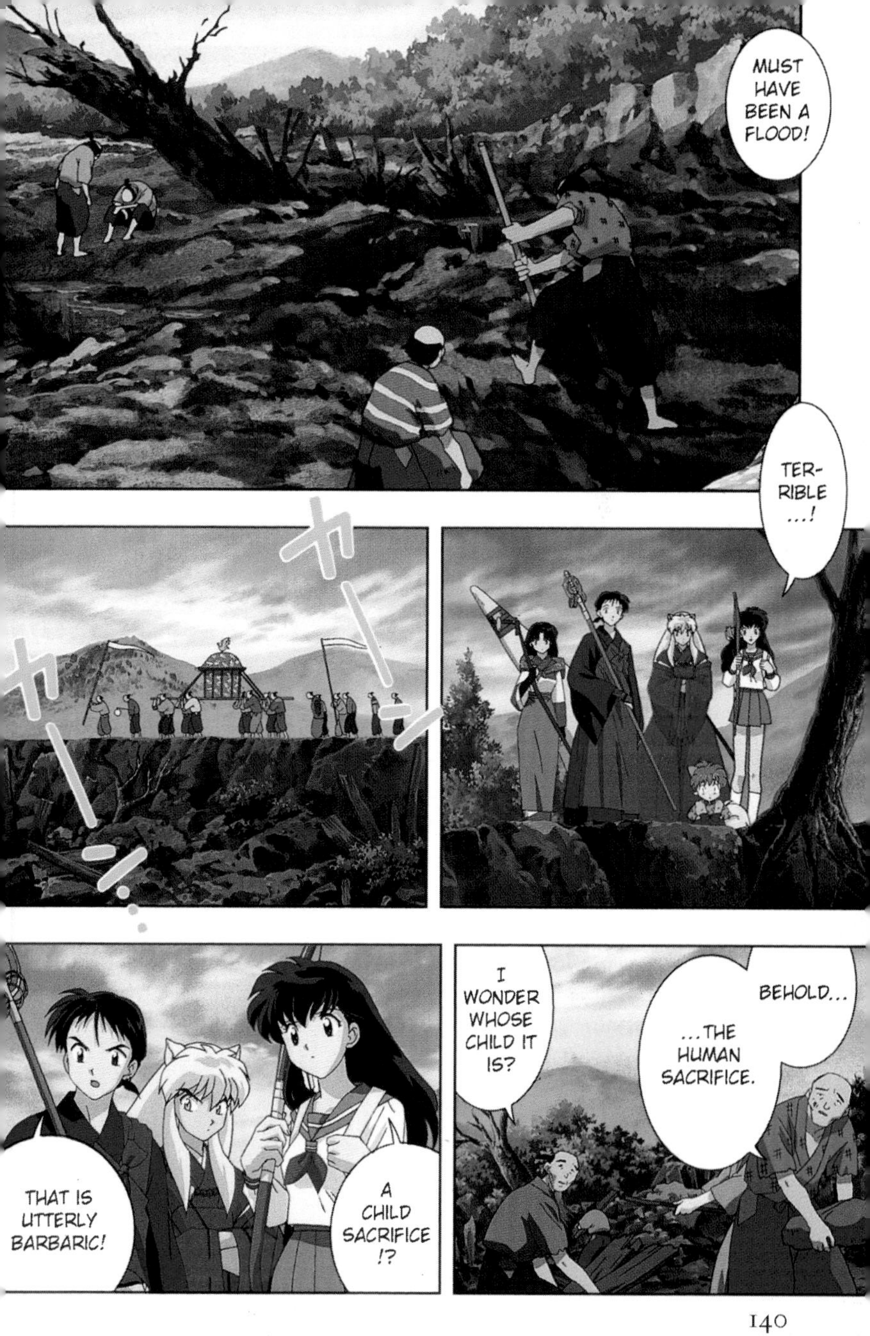
MUST HAVE BEEN A FLOOD!
TER-RIBLE...!
BEHOLD...
...THE HUMAN SACRIFICE.
I WONDER WHOSE CHILD IT IS?
A CHILD SACRIFICE!?
THAT IS UTTERLY BARBARIC!

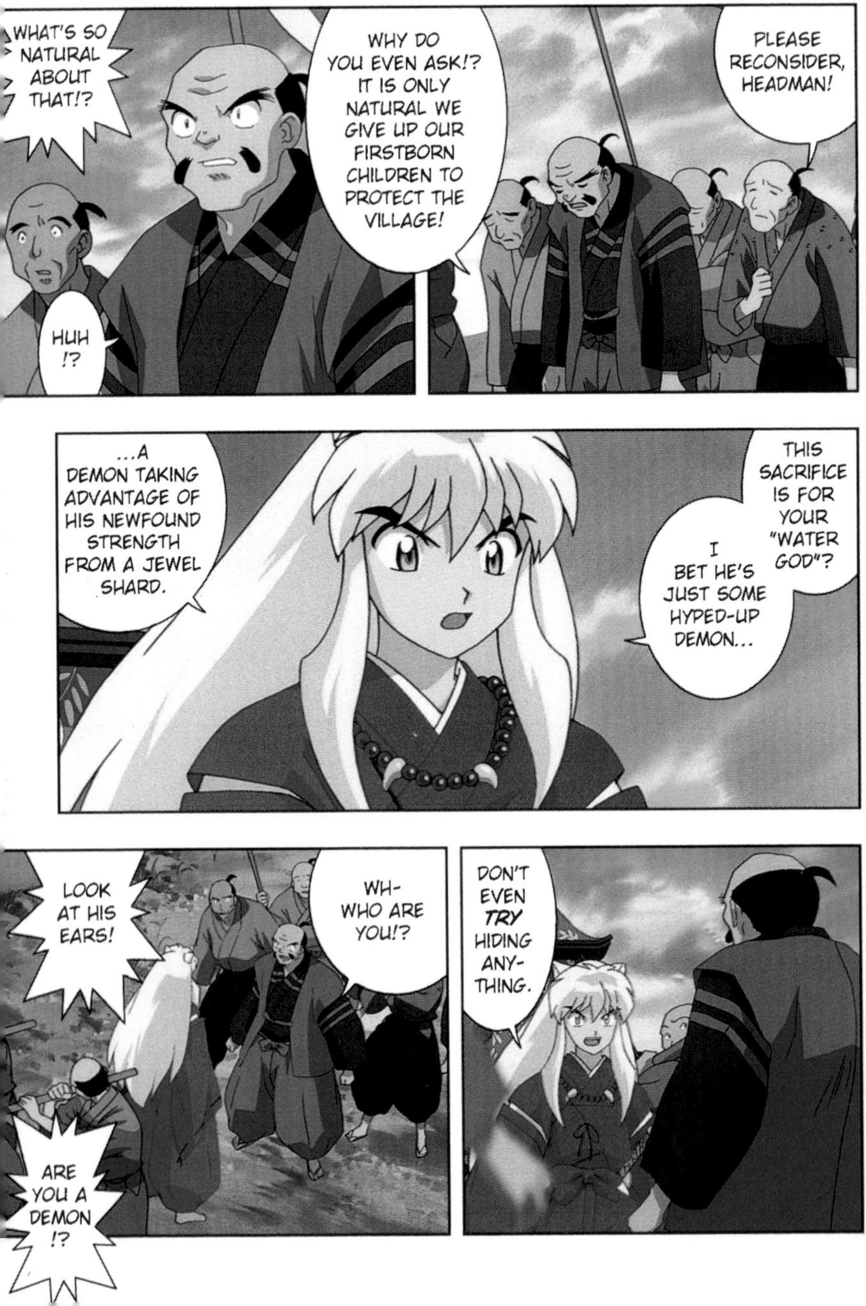
PLEASE RECONSIDER, HEADMAN!
WHY DO YOU EVEN ASK!? IT IS ONLY NATURAL WE GIVE UP OUR FIRSTBORN CHILDREN TO PROTECT THE VILLAGE!
WHAT'S SO NATURAL ABOUT THAT!?
HUH !?
THIS SACRIFICE IS FOR YOUR "WATER GOD"?
I BET HE'S JUST SOME HYPED-UP DEMON...
...A DEMON TAKING ADVANTAGE OF HIS NEWFOUND STRENGTH FROM A JEWEL SHARD.
DON'T EVEN *TRY* HIDING ANYTHING.
WH- WHO ARE YOU!?
LOOK AT HIS EARS!
ARE YOU A DEMON !?

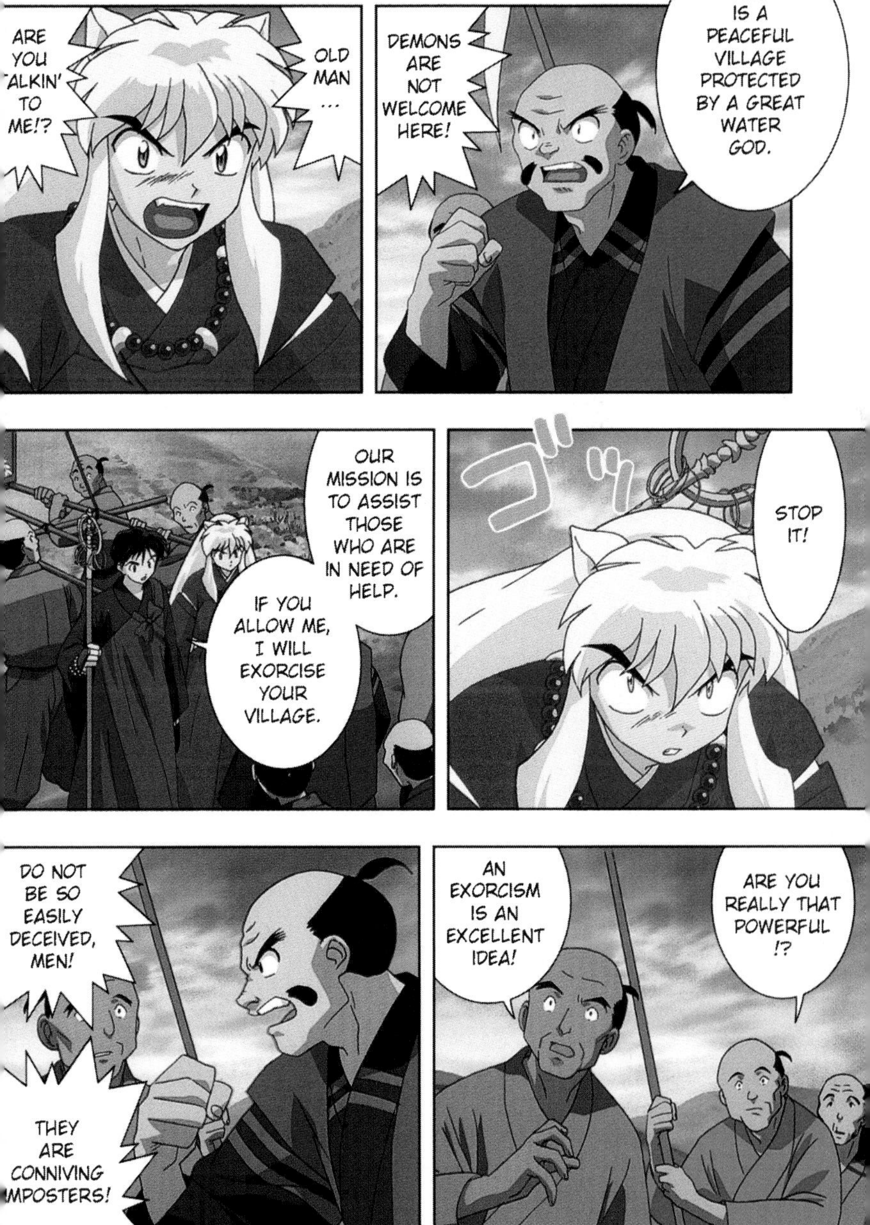
THIS IS A PEACEFUL VILLAGE PROTECTED BY A GREAT WATER GOD.
DEMONS ARE NOT WELCOME HERE!
OLD MAN ...
ARE YOU ALKIN' TO ME!?
STOP IT!
OUR MISSION IS TO ASSIST THOSE WHO ARE IN NEED OF HELP.
IF YOU ALLOW ME, I WILL EXORCISE YOUR VILLAGE.
ARE YOU REALLY THAT POWERFUL !?
AN EXORCISM IS AN EXCELLENT IDEA!
DO NOT BE SO EASILY DECEIVED, MEN!
THEY ARE CONNIVING MPOSTERS!

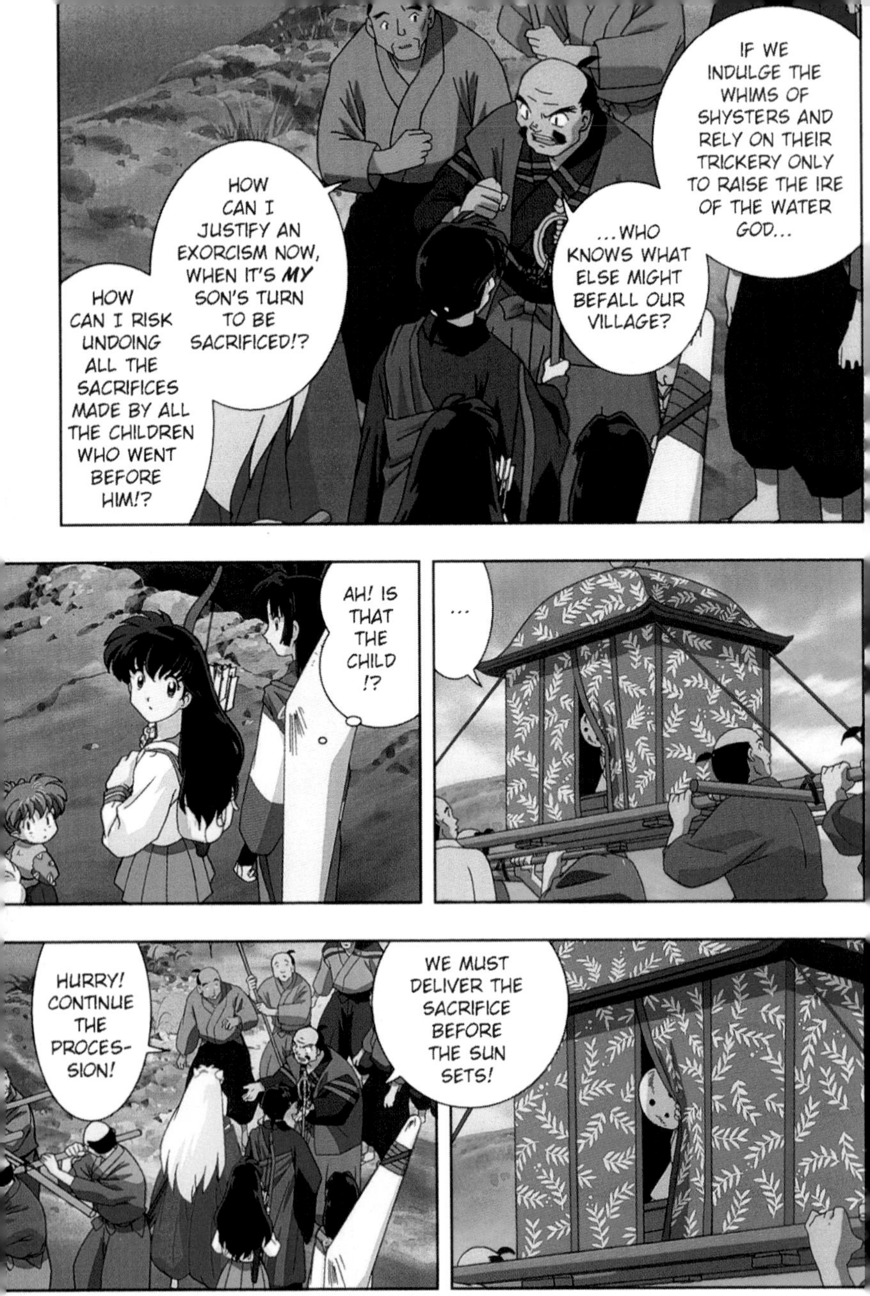
IF WE INDULGE THE WHIMS OF SHYSTERS AND RELY ON THEIR TRICKERY ONLY TO RAISE THE IRE OF THE WATER GOD...
...WHO KNOWS WHAT ELSE MIGHT BEFALL OUR VILLAGE?
HOW CAN I JUSTIFY AN EXORCISM NOW, WHEN IT'S *MY* SON'S TURN TO BE SACRIFICED!?
HOW CAN I RISK UNDOING ALL THE SACRIFICES MADE BY ALL THE CHILDREN WHO WENT BEFORE HIM!?
...
AH! IS THAT THE CHILD !?
WE MUST DELIVER THE SACRIFICE BEFORE THE SUN SETS!
HURRY! CONTINUE THE PROCES-SION!

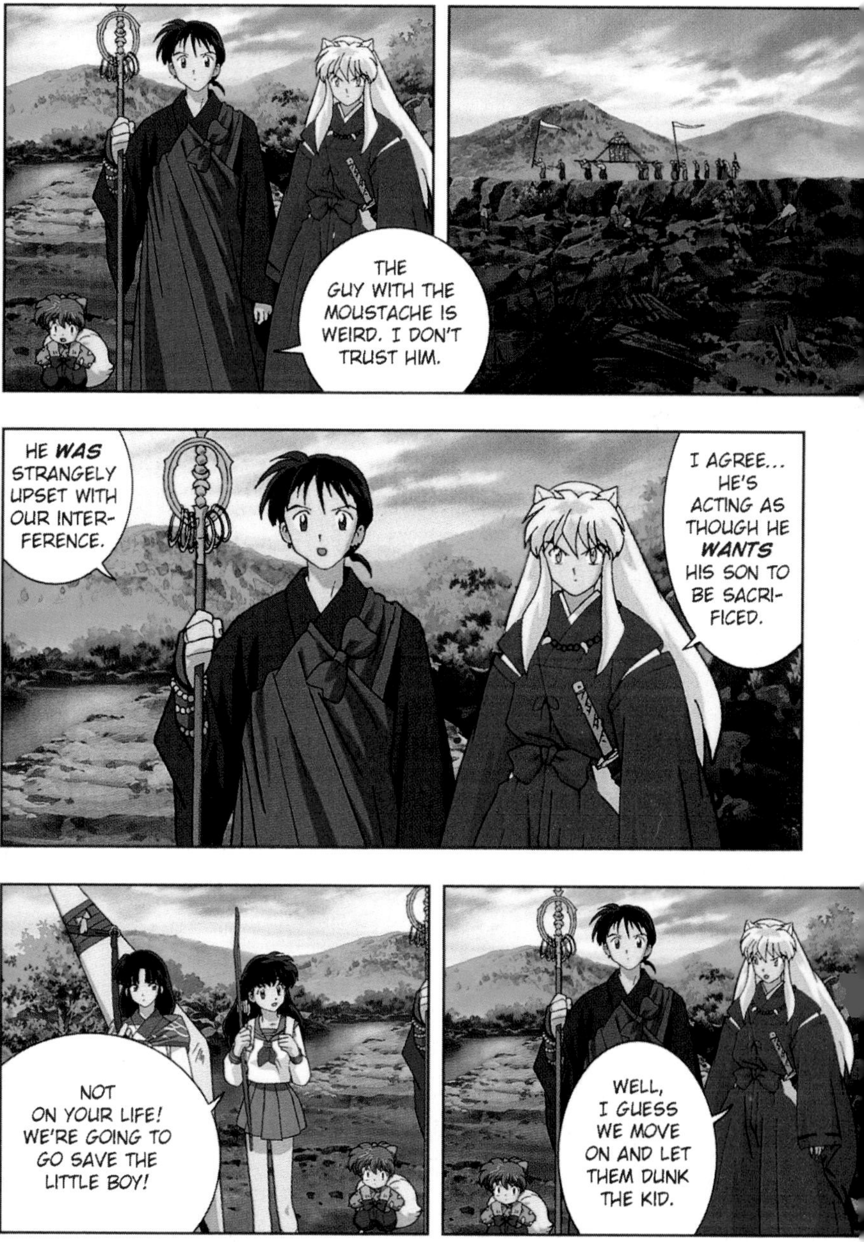
THE GUY WITH THE MOUSTACHE IS WEIRD. I DON'T TRUST HIM.
I AGREE... HE'S ACTING AS THOUGH HE *WANTS* HIS SON TO BE SACRI-FICED.
HE *WAS* STRANGELY UPSET WITH OUR INTER-FERENCE.
WELL, I GUESS WE MOVE ON AND LET THEM DUNK THE KID.
NOT ON YOUR LIFE! WE'RE GOING TO GO SAVE THE LITTLE BOY!

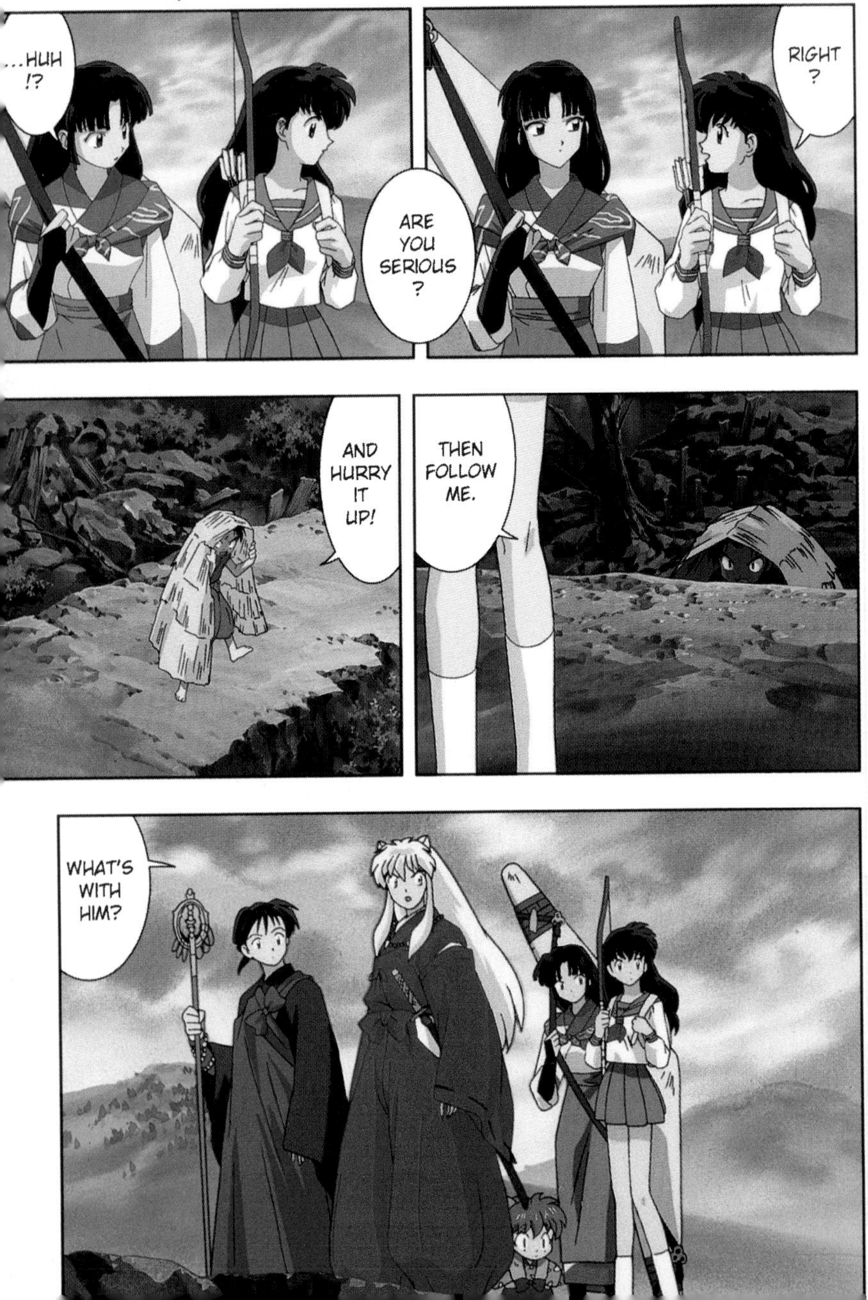
RIGHT ?
ARE YOU SERIOUS ?
...HUH !?
THEN FOLLOW ME.
AND HURRY IT UP!
WHAT'S WITH HIM?

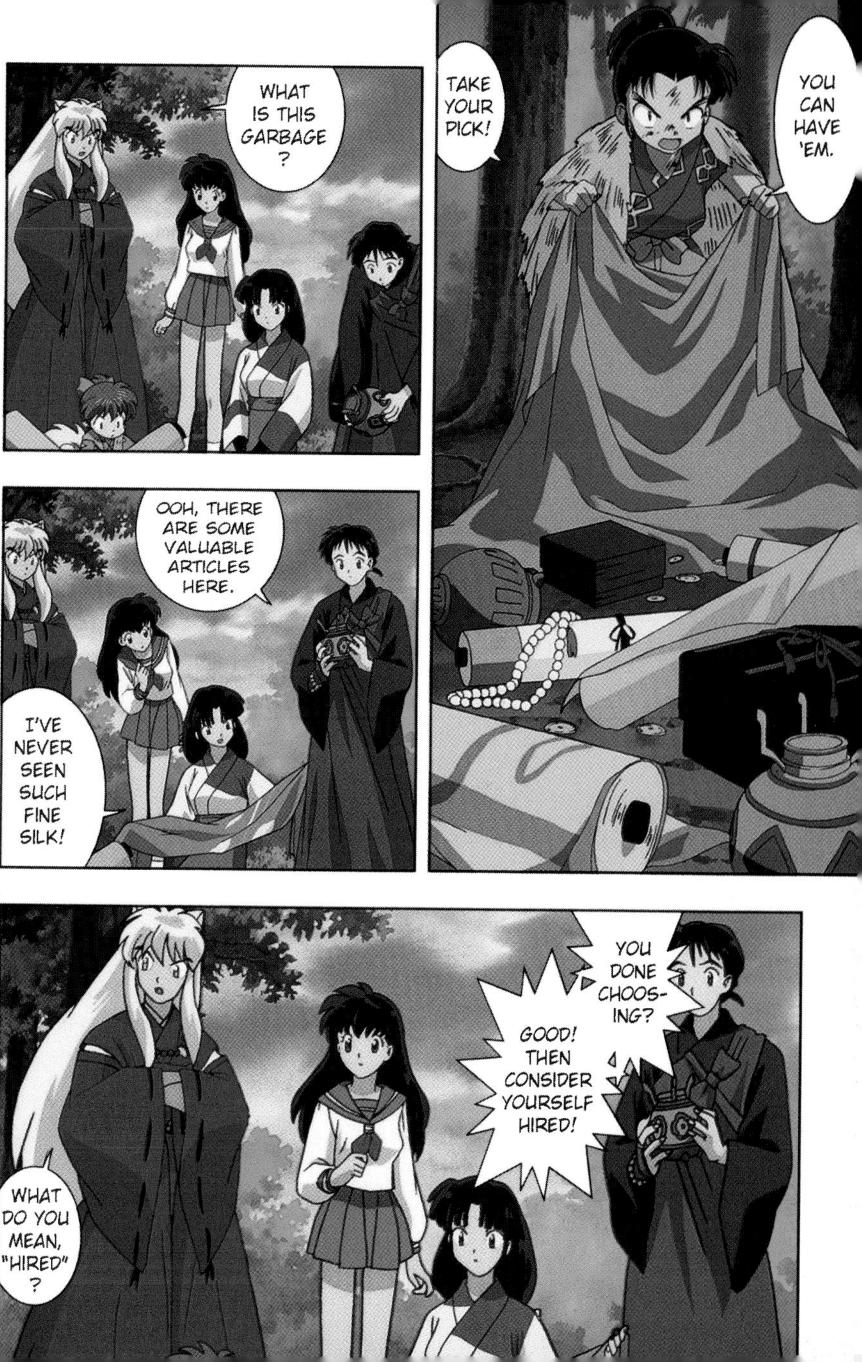
YOU CAN HAVE 'EM.
TAKE YOUR PICK!
WHAT IS THIS GARBAGE?
OOH, THERE ARE SOME VALUABLE ARTICLES HERE.
I'VE NEVER SEEN SUCH FINE SILK!
YOU DONE CHOOSING?
GOOD! THEN CONSIDER YOURSELF HIRED!
WHAT DO YOU MEAN, "HIRED"?

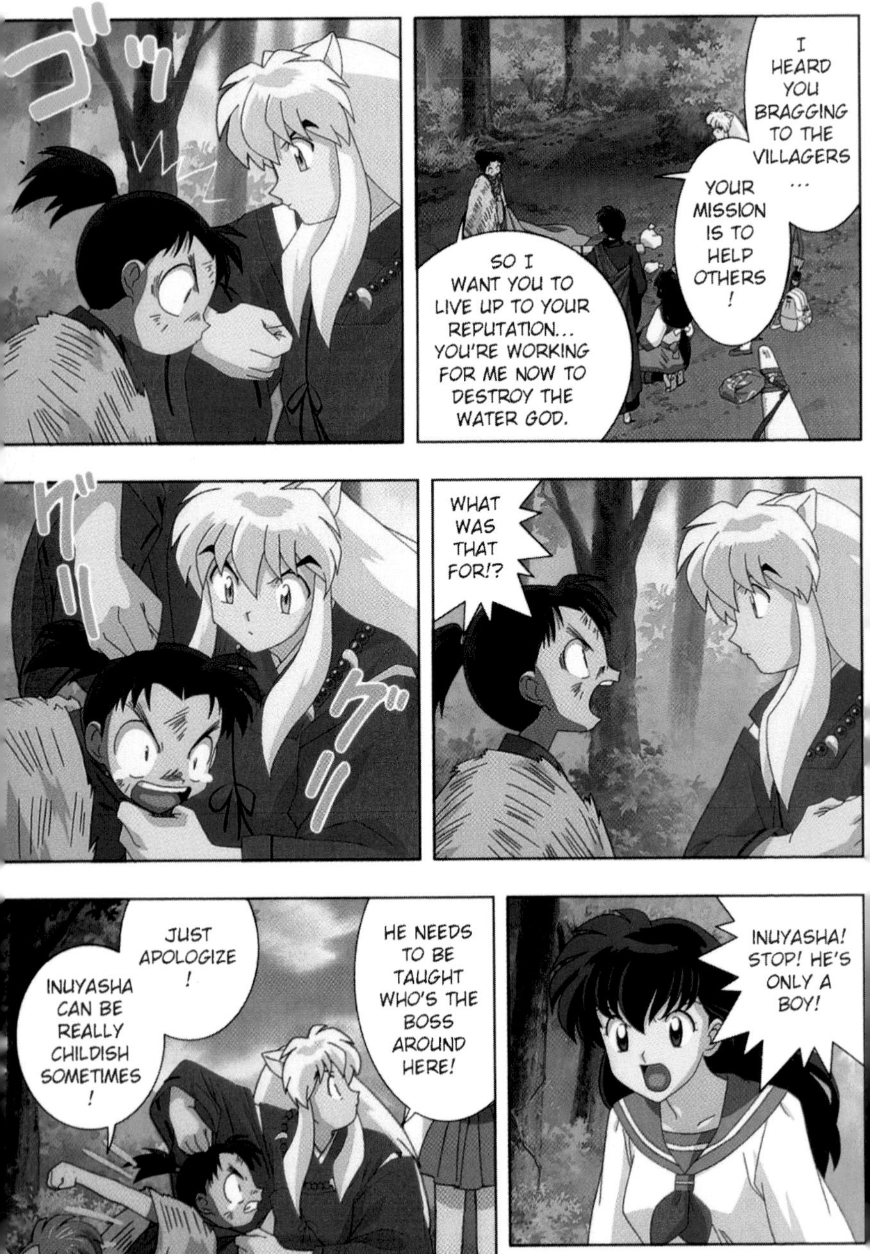
I HEARD YOU BRAGGING TO THE VILLAGERS...
YOUR MISSION IS TO HELP OTHERS!
SO I WANT YOU TO LIVE UP TO YOUR REPUTATION... YOU'RE WORKING FOR ME NOW TO DESTROY THE WATER GOD.
ゴッ
WHAT WAS THAT FOR!?
INUYASHA! STOP! HE'S ONLY A BOY!
HE NEEDS TO BE TAUGHT WHO'S THE BOSS AROUND HERE!
JUST APOLOGIZE!
INUYASHA CAN BE REALLY CHILDISH SOMETIMES!

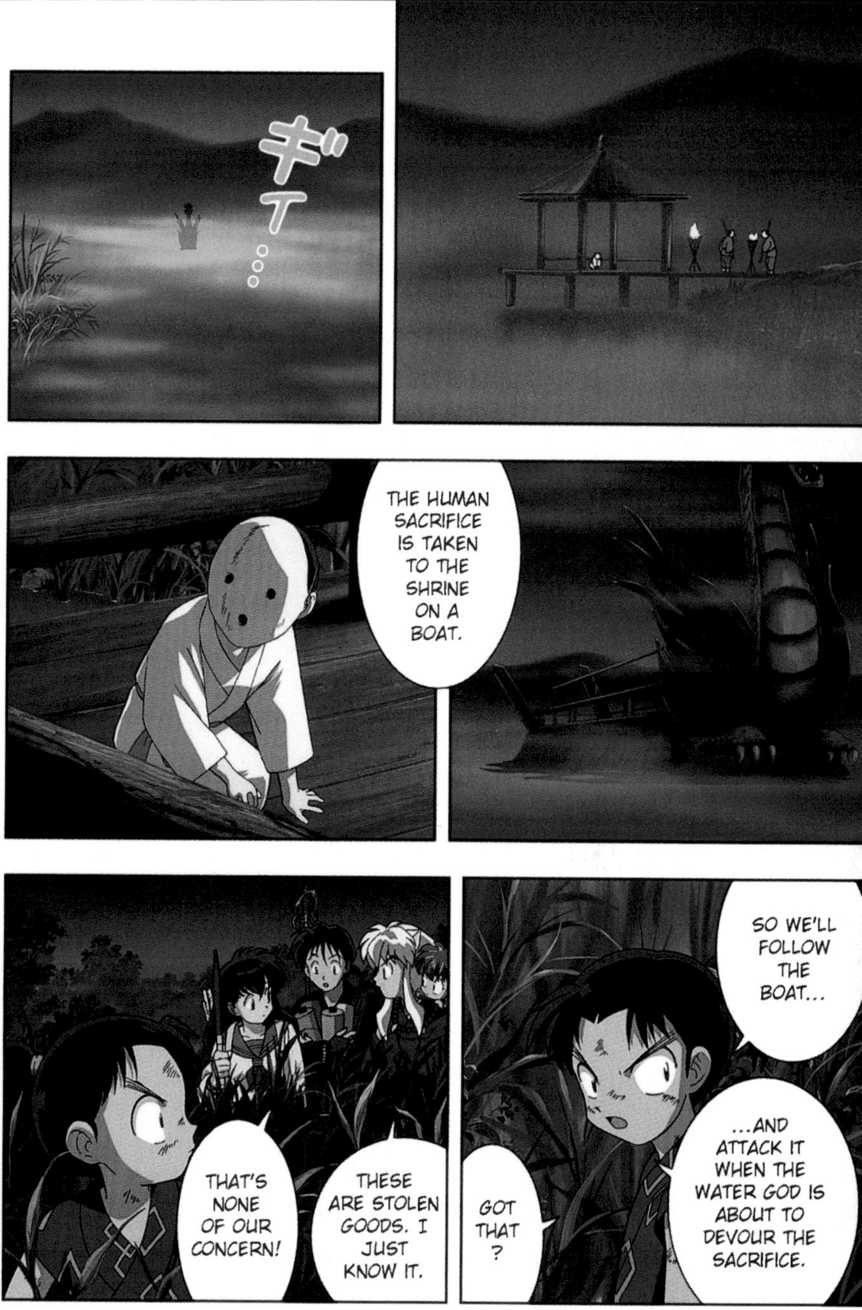
ギイ...
THE HUMAN SACRIFICE IS TAKEN TO THE SHRINE ON A BOAT.
SO WE'LL FOLLOW THE BOAT...
...AND ATTACK IT WHEN THE WATER GOD IS ABOUT TO DEVOUR THE SACRIFICE.
GOT THAT?
THESE ARE STOLEN GOODS. I JUST KNOW IT.
THAT'S NONE OF OUR CONCERN!

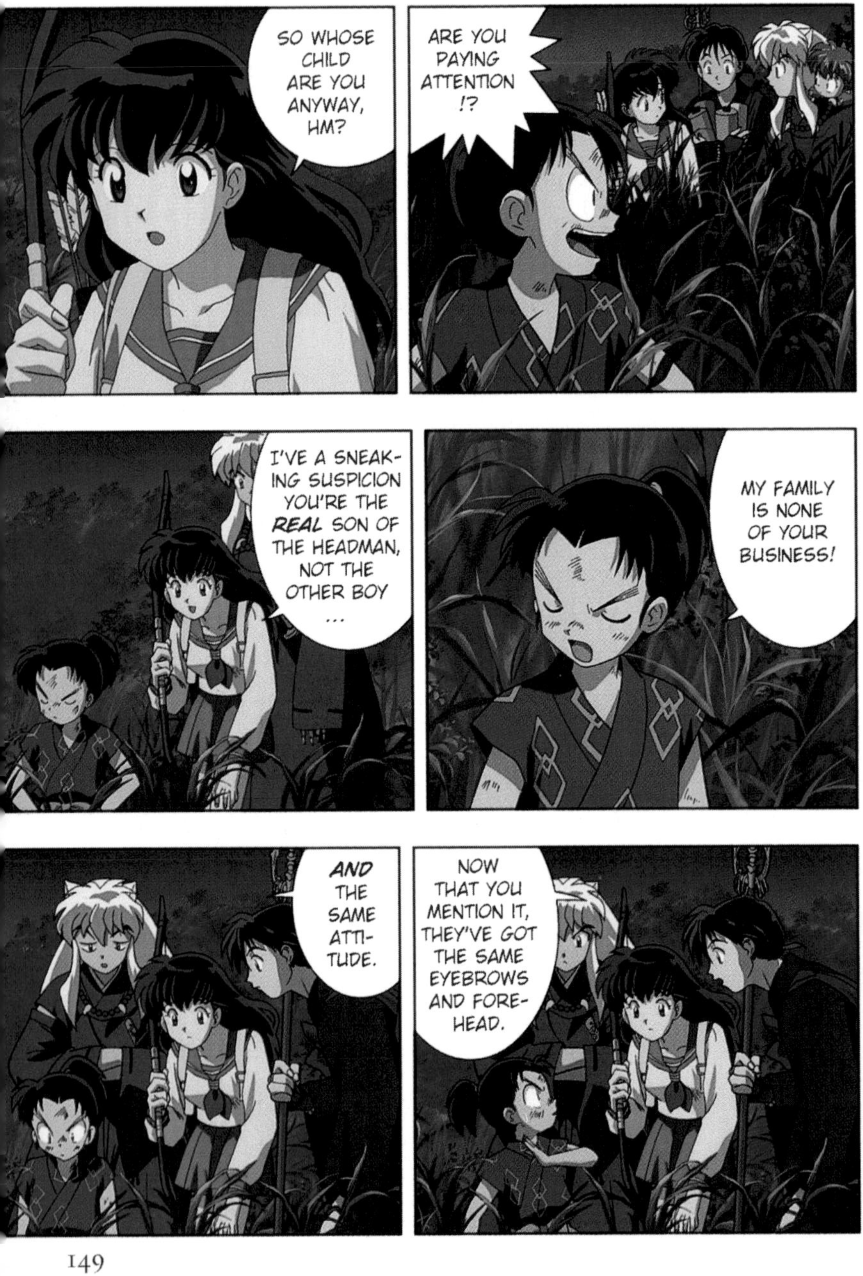
ARE YOU PAYING ATTENTION !?
SO WHOSE CHILD ARE YOU ANYWAY, HM?
MY FAMILY IS NONE OF YOUR BUSINESS!
I'VE A SNEAK-ING SUSPICION YOU'RE THE *REAL* SON OF THE HEADMAN, NOT THE OTHER BOY ...
NOW THAT YOU MENTION IT, THEY'VE GOT THE SAME EYEBROWS AND FORE-HEAD.
AND THE SAME ATTI-TUDE.

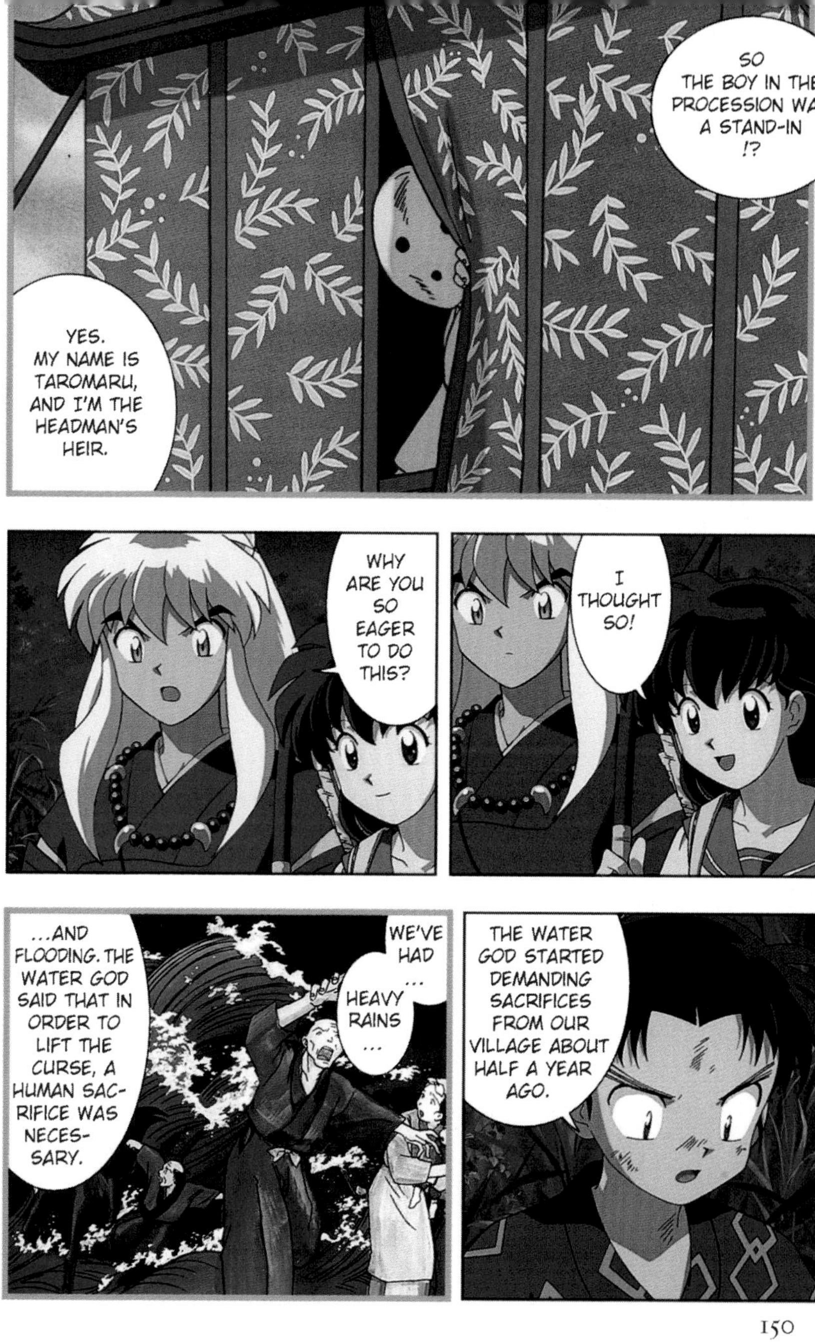
SO THE BOY IN THE PROCESSION WAS A STAND-IN !?
YES. MY NAME IS TAROMARU, AND I'M THE HEADMAN'S HEIR.
I THOUGHT SO!
WHY ARE YOU SO EAGER TO DO THIS?
THE WATER GOD STARTED DEMANDING SACRIFICES FROM OUR VILLAGE ABOUT HALF A YEAR AGO.
WE'VE HAD ...
HEAVY RAINS ...
...AND FLOODING. THE WATER GOD SAID THAT IN ORDER TO LIFT THE CURSE, A HUMAN SACRIFICE WAS NECESSARY.

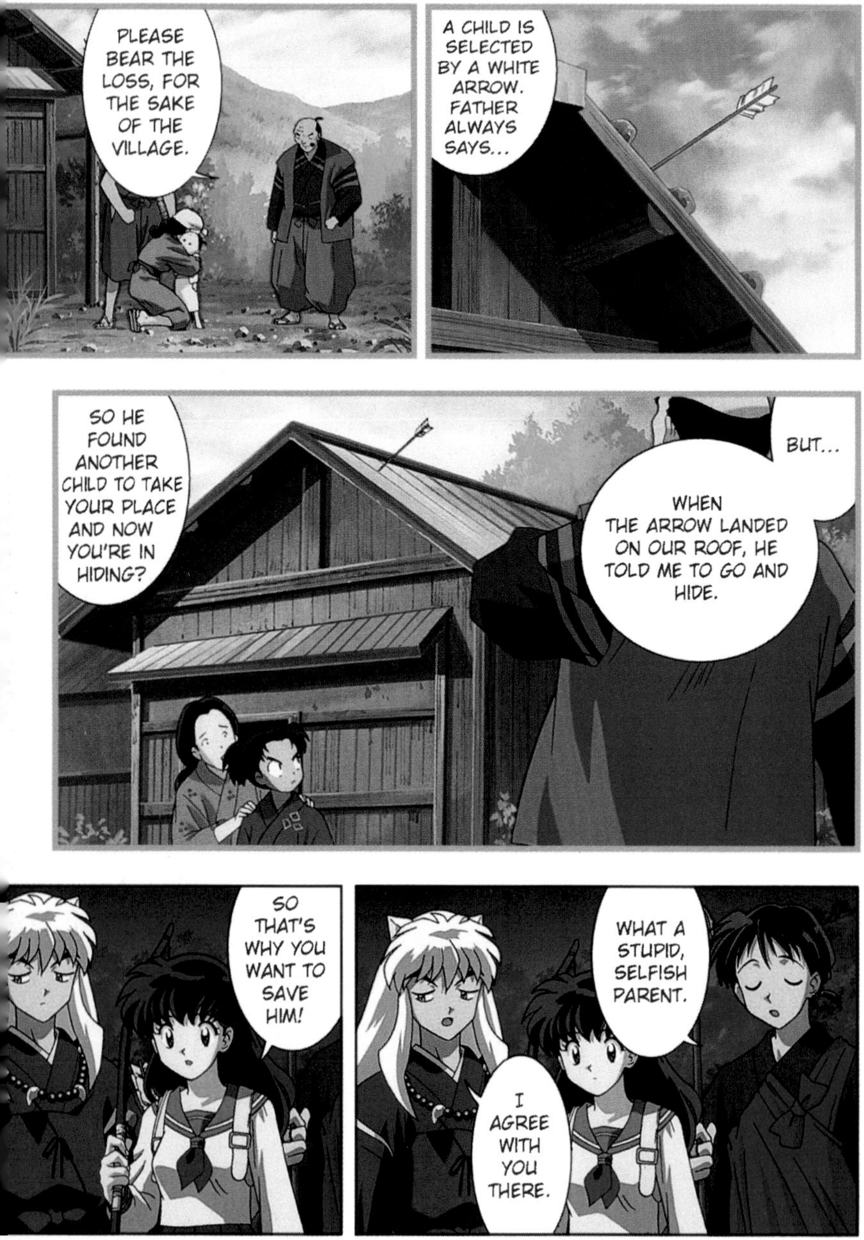
A CHILD IS SELECTED BY A WHITE ARROW. FATHER ALWAYS SAYS...
PLEASE BEAR THE LOSS, FOR THE SAKE OF THE VILLAGE.
BUT...
WHEN THE ARROW LANDED ON OUR ROOF, HE TOLD ME TO GO AND HIDE.
SO HE FOUND ANOTHER CHILD TO TAKE YOUR PLACE AND NOW YOU'RE IN HIDING?
WHAT A STUPID, SELFISH PARENT.
I AGREE WITH YOU THERE.
SO THAT'S WHY YOU WANT TO SAVE HIM!

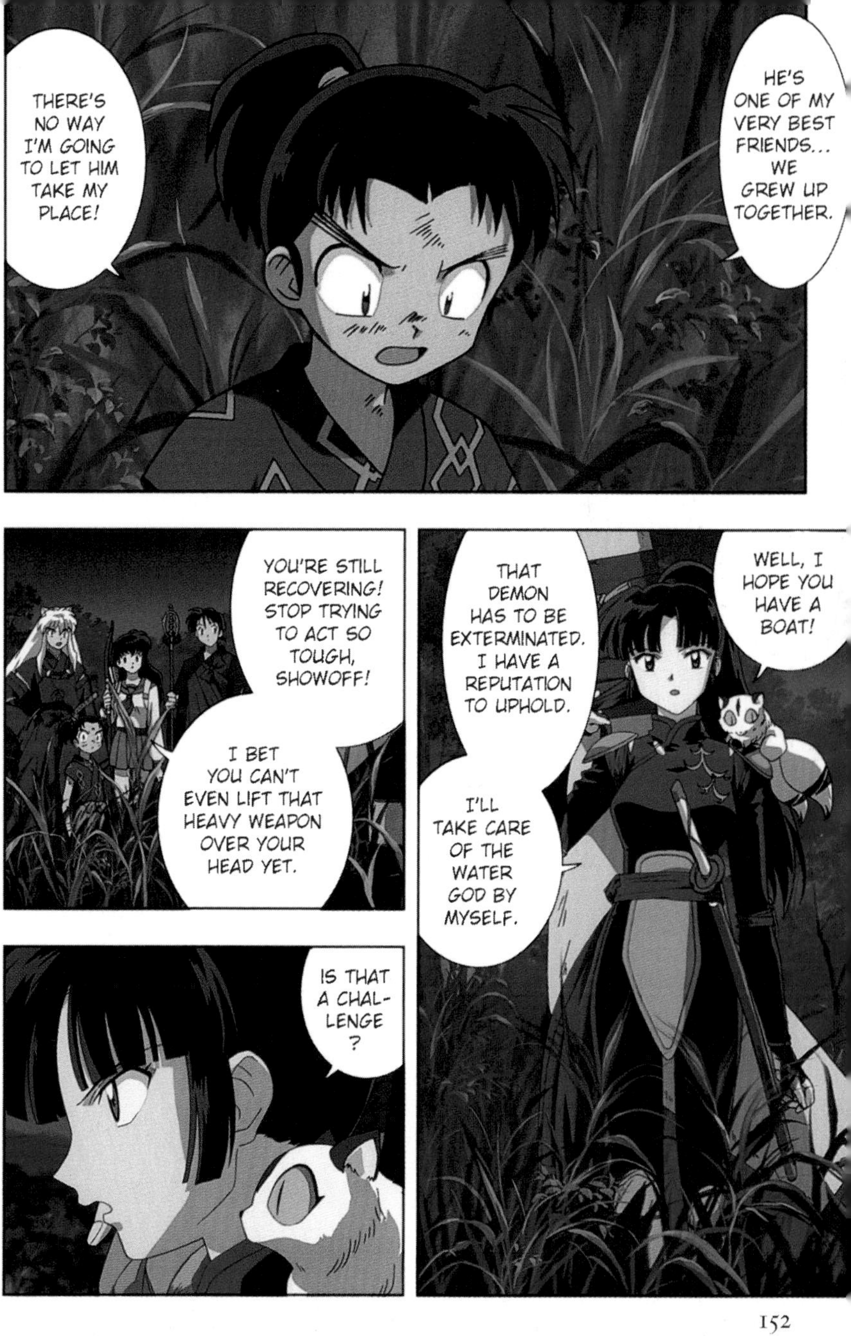
HE'S ONE OF MY VERY BEST FRIENDS... WE GREW UP TOGETHER.
THERE'S NO WAY I'M GOING TO LET HIM TAKE MY PLACE!
WELL, I HOPE YOU HAVE A BOAT!
THAT DEMON HAS TO BE EXTERMINATED. I HAVE A REPUTATION TO UPHOLD.
I'LL TAKE CARE OF THE WATER GOD BY MYSELF.
YOU'RE STILL RECOVERING! STOP TRYING TO ACT SO TOUGH, SHOWOFF!
I BET YOU CAN'T EVEN LIFT THAT HEAVY WEAPON OVER YOUR HEAD YET.
IS THAT A CHAL-LENGE?

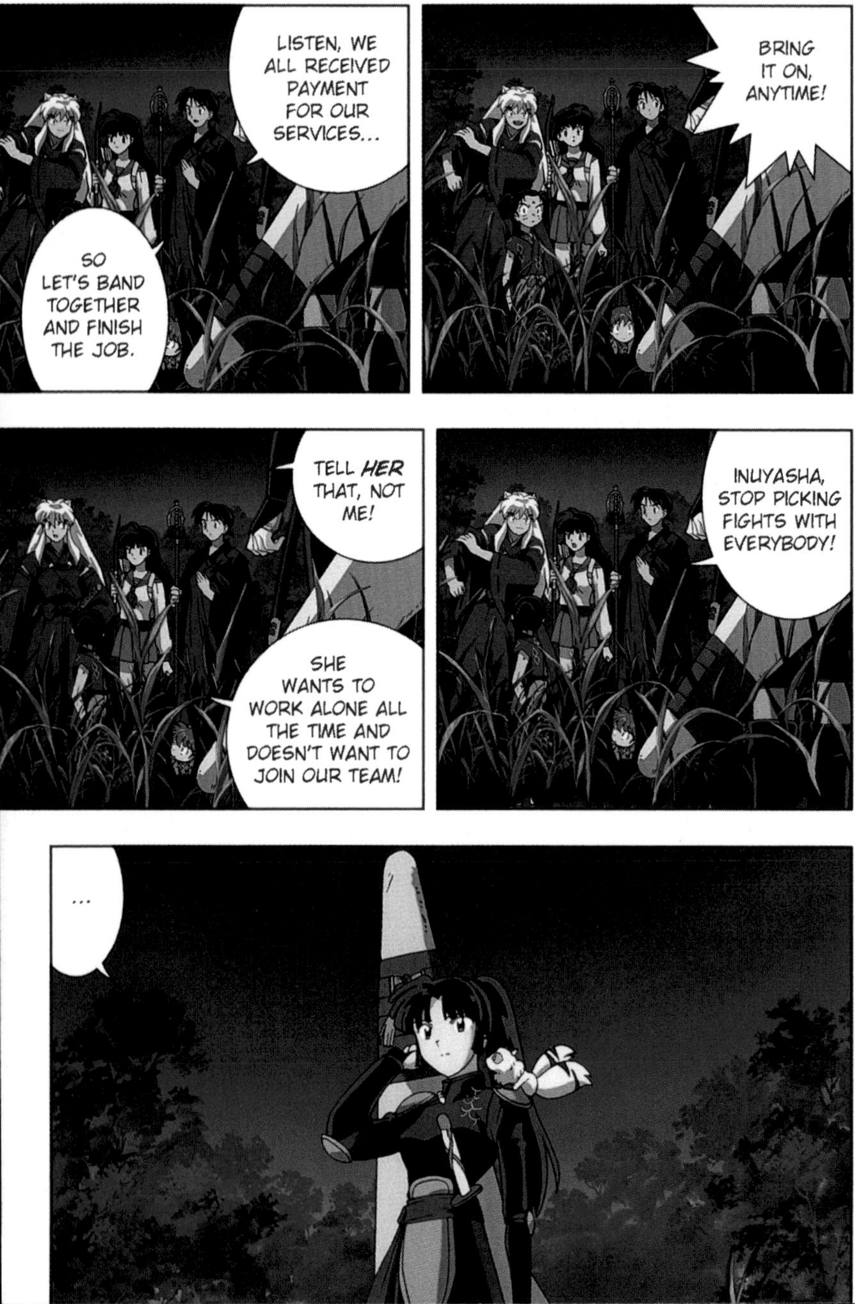
BRING IT ON, ANYTIME!
LISTEN, WE ALL RECEIVED PAYMENT FOR OUR SERVICES...
SO LET'S BAND TOGETHER AND FINISH THE JOB.
INUYASHA, STOP PICKING FIGHTS WITH EVERYBODY!
TELL *HER* THAT, NOT ME!
SHE WANTS TO WORK ALONE ALL THE TIME AND DOESN'T WANT TO JOIN OUR TEAM!
...

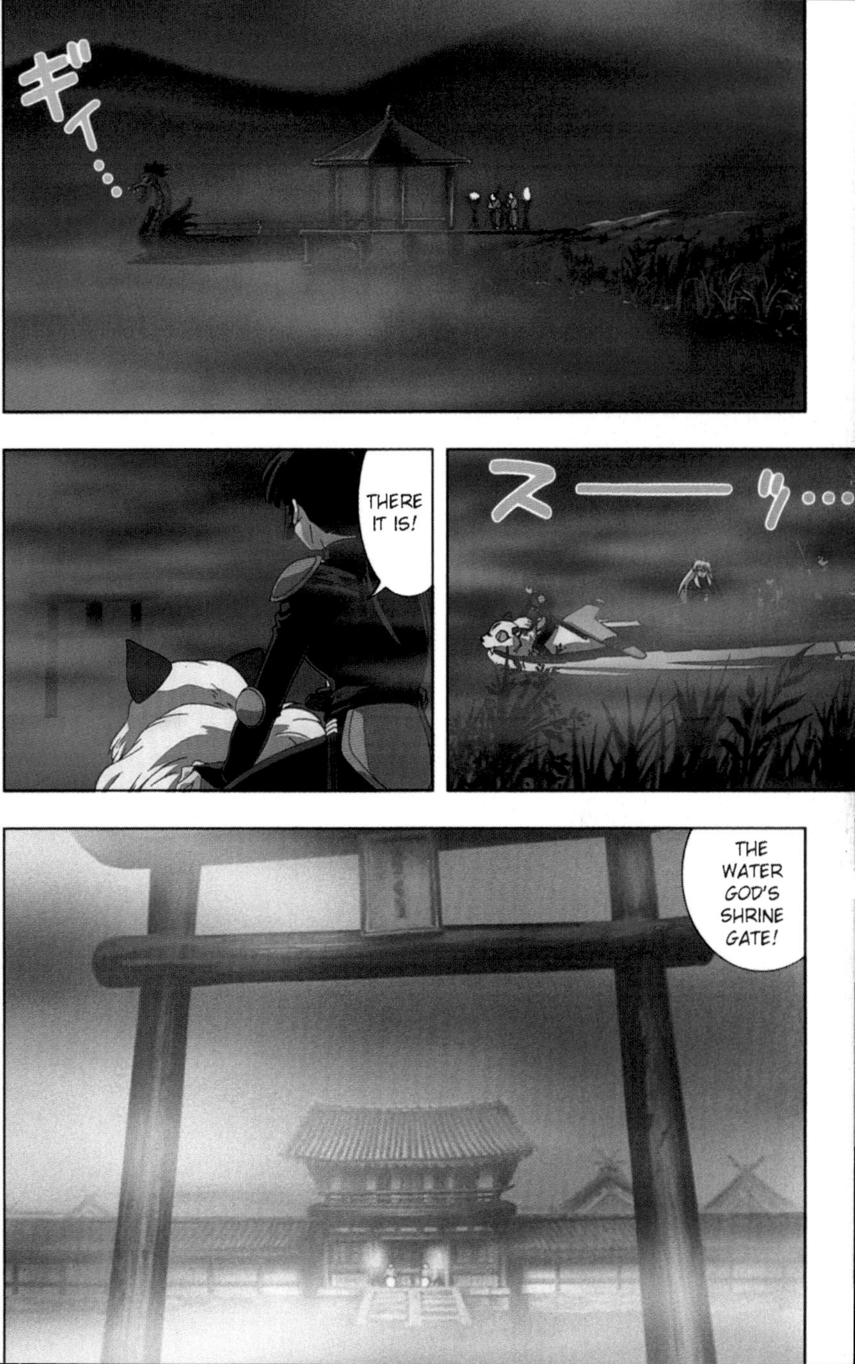
ギィ…
スーーッ…
THERE IT IS!
THE WATER GOD'S SHRINE GATE!

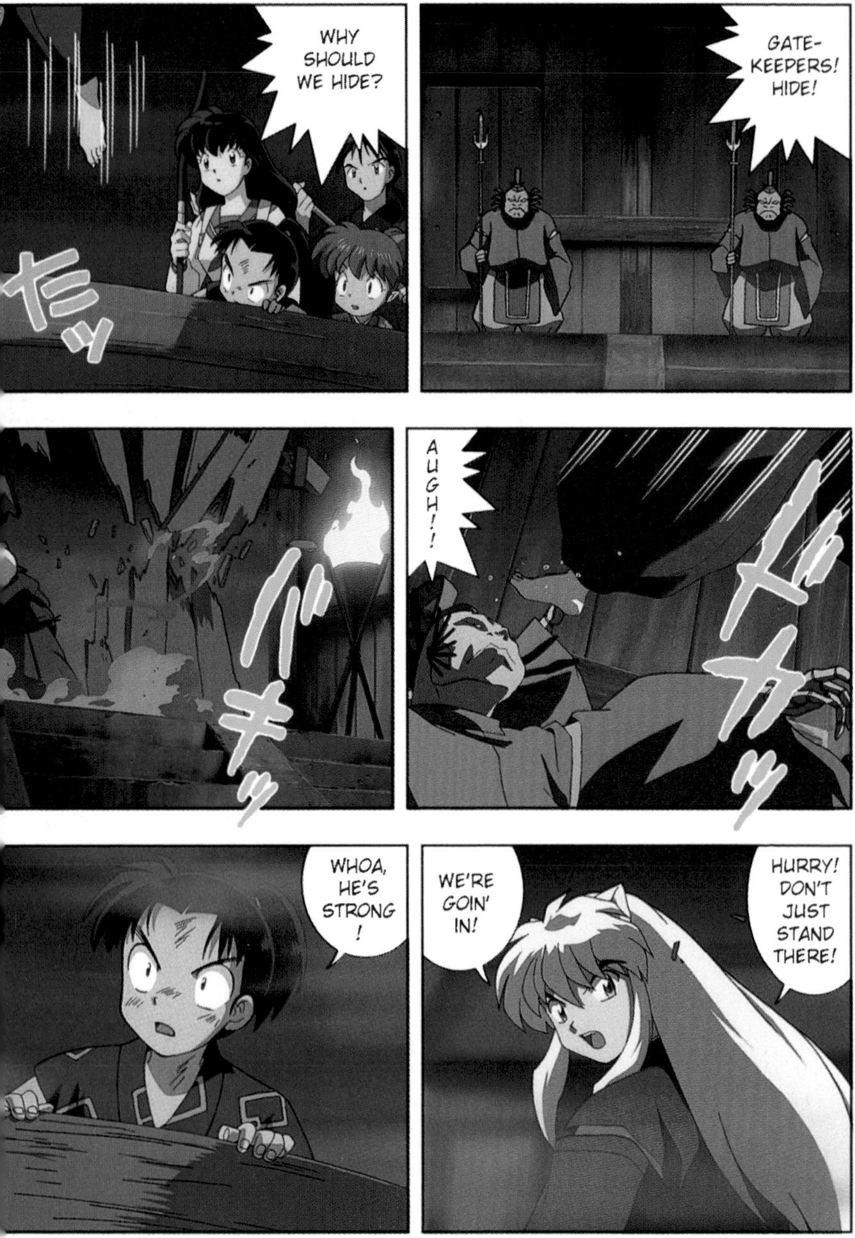
GATE-KEEPERS! HIDE!
WHY SHOULD WE HIDE?
AUGH!!
HURRY! DON'T JUST STAND THERE!
WE'RE GOIN' IN!
WHOA, HE'S STRONG!

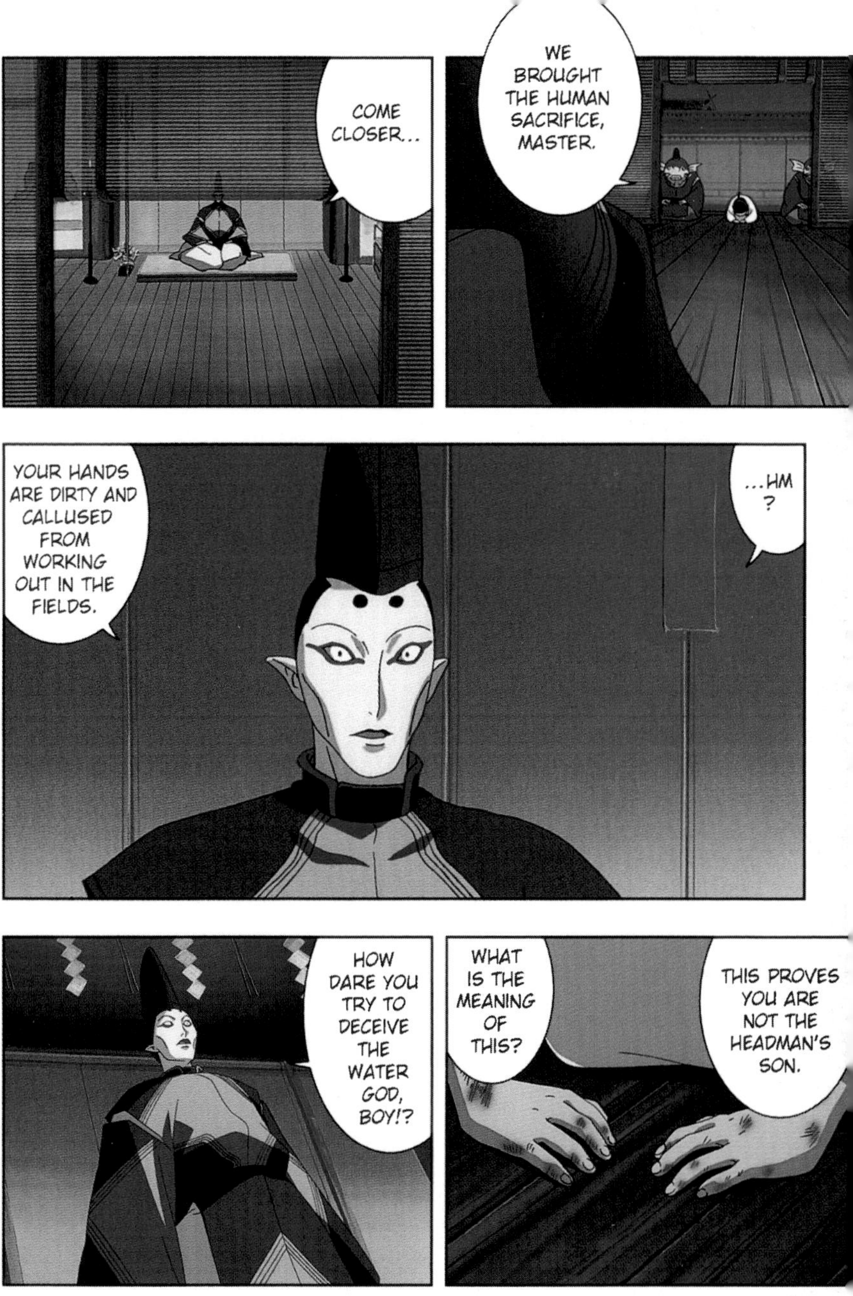
WE BROUGHT THE HUMAN SACRIFICE, MASTER.
COME CLOSER...
...HM ?
YOUR HANDS ARE DIRTY AND CALLUSED FROM WORKING OUT IN THE FIELDS.
THIS PROVES YOU ARE NOT THE HEADMAN'S SON.
WHAT IS THE MEANING OF THIS?
HOW DARE YOU TRY TO DECEIVE THE WATER GOD, BOY!?

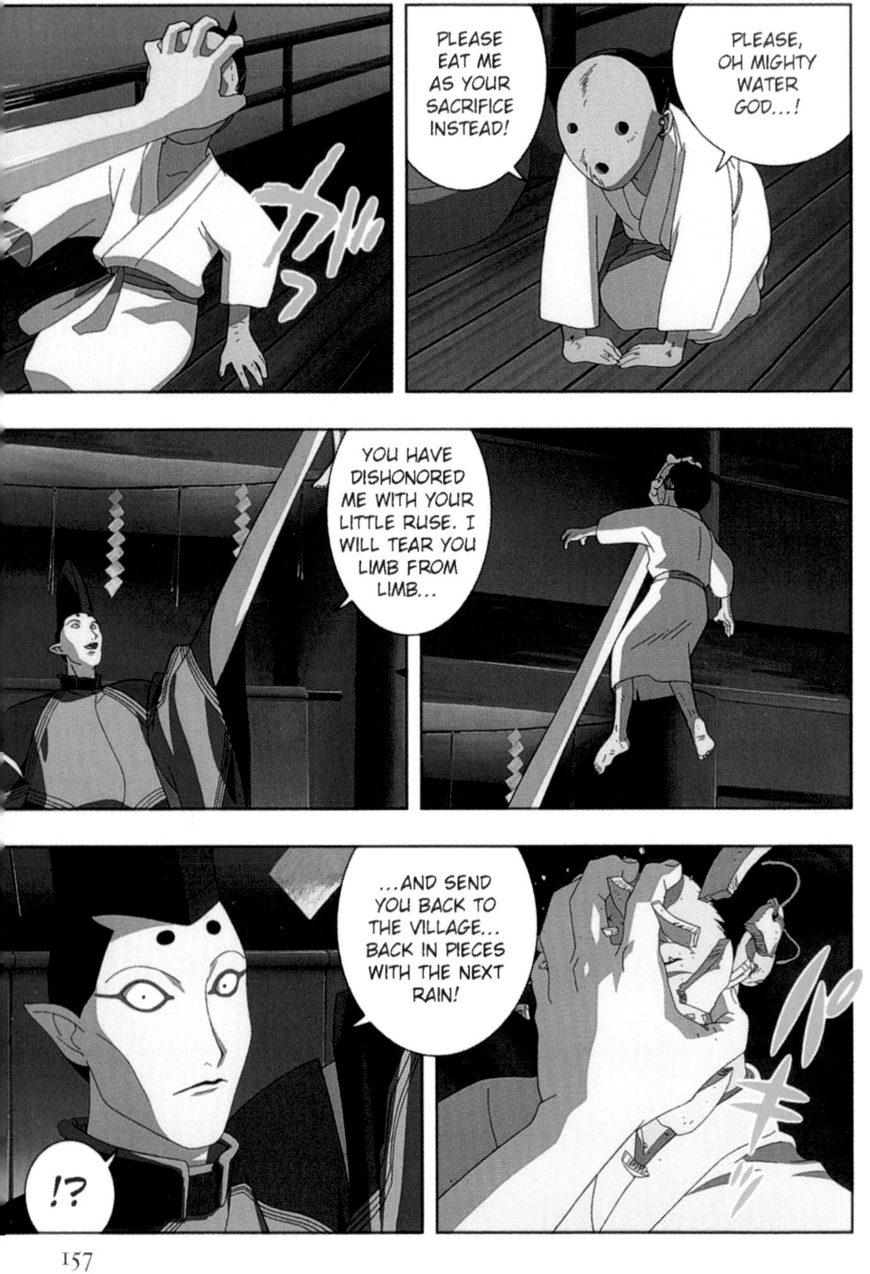
PLEASE, OH MIGHTY WATER GOD...!
PLEASE EAT ME AS YOUR SACRIFICE INSTEAD!
YOU HAVE DISHONORED ME WITH YOUR LITTLE RUSE. I WILL TEAR YOU LIMB FROM LIMB...
...AND SEND YOU BACK TO THE VILLAGE... BACK IN PIECES WITH THE NEXT RAIN!
!?

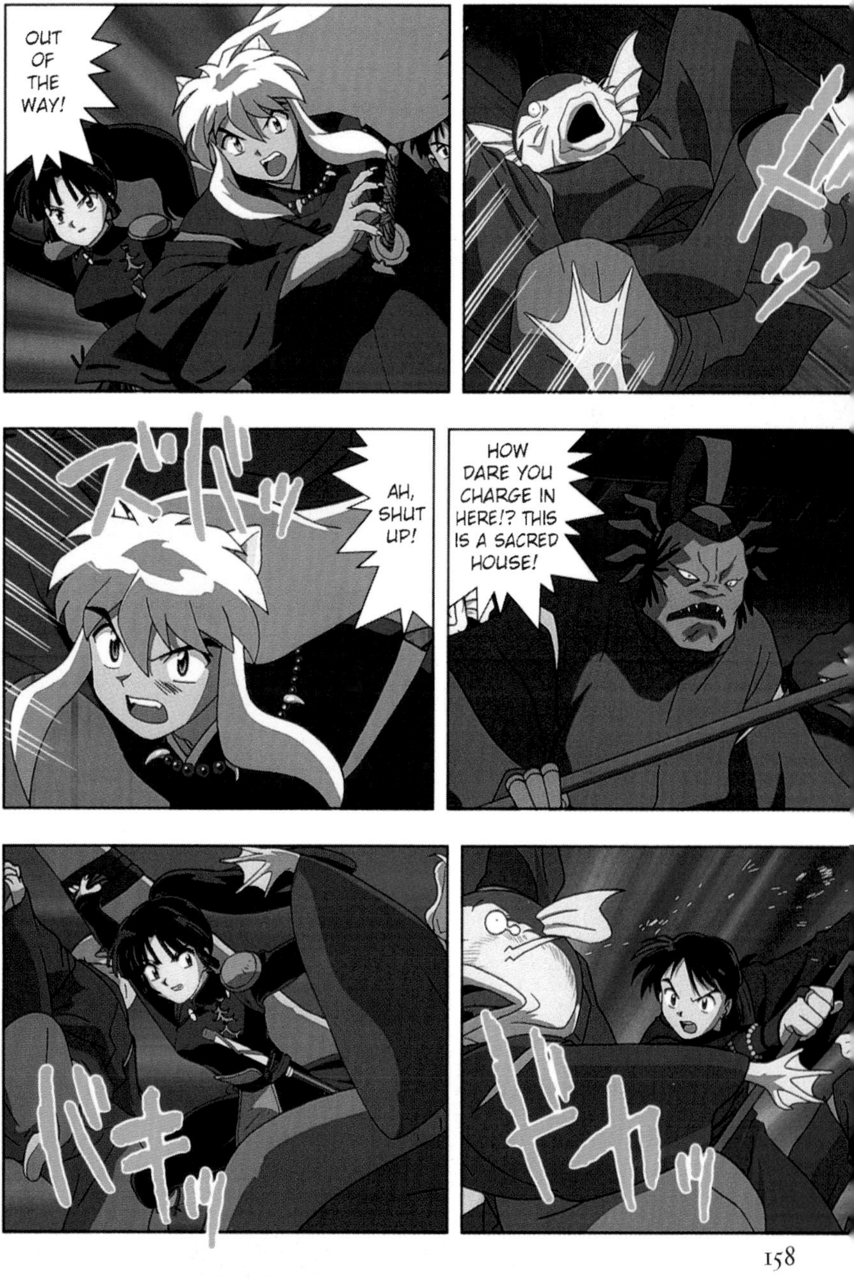
OUT OF THE WAY!
HOW DARE YOU CHARGE IN HERE!? THIS IS A SACRED HOUSE!
ズバッ
AH, SHUT UP!
ドカッ
バキッ

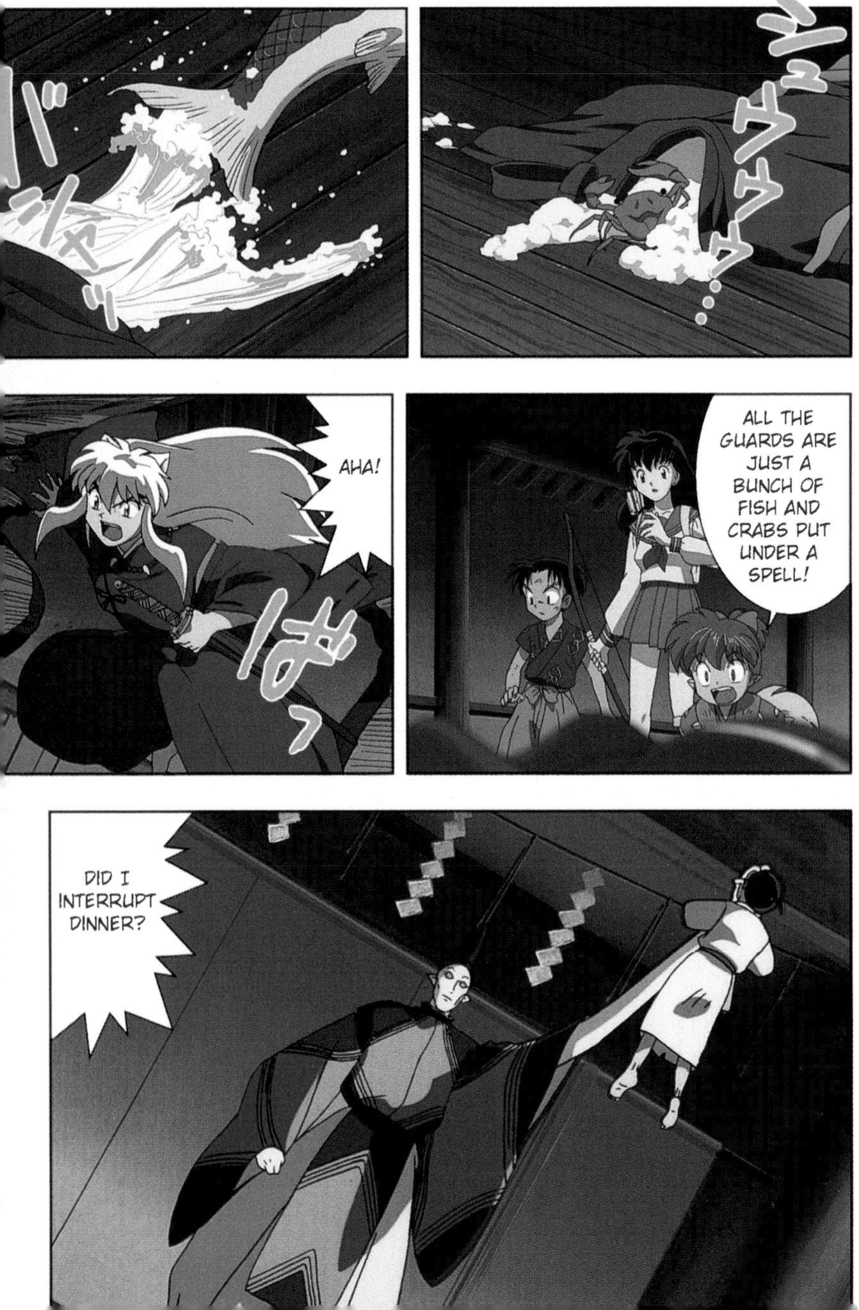
バシャッ
ALL THE GUARDS ARE JUST A BUNCH OF FISH AND CRABS PUT UNDER A SPELL!
AHA!
ばっ
DID I INTERRUPT DINNER?

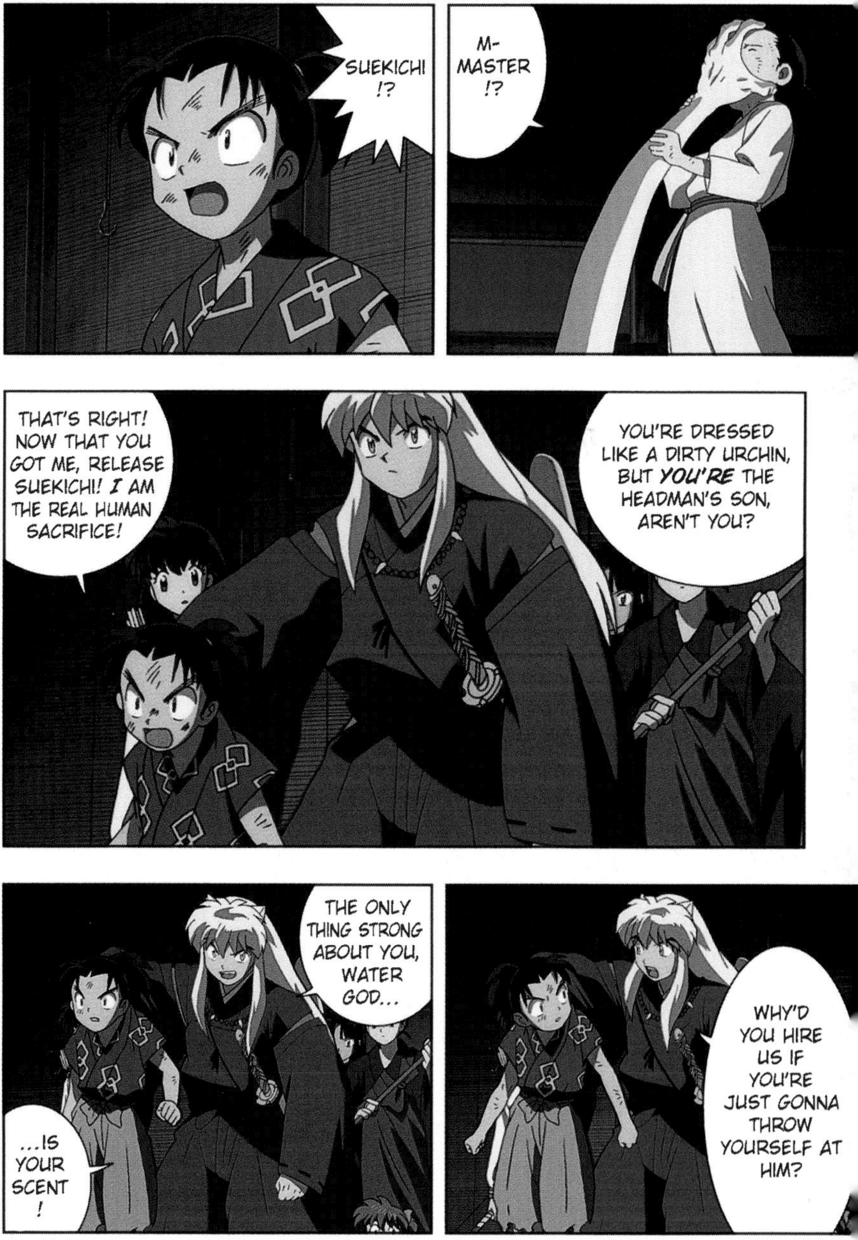
M-MASTER!?
SUEKICHI!?
YOU'RE DRESSED LIKE A DIRTY URCHIN, BUT *YOU'RE* THE HEADMAN'S SON, AREN'T YOU?
THAT'S RIGHT! NOW THAT YOU GOT ME, RELEASE SUEKICHI! *I* AM THE REAL HUMAN SACRIFICE!
WHY'D YOU HIRE US IF YOU'RE JUST GONNA THROW YOURSELF AT HIM?
THE ONLY THING STRONG ABOUT YOU, WATER GOD...
...IS YOUR SCENT!

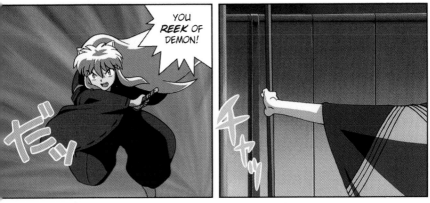

YOU *REEK* OF DEMON!

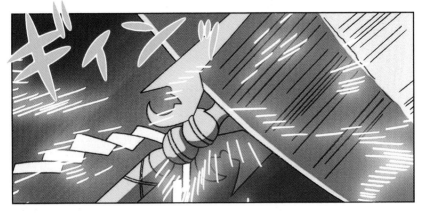

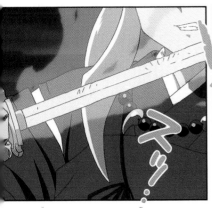

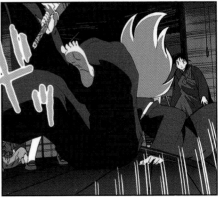

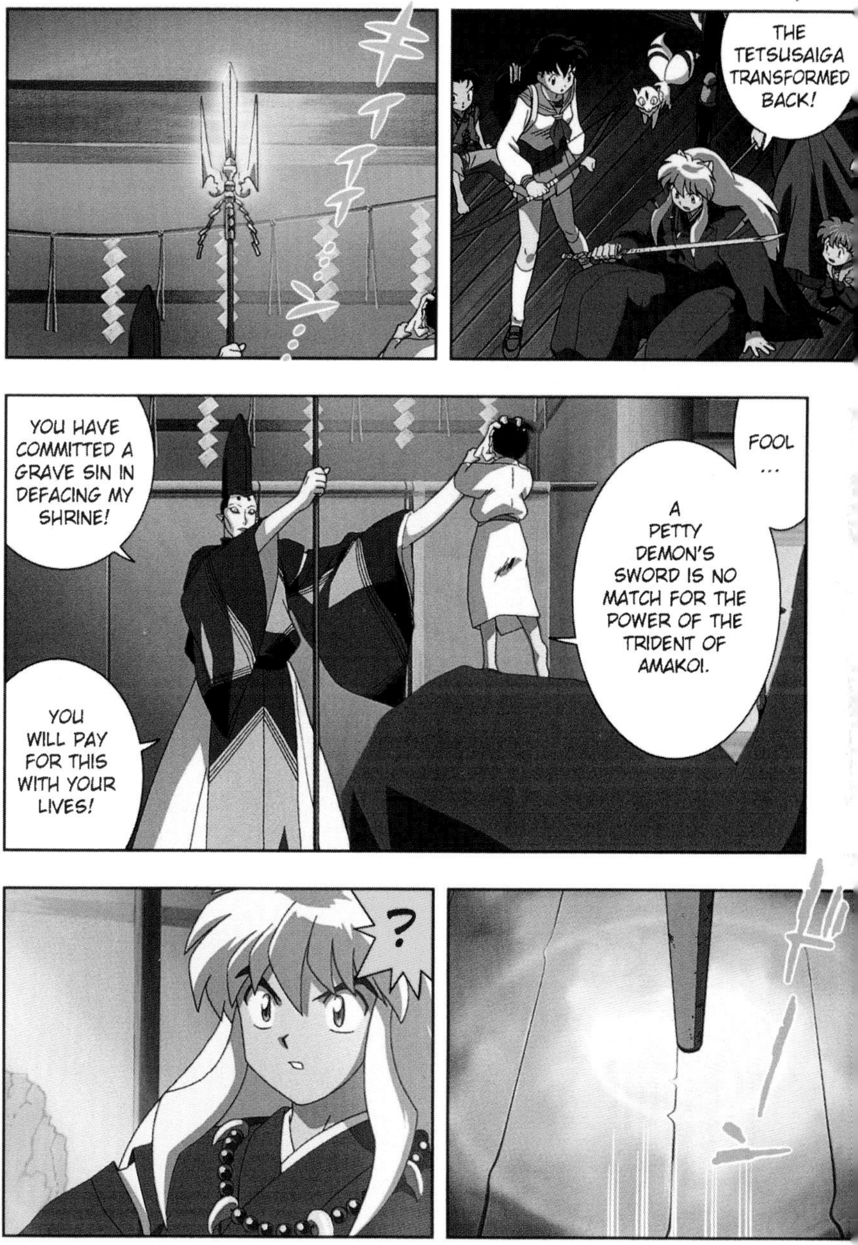
THE TETSUSAIGA TRANSFORMED BACK!
FOOL...
A PETTY DEMON'S SWORD IS NO MATCH FOR THE POWER OF THE TRIDENT OF AMAKOI.
YOU HAVE COMMITTED A GRAVE SIN IN DEFACING MY SHRINE!
YOU WILL PAY FOR THIS WITH YOUR LIVES!
?

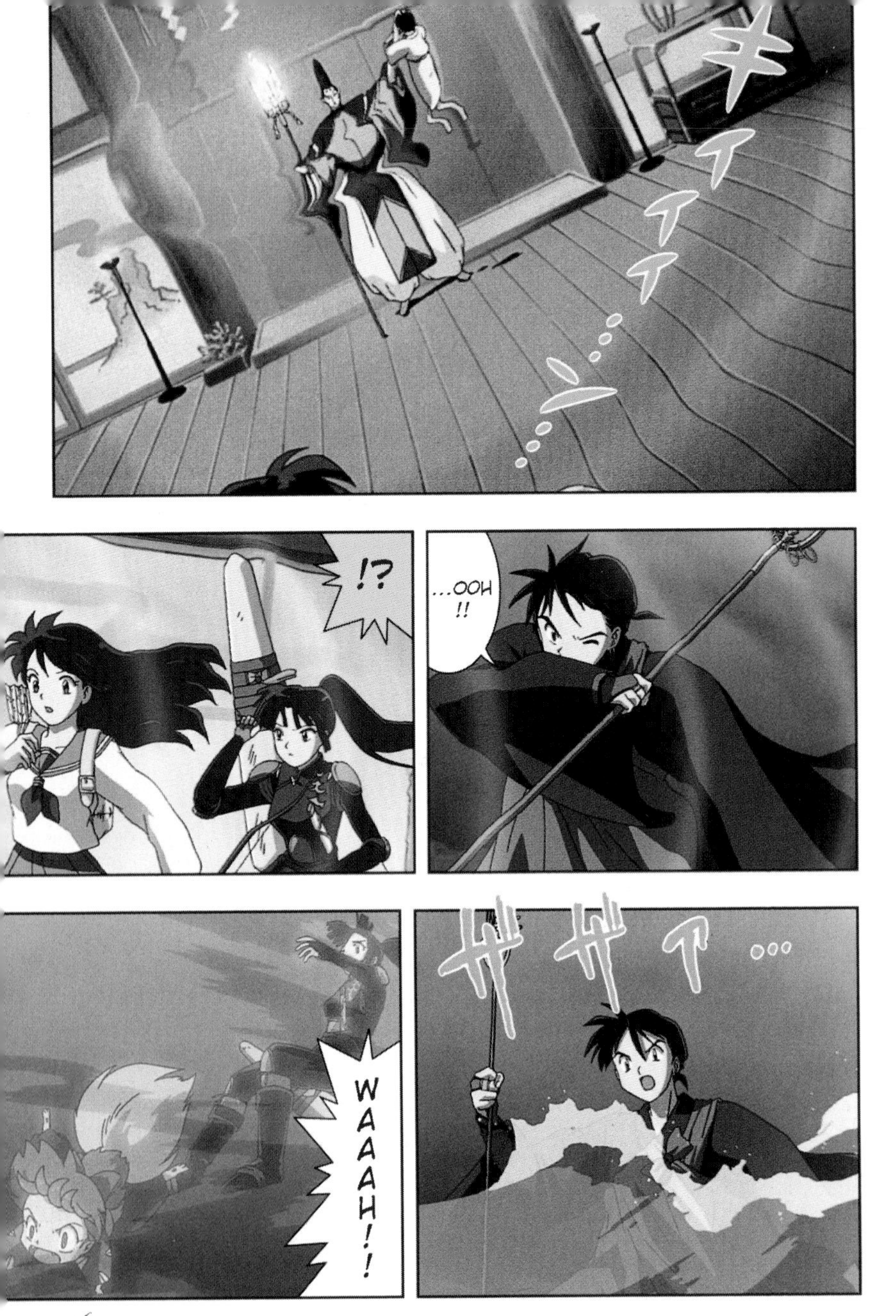
キィィィィ…ン
...OOH!!
!?
ザザァ…
WAAAAH!!

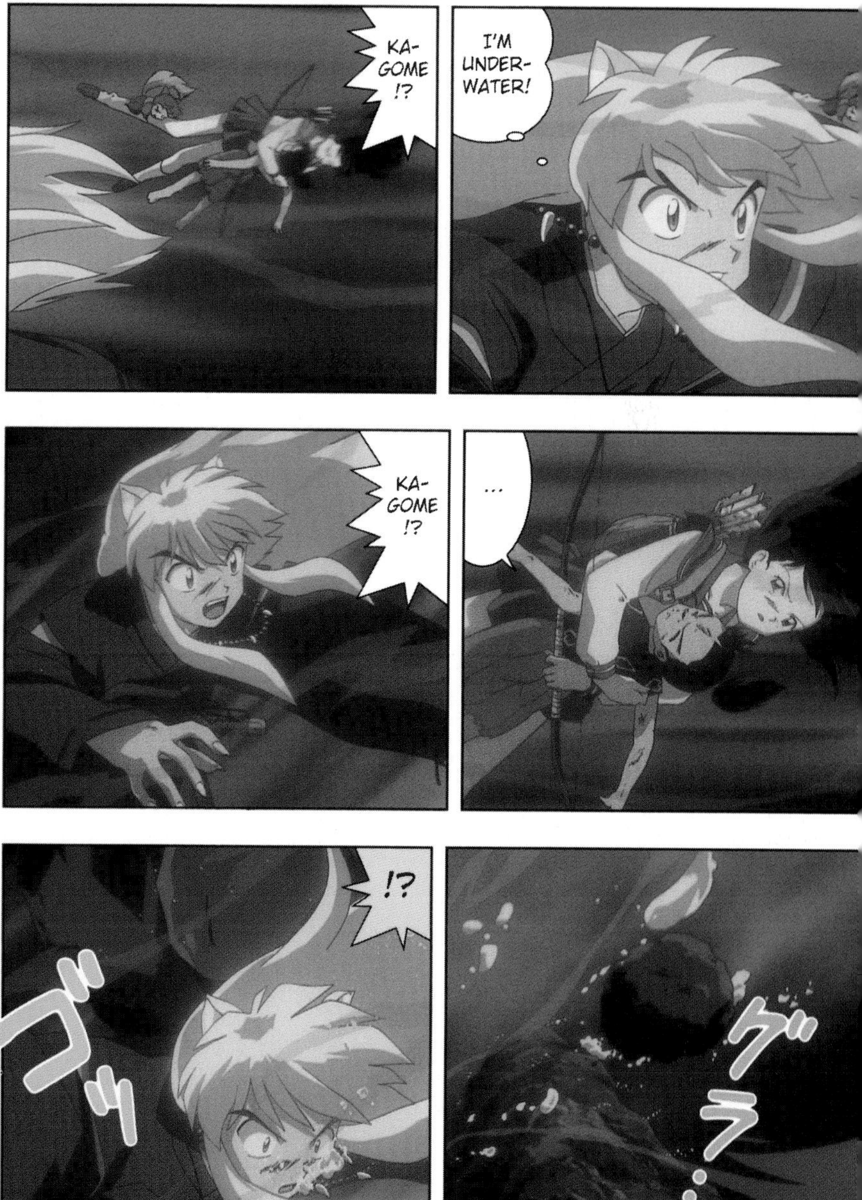
I'M UNDER-WATER!
KA-GOME !?
...
KA-GOME !?
グラ…
!?
ゴッ

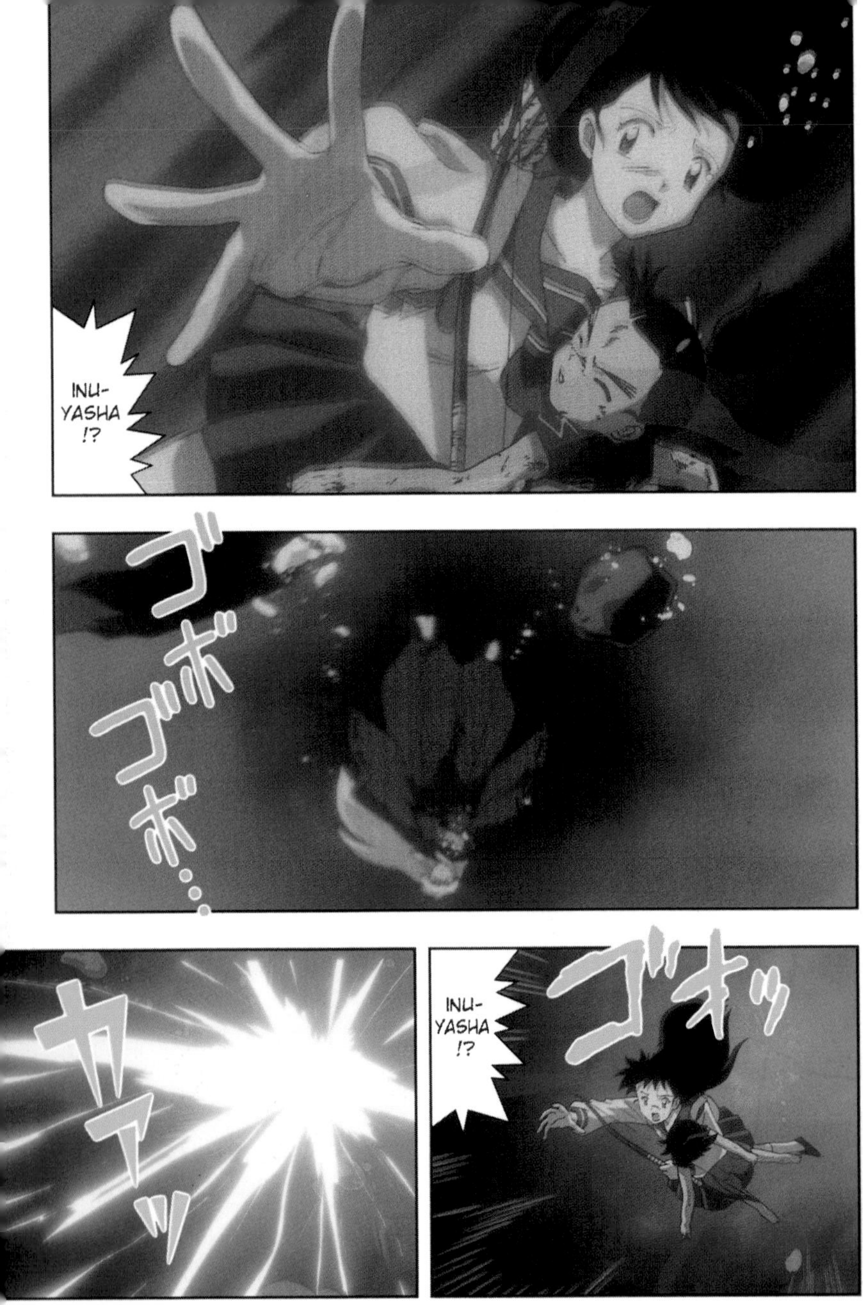
INU-YASHA!?
ゴボゴボ…
ゴオッ
INU-YASHA!?
ヤァァッ

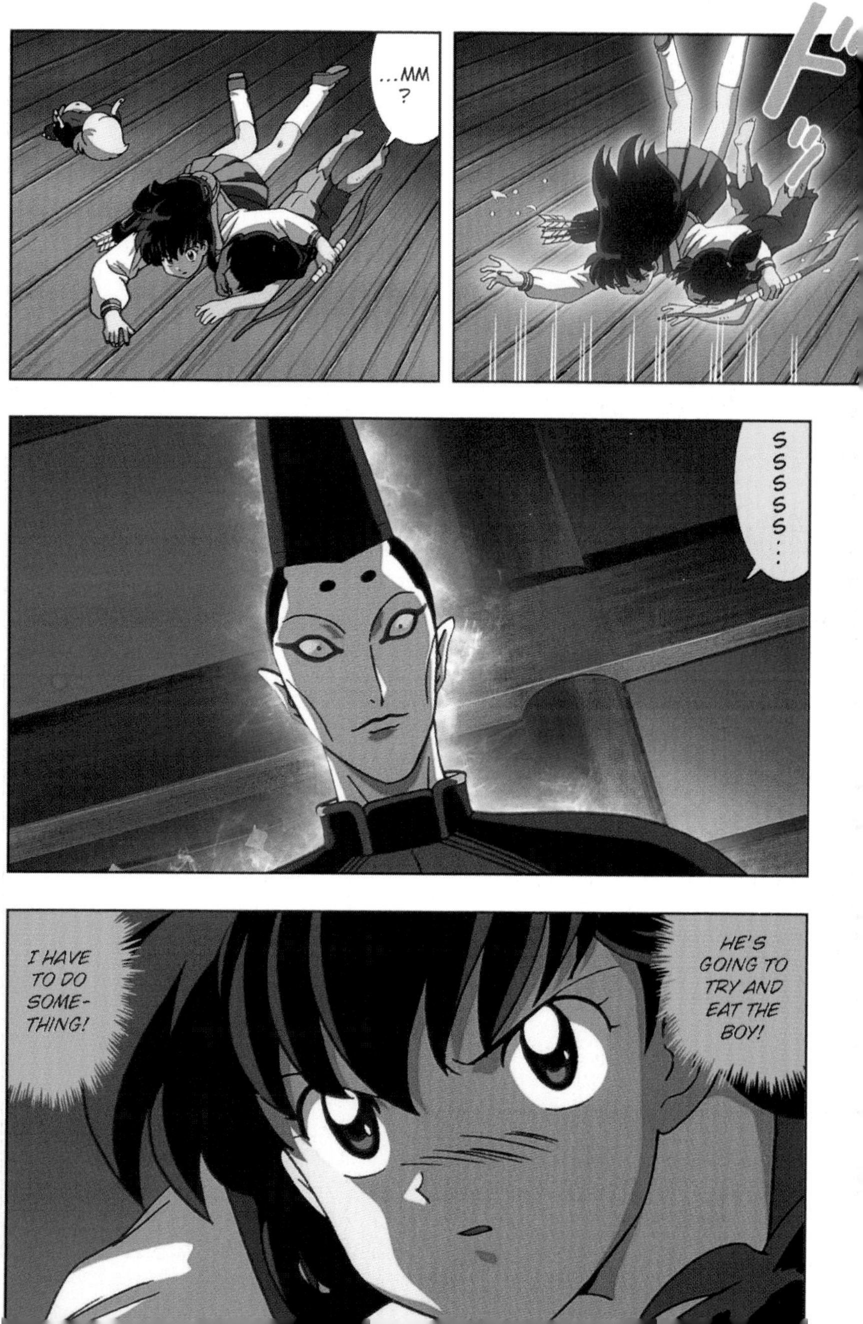
ドッ
...MM ?
SSSSS...
HE'S GOING TO TRY AND EAT THE BOY!
I HAVE TO DO SOME-THING!

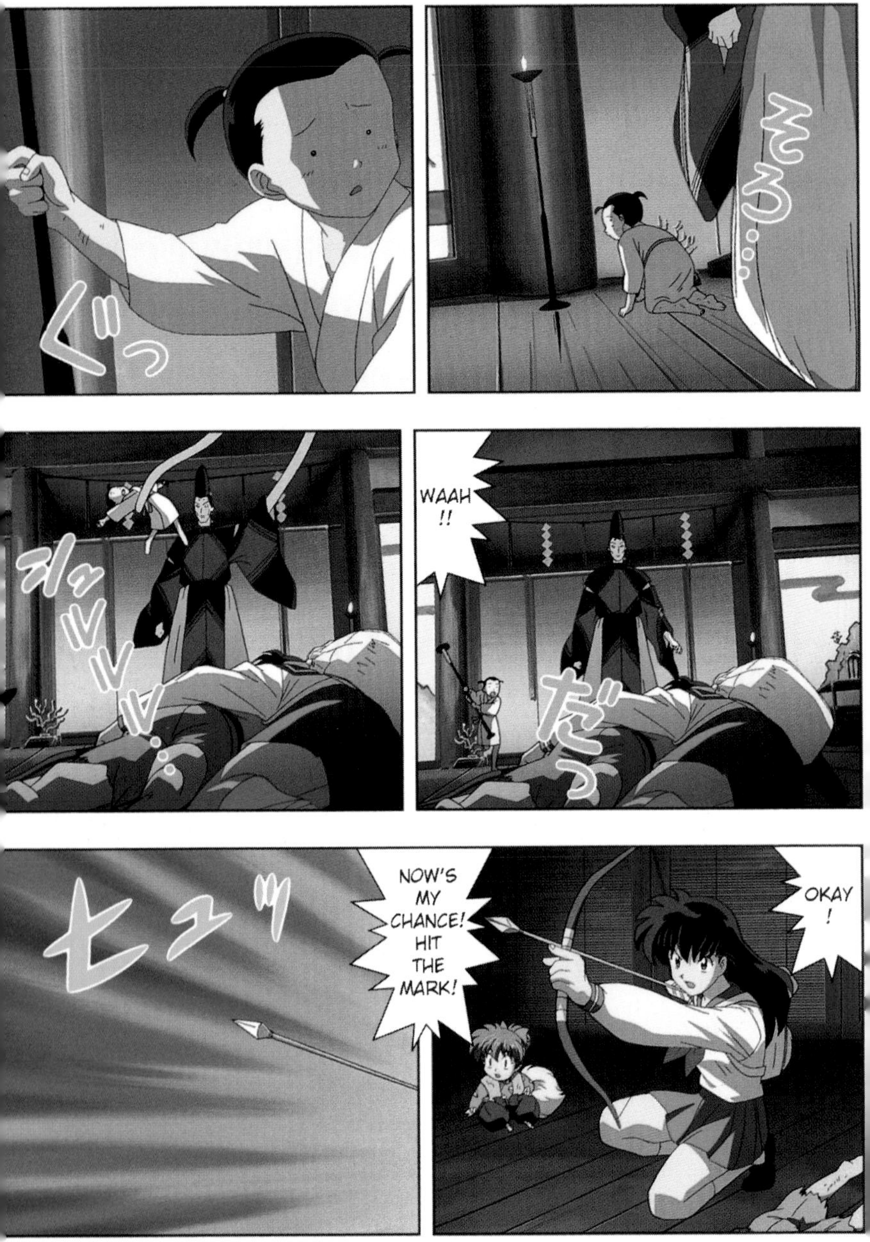
ぐっ
WAAH !!
だっ
OKAY!
NOW'S MY CHANCE! HIT THE MARK!
ヒュッ

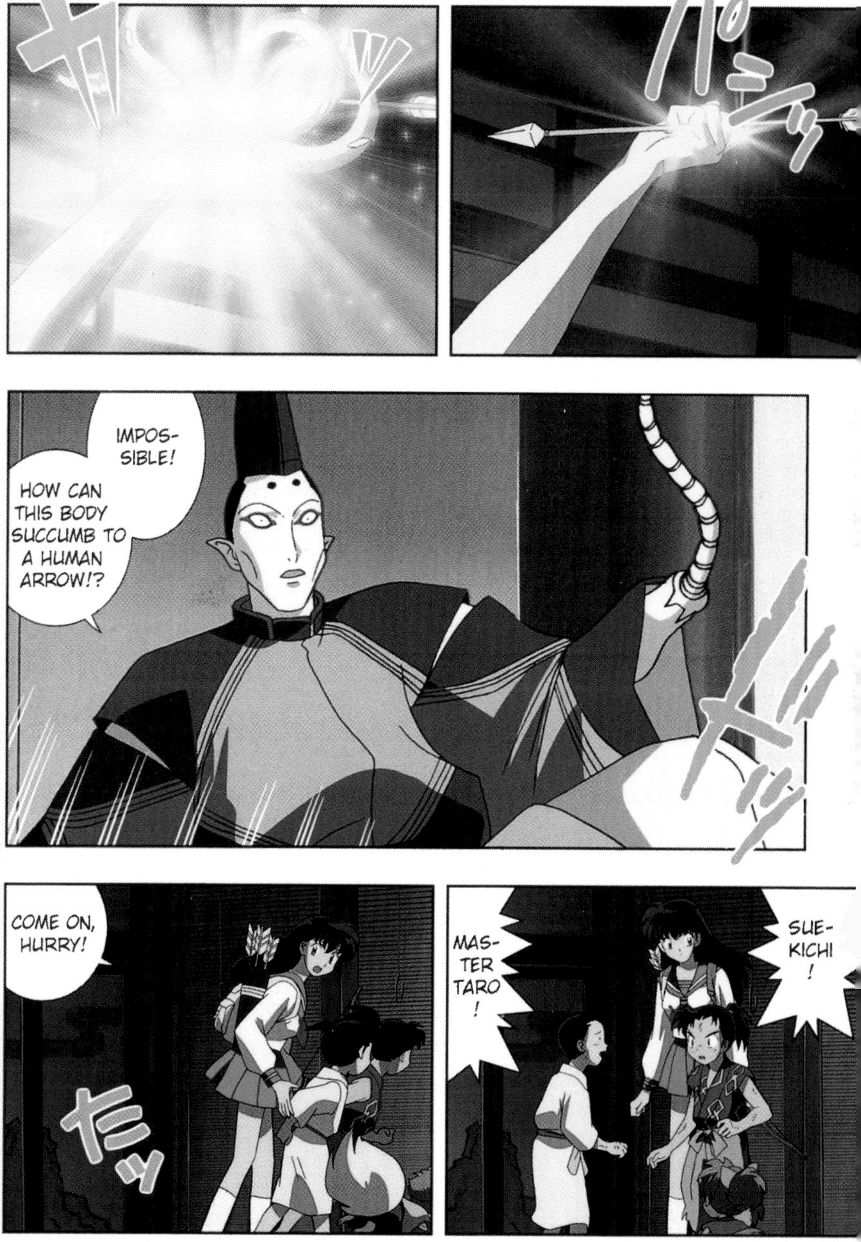
パシッ
IMPOSSIBLE!
HOW CAN THIS BODY SUCCUMB TO A HUMAN ARROW!?
SUEKICHI!
MASTER TARO!
COME ON, HURRY!
タッ

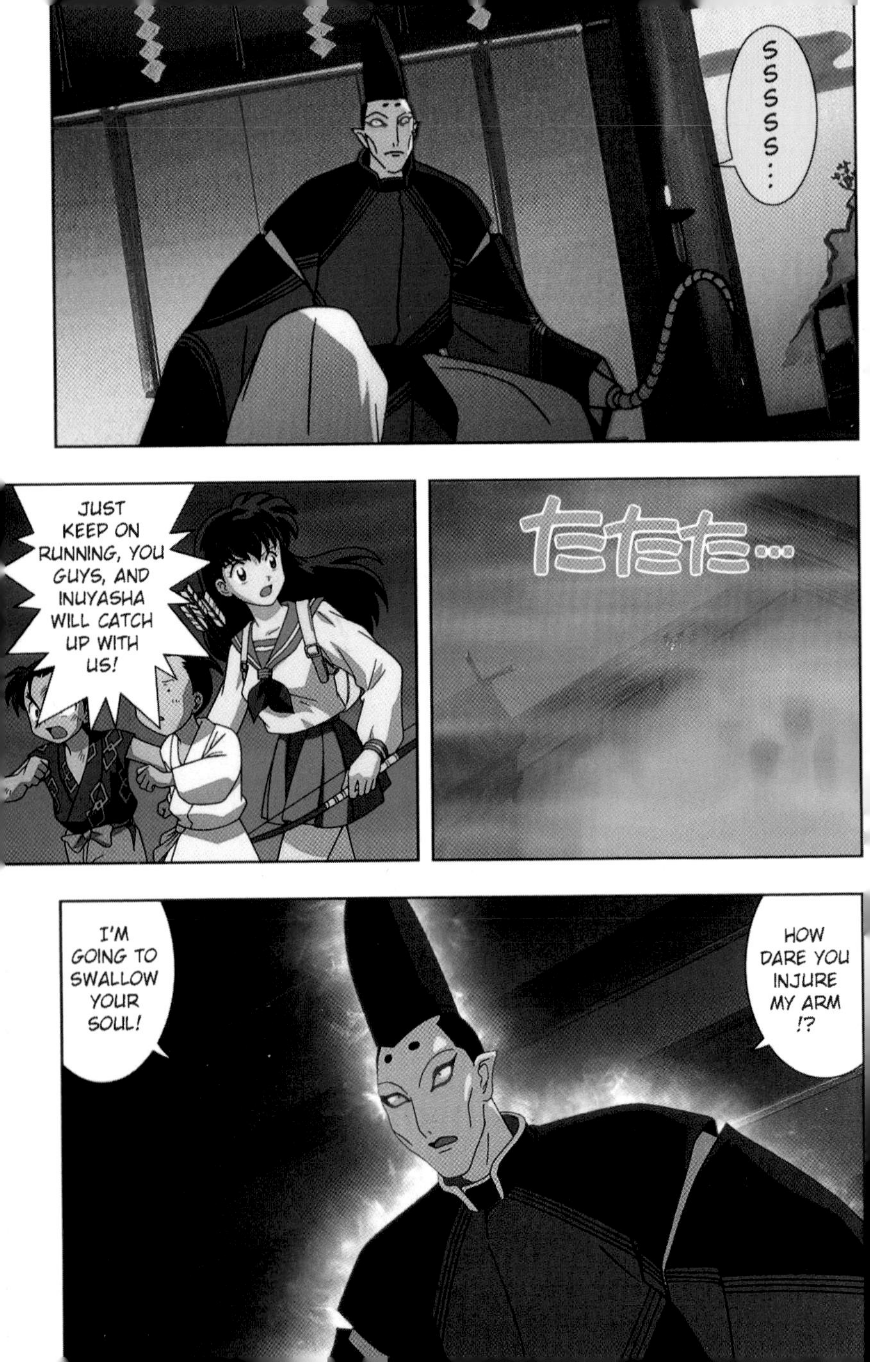
SSSSS...
たたた…
JUST KEEP ON RUNNING, YOU GUYS, AND INUYASHA WILL CATCH UP WITH US!
HOW DARE YOU INJURE MY ARM !?
I'M GOING TO SWALLOW YOUR SOUL!

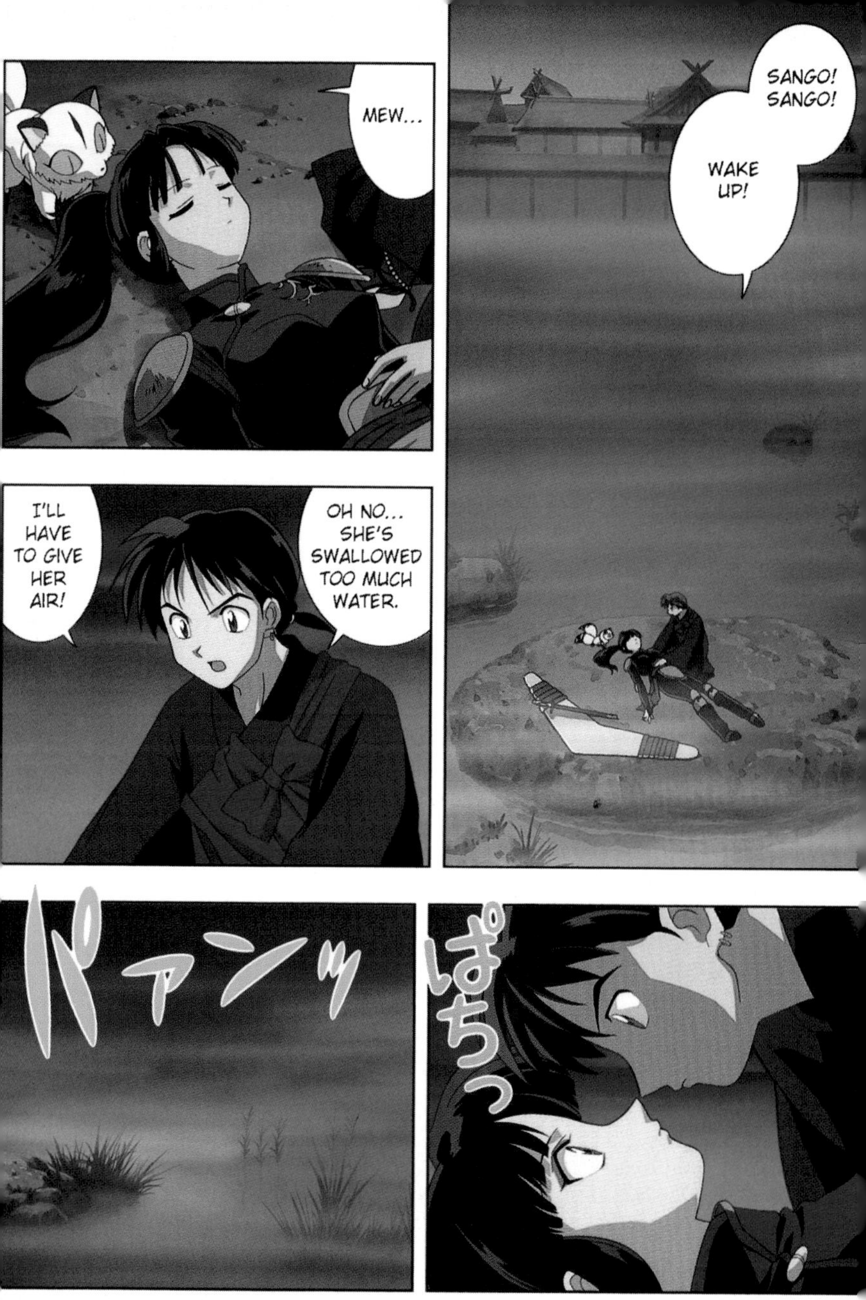
SANGO! SANGO!
WAKE UP!
MEW...
OH NO... SHE'S SWALLOWED TOO MUCH WATER.
I'LL HAVE TO GIVE HER AIR!
ぱちっ
パァンッ

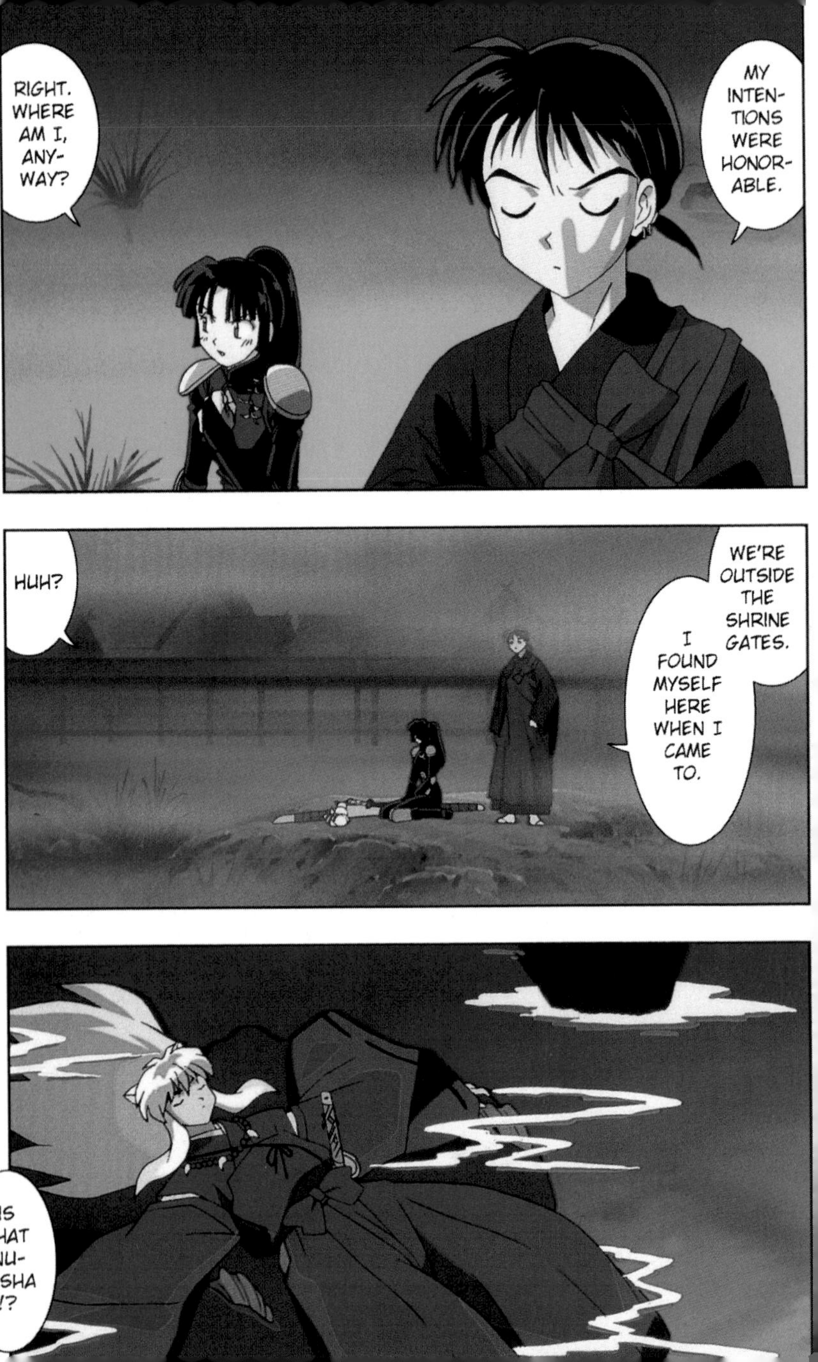
MY INTEN-TIONS WERE HONOR-ABLE.
RIGHT. WHERE AM I, ANY-WAY?
WE'RE OUTSIDE THE SHRINE GATES.
I FOUND MYSELF HERE WHEN I CAME TO.
HUH?
IS THAT INU-YASHA!?

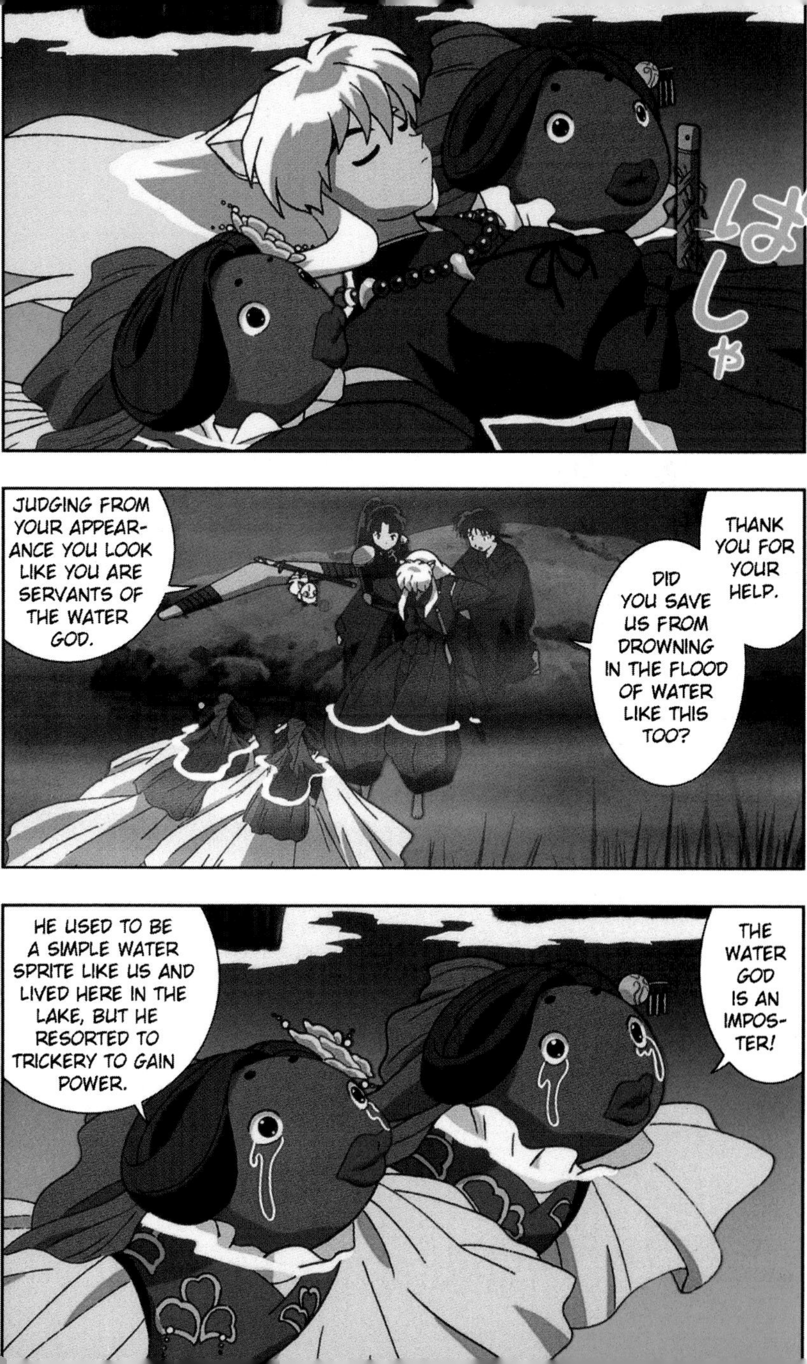
ぱしゃ
THANK YOU FOR YOUR HELP.
DID YOU SAVE US FROM DROWNING IN THE FLOOD OF WATER LIKE THIS TOO?
JUDGING FROM YOUR APPEARANCE YOU LOOK LIKE YOU ARE SERVANTS OF THE WATER GOD.
THE WATER GOD IS AN IMPOSTER!
HE USED TO BE A SIMPLE WATER SPRITE LIKE US AND LIVED HERE IN THE LAKE, BUT HE RESORTED TO TRICKERY TO GAIN POWER.

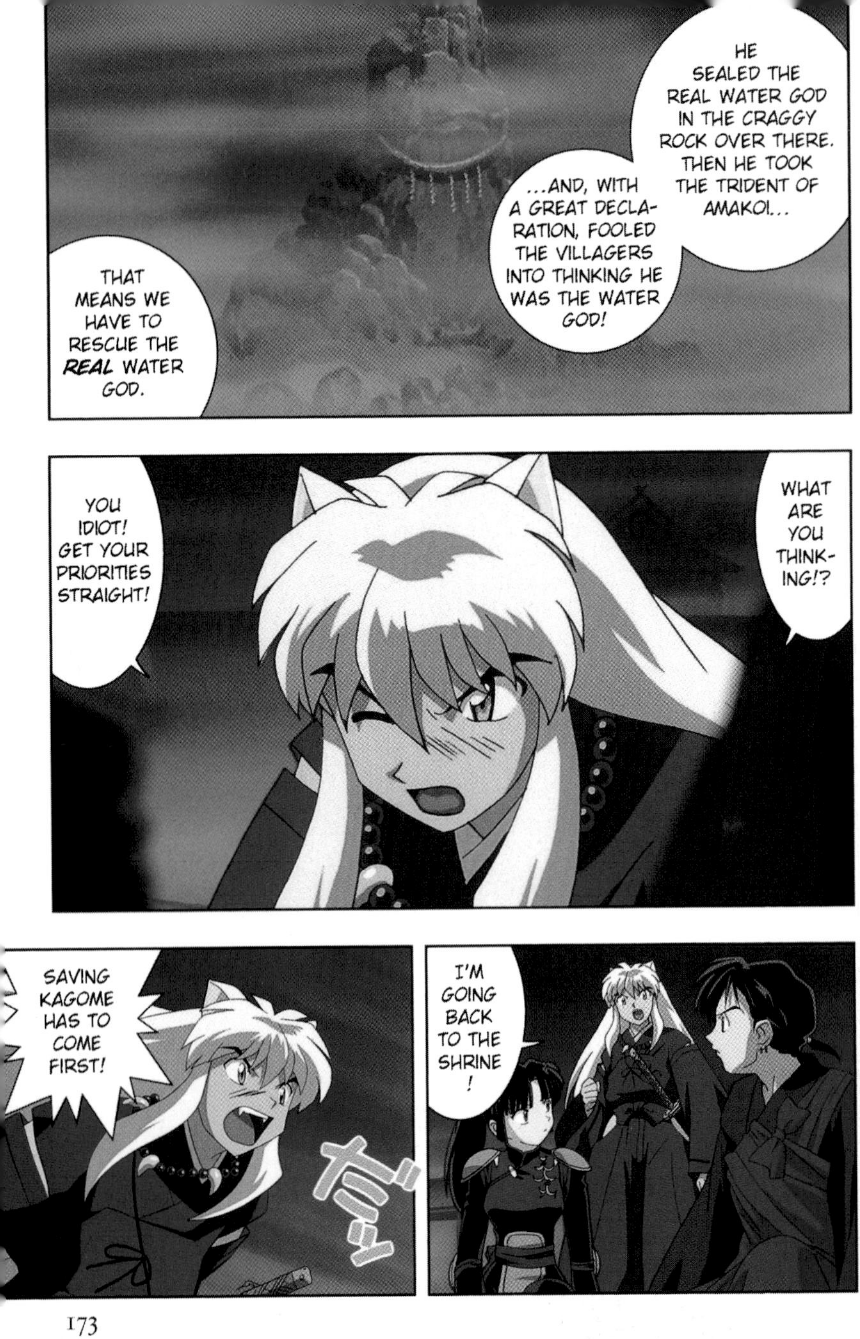
HE SEALED THE REAL WATER GOD IN THE CRAGGY ROCK OVER THERE. THEN HE TOOK THE TRIDENT OF AMAKOI...
...AND, WITH A GREAT DECLA-RATION, FOOLED THE VILLAGERS INTO THINKING HE WAS THE WATER GOD!
THAT MEANS WE HAVE TO RESCUE THE *REAL* WATER GOD.
WHAT ARE YOU THINK-ING!?
YOU IDIOT! GET YOUR PRIORITIES STRAIGHT!
I'M GOING BACK TO THE SHRINE!
SAVING KAGOME HAS TO COME FIRST!
ダッ

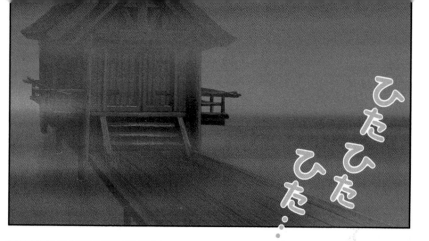

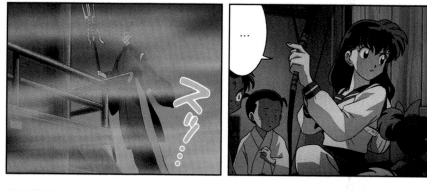

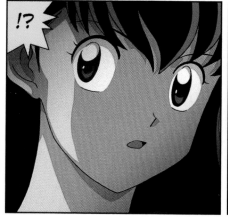

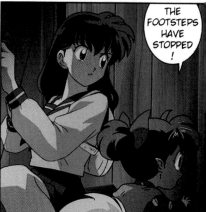

THE
FOOTSTEPS
HAVE
STOPPED
!

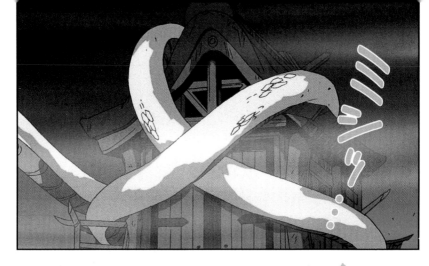

...?

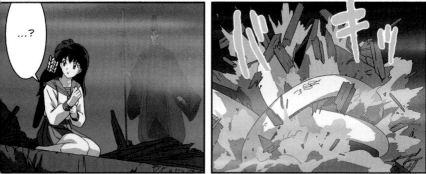

!!

I WILL DESTROY *YOU* FIRST, WENCH.

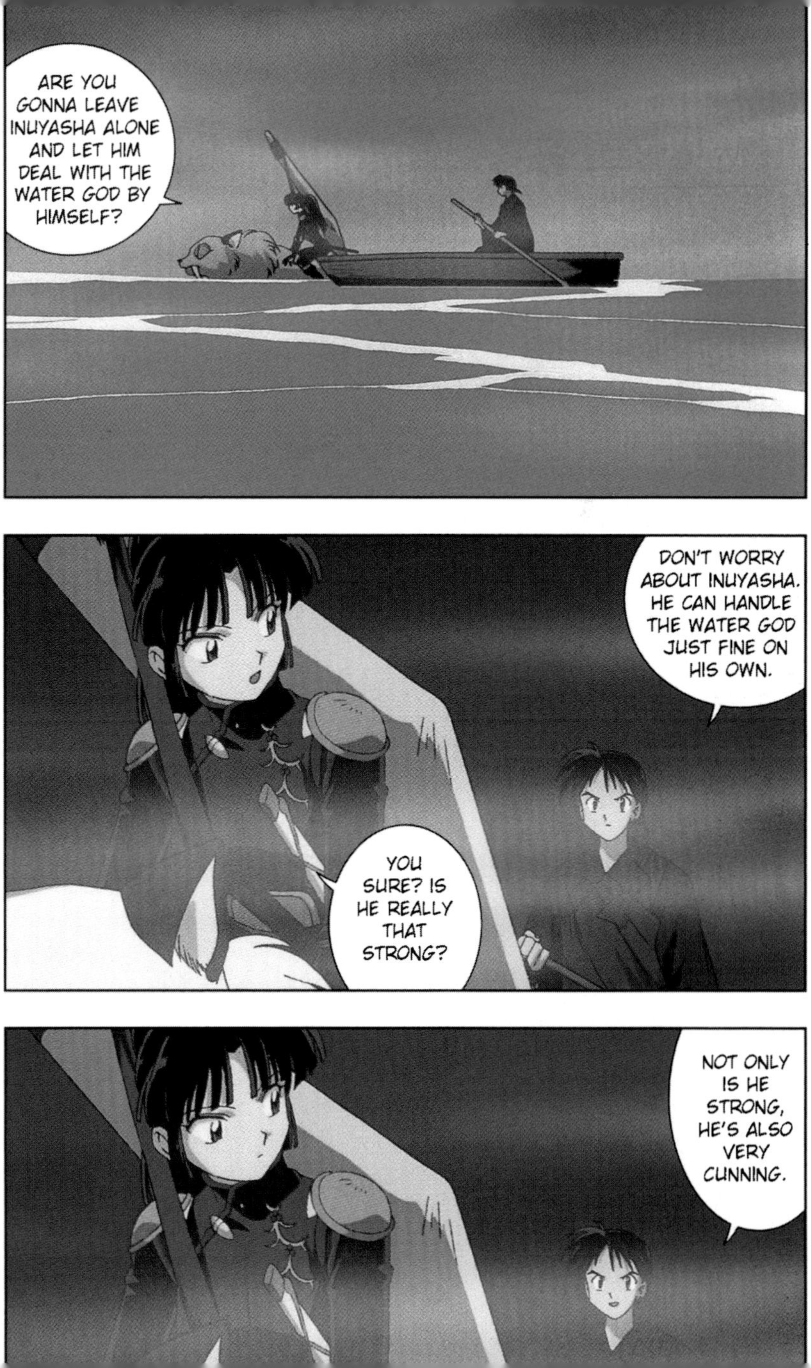
ARE YOU GONNA LEAVE INUYASHA ALONE AND LET HIM DEAL WITH THE WATER GOD BY HIMSELF?
DON'T WORRY ABOUT INUYASHA. HE CAN HANDLE THE WATER GOD JUST FINE ON HIS OWN.
YOU SURE? IS HE REALLY THAT STRONG?
NOT ONLY IS HE STRONG, HE'S ALSO VERY CUNNING.

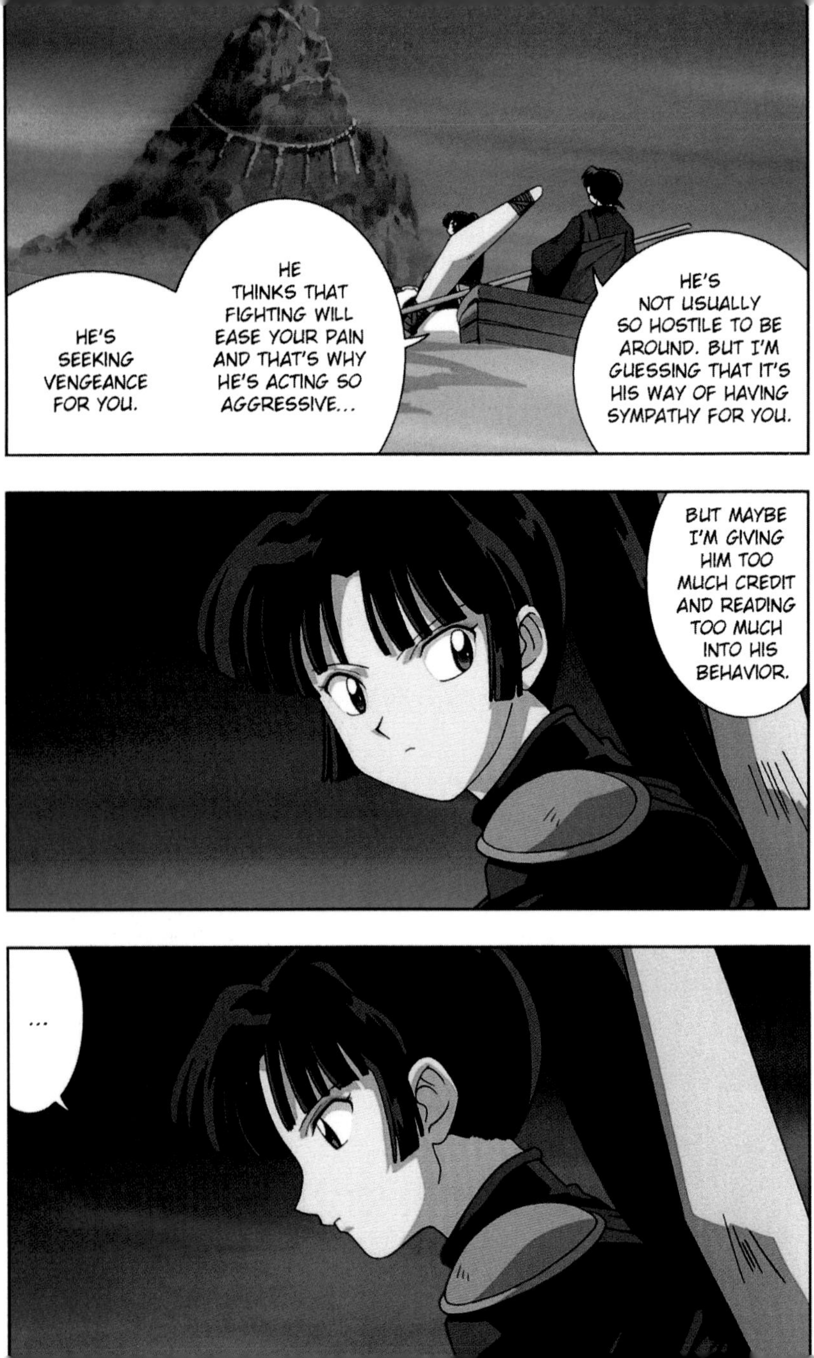
HE'S NOT USUALLY SO HOSTILE TO BE AROUND. BUT I'M GUESSING THAT IT'S HIS WAY OF HAVING SYMPATHY FOR YOU.
HE THINKS THAT FIGHTING WILL EASE YOUR PAIN AND THAT'S WHY HE'S ACTING SO AGGRESSIVE...
HE'S SEEKING VENGEANCE FOR YOU.
BUT MAYBE I'M GIVING HIM TOO MUCH CREDIT AND READING TOO MUCH INTO HIS BEHAVIOR.
...

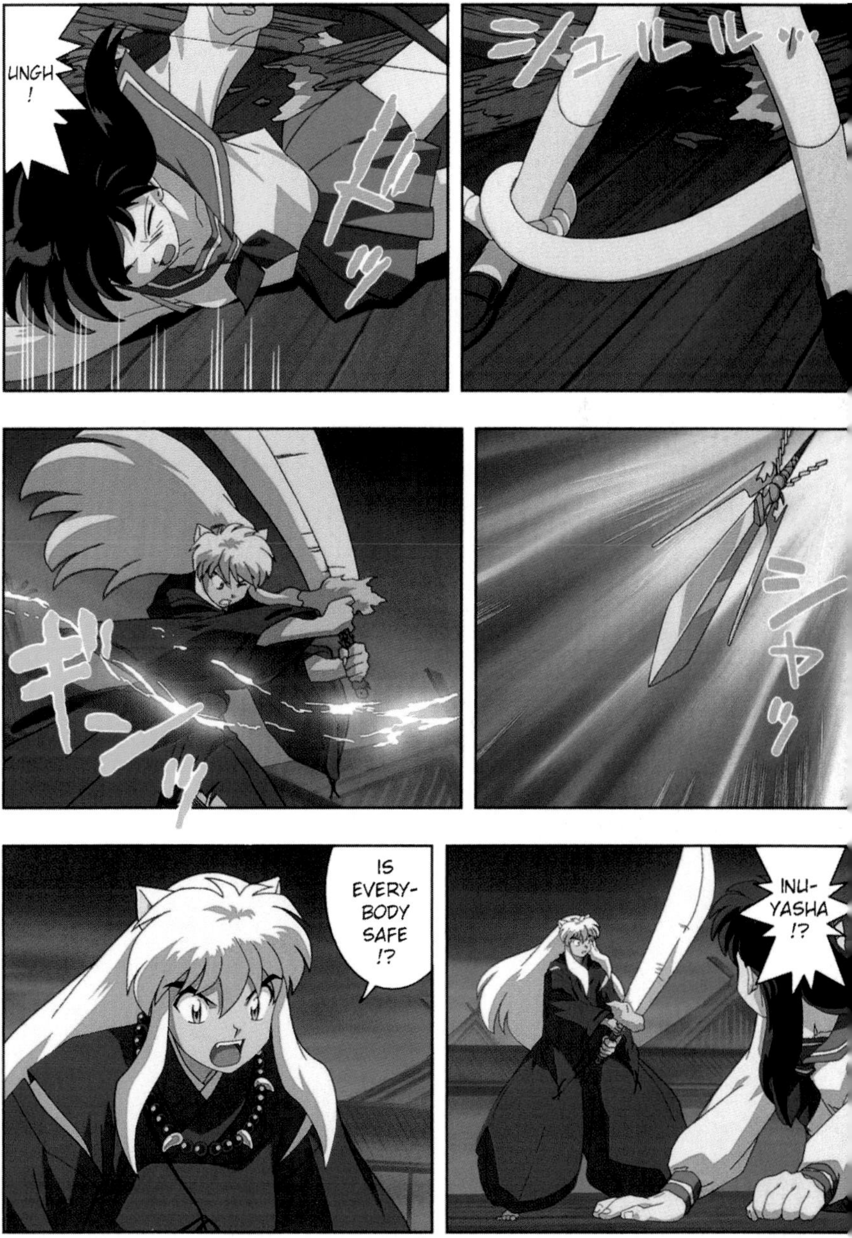
シュルルッ
UNGH !
ドッ
シャッ
ギーンッ
INU-YASHA !?
IS EVERY-BODY SAFE !?

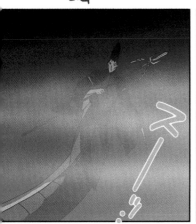

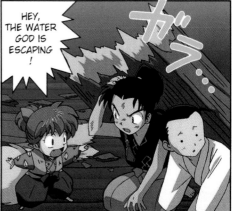

HEY, THE WATER GOD IS ESCAPING!

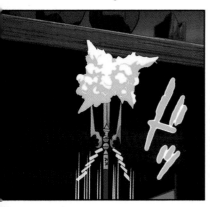

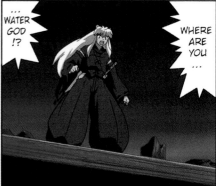

...WATER GOD!?

WHERE ARE YOU...

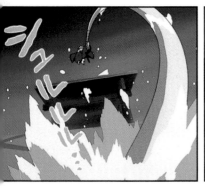

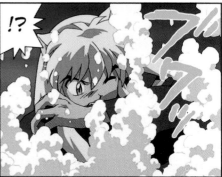

!?

179

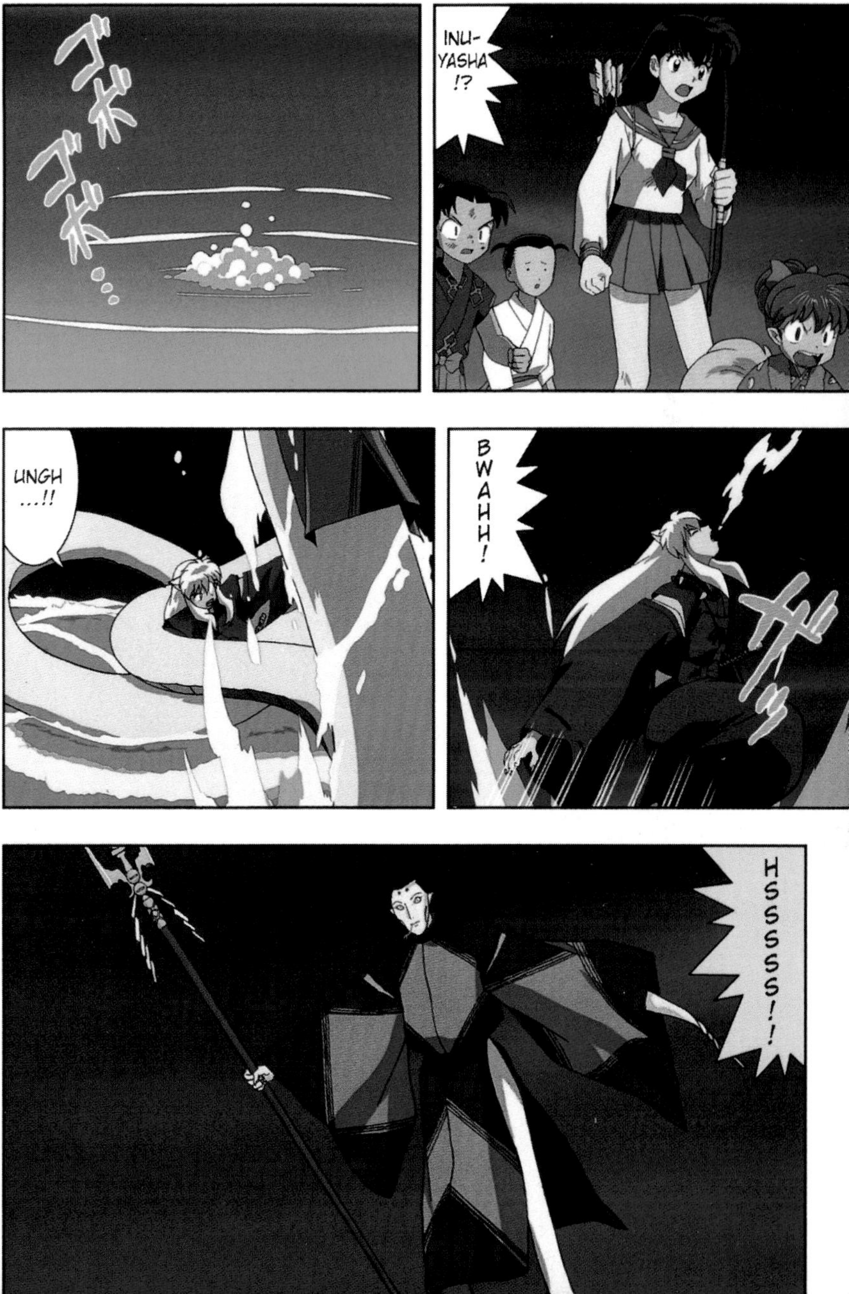
INU-YASHA!?
ゴボゴボ
BWAHH!
UNGH...!!
HSSSSS!!

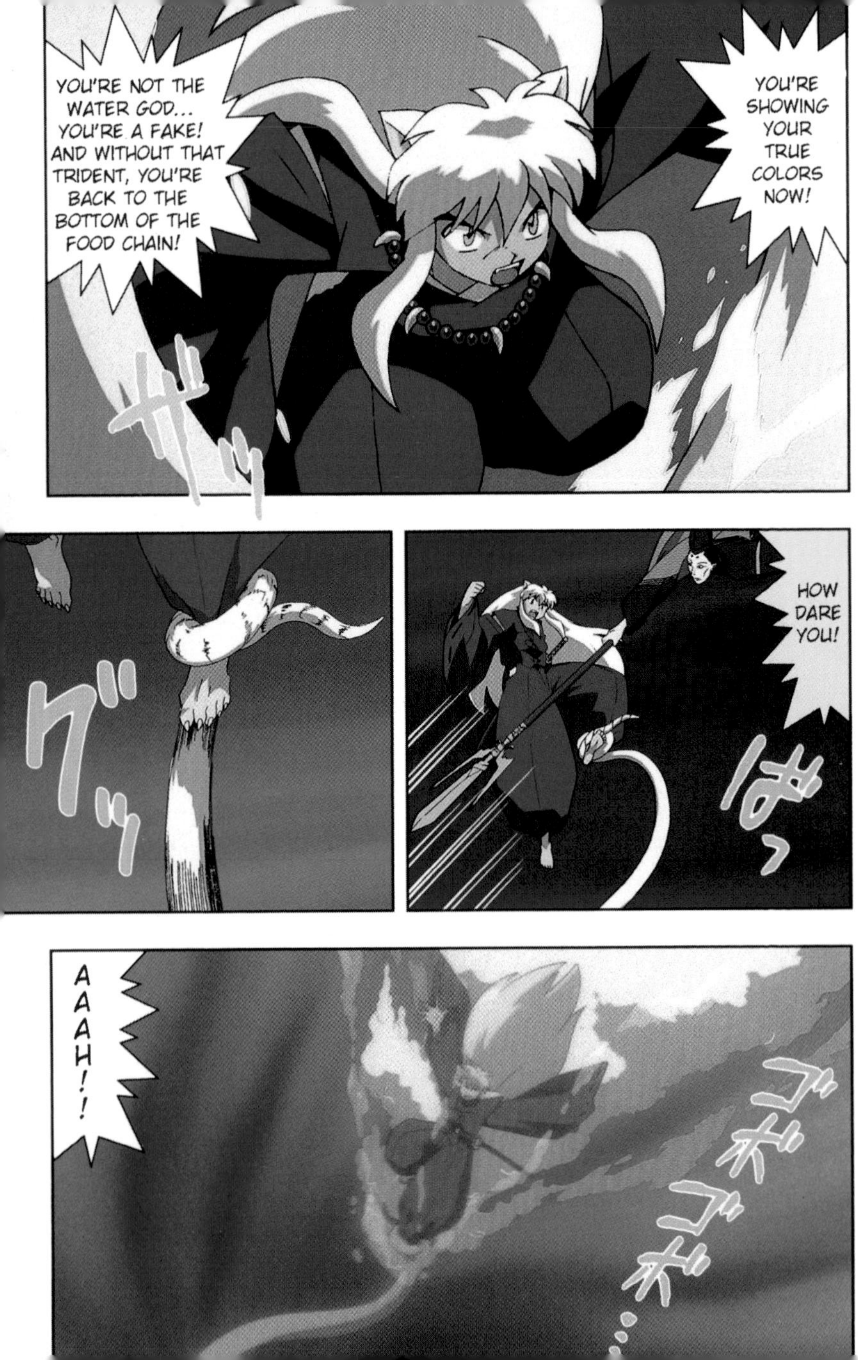
YOU'RE SHOWING YOUR TRUE COLORS NOW!
YOU'RE NOT THE WATER GOD... YOU'RE A FAKE! AND WITHOUT THAT TRIDENT, YOU'RE BACK TO THE BOTTOM OF THE FOOD CHAIN!
ザッ
HOW DARE YOU!
ばっ
グッ
ゴボゴボ…
AAAAH!!

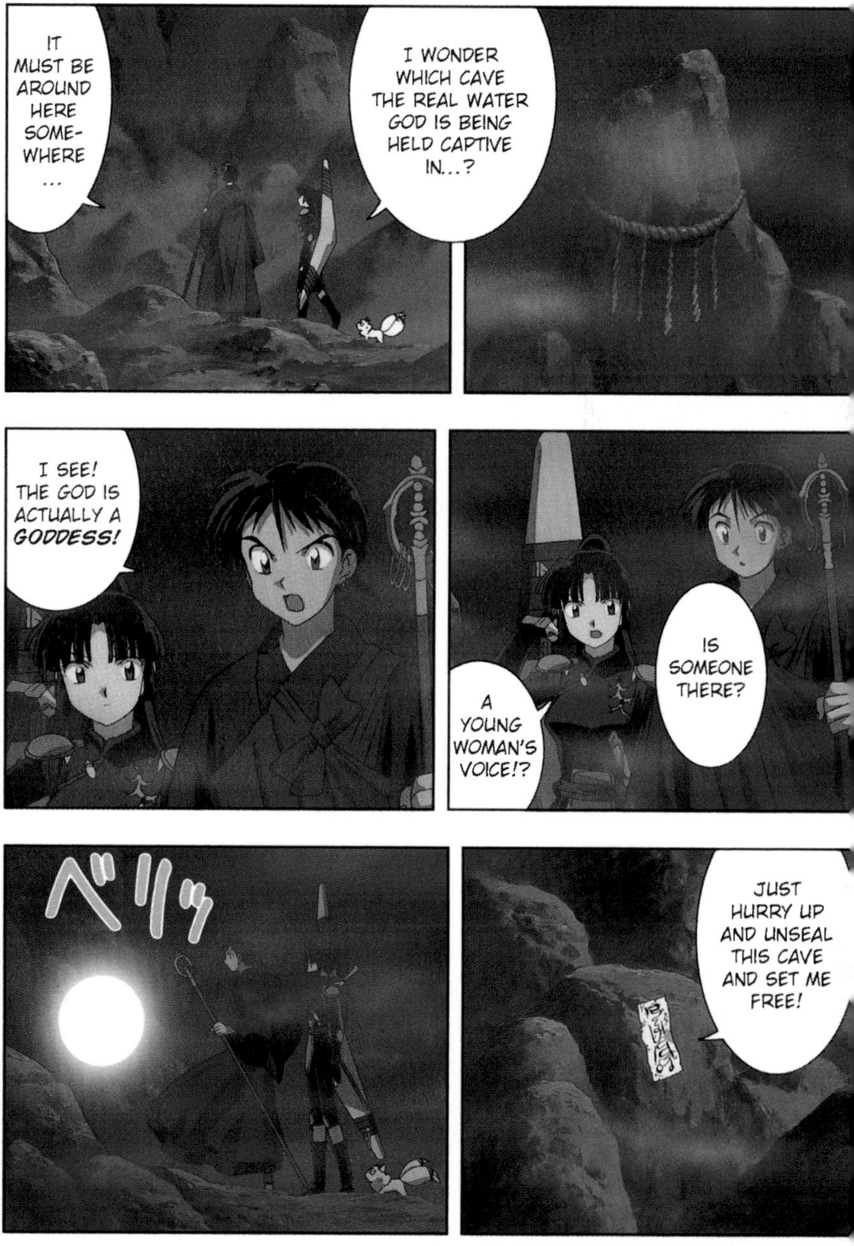
I WONDER WHICH CAVE THE REAL WATER GOD IS BEING HELD CAPTIVE IN...?
IT MUST BE AROUND HERE SOME-WHERE ...
IS SOMEONE THERE?
A YOUNG WOMAN'S VOICE!?
I SEE! THE GOD IS ACTUALLY A ***GODDESS!***
JUST HURRY UP AND UNSEAL THIS CAVE AND SET ME FREE!
ベリッ

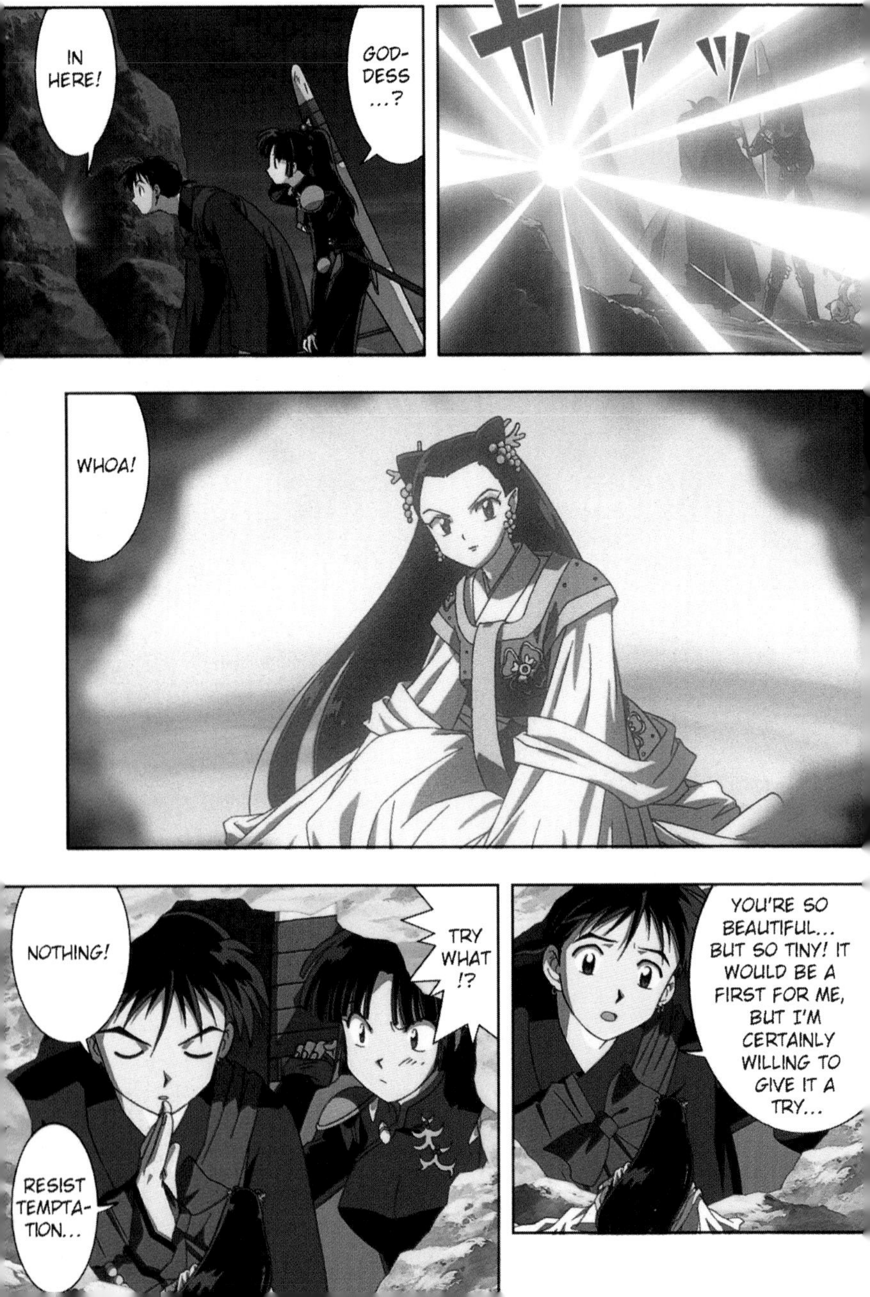
カァッ
GOD-DESS...?
IN HERE!
WHOA!
YOU'RE SO BEAUTIFUL... BUT SO TINY! IT WOULD BE A FIRST FOR ME, BUT I'M CERTAINLY WILLING TO GIVE IT A TRY...
TRY WHAT!?
NOTHING!
RESIST TEMPTA-TION...

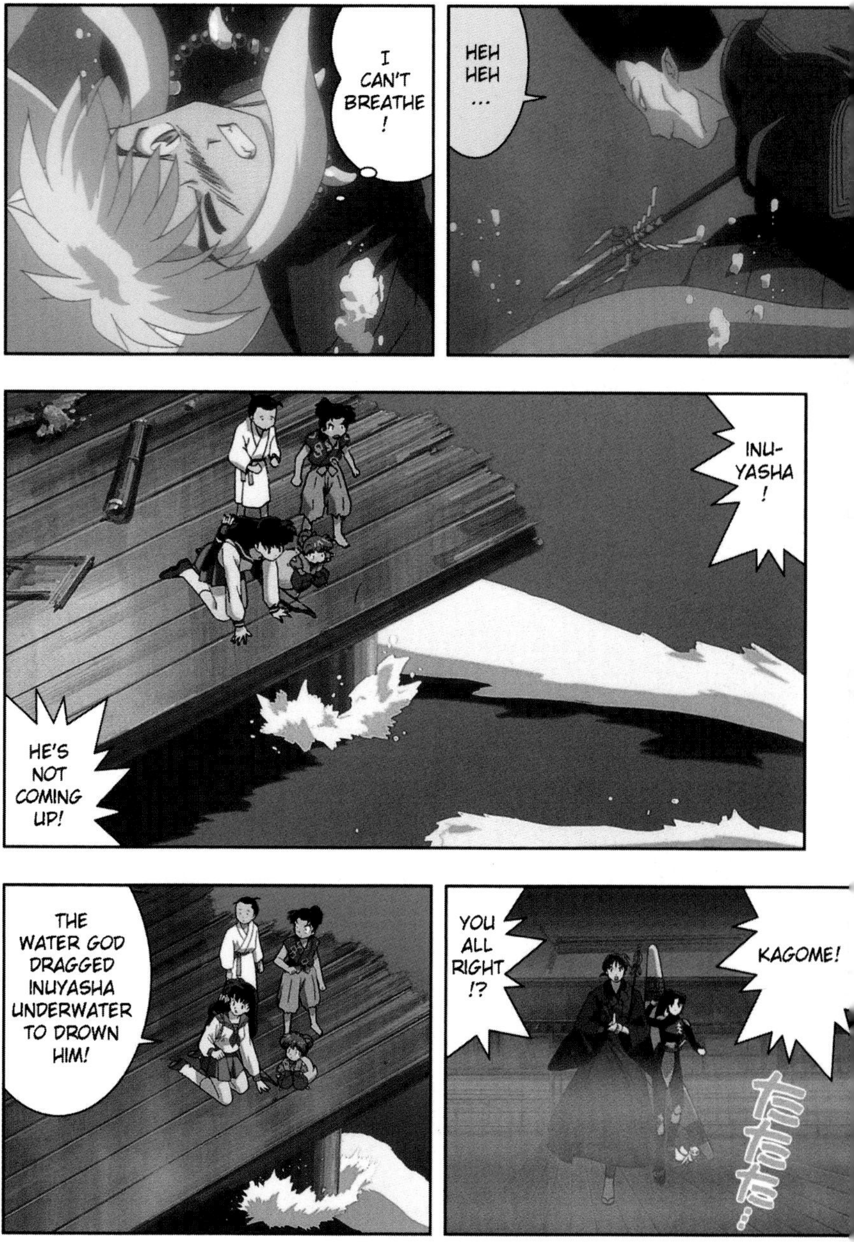
HEH HEH ...
I CAN'T BREATHE!
INU-YASHA!
HE'S NOT COMING UP!
KAGOME!
YOU ALL RIGHT!?
たたた...
THE WATER GOD DRAGGED INUYASHA UNDERWATER TO DROWN HIM!

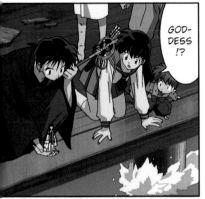

GOD-DESS
!?

YES, GODDESS!

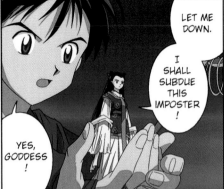

LET ME DOWN.

I SHALL SUBDUE THIS IMPOSTER!

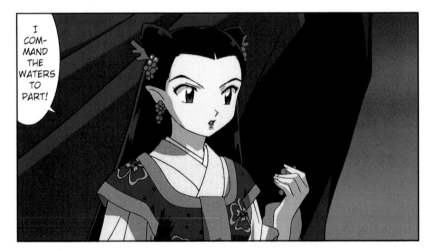

I COM-MAND THE WATERS TO PART!

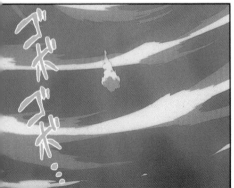

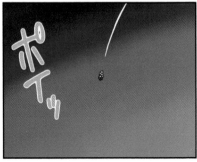

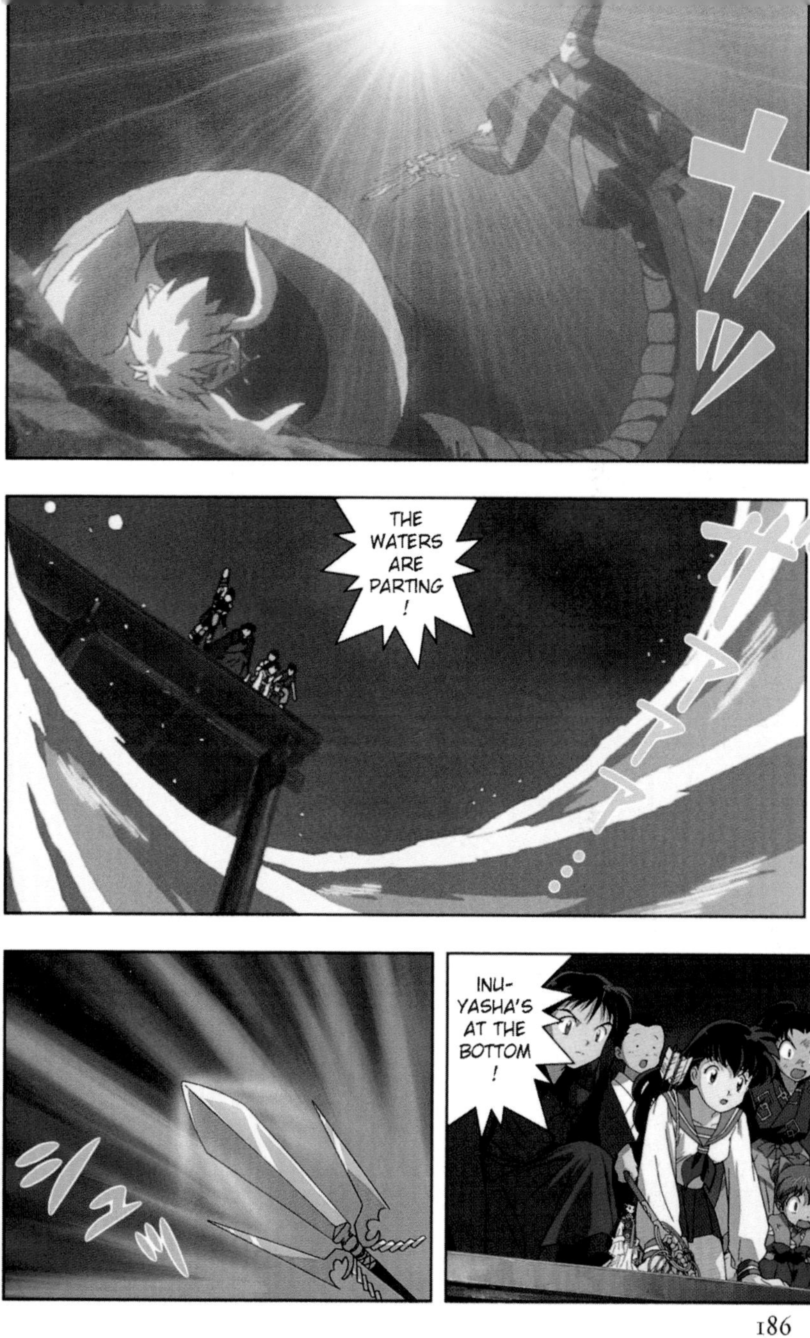
THE WATERS ARE PARTING!
INU-YASHA'S AT THE BOTTOM!

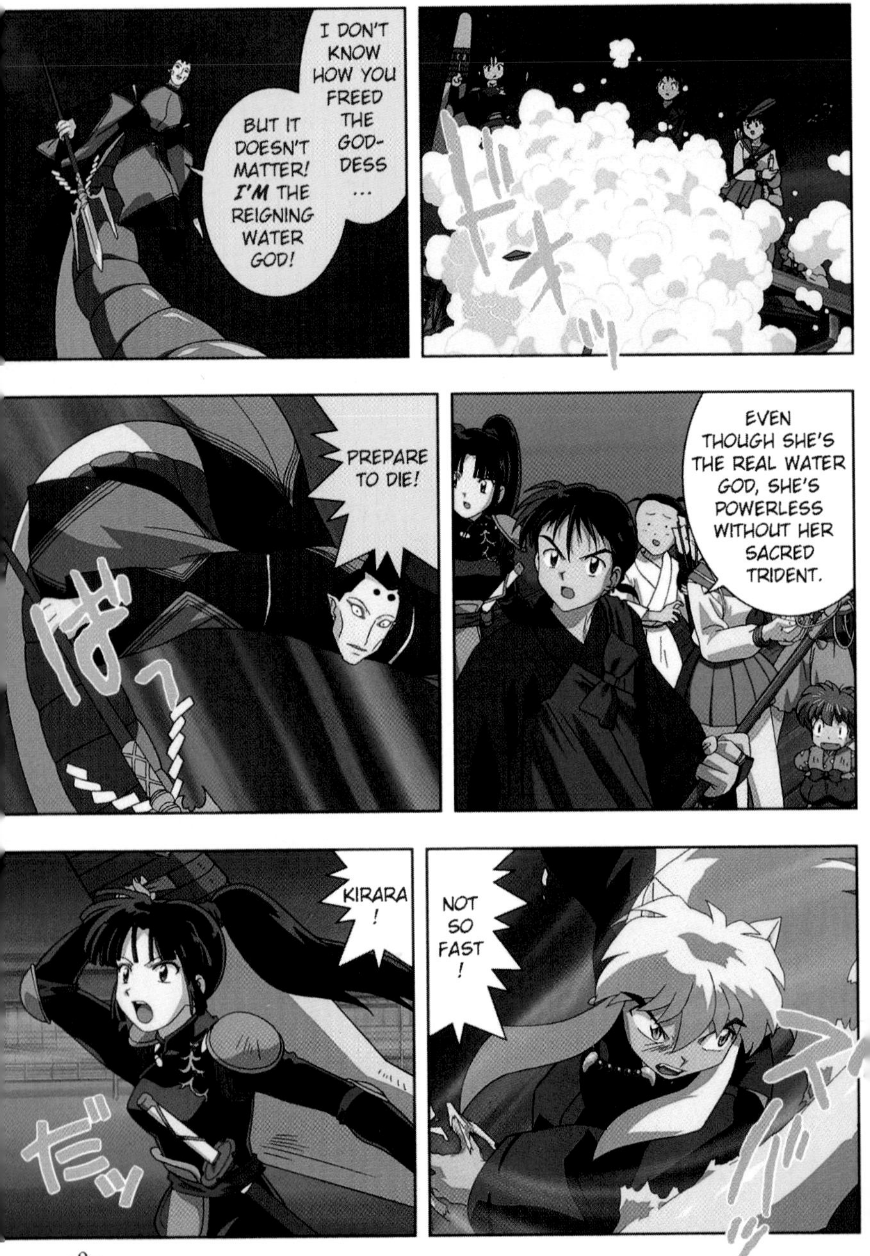
I DON'T KNOW HOW YOU FREED THE GOD-DESS ...
BUT IT DOESN'T MATTER! *I'M* THE REIGNING WATER GOD!
EVEN THOUGH SHE'S THE REAL WATER GOD, SHE'S POWERLESS WITHOUT HER SACRED TRIDENT.
PREPARE TO DIE!
NOT SO FAST!
KIRARA!

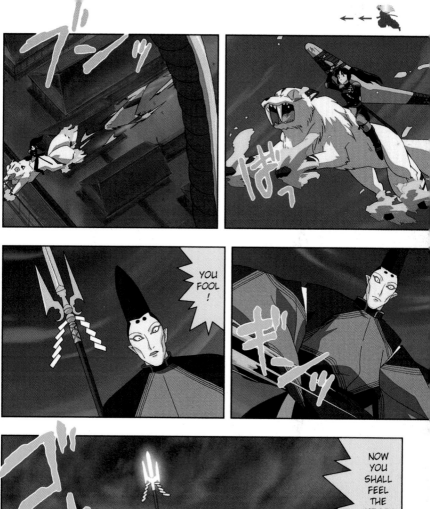

YOU FOOL!

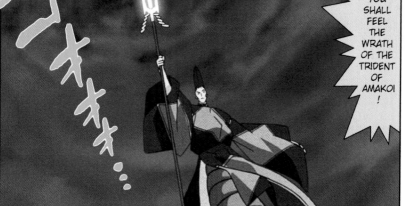

NOW YOU SHALL FEEL THE WRATH OF THE TRIDENT OF AMAKOI!

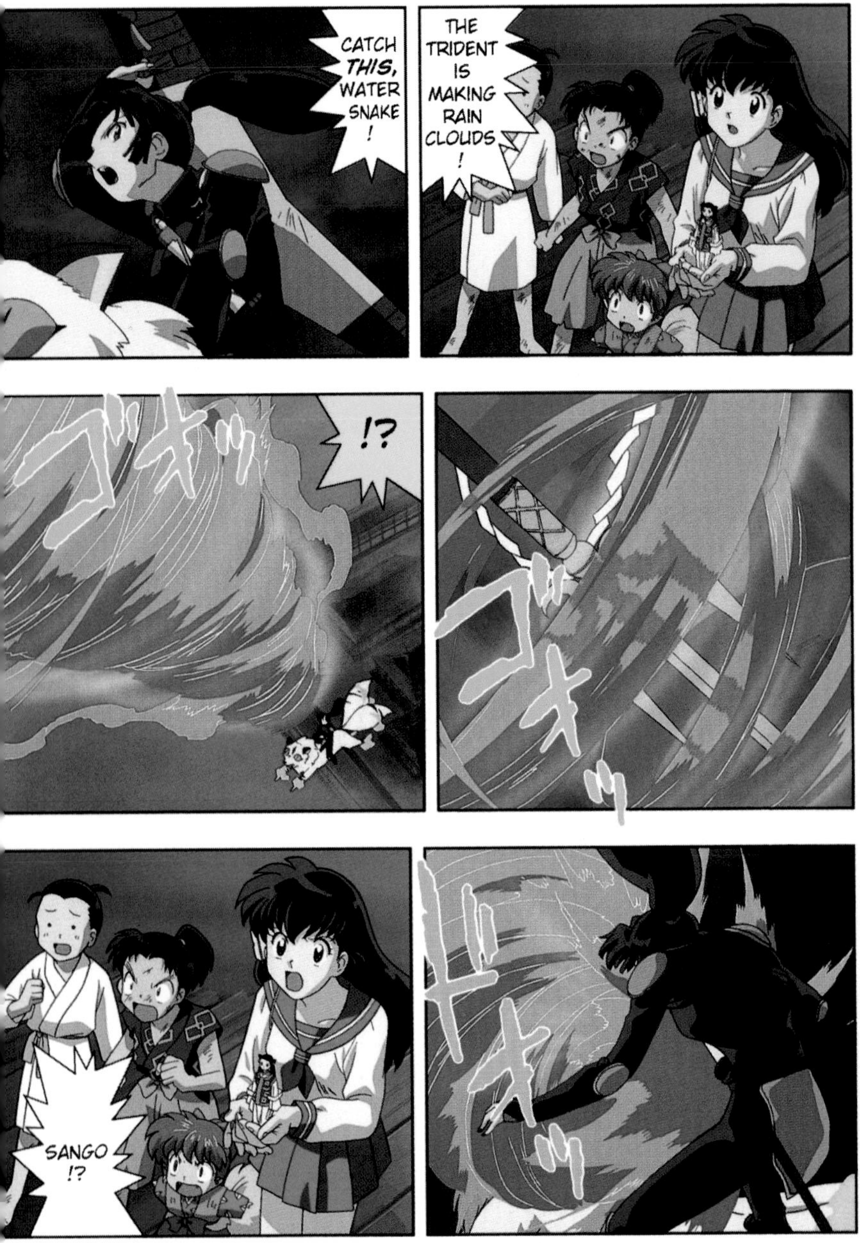
THE TRIDENT IS MAKING RAIN CLOUDS!
CATCH *THIS*, WATER SNAKE!
!?
SANGO!?

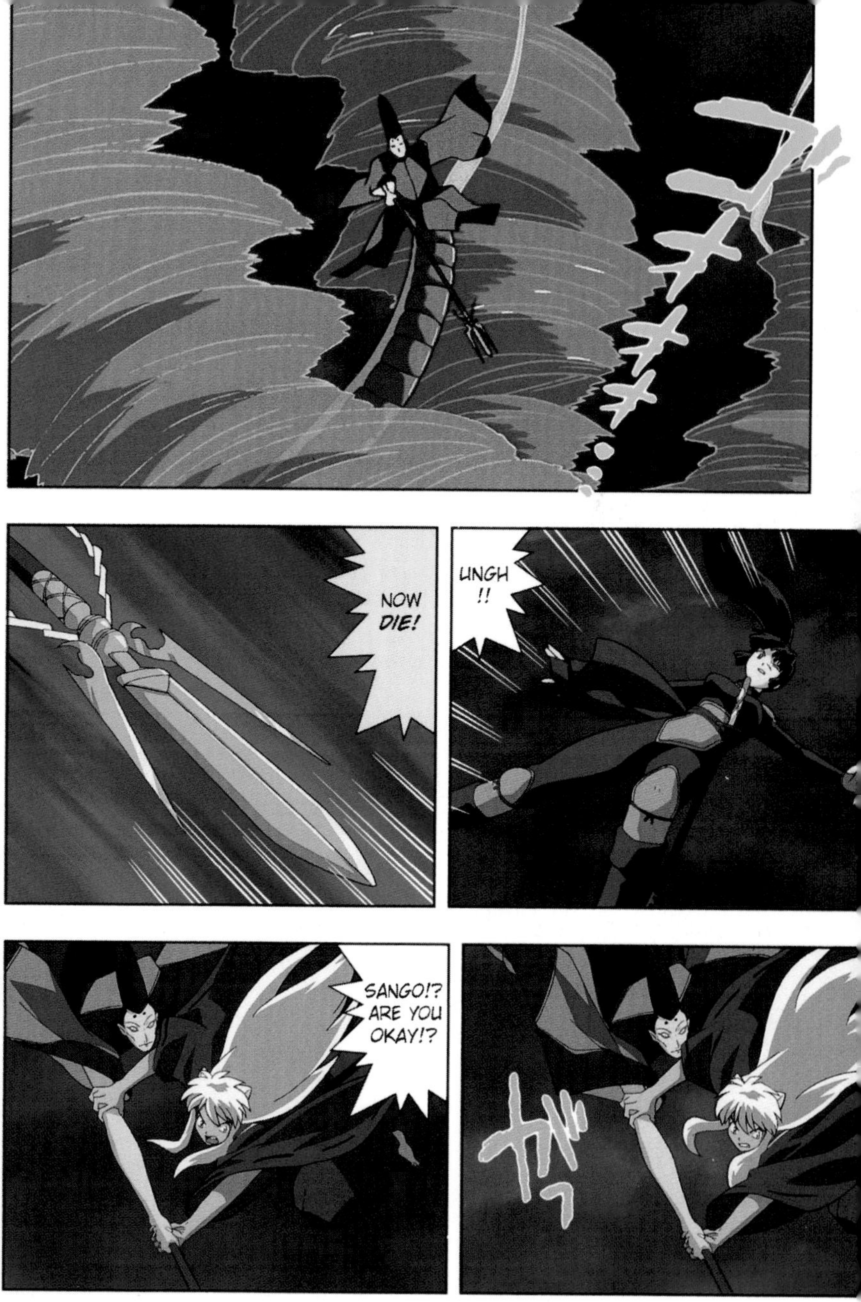
UNGH !!
NOW DIE!
SANGO!? ARE YOU OKAY!?

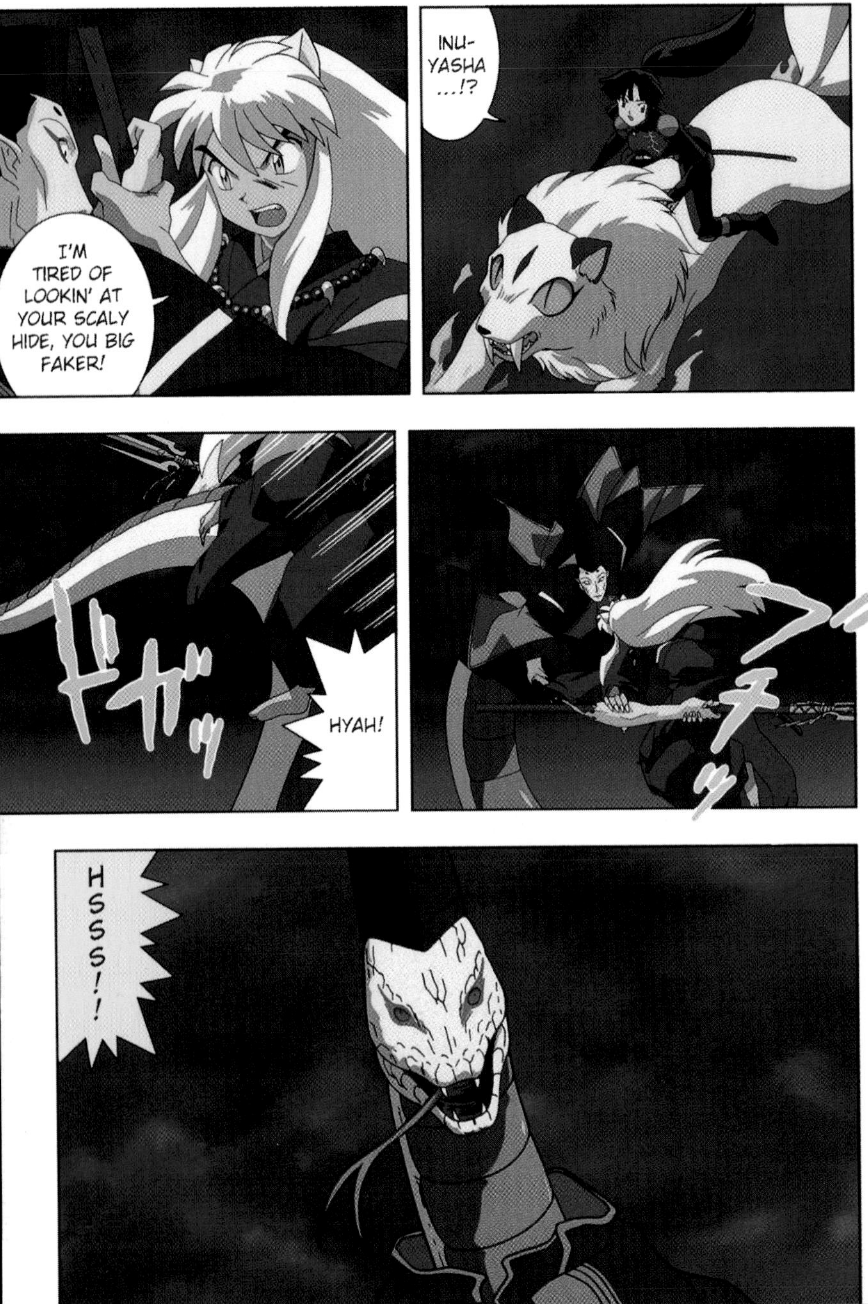
INU-YASHA ...!?
I'M TIRED OF LOOKIN' AT YOUR SCALY HIDE, YOU BIG FAKER!
ドガッ
HYAH!
HSSS!!

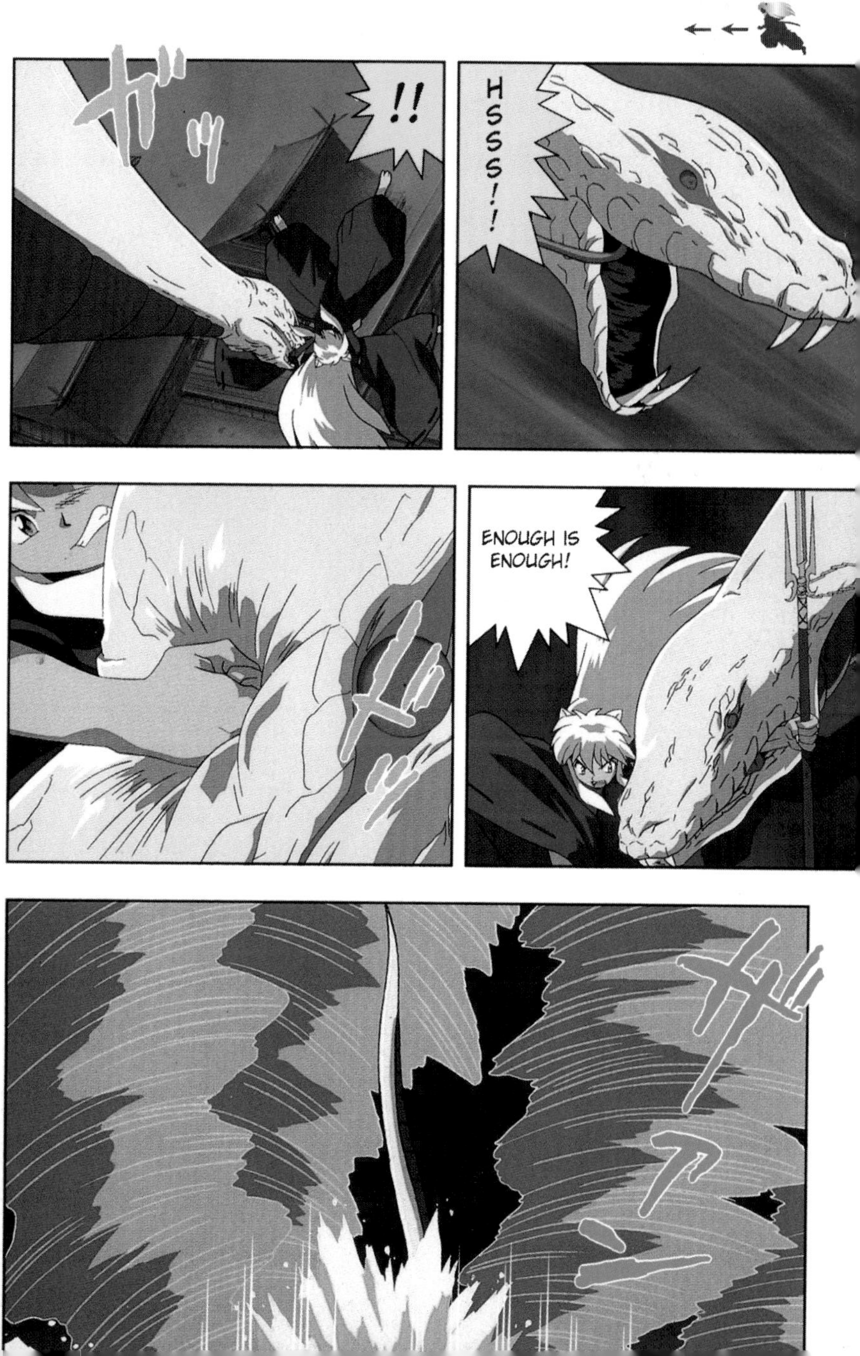
HSSS!!
!!
ENOUGH IS ENOUGH!

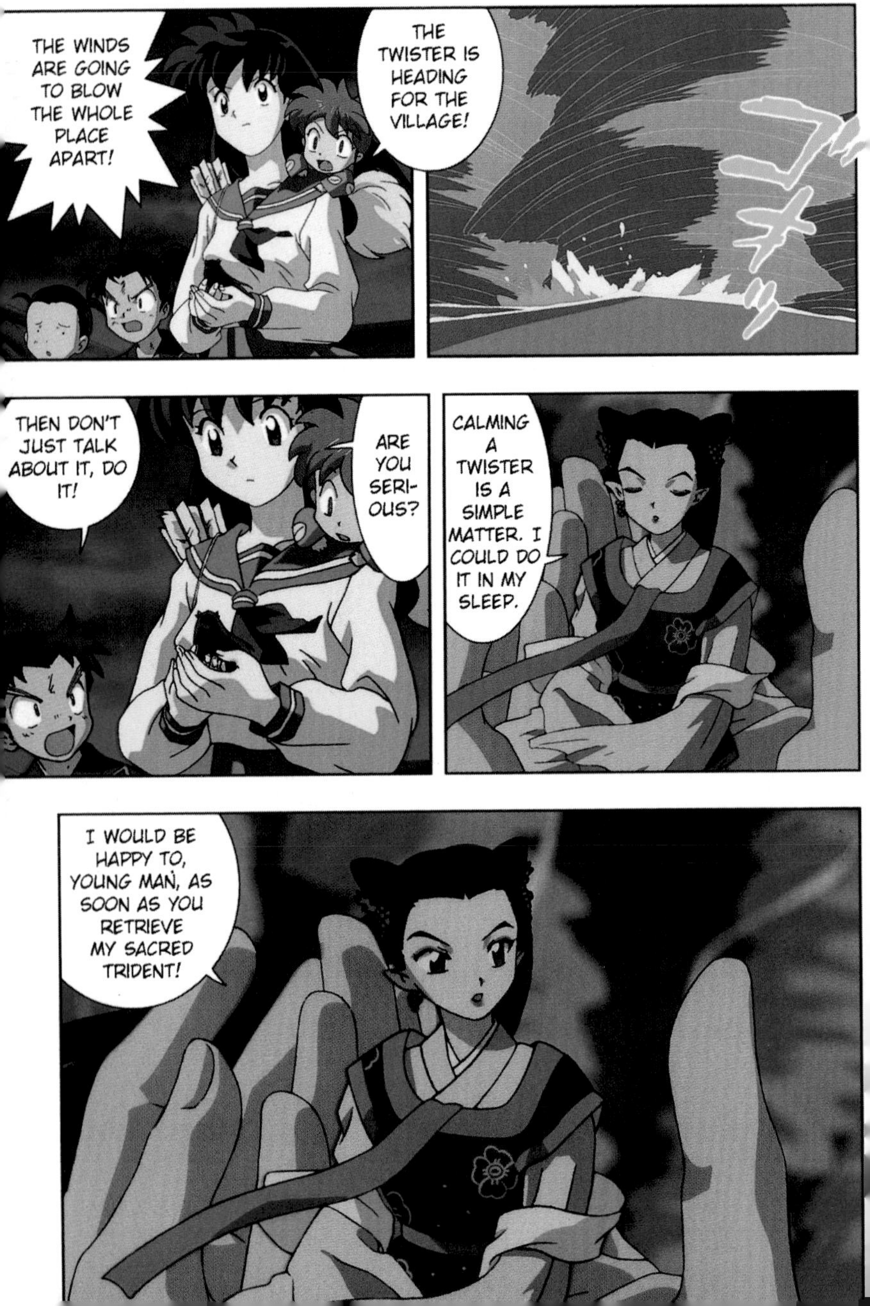
THE TWISTER IS HEADING FOR THE VILLAGE!
THE WINDS ARE GOING TO BLOW THE WHOLE PLACE APART!
CALMING A TWISTER IS A SIMPLE MATTER. I COULD DO IT IN MY SLEEP.
ARE YOU SERI-OUS?
THEN DON'T JUST TALK ABOUT IT, DO IT!
I WOULD BE HAPPY TO, YOUNG MAN, AS SOON AS YOU RETRIEVE MY SACRED TRIDENT!

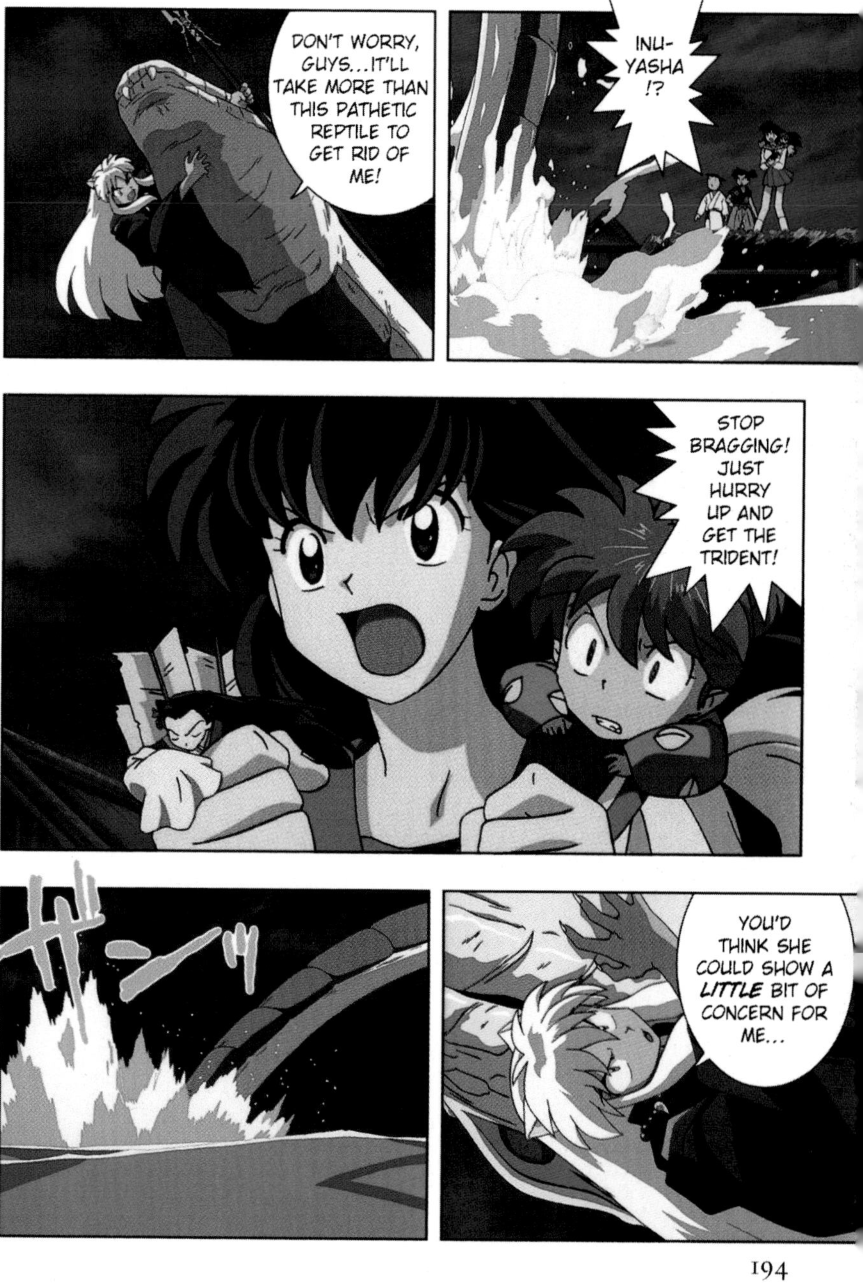
INU-YASHA!?
DON'T WORRY, GUYS...IT'LL TAKE MORE THAN THIS PATHETIC REPTILE TO GET RID OF ME!
STOP BRAGGING! JUST HURRY UP AND GET THE TRIDENT!
YOU'D THINK SHE COULD SHOW A *LITTLE* BIT OF CONCERN FOR ME...
ザーンッ

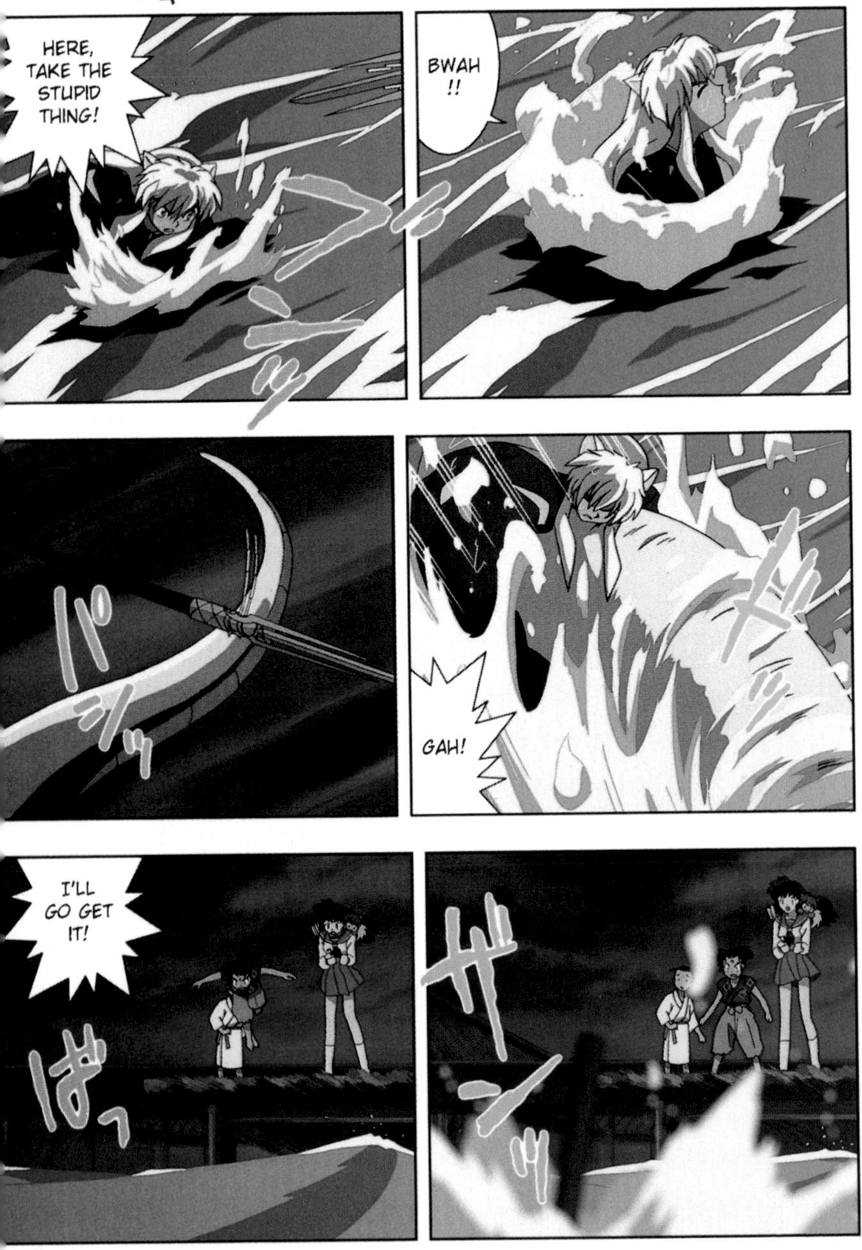
BWAH !!
HERE, TAKE THE STUPID THING!
GAH!
パシッ
I'LL GO GET IT!
ぱっ

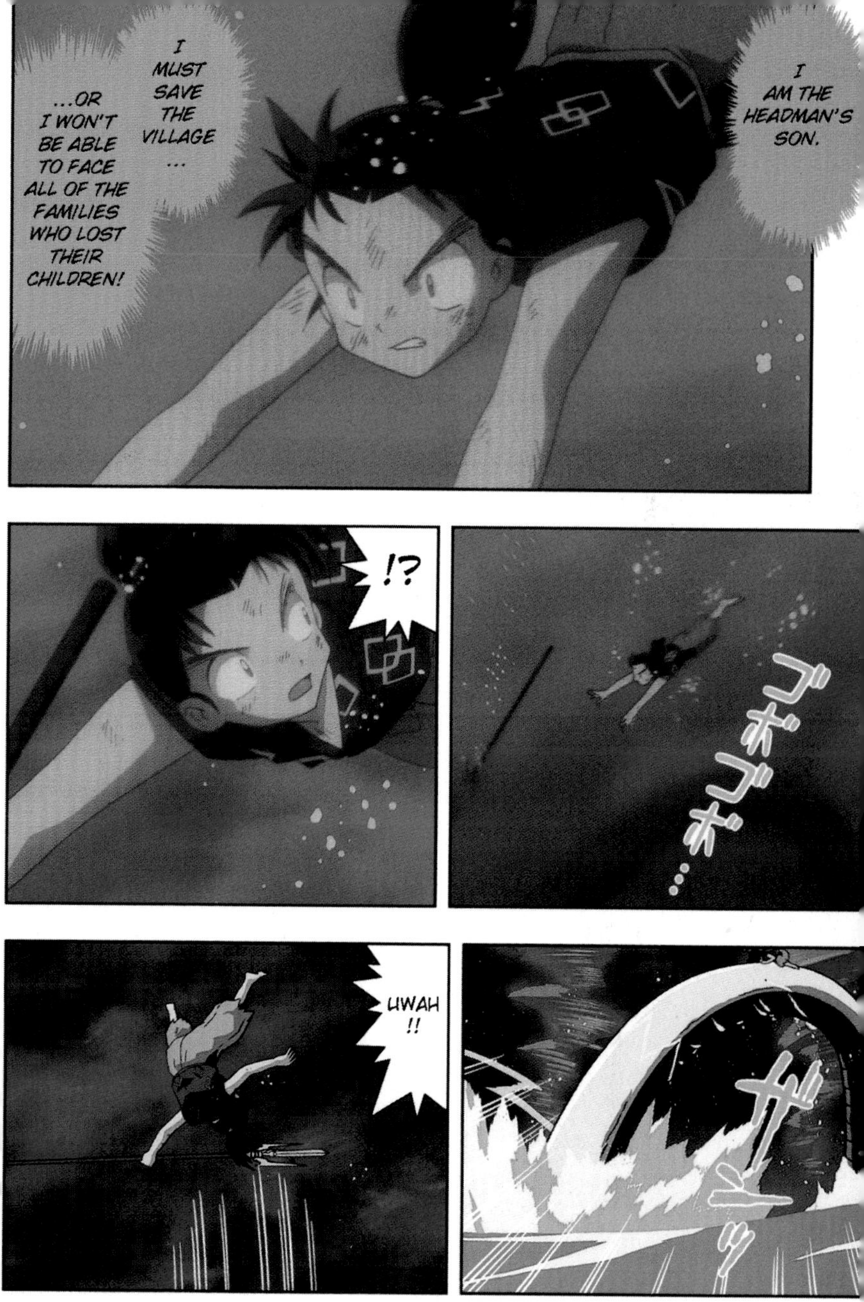
I AM THE HEADMAN'S SON.
I MUST SAVE THE VILLAGE...
...OR I WON'T BE ABLE TO FACE ALL OF THE FAMILIES WHO LOST THEIR CHILDREN!
ゴボゴボ…
!?
UWAH!!

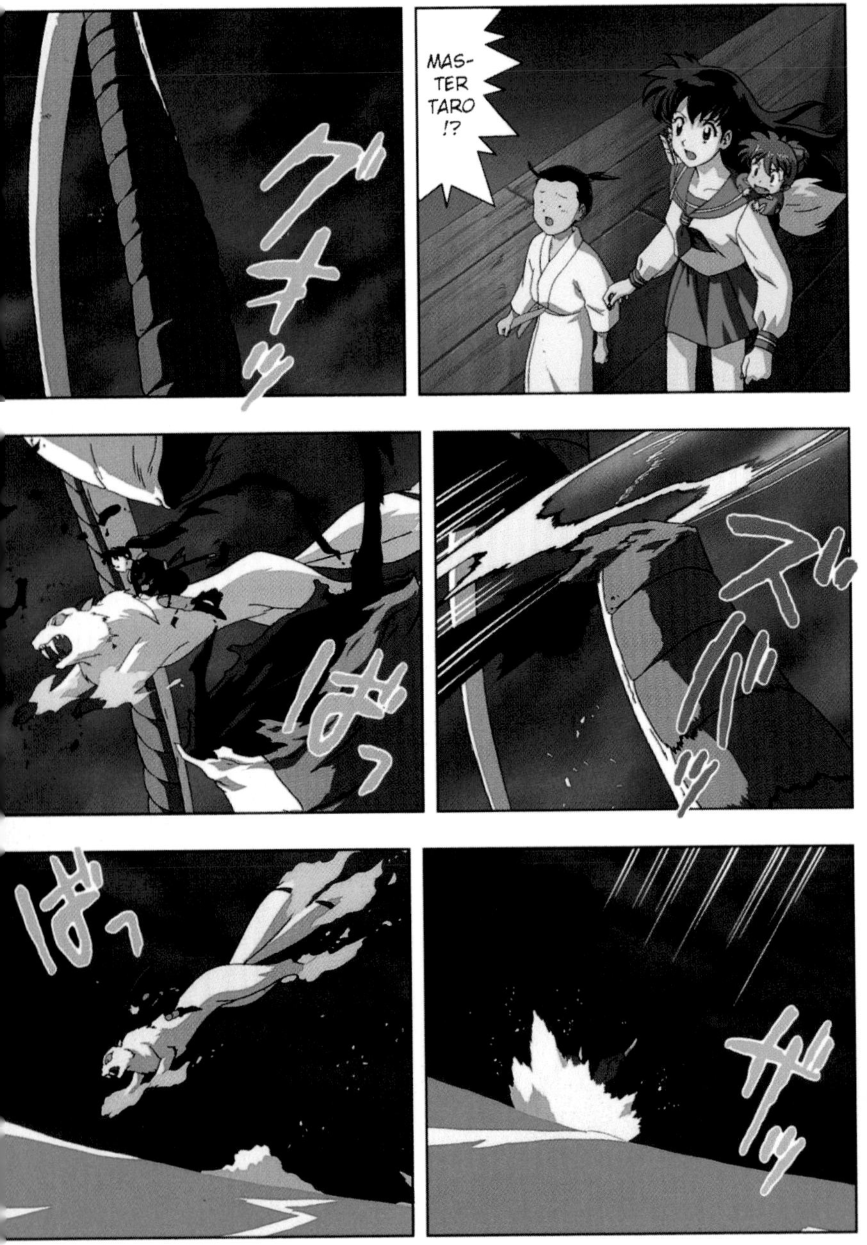
MASTER TARO!?

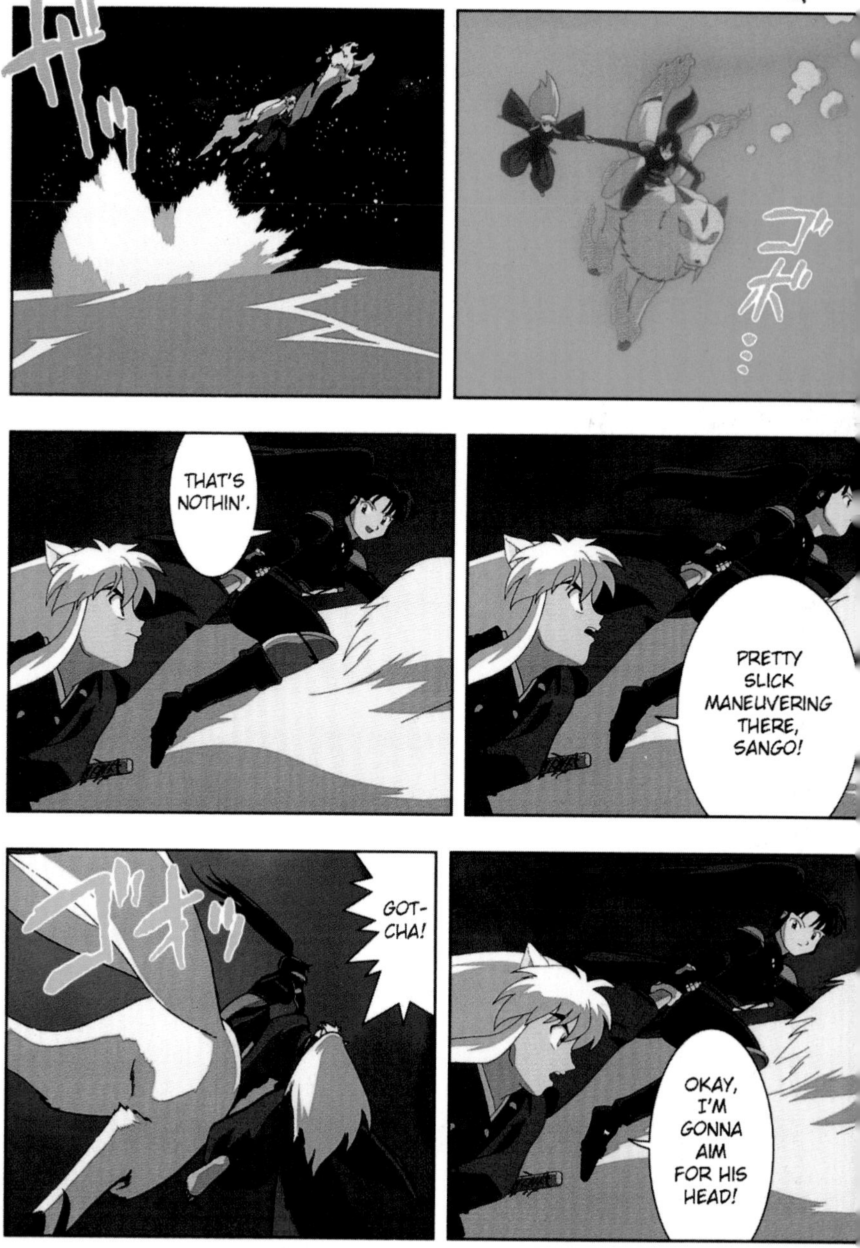
ゴォ
ザッ
PRETTY SLICK MANEUVERING THERE, SANGO!
THAT'S NOTHIN'.
OKAY, I'M GONNA AIM FOR HIS HEAD!
GOT-CHA!
ゴオッ

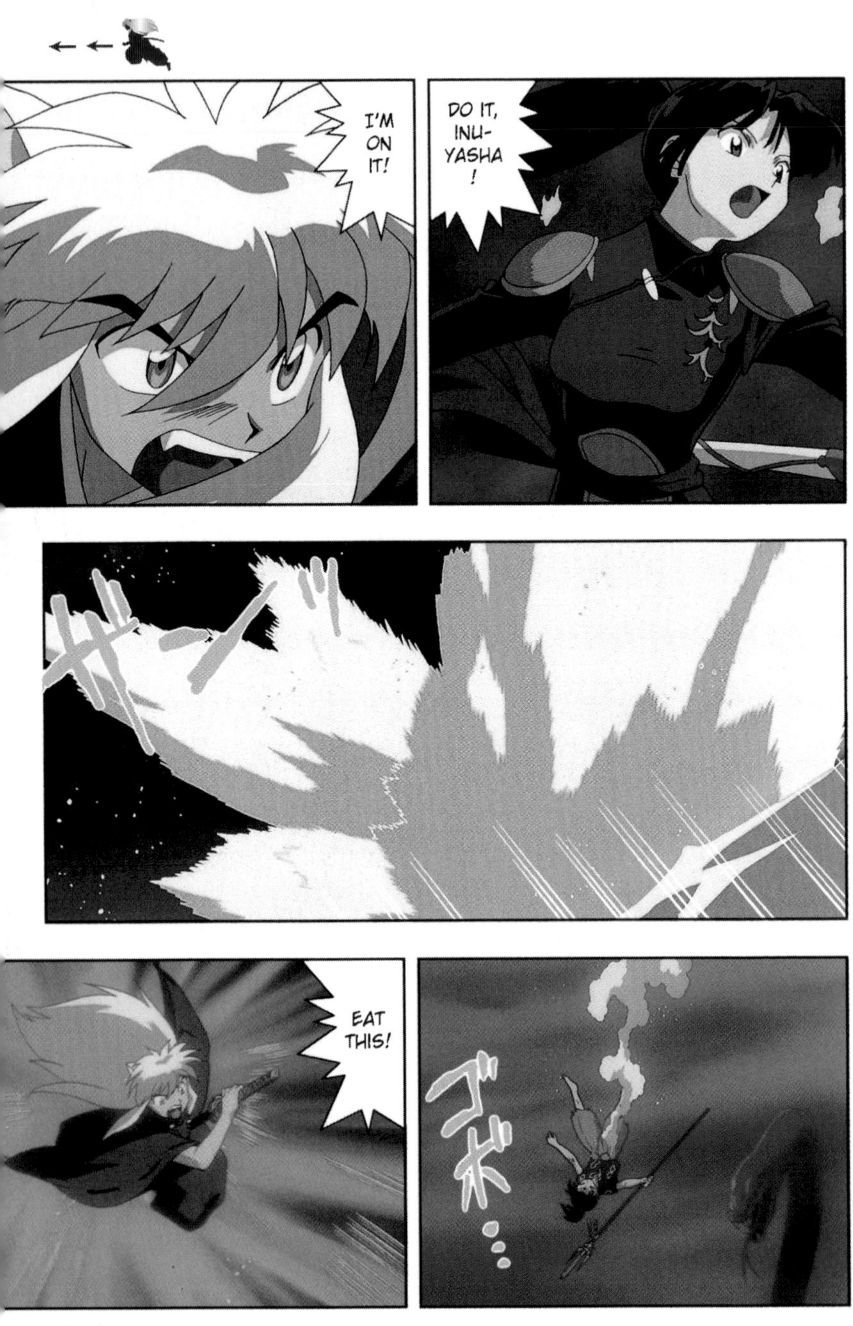
DO IT, INU-YASHA!
I'M ON IT!
ゴボ…
EAT THIS!

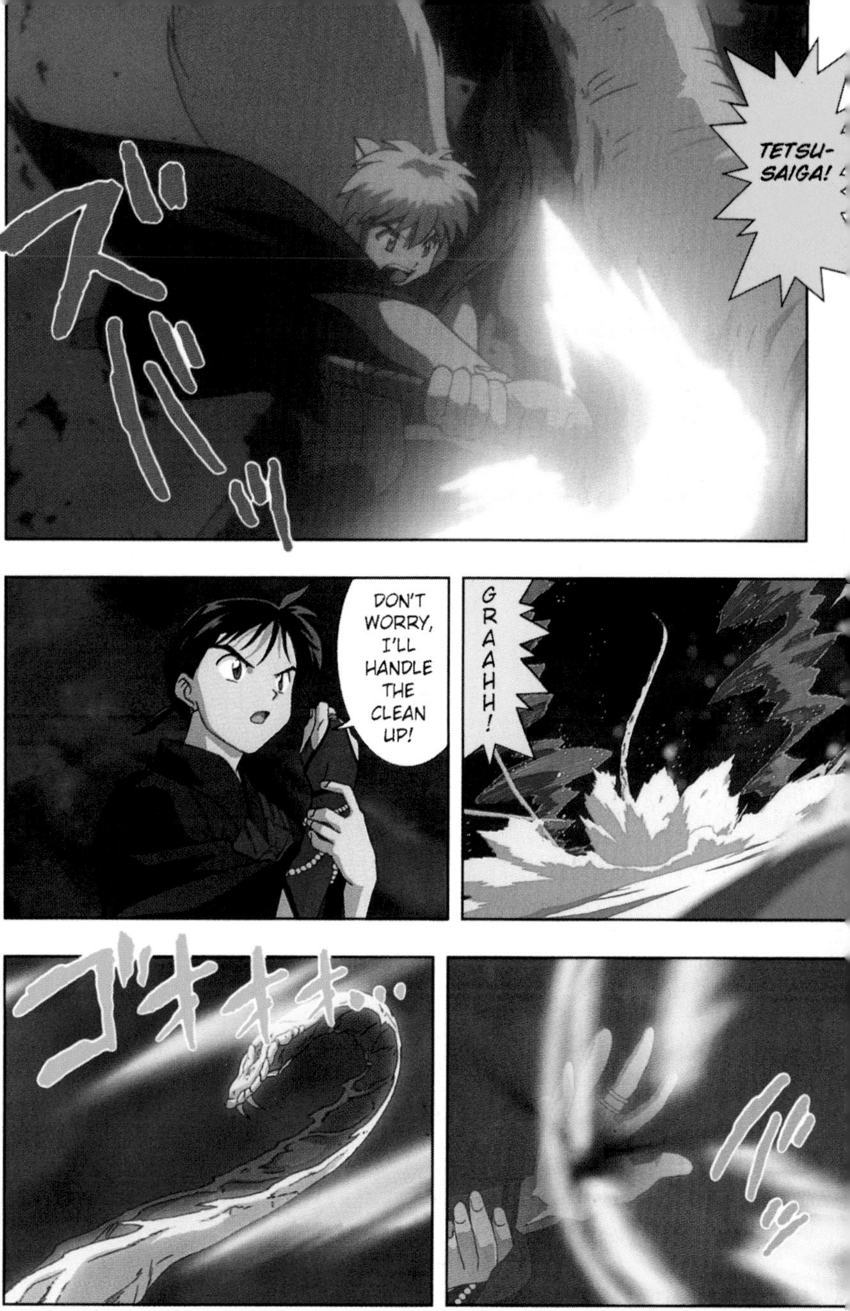
TETSU-SAIGA!
ズバッ
GRAAHH!
DON'T WORRY, I'LL HANDLE THE CLEAN UP!
グッ
ゴオオオ…

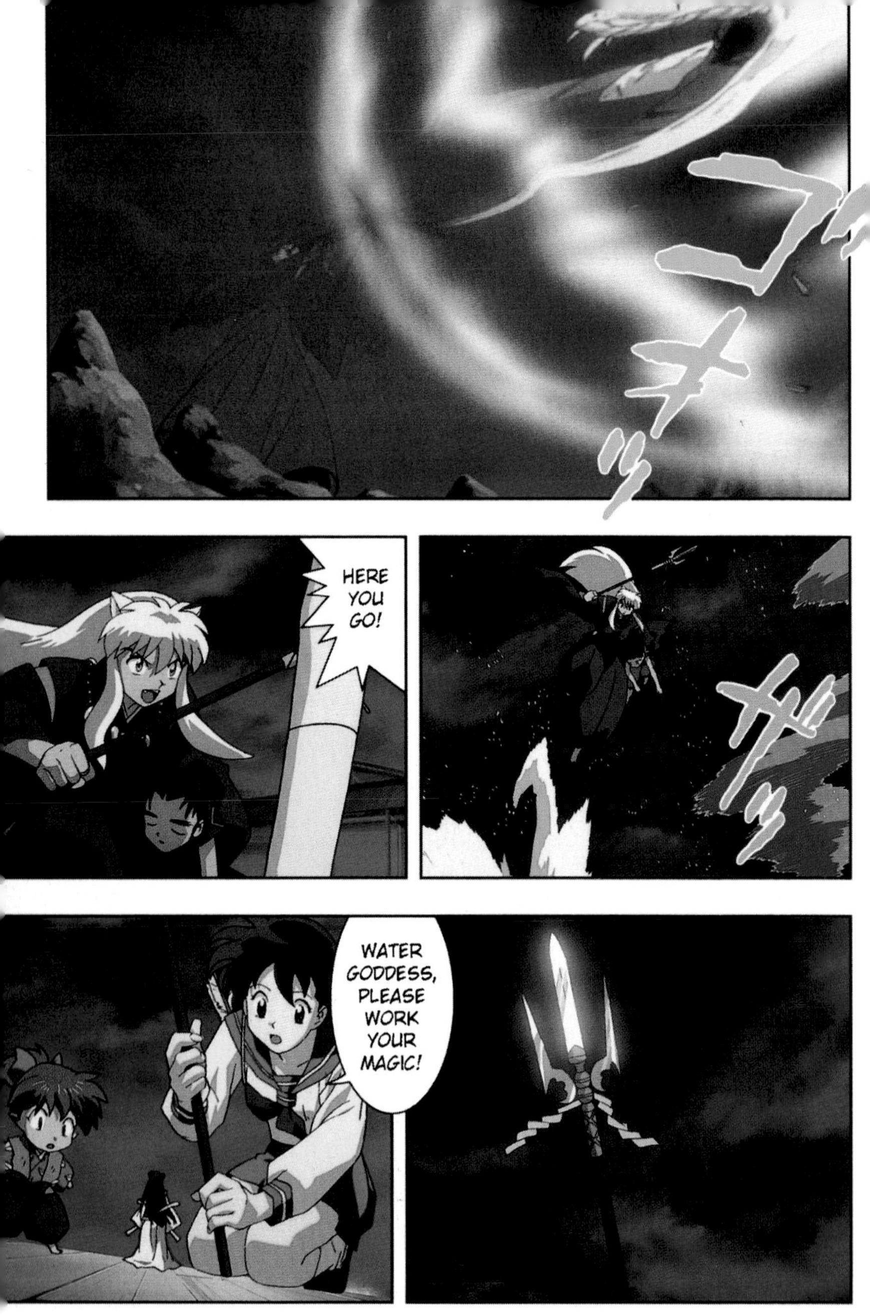
HERE YOU GO!
WATER GODDESS, PLEASE WORK YOUR MAGIC!

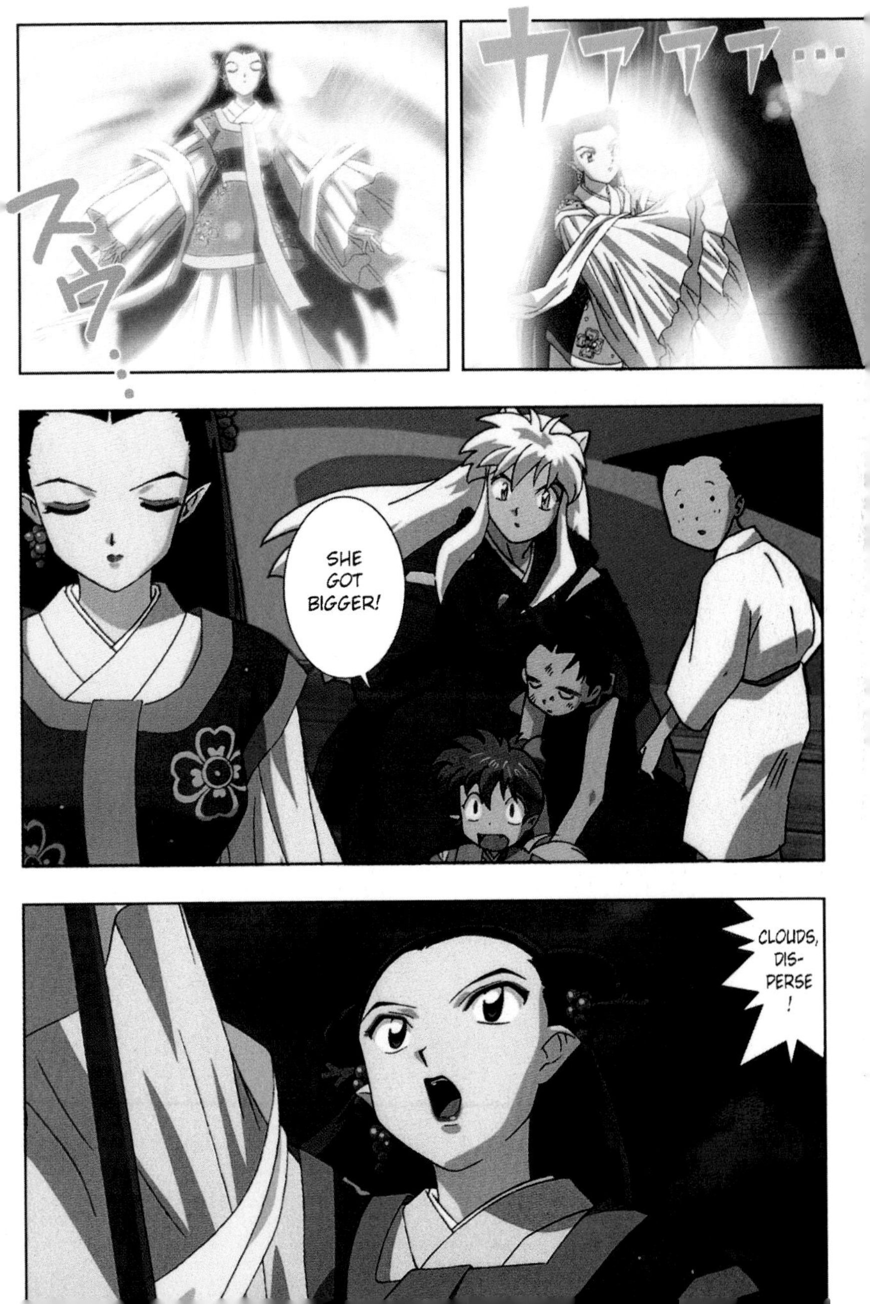
カァァァ…
スゥ…
SHE GOT BIGGER!
CLOUDS, DIS-PERSE!

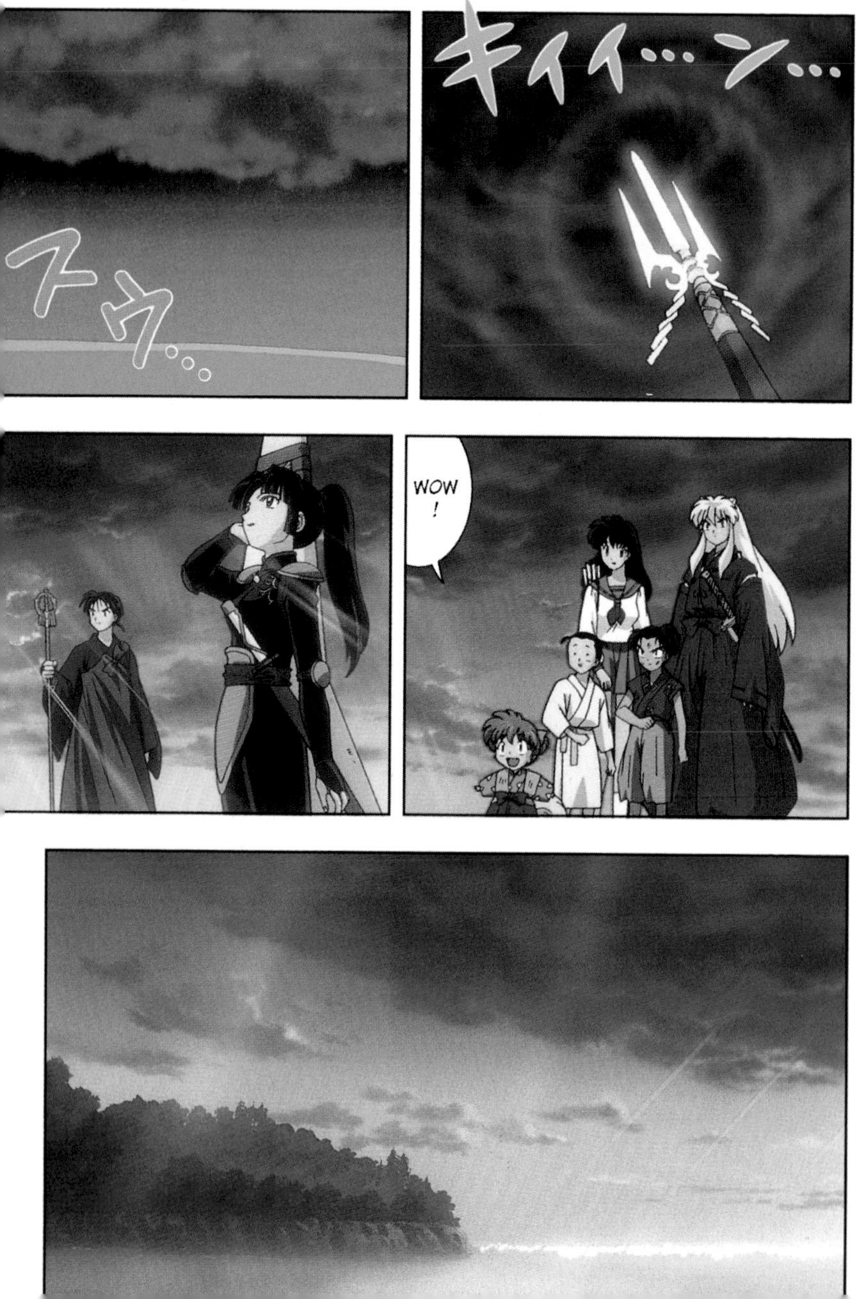
キイイ…ン…
スゥ…
WOW!

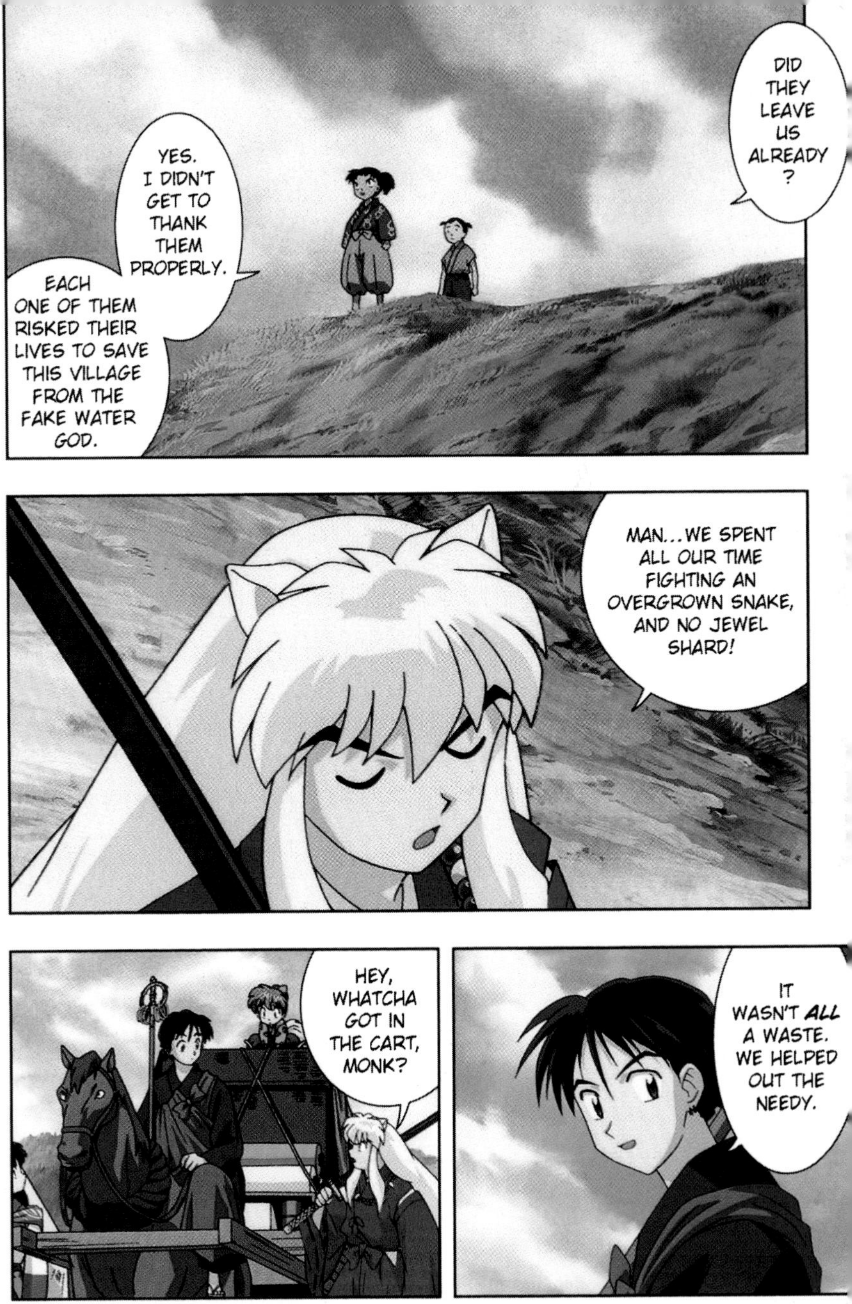
DID THEY LEAVE US ALREADY?
YES. I DIDN'T GET TO THANK THEM PROPERLY.
EACH ONE OF THEM RISKED THEIR LIVES TO SAVE THIS VILLAGE FROM THE FAKE WATER GOD.
MAN...WE SPENT ALL OUR TIME FIGHTING AN OVERGROWN SNAKE, AND NO JEWEL SHARD!
IT WASN'T ***ALL*** A WASTE. WE HELPED OUT THE NEEDY.
HEY, WHATCHA GOT IN THE CART, MONK?

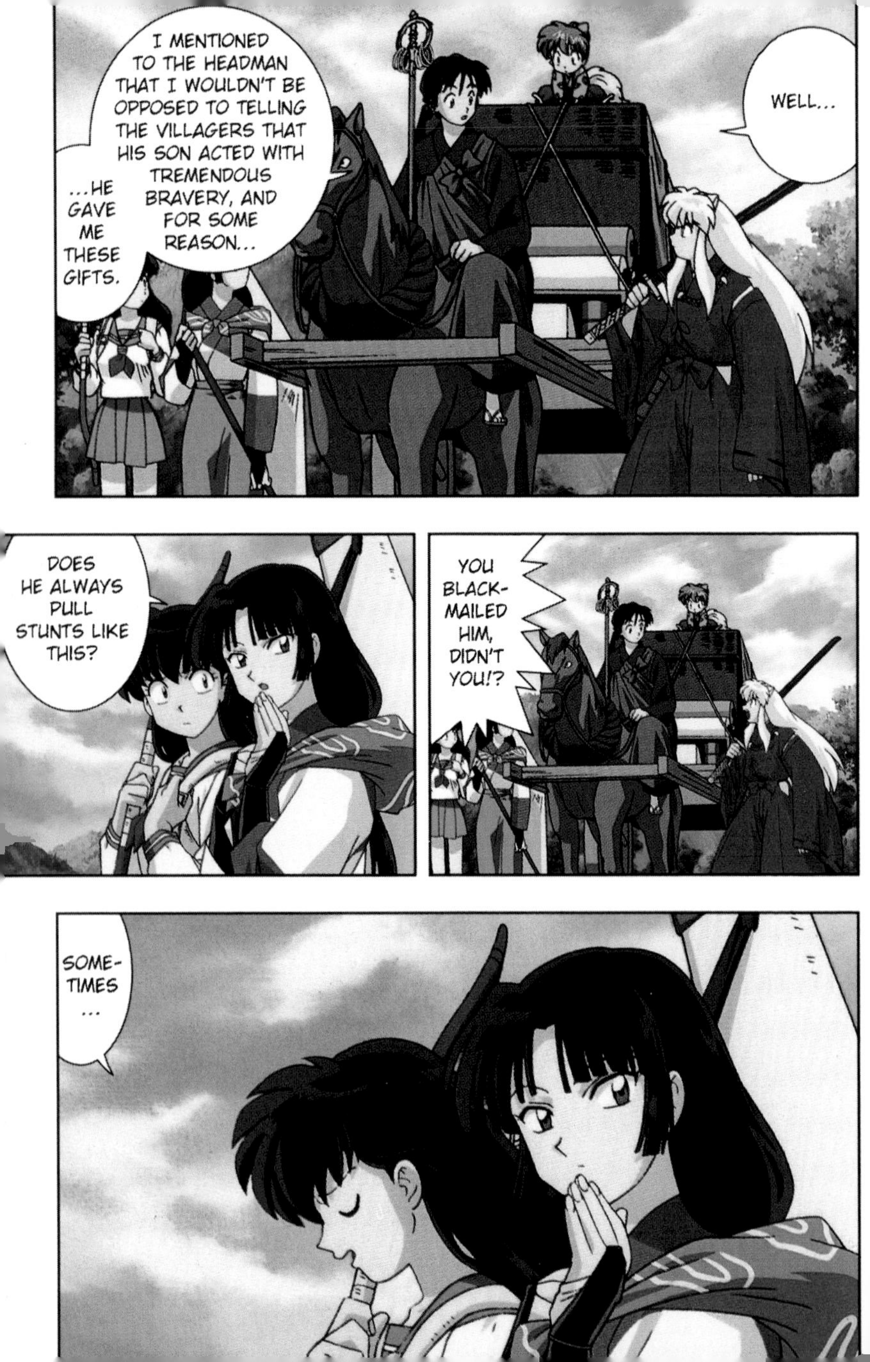
WELL...
I MENTIONED TO THE HEADMAN THAT I WOULDN'T BE OPPOSED TO TELLING THE VILLAGERS THAT HIS SON ACTED WITH TREMENDOUS BRAVERY, AND FOR SOME REASON...
...HE GAVE ME THESE GIFTS.
YOU BLACK-MAILED HIM, DIDN'T YOU!?
DOES HE ALWAYS PULL STUNTS LIKE THIS?
SOME-TIMES ...

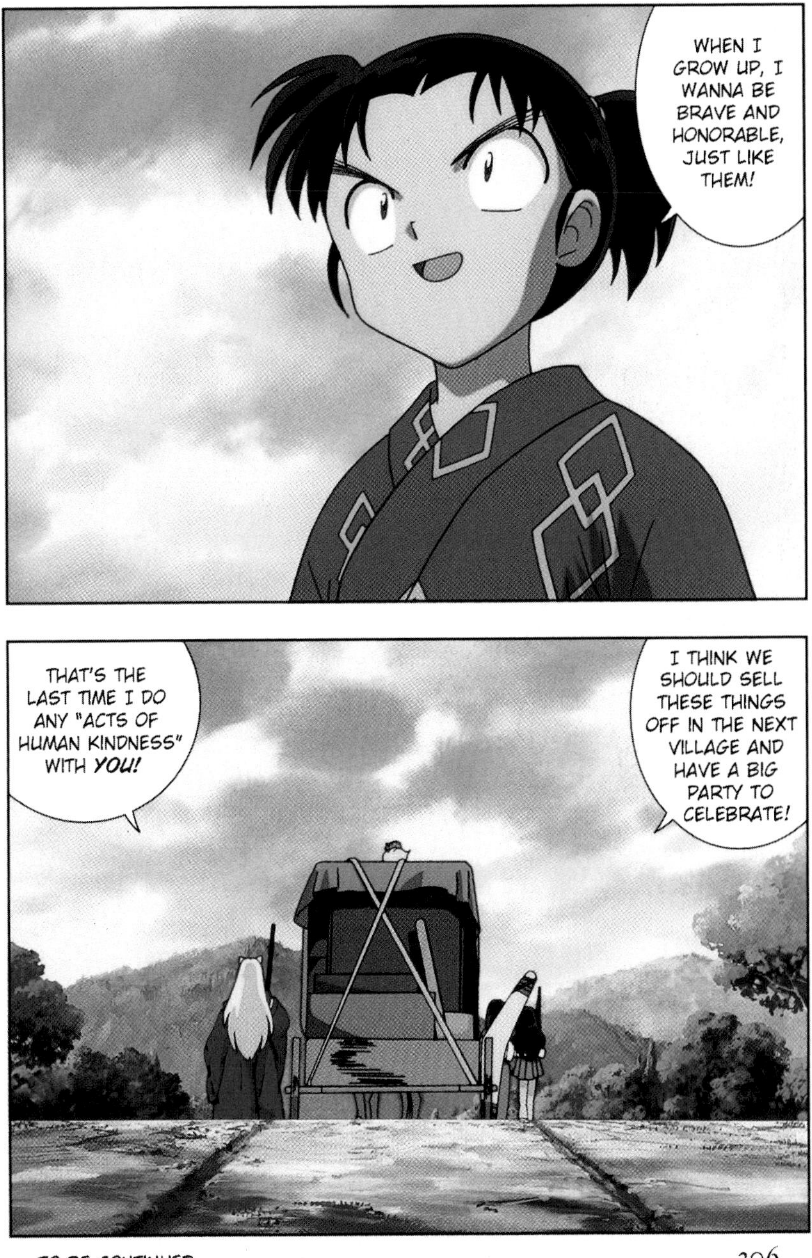
WHEN I GROW UP, I WANNA BE BRAVE AND HONORABLE, JUST LIKE THEM!
I THINK WE SHOULD SELL THESE THINGS OFF IN THE NEXT VILLAGE AND HAVE A BIG PARTY TO CELEBRATE!
THAT'S THE LAST TIME I DO ANY "ACTS OF HUMAN KINDNESS" WITH *YOU!*

TO BE CONTINUED...

Glossary of Sound Effects

Each entry includes: the location, indicated by page number and panel number (so 3.1 means page 3, panel number 1); the phonetic romanization of the original Japanese; and our English "translation"—we offer as close an English equivalent as we can.

26.5 FX: Shurururu...
(boomerang flies back toward Sango)

27.1 FX: Pashi (Sango catches boomerang)
27.3 FX: Bun (Sango throws boomerang)
27.4 FX: Zuga (wham)

28.2 FX: Gyururu...
(boomerang whooshing through air)
28.3 FX: Doga (boomerang slams into ground)
28.5 FX: Ba
(Miroku removes glove and prayer beads)

29.1 FX: Gohh (whoosh of wind tunnel)
29.2 FX: Shurururu... (boomerang flies through air)
29.4 FX: Bu bu bu bu (buzzing of Naraku's bees)

30.2 FX: Pashi (Miroku closes his wind tunnel)

31.3 FX: Ba (Inuyasha springs)
31.4 FX: Jara (chain wraps around Inuyasha's ankle)
31.5 FX: Doh
(Sango brings Inuyasha down with chain)

33.1 FX: Ba (Sango throws boomerang)
33.2 FX: Kira (jewel shard sparkling)
33.4 FX: Giin (clang of weapon against weapon)
33.5 FX: Da (Sango touches down)

34.1 FX: Ba (powder is thrown)
34.2 FX: Buwa (powder expands into cloud)

35.3 FX: Cha (Naraku draws sword)
35.4 FX: Giin (clang)

36.1 FX: Zan (Miroku slashes at Naraku)
36.3 FX: Doh
(Naraku's severed hand falls to the ground)
36.4 FX: Chari (Miroku's staff jingling)

Chapter 25:
Naraku's Insidious Plot!

7.3 FX: Yoro... (Sango being unsteady on her feet)

10.2 FX: Gara gara (rolling of wheels)

11.1 FX: Gohhh... (whoosh sound of cave)

12.3 FX: Pyon (Myoga hops about, affronted)

13.1 FX: Bachi (smack!)
13.2 FX: Doh (Inuyasha falls backwards)

14.3 FX: Zan
(Kohaku's blade thumps into Sango's back)

15.4 FX: Doh (Sango drops to her knees)

18.2 FX: Gin (clang)
18.3 FX: Doh (Inuyasha falls over backwards)

20.5 FX: Ta (Kagome running)

22.2 FX: Piku... (Kirara notices something)
22.5 FX: Za za za (crashing through the underbrush)

23.1 FX: Doka (boomerang chops through tree)
23.2 FX: Gohh (whoosh)
23.3 FX: Gohhh... (whoosh)
23.4 FX: Pashi (boomerang returns to Sango)

25.4 FX: Bun (Sango throws boomerang)
25.6 FX: Ba (Inuyasha draws sword)

26.1 FX: Giin (Tetsusaiga clangs against boomerang)
26.2 FX: Zuzaza...
(friction of Tetsusaiga against boomerang)
26.3 FX: Bun (boomerang deflected away)

37.2 FX: Gohh (Naraku's hand flying after Kagome)
37.5 FX: Ba (Naraku's hand grabs Kagome)

38.1 FX: Shuuu (arms reaffixes itself to Naraku)
38.5 FX: Da (Inuyasha runs toward Naraku)

39.1 FX: Gohh (fog rolling out from around Naraku)
39.3 FX: Gohhhhh… (more fog, Naraku is lifted up)
39.4 FX: Gohhhhh…
(Naraku goes up, up and away)

40.4 FX: Gohh (Kirara turns into a big cat)
40.5 FX: Ba (Kirara flies off)

41.1 FX: Ta (running)
41.2 FX: Da (Inuyasha steps to attack)
41.3 FX: Gohh (boomerang flies)
41.4 FX: Doga
(boomerang lands in front of Inuyasha)

42.1 FX: Da (running)
42.3 FX: Bun (boomerang thrown)
42.4 FX: Doga (boomerang lands in dirt)

43.2 FX: Bun (boomerang thrown)
43.3 FX: Doka (Inuyasha throws the Tetsusaiga)
43.4 FX: Gyurururu… (boomerang flies through air)
43.6 FX: Ta (Inuyasha runs)

44.2 FX: Ta (Inuyasha jumps)
44.3 FX: Bun (Inuyasha smacks off Sango's mask)
44.6 FX: Ga (Inuyasha grabs Sango)

45.1 FX: Gohh (whoosh)
45.4 FX: Toh (Inuyasha touches down)
45.5 FX: Chari (Sango draws sword)

46.1 FX: Doh (Sango stabs him with sword)
46.3 FX: Ba (Inuyasha yanks out the sword)

47.1 FX: Bota bota… (blood dripping)

49.1 FX: Shurururu… (arrows flying)
49.2 FX: Doh (arrows hit)

50.2 FX: Furaa (Sango collapses in a faint)
50.3 FX: Dosa… (Sango hits ground)

52.1 FX: Ta ta ta… (running)
52.3 FX: Hyohhhh… (Kirara whooshing about)
52.5 FX: Ba (Kirara lands and scoops up Miroku)

53.1 FX: Goh (whoosh)
53.4 FX: Doga (Miroku whacks Naraku with staff)

54.1 FX: Shurururu…
(root-like tentacles swarm out)
54.2 FX: Meki… (arms grow from Naraku)
54.4 FX: Buoh (Kirara jumps)
54.5 FX: Zuba (Miroku strikes at Naraku's arms)

55.1 FX: Ga (Naraku's branchy hand grabs Kirara
by the throat)
55.2 FX: Shururu…
(branchy thing from Naraku grabs Miroku)
55.3 FX: Doh (Kirara and Miroku land on ground)

56.1 FX: Ta ta ta… (running)
56.2 FX: Gohh (wind starts to blow)

57.3 FX: Da (Inuyasha leaping)

59.3 FX: Da (Inuyasha leaping)

60.2 FX: Shurururu…
(branchy arms unroll toward Miroku)
60.3 FX: Zuba (Miroku cuts off some branchy arms)
60.4 FX: Doh (arms strike ground)

61.1 FX: Shuuuu… (arm snakes out)
61.3 FX: Shurururu… (arm flying through air)
61.4 FX: Ga (hand grabs Miroku's foot)
61.5 FX: Shurururu…
(Miroku and arm flying through air)

62.1 FX: Doh (branchy arm strikes Miroku in midriff)
62.3 FX: Ba (Inuyasha slashes)
62.4 FX: Zuba (Inuyasha lands, Miroku falls)

63.1 FX: Shurururu… (Naraku's branchy tentacles
fly toward Inuyasha)
63.2 FX: Zan (Inuyasha cuts tentacles)

66.2 FX: Da (Sango prepares to attack)
66.3 FX: Fu (Sango collapses)
66.4 FX: Doh (Sango falls)

68.1 FX: Bun (Inuyasha strikes)
68.3 FX: Zuba (Naraku's head is lopped off)

114.3 FX: Pori pori (Kirara scratching)
114.4 FX: Pyon (Myoga jumps off)

116.1 FX: Pyon pyon (hop, hop)

117.1 FX: Zu—n… (ominous rumbling)
117.2 FX: Tsuru (Myoga slips and drops the jewel)
117.3 FX: Charin (jewel bounces away)
117.4 FX: Zu zu (shaking)
117.5 FX: Zu zu (more shaking)

118.1 FX: Gohh (flames of demons' roar)
118.3 FX: Gohh (demon balls whooshing)

119.1 FX: Dohh (demons expanding)
119.2 FX: Suto (Kirara jumps down)
119.3 FX: Gohh (Kirara transforms)

120.4 FX: Ta (Inuyasha runs)

122.1 FX: Gohhhh… (demon balls whooshing)
122.2 FX: Gohh (demons balls whooshing)
122.4 FX: Doga (demon balls strike ground where Kirara was)
122.5 FX: Da (Kirara dodges)

123.1 FX: Dohh (demons balls whoosh)
123.2 FX: Ta (Kirara lands)
123.4 FX: Da (Kirara runs)

124.2 FX: Ta (Kirala running)
124.3 FX: Go go go (whooshing)
124.4 FX: Go go go (whooshing)
124.5 FX: Ga (Kirara gets pinched by demon)
124.6 FX: Gishi… (Kirara is squeezed)

125.3 FX: Mishi… (Kirara gets squeezed more)

126.2 FX: Kaaaa… (shining)
126.3 FX: Kaaaaa… (shining)
126.4 FX: Suu… (Midoriko reanimates, sparkling)
126.5 FX: Fuu… (sound of wind chimes)

127.2 FX: Guoh (whoosh)
127.3 FX: Zuba (Midoriko strikes)
127.4 FX: Kaa (bright shining)

128. 1 FX: Fuu… (more sparkly wind chime sound)
128.2-3FX: Suuu… (Midoriko becomes Inuyasha)
128.4 FX: Toh (Inuyasha touches down)

68.4 FX: Dohh (Naraku erupts in light and apparently dies)

70.1 FX: Zawa… (Naraku reanimates even without his head)
70.2 FX: Doga (branchy arm smacks into ground)

71.1 FX: Zuba (slash)
71.2 FX: Doga (strike)
71.3 FX: Shuuu… (branchy arm glows)

73.4 FX: Ba (Inuyasha jumps)
73.5 FX: Zuba (slash)

74.1 FX: Hyururu… (head flies through air)
74.2 FX: Pan (Naraku's head explodes)
74.3 FX: Zu zu zu (Naraku dissolves)

76.2 FX: Koto (demon puppet falls apart)

78.3 FX: Suri (Naraku slides open fusuma door)

Chapter 26:
The Secret of the Sacred Jewel Revealed!

80.2 FX: Goshi goshi (rubbing on a washboard)

83.3 FX: Gohn (Miroku beans Inuyasha with something to get his attention)

85.4 FX: Ta tat a… (Kagome running)

93.1 FX: Su… (party passes through barrier)
93.4 FX: Bari bari (crackling)

104.3 FX: Kaa… (Inuyasha starts to glow)

105.1 FX: Gohh (Inuyasha being thrown out of cave)
105.3 FX: Dohn (Inuyasha passes back through barri-er)
105.4 FX: Hyurururu… (Inuyasha flies through the air)

112.5 FX: Piku (Kirara's eyes open)

113.1 FX: Ta (quiet little footfalls)
113.4 FX: Charin charin… (glimmering)
113.5 FX: Charin charin… (more glimmering)

114.2 FX: Charin charin… (glimmering)

161.5 FX: Su...
(Tetsusaiga steaming and transforming)

162.2 FX: Kiiii...n (trident ringing)
162.4 FX: Doh—n (trident plunked down)

163.1 FX: Kiiii...n... (sound of trident's magic)
163.4 FX: Za zaa... (water rushing in)

164.5 FX: Gura... (Kagome gurgles, losing air)
164.6 FX: Go (Kagome whooshes toward surface)

165.2 FX: Gobo gobo (sound of going underwater)
165.3 FX: Gohh (roar of rushing water)
165.4 FX: Kaa (shining)

166.1 FX: Doh (Kagome and Taromaru land on floor)

167.1 FX: Soro... (Suekichi scoots away)
167.2 FX: Gu (Suekichi grips trident)
167.3 FX: Da (Suekichi rushes the Water god)
167.4 FX: Shururuu... (Suekichi whooshing through air as flung about by water god)
167.6 FX: Hyu (arrow flies)

168.1 FX: Pashi (water god catches arrow)
168.2 FX: Ka (shining)
168.3 FX: Doh (water god collapses)
168.5 FX: Ta (running)

169.2 FX: Ta ta ta... (running)

170.4 FX: Pachi (Sango's eyes open)
170.5 FX: Paan (a resounding slap)

172.1 FX: Pasha (splashing)

173.3 FX: Da (running)

174.1 FX: Hita hita hita... (mysterious footsteps)
174.3 FX: Su... (water god encircles structure with his tentacles)

175.1 FX: Mishi (squeezing)
175.2 FX: Baki (breaking and splintering)

178.1 FX: Shururu... (water god tentacle snakes around Kagome's legs)
178.2 FX: Doh (tentacle pulls Kagome to ground)
178.3 FX: Sha (trident flies)

129.4 FX: Mozo... (Inuyasha searches in Kirara's fur)

131.3 FX: Pashi (Inuyasha swipes in Myoga's general direction)
131.5 FX: Peshi
(Inuyasha practices flea demon hurling)

Chapter 27:
The Lake of the Evil Water God

138.1 FX: Gyuuu... (Sango pinches Miroku)

139.1 FX: Fuwa—... (Shippo floating)
139.3 FX: Pon (Shippo pops)

140.3 FX: Ka—n ka—n (tolling bell)

142.3 FX: Goh (whack)

147.2 FX: Go (smack)
147.4 FX: Guri guri (pound, pound)

148.2 FX: Gii...(dragon boat appears)

154.1 FX: Gii... (flickering torches)
154.2 FX: Su—... (boat moves eerily through water)

155.2 FX: Ta (Inuyasha jumps)
155.3 FX: Doka (kick)
155.4 FX: Baki (Inuyasha smashes wall)

157.2 FX: Ga (water god's hand clutches Suekichi by the face)
157.5 FX: Paki (water god crushes Suekichi's mask)

158.1 FX: Doh (smack)
158.4 FX: Zuba (Inuyasha smacks away crab guard)
158.5 FX: Doka (strike)
158.6 FX: Baki (strike)

159.1 FX: Shuuuu... (fizzy sound as guard turns back into a crab)
159.2 FX: Basha (guard turns back into fish)
159.4 FX: Ba (Inuyasha breaks through bamboo partition)

161.1 FX: Chari (Water god grabs trident)
161.2 FX: Da (running)
161.3 FX: Giin (sword strikes trident)
161.4 FX: Doh (Inuyasha falls)

178.4 FX: Gin (clang)

179.1 FX: Gara… (Shippo and kids poke their heads out from rubble)
179.2 FX: Su—… (water god moving)
179.4 FX: Doh (trident comes flying)
179.5 FX: Buwa (foam appears)
179.6 FX: ShururuRU… (Inuyasha flung around)

180.2 FX: Gobo gobo… (bubbles coming up from the deep)
180.3 FX: Za (Inuyasha leaps out of water)

181.1 FX: Za (Inuyasha jumps forward)
181.2 FX: Ba (water god swipes with trident)
181.3 FX: Gu (tentacle wraps around Inuyasha's ankle)
181.4 FX: Gobo gobo… (blubs as Inuyasha is pulled underwater)

182.6 FX: Beri (glowing)

183.1 FX: Kaa (burst of bright light)

184.4 FX: Ta ta ta… (running)

185.4 FX: Poi (petal falls in water)
185.5 FX: Gobo gobo (petal sinks)

186.1 FX: Ka (shining)
186.2 FX: Zaaaa… (waters part)
186.4 FX: Shu (trident flies)

187.1 FX: Dohh (trident smashes into pier)
187.4 FX: Ba (water god strikes)
187.5 FX: Zuba (Inuyasha strikes)
187.6 FX: Da (Sango jumps forward)

188.1 FX: Ba (Kirara leaps off)
188.2 FX: Bun (Sango throws boomerang)
188.3 FX: Gin (boomerang clangs off trident)
188.5 FX: Gohhhh… (whooshing of wind)

189.3 FX: Gohh (whooshing)
189.4 FX: Gohh (more whooshing)
189.5 FX: Dohh (Sango knocked off Kirara)

190.1 FX: Gohhhh… (more wind whooshing)
190.4 FX: Ga (Inuyasha grabs water god's arm)

191.3 FX: Buchi (Inuyasha strikes water god)
191.4 FX: Doga (water god strikes Inuyasha)

192.2 FX: Ga (water god dives toward water)
192.4 FX: Doh (punch)
192.5 FX: Zaan (whirlwind)

193.1 FX: Gohh (roar of whirlwind)

194.5 FX: Zan (tentacle splashes into water)

195.2 FX: Bun (Inuyasha throws trident toward Kagome)
195.3 FX: Doh (Inuyasha knocked away)
195.4 FX: Pashi (tentacle nicks trident)
195.5 FX: Zan (trident splashes down)
195.6 FX: Ba (Taromaru dives off pier)

196.2 FX: Gobo gobo… (trident sinking)
196.4 FX: Zan (tentacle splashes into water)

197.2 FX: Guoh (tentacle reaches up)
197.3 FX: Zuba (boomerang slashes off tentacle)
197.4 FX: Ba (Sango and Kirara fly by)
197.5 FX: Za (Inuyasha lands in water)
197.6 FX: Ba (Kirara dashes off)

198.1 FX: Gobo… (diving under water)
198.2 FX: Za (coming up out of water)
198.6 FX: Gohh (whooshing down)

199.3 FX: Zan (splash)
199.4 FX: Gobo (Taromaru and trident continue to sink)

200.1 FX: Zuba (big Tetsusaiga slice)
200.4 FX: Ba (Miroku opens wind tunnel)
200.5 FX: Gohhh… (whoosh of wind tunnel)

201.1 FX: Gohh (whoosh of water god being sucked in)
201.2 FX: Za (Inuyasha jumps down)

202.1 FX: Kaaaa… (glow as magic works)
202.2 FX: Suu… (goddess returns to true size)

203.1 FX: Kiii…n… (trident radiates magic)
203.2 FX: Suu… (wind and waters calm down)

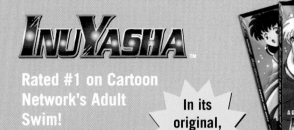

Rated #1 on Cartoon Network's Adult Swim!

In its original, unedited form!

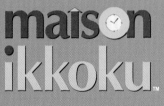

The beloved romantic comedy of errors—a fan favorite!

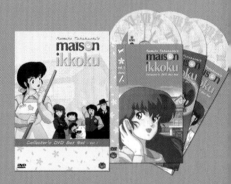

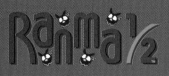

The zany, wacky study of martial arts at its best!

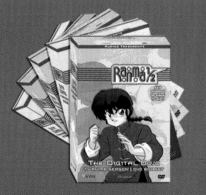

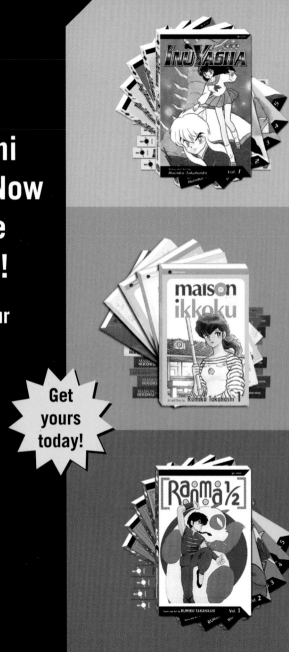

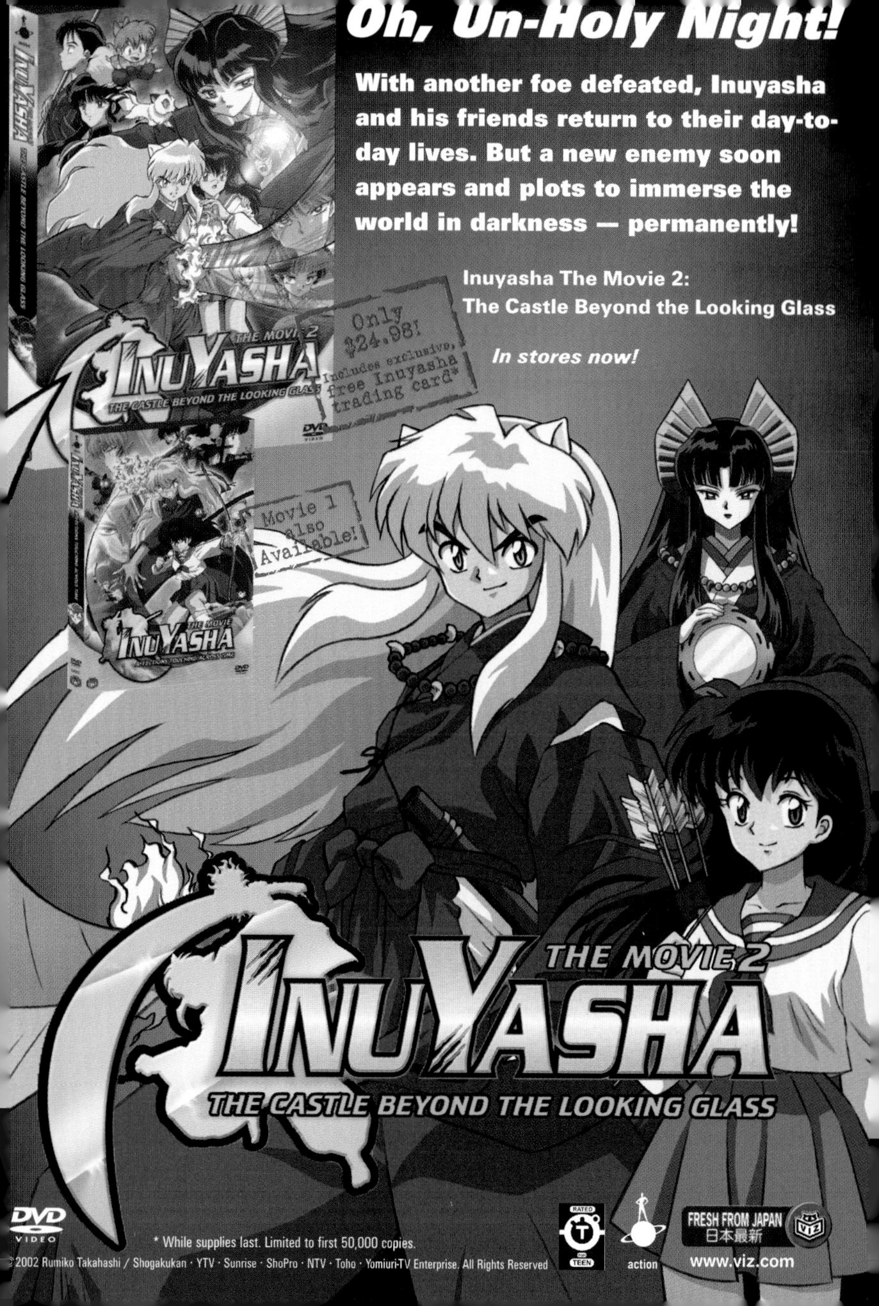

Oh, Un-Holy Night!
With another foe defeated, Inuyasha and his friends return to their day-to-day lives. But a new enemy soon appears and plots to immerse the world in darkness — permanently!
Inuyasha The Movie 2:
The Castle Beyond the Looking Glass
In stores now!
Only $24.98!
Includes exclusive, free Inuyasha trading card*
THE MOVIE 2
INUYASHA
THE CASTLE BEYOND THE LOOKING GLASS
Movie 1 also Available!
THE MOVIE
INUYASHA
THE MOVIE 2
INUYASHA
THE CASTLE BEYOND THE LOOKING GLASS
DVD VIDEO
* While supplies last. Limited to first 50,000 copies.
© 2002 Rumiko Takahashi / Shogakukan · YTV · Sunrise · ShoPro · NTV · Toho · Yomiuri-TV Enterprise. All Rights Reserved
RATED T TEEN
action
FRESH FROM JAPAN
日本最新
VIZ
www.viz.com

COMPLETE OUR SURVEY AND LET US KNOW WHAT YOU THINK!

☐ Please do NOT send me information about VIZ products, news and events, special offers, or other information.

☐ Please do NOT send me information from VIZ's trusted business partners.

Name: _____

Address: _____

City: _____ **State:** _____ **Zip:** _____

E-mail: _____

☐ Male ☐ Female **Date of Birth** (mm/dd/yyyy): ___ / ___ / ___ (Under 13? Parental consent required)

What race/ethnicity do you consider yourself? (please check one)

☐ Asian/Pacific Islander ☐ Black/African American ☐ Hispanic/Latino

☐ Native American/Alaskan Native ☐ White/Caucasian ☐ Other: _____

What VIZ product did you purchase? (check all that apply and indicate title purchased)

☐ DVD/VHS _____

☐ Graphic Novel _____

☐ Magazines _____

☐ Merchandise _____

Reason for purchase: (check all that apply)

☐ Special offer ☐ Favorite title ☐ Gift

☐ Recommendation ☐ Other _____

Where did you make your purchase? (please check one)

☐ Comic store ☐ Bookstore ☐ Mass/Grocery Store

☐ Newsstand ☐ Video/Video Game Store ☐ Other: _____

☐ Online (site: _____)

What other VIZ properties have you purchased/own? _____

How many anime and/or manga titles have you purchased in the last year? How many were VIZ titles? **(please check one from each column)**

ANIME	MANGA	VIZ
☐ None	☐ None	☐
☐ 1-4	☐ 1-4	☐
☐ 5-10	☐ 5-10	☐ 5-10
☐ 11+	☐ 11+	☐ 11+

I find the pricing of VIZ products to be: **(please check one)**

☐ Cheap ☐ Reasonable ☐ Expensive

What genre of manga and anime would you like to see from VIZ? **(please check two)**

☐ Adventure ☐ Comic Strip ☐ Science Fiction ☐ Fighting

☐ Horror ☐ Romance ☐ Fantasy ☐ Sports

What do you think of VIZ's new look?

☐ Love It ☐ It's OK ☐ Hate It ☐ Didn't Notice ☐ No Opinion

Which do you prefer? **(please check one)**

☐ Reading right-to-left

☐ Reading left-to-right

Which do you prefer? **(please check one)**

☐ Sound effects in English

☐ Sound effects in Japanese with English captions

☐ Sound effects in Japanese only with a glossary at the back

THANK YOU! Please send the completed form to:

VIZ Survey
42 Catharine St.
Poughkeepsie, NY 12601

All information provided will be used for internal purposes only. We promise not to sell or otherwise divulge your information.